GOD'S RIGHT HAND

GOD'S RIGHT HAND

How Jerry Falwell Made God a Republican

and Baptized the American Right

WITHDRAWN

Michael Sean Winters

HarperOne
An Imprint of HarperCollinsPublishers

HarperOne

HarperCollins books may be purchased for educational, business, or sales promotional use. For information please write: Special Markets Department, Harper-Collins Publishers, 10 East 53rd Street, New York, NY 10022.

HarperCollins website: http://www.harpercollins.com

HarperCollins®, 🏭®, and HarperOne™ are trademarks of HarperCollins Publishers.

FIRST EDITION

Library of Congress Cataloging-in-Publication Data

Winters, Michael Sean.
    God's right hand : how Jerry Falwell made God a Republican and baptized the American right / Michael Sean Winters.
        p. cm.
    ISBN 978–0–06–197067–2
    1. Christianity and politics—United States. 2. Church and state—United States. 3. Religious right—United States. 4. Falwell, Jerry. 5. Baptists—United States—Clergy—Biography. 6. United States—Moral conditions. 7. United States—Social conditions. 8. Moral Majority, Inc. 9. Fundamentalism. I. Title.
    BR115.P7W56 2012
    322'.10973—dc23   2011031293

    12   13   14   15   16   RRD(H)   10   9   8   7   6   5   4   3   2   1

THIS BOOK IS DEDICATED TO
THE MOST SAINTLY MAN I KNOW,
MY FATHER,
FELIX J. WINTERS.

Contents

Introduction

Jerry Falwell lived one of the most consequential lives of any American in the last half of the twentieth century. Other preachers became televangelists, and some had larger audiences, but Falwell became the face of televangelism, the preacher whom Phil Donohue or Ted Koppel was most likely to call for an interview. Some men, and a few women, had more direct influence on the nation's politics. While there is some debate about whether Reagan could have won without the votes of the millions of evangelical voters Falwell energized and organized, there is no doubt that the moral concerns that mattered to Falwell and his voters became an integral part of the Reagan Revolution. Others began colleges and universities in the last half of the twentieth century, but none grew faster than Falwell's Liberty University. Many people affected the culture in myriad ways, from the Beatles to Bill Gates, but Jerry Falwell changed the perception of what it meant to be a Christian, and in America, the most religiously observant industrialized nation in the world, that was no small accomplishment.

Jerry Falwell was trying to bring the Gospel of Jesus Christ to bear on his culture. He built institutions to carry out his work, with all the minor and not so minor missteps that attend such institution building. And however much one disagrees with any particular position he took, astute observers will find themselves appalled at the coarseness displayed by many of his critics. Those secular liberals who denounced the bringing of dogma into the public realm brought their own dogmas. Those who denounced Falwell as intolerant had their own intolerances. Those who criticized his views of America or its founding as deeply flawed had plenty of deep flaws in their own views.

In the end, it is impossible to avoid a frank admiration for Falwell's gifts, his perseverance, the sheer energy he brought to his task, even if one also experiences an ambivalence, or even disdain, about his career and its consequences. The political gospel he preached was unrecognizable to anyone schooled in the tradition of Catholic social thought or the writings of Reinhold Niebuhr. At times Falwell's exuberance led him to be demeaning toward others who did not share his views, but he usually engaged his interlocutors with a warm and disarming personality. Few Americans can say that they have achieved the profound impact on their times and country that Falwell could rightly claim.

The British philosopher Isaiah Berlin penned a justly famous essay entitled "The Hedgehog and the Fox." The title is drawn from the fragment of an ancient Greek poem that reads: "The fox knows many things, but the hedgehog knows one big thing." Berlin characterized how different men, in different epochs, have evidenced the genius unique to each way of knowing, the monists versus the pluralists, those seized with one great idea and those whose minds sought the many, not the one. Berlin gives a few examples: Plato, Dante, Pascal, Hegel, Dostoyevsky, Nietzsche, and Ibsen, obviously, were hedgehogs, while Aristotle, Shakespeare, Erasmus, and Pushkin were foxes. In Berlin's telling, Tolstoy, the subject of the essay, was a fox who desperately wanted to be a hedgehog. Using Berlin's classification and applying it to a few prominent religious figures, we could say that Augustine, Luther, Jonathan Edwards, and Billy Graham were all hedgehogs, while Aquinas, Calvin, Bellarmine, and Father Drinan were foxes.

Jerry Falwell was a hedgehog, and he did not wish to be anything else. He knew "one big thing," and that big thing was the Bible. In all of his actions and activities, Falwell saw himself as advancing toward the singular goal of evangelization, spreading the Gospel of Jesus Christ and helping the converted to live their lives in a godly way.

Falwell was, consequently, first and last a preacher. From the time he founded the Thomas Road Baptist Church in 1956 with thirty-five members, all of his activities were directed at, or flowed from, his efforts to build the church. The home for alcoholics, the Lynch-burg Christian Academy, the home for unwed mothers, his television ministry, Liberty University—all grew out of his ministry at Thomas Road Baptist. Even his political involvement grew out of the belief that his church could scarcely survive if the ambient culture contin-ued on what Falwell deemed to be a steep moral decline.

Built on the strength of Falwell's ceaseless activities and win-some personality, Thomas Road Baptist Church became a prototype for the modern megachurch. More than size makes a megachurch, although Falwell's congregation grew so quickly that he had to build a new and larger sanctuary three different times. A megachurch has the kind of cradle-to-grave social services that we associate with large, urban, ethnic Catholic parishes at the end of the nineteenth century. A megachurch has an elementary school and a high school and a preschool, and Falwell's even had a university. A megachurch has ministries for the homeless and for the addicted, social clubs for the lonely, sports leagues for the competitive, job training semi-nars, and social support groups for teens and young mothers and the elderly. A megachurch is a sort of village organized around the church, providing alternatives to the social, educational, and cultural offerings found in the wider culture.

The many and varied activities of a megachurch are signs of social and cultural vibrancy, to be sure, but they are also prey to the men-talities and inhibitions we associate with any cultural ghetto. Mem-bership has its privileges, as the old American Express ads used to say, but it also has its limits. The educational and cultural exchanges within the megachurch become univocal. The lack of interchange with the ambient culture leads to a certain inflexibility of ideas and attitudes. And as long as the numbers continue to grow, a sense of self-satisfaction can take hold.

Falwell began his television and radio ministry shortly after he launched his church. He was neither the first nor the most popular television evangelist, but he was one of the most prominent. He built his outreach on the network of fundamentalist institutions and organizations that had been erected in the first half of the century and had grown steadily, out of sight of the mainstream culture. Then television and radio allowed him to reach beyond that network. In later years Falwell would use his plane, his fax machine, e-mail, and any other technological advance to get his message out. He was a master communicator in the pulpit, but he saw almost every new technology as a pulpit too. Whether he was in Lynchburg on Sunday morning or on a television show broadcast nationally, Falwell was, in a sense, always in his pulpit. It went with him. He was always preaching in one way or another.

Falwell was not just any preacher. He was a fundamentalist Baptist preacher. He believed that the Bible is the inerrant Word of God in every particular. While all Christians turn to the scriptures for understanding and inspiration, in some sense as definitively true, fundamentalists view the Bible as literally true. They eschew centuries of biblical interpretation, believing that any baptized person can readily grasp the meaning of the Bible. As a Baptist, Falwell believed that a preacher brings learning to his task but does not enjoy any particular privileged hermeneutic by reason of his office. Baptists are a fiercely independent lot, with a completely decentralized organizational structure. If some denominations believe that ordination confers a distinct status upon the preacher, in the Baptist tradition the preacher has no such distinct priestly status, so he must be more entrepreneurial, more attuned to his audience.

Fundamentalism is a self-contained intellectual whole. From the inside, it is supremely coherent and everything fits neatly into place. There is a certainty and a clarity to fundamentalism: all the answers to all life's questions are found in the Bible if you know where to look. This certainty and clarity are opaque to those on the outside, and fundamentalism is ill suited to dialogue with nonfundamentalist believers. Fundamentalists do not recognize the kind of mediating intellectual traditions by which people of different points of view find common ground or, at least, clarify their differences. Conversely, most modern thinkers, even most modern religious thinkers, who do not share the fundamentalists' views about biblical inerrancy, find fundamentalist discourse and methods of analysis confounding. Fundamentalism is forceful but blunt. It is morally rigorous but not intellectually curious. Fundamentalism is accessible but not dexterous. Fundamentalism conforms easily to parts of American culture but is profoundly countercultural in other parts. In all these regards, fundamentalism conformed well to Falwell's personality. It is difficult to imagine him as a Catholic priest or an Episcopalian minister.

Fundamentalism is different from, but related to, what is usually meant by the word "evangelical." While all fundamentalists are in a sense evangelicals, not all evangelicals are fundamentalists. Evangelicalism of the kind exhibited by Rev. Billy Graham has a lighter touch than fundamentalism and is less strident and less fixated on doctrinal particulars. Both evangelicals and fundamentalists have a loose church structure, rooting their beliefs in scripture, not in church hierarchies. Both often work in tandem. But just as it is impossible to imagine Falwell as a Catholic priest, it is difficult to imagine him as a more moderate evangelical pastor. Billy Graham might have had as much in the way of zeal as any fundamentalist preacher, but he shied away from the role of zealot. Falwell relished that role. And one of Falwell's political achievements was to reach beyond his fundamentalist colleagues and tap into the conservative attitudes of evangelicals. As the reader will see, Falwell continually reached out to conservative evangelicals who were not fundamentalists, and to conservative Catholics and Jews as well.

Falwell's entry into the world of politics is what made his a household name. Disgusted with what he saw as the moral decline of the nation, as exemplified by legalized abortion and the push for gay rights, Falwell decided to break with his prior aloof stance toward politics. That stance had been symptomatic of fundamentalism's self-imposed cultural exile from mainstream culture throughout most of the twentieth century. Falwell's Moral Majority ended that exile.

Falwell organized, energized, and educated fundamentalists about politics. They became not only a part of the Reagan Revolution but an integral constituency of the Republican Party. Conservative southerners had been abandoning their long-standing allegiance to the Democratic Party for years, so in part, Falwell rode a wave that had begun earlier. But when he brought fundamentalists, most of whom had abstained from political involvement, to the polls, the electoral shift in the South toward the Republicans became a tsunami. Indeed, one of the problems facing the Republican Party on the national stage in the future is that Falwell succeeded so thoroughly: today the GOP is often perceived as too white, too southern, too conservative, and too Christian.

The Republican Party welcomed not only Falwell and his flock but his ideas, and those ideas continue to shape the Republican Party today. He cast a long shadow. Apart from her riffs on the natural beauty of Alaska, there are few phrases that Sarah Palin utters that were not spoken first by Falwell. The preacher devised many of the tropes of American exceptionalism, specifically the religiously infused exceptionalism that Palin has made her hallmark. Falwell opposed "socialized medicine" and "government-run health care" when he fought the Clinton health care reform proposals, and Texas governor Rick Perry used the same language to fight the Obama health care proposals. Both Falwell and Mitt Romney speak of the free enterprise system in terms of small businesses and family farms, despite the fact that the dominant actors in modern capitalism are multinational corporations and Wall Street financial firms. Falwell developed a highly populist critique of cultural elites that Michele Bachmann has turned into an art form.

Most important, Falwell did more than simply identify key issues for his constituency and make them central planks in the GOP platform—he introduced the language and the logic of orthodoxy into politics. The religion he brought into the public square had nothing in common with the "civic religion" of earlier times; indeed, his fundamentalism was completely at odds with the generic, nondenominational religious references that had previously been the way religion found expression in the political life of the nation. Dwight Eisenhower gave voice to that civic religion perfectly when he stated, "Our form of government has no sense unless it is founded in a deeply felt religious faith, and I don't care what it is." Falwell cared what it is. He brought all the sense of certainty that he had found in his fundamentalist Christianity into the political realm, and he did so at a time when many Americans were afraid that the nation suffered from too much uncertainty. Many who did not share all of Falwell's views nonetheless appreciated his commitment to stand as a bulwark against the self-doubt and malaise that plagued America in the late 1970s.

This language and logic of orthodoxy did not always fit well with American politics. Economic policy, for example, had normally been about the adjudication of interests. If liberals wanted to raise the minimum wage by one dollar and conservatives did not want to raise it at all, they could reach compromise with a fifty-cent increase. But in Falwell's view of the world, raising taxes and increasing the size and reach of government were evidence of creeping socialism, which was the kissing cousin of communism, and communism was evil. Falwell's procapitalist stance—specifically his commitment to lower taxes and smaller government, a commitment he shared with Ronald Reagan—has become the most widely shared article of the Republican faith ever since. A preference for lower taxes became an ideological commitment that could never be compromised.

On the other hand, in the debate about abortion, which really did entail categorical distinctions, Falwell's intervention brought a much-needed clarity. The Supreme Court's 1973 *Roe v. Wade* decision had tried to balance a woman's right to privacy with the state's interest in protecting life, but Falwell recognized that such a formulation was inadequate. To him, the unborn baby was a baby nonetheless, and if it was a baby, then it deserved to have the full protection of the law. The issue of abortion, cast in such categorical terms, has become a perennial issue precisely because Falwell succeeded in redefining it in categorical terms.

Falwell's frequent claim that America was a "Christian nation" was contentious to say the least. He developed the belief, still evident in conservative political circles, that America's Founders were profoundly influenced by their faith and that he and other religious believers could better appreciate what the Founders had intended. Those who did not share these views were betraying the founding. This overlooks the fact that the American founding happened in the heyday of Deism, whose conception of a God who is uninvolved with human affairs is easier to keep out of the way of achieving political objectives. The Deist God that Thomas Jefferson acknowledged had little in common with the personal, miracle-producing God whom Jerry Falwell worshiped. The claim also overlooks the fact that different Founders wanted different things from their achievements, as evidenced by the fact that they immediately broke into parties contending for control of the country they had helped birth.

It is perhaps wrong to fault Falwell for failing to craft a more satisfying synthesis between the founding ideals of America and traditional Christianity. The "freedom of the children of God" of which St. Paul wrote bears little resemblance to the negative liberty, a freedom from government coercion, that was at the heart of the American founding. For Protestants faith is private, a point on which the Founders would have agreed, but for the Founders, unlike Falwell, that point presumed a moral consensus that was dead by the time Falwell entered the public sphere. He wanted faith to be more than private, he wanted it to be public, and that is where the trouble began.

The "Christian nation" claim also got Falwell into trouble with American Jews, and eventually he abandoned the phrase. Falwell's relationship with Jews and Israel is both more ironic and more decidedly positive than many of his other political activities. The irony is found in the twin facts that Falwell's belief in the need to support Israel was rooted in the Bible, while the modern state of Israel was founded by thoroughly secular, European socialists and was opposed by religiously Orthodox Jews. (Orthodox Jews viewed the man-made state as an infringement on the divine prerogative to reconstitute Israel by sending the Messiah.) Falwell himself never recognized the irony. This did not keep him from succeeding in removing the stain of anti-Semitism from conservative political circles and developing long-standing relationships with Jewish leaders, both in America

and in Israel. Before Falwell, anti-Semitism was found
sively among conservatives, and after him it was found
sively in some liberal quarters.

There was one sense in which Falwell's fundamentalism did mimic the
civic religion of earlier times: both ended up reducing religion to ethics. Once he entered the realm of politics, Falwell recognized that he
needed to appeal to nonfundamentalists too, and that whatever their
doctrinal differences, conservative Jews and Christians could share in
advocating for certain moral propositions. He brought the fervor of
orthodoxy, but he began leaving the orthodoxy itself at the door. He
succumbed to the temptation to gain access to the public square as a
moral authority. He continued to preach the saving Gospel of Jesus
Christ from the pulpit of Thomas Road Baptist Church, but on *The
Phil Donohue Show* or *Nightline* he played the role of a moral expert.

Falwell was completely unalert to the danger of reducing religion to ethics, thereby casting religion in a utilitarian role, as a prop
for Americanism, albeit his version of Americanism. He could not
see that once divorced from the core, doctrinal claims of his faith,
morality would become moralism, one ideology among many, something to be justified at the polls, not confirmed by the dictates of
God. A moralism that is not rooted in doctrine risks that the faithful
will lose the forest for the trees and that what is distinctive about
Christianity, how and whom it worships, will cease to be of central
concern. Religion becomes about us and not about God, about principles and not a personal relationship with the divine. Such a religion
is halfway to extinction.

Furthermore, if the moral arguments advanced by the churches
are divorced from their doctrinal roots and become accessible to
all reasonable people, those arguments are, strictly speaking, secular arguments. Secularism is acting as if God does not exist. Falwell
sought to bring his moral views into what he perceived as a godless,
overly secular culture. But by reducing religion to ethics in his arguments, he helped achieve the perverse result of secularizing a central function of any Christian church, the proclamation of a moral

vision. Instead of bringing Christ to the secularists, he brought some degree of secularism to the church. This tension between the premises of modern political culture and religious faith was commented upon throughout Falwell's involvement on the national scene, but almost no attention was paid at the time to this reduction of religion to ethics. It remains the fault line, capable of eruption, between religious faith and American politics, and no one, including Falwell, has been able to resolve the tension.

This reduction of religion to ethics, imposed by the nature of public, political debate, profoundly affects the way Christians view themselves. Whether Christianity is reduced to social justice or to conservative sexual practices or to being kind, it is robbed of its core doctrinal claims and loses its power to save. Falwell, whose own conversion had been so dramatic and thorough, surely should have recognized that the belief that God Himself came down from heaven, was born of a virgin, walked on the earth, and was crucified and raised from the dead was the stuff of evangelization and conversion. Arguing for the morality of lower tax rates or aid to the South African government did not produce conversions. Even today, when religious leaders take stances on environmental issues or deficit reduction, their arguments tend to lack the kind of explicitly doctrinal language that animates believers.

Falwell's explicitly moral political engagement did, however, produce something. Just as the Moral Majority had been, in part, a reaction to the prominence of liberal Christianity in the public square, an effort to displace the politics of Rev. King and Father Drinan, the Moral Majority, in turn, also produced a reaction. In the early 1990s, for the first time in the history of the Pew surveys, and after ten years of frantic, unrelenting activity by the Moral Majority, an appreciable number of Americans began to answer "none" when asked their religious affiliation. In the 2008 Pew survey of religious affiliation, more than 16 percent of Americans claimed the mantle of the "nones."

It is impossible not to admire Falwell's many gifts, his intelligence, his drive, the sheer energy he brought to his tasks, the delight he took in his adventures. Falwell's life is an amazing story, filled with larger-than-life characters, occasional intrigues, large ideas, and even larger personalities, running into each other. His life intersected with some of the most notable figures of his time, from Ronald Reagan, whom he helped elect president, to his frustrating involvement with the scandal-ridden Jim and Tammy Faye Bakker. He helped create the megachurch movement that continues to change the religious landscape of America. He stared down pornographers and wrestled with women's groups. Falwell battled with liberals and enforced a brand of orthodoxy on conservatives. Most especially, he knew his own views and knew that those views were shared by millions of Americans who had become disengaged from American public life. Falwell led them into the public square, articulated a coherent rationale for their involvement in politics, and made them the largest and most organized constituency in the contemporary Republican Party. He baptized the American Right.

Falwell's life is filled with seeming contradictions. Even his critics, such as pornographer Larry Flynt and liberal icon Sen. Edward Kennedy, acknowledged him as a friend. He vowed to stay out of politics in the 1960s, but then jumped in at the end of the 1970s; he subsequently vowed to stay away in the late 1980s, but still found himself at the center of political controversy until his death in 2007. A preacher first and last, he remains best known not for his sermons but for his political repartee on *The Phil Donohue Show* and *Nightline*.

Falwell's life was also filled with consequences for both the religious and political life of the nation. He set out to change the face of America, and he largely succeeded. The Moral Majority may have never represented the views of the majority of Americans, but its views have had a lasting impact on America's political dialogue, as witnessed by the ongoing debates about funding for Planned Parenthood and the legal status of same-sex unions. And at a time when many more liberal denominations are in decline, fundamentalist churches continue to grow, or to at least not lose members, as many more mainline churches have done. Even had all of his many religious and political enterprises followed Falwell into the grave, he would still be one of the most consequential figures in American public life.

But Falwell was also a builder of institutions, and so his legacy has outlived him. Liberty University, presided over by Jerry Falwell Jr., is now the largest fundamentalist university in the world, producing first-rate lawyers and teachers and politicians and preachers. One of the first lawsuits against President Barack Obama's health care reforms was brought by Liberty University. Liberty Counsel, the legal advocacy organization affiliated with the law school, frequently joins lawsuits on a variety of matters ranging from same-sex marriage to conscience protections.

Thomas Road Baptist Church remains one of the largest fundamentalist churches in the country. Falwell's son Jonathan leads the church, preaching every Sunday to thousands of congregants, but unlike his dad, Jonathan is rarely in the pulpit. He walks from one end of the stage to the next, engaging his audience in a less formal, conversational style than evidenced in his father's preaching. But the point is not the style, the point is the engagement, and in Jonathan's successful cultivation of his flock, the fruit did not fall far from the tree.

Throughout America, fundamentalists remain an organized voting bloc that is decisive in countless local elections for school boards and city councils. No candidate can hope to win the Republican presidential primaries without significant support from evangelical and fundamentalist voters. A majority of the Tea Party members report that they hold conservative social views of the kind first brought onto the national stage by Jerry Falwell. The anti–big government tropes that Falwell articulated remain a political belief held as dearly among these voters as the inerrancy of the Bible is held religiously. Falwell did not eliminate the divide between religion and politics. Nor did he blur it. He jumped over it, bringing millions of voters with him, and he never looked back.

Chapter One

The Prodigal

Falwell's Early Years

Jerry Falwell and his twin brother, Gene, were born August 11, 1933, into a family beset by dysfunction, in a provincial Appalachian city, in a South still practicing strict racial segregation, and in a country struggling to overcome the economic misery and social dislocation caused by the Great Depression. Curiously, given Falwell's subsequent rise to fame, he was not born into a church family. By the end of the century his own family would be highly successful, his city would be less provincial in large part because of his efforts, legal racial segregation would be consigned to the history books, and America would find itself flourishing politically and economically. What is more, by the end of the century Falwell would become the face of Christianity in American culture.

Carey Falwell, Jerry's father, was a very ambitious and successful businessman in Lynchburg, Virginia, the small city in which the Falwell clan had lived since it was founded in the mid-eighteenth century. While previous generations were mostly farmers, Carey Falwell was an entrepreneur. He had opened his first grocery store in 1915 at the age of twenty-two. In 1921 he opened the first of seventeen service stations in Lynchburg, each of which would have a small store or restaurant

attached to it. This enterprise led to his becoming a gas and oil dis-
tributor for sixteen Virginia counties. He opened an inn near the ruins
of a Confederate fort just outside the city and a dance hall at one of
his restaurants. Carey Falwell also sponsored cockfights and dogfights,
which were as profitable as they were illegal. With his brother Garland,
Carey ran a very successful bootlegging business, using the oil and gas
trucks belonging to his legitimate business to distribute the contra-
band liquor to the stores and restaurants he owned. In 1927 Carey
Falwell started the first bus company with service between Lynchburg
and Washington, D.C., and the company soon expanded to include a
range of routes throughout central Virginia. All of this business activity made the Falwell family affluent, although Carey Falwell's shadier
business activities also prevented the Falwells from ever being considered part of the social elite of Lynchburg—which was, and remains,
the kind of small southern city where such social distinctions matter
greatly. In addition to the sketchy sources of some of his wealth, Carey
Falwell did not belong to a church and was a second-generation atheist, a fact that further alienated the family from the rigid social norms
of Lynchburg. Indeed, Jerry Falwell would later describe his father as
"an atheist, a racist and an anti-Semite."[1]

Jerry Falwell would later recall that his father was a prankster.
Jerry once brought a friend home who admitted he was scared of Carey.
Jerry told his father of his friend's fear, half cautioning, half goading
Carey as he brought the young man into the house. When the young
friend walked in, Carey shouted, "Stop!," aimed a pistol at the boy's
feet, and shot a hole in the floor a few inches in front of his shoes. "I've
been trying to get that fly all day," Jerry's father announced, returning
to his newspaper while the boy fled the house. Jerry admitted that he
and his father howled with laughter. Some of the pranks were cruel,
however, as when Carey decided he had had enough complaints from
one of his workers. When the man called in sick, Carey offered to have
lunch brought to his house, then killed and skinned the man's cat, put
it into a "squirrel stew," and sent it to the man's home for lunch. The
next day the man complained that the squirrel meat in the stew had
been tough, and Carey told him he had eaten his own cat.[2]

Carey Falwell was also an alcoholic. Unlike his brother Garland, who had several serious alcohol-related run-ins with the law, Carey Falwell was a solitary drinker. He did not fly into rages. He just sat at home and drank himself into a stupor. His drinking grew especially bad after his daughter Rosha died suddenly at the age of ten in 1931. Carey Falwell did not believe in hospitals, so he had not brought his daughter to be treated for the appendicitis that was afflicting her. When her appendix burst, she died of peritonitis.[3]

Later that same year Carey shot and killed his brother Garland in what one biographer has called a "duel," but which could more properly be considered an act of self-defense. Garland, recently released from jail for shooting at some teenagers who had angered him, was partying with some friends and setting off firecrackers. Someone called the police to report what they thought was gunfire. Garland became convinced that his brother had called the police, and he rushed to one of the Falwell restaurants to track him down. Garland was both intoxicated by alcohol and high on the drug Veronal when he began shooting at Carey. A chase ensued. Carey retrieved a shotgun and returned to the office. Garland also returned and began shooting. Carey fired his shotgun, killing Garland instantly. "Garland Falwell is dead," read the account in the local newspaper. "Thus his turbulent career of terrorizing the police and populace was brought to an abrupt close." The authorities concluded that Carey had acted in self-defense, and no charges were brought against him, but no court could remove the psychological pain. The Falwell children would recall that whenever Carey got very drunk, he would talk about killing his brother and losing his daughter.[4]

Falwell's mother, Helen Beasley, was of an entirely different character. She was soft-spoken and reserved, where her husband was intemperate and bold. She came from a strict Baptist family who lived in rural Appomattox County, not far from Appomattox Courthouse, where Gen. Robert E. Lee had surrendered the Army of Northern Virginia to Gen. Ulysses S. Grant, bringing the Civil War to a close. She had met Carey and married him in 1913, then moved to Lynchburg to start a family. There is some dispute about when she was "saved." Jerry would write that she met the Lord when she was still a child, but an earlier, authorized biography with nothing but praise for the Falwells claims that she was "saved" several years after her son began his ministry. The actions of the Holy Spirit are opaque to the eyes of historians, alas, but Helen Falwell was always a religious woman. She attended the Franklin Street Baptist Church every Sunday by the time the twins, Jerry and Gene, were born, and she had all the stern and pious qualities one would expect from a southern Baptist mother circa 1933.[5]

Jerry and Gene had two older siblings. Virginia, the oldest, had been born in 1917. She married her high school sweetheart, Lawrence Jennings, when Jerry was still young, and the newlyweds moved in with the Falwell family. Lawrence would often stay up into the early hours of the morning keeping Carey company while he drank. The twins' older brother, Lewis, was drafted and joined the navy during the war and saw action in the Pacific. Lewis would go into the family business.[6]

Both sides of Jerry Falwell's extended family lived close by, and like his parents, they were a study in contrasts. The Falwells were all involved in various businesses in Lynchburg, reasonably successful in the difficult years of the Depression, and unchurched. When they met, it was usually at one of the family's restaurants, and their gatherings were rowdy affairs. The Beasleys lived on farms in the rural areas of Appomattox County. They would frequently gather for family celebrations at one of the farms, where the meals were always preceded by the saying of grace and alcohol was not permitted. From later accounts, it appears that both extended families were close and family gatherings were frequent.[7]

Lynchburg was the archetypal sleepy southern city in the 1930s and 1940s. It had been founded by John Lynch, who ran a ferry across the James River in the eighteenth century. He hired a surveyor to lay out a series of half-acre lots, which he offered for free to anyone who promised to build a home with a stone chimney within three years. Lynch constructed bridges over the many small streams that fed the river, making it easier to move around town. He also lent his name to a more sinister activity. During the American Revolution he would arrest Tories and hang them up by their thumbs until they pledged themselves to the cause of American independence. The practice became known as lynching.[8]

Two American patriots had associations with Lynchburg. Patrick Henry delivered his "give me liberty or give me death" speech to the Virginia colonial legislature in 1775, advancing the patriot cause and clarifying the stakes as the colonial body considered whether or not to resist British encroachments by mustering the militia. Henry lived at Red Hill, a plantation in nearby Charlotte County, and after serving as the commonwealth's first governor and in several other public offices, he retired to this farm. It was there he died in 1799. The other patriot was Thomas Jefferson, who inherited 4,819 acres just west of Lynchburg from his father in 1773. He would hide at the overseer's cottage on this property in 1781, after barely escaping capture by British troops at his home outside Charlottesville. During his presidency Jefferson decided to build a retreat for himself on the property and designed an octagonal villa he named Poplar Forest. He would visit his second home three or four times a year, for a week or two at a time, reading and writing in relative seclusion.[9]

Like many cities in the foothills of the Blue Ridge Mountains and along the James River, Lynchburg became an important transportation hub, first with bateau barges carrying tobacco and other produce down the river, and later as an important rail depot where the Virginia & Tennessee railroad intersected with the Southern Railways, Chesapeake & Ohio, and Norfolk & Western rail lines. During the Civil War, Lynchburg's status as a transportation hub and munitions center made it a target for invading Union armies. In 1864 Gen. David "Black Dave" Hunter, with two future presidents among his troops—Rutherford B. Hayes and William McKinley— tried to take the town, but after a brief skirmish turned back his first assault and Gen. Jubal Early rushed in Confederate reinforcements, Hunter withdrew and Lynchburg was spared the devastation that struck many other southern cities during the Civil War, which would end the next year when General Lee surrendered his army to General Grant at Appomattox Courthouse, twenty-five miles east of Lynchburg.[10]

Lynchburg remained a transportation hub into the twentieth century, and the town grew accordingly. It became a natural location for mills, foundries, and small-scale factories. The Craddock-Terry Shoe Company became the largest shoemaker in the South, and a large pharmaceutical company, C. B. Fleet, also set up shop in the city. Sweet Briar College, a small liberal arts college for women, was opened in 1901, and Lynchburg College opened in 1903. Farmers brought their crops to town to be sent by boat downriver to Richmond or by train to anywhere in the country. In 1905 the Academy of Music opened its doors as a performing arts center, and in 1907 the first public library in the city was established. Lynchburg was provincial, to be sure, but not without its charms.[11]

Everything that caught the eye in the South suggested great stability. The omnipresent church bazaars and family picnics, the biscuits and gravy for breakfast and homemade pies for dessert, and the steady rhythms of the seasons unmodified by air-conditioning, all characterized the American South into which Jerry Falwell was born. But, in fact, the South was undergoing major changes beneath the surface. The New Deal and World War II both brought about significant changes in the economic and social character of the South. These changes played themselves out while Falwell and his brother were still frequenting the playground, but they were not always apparent, even to older observers.

President Franklin Delano Roosevelt considered himself an adopted son of the South because of his frequent visits to Warm Springs, Georgia, where he went for polio treatments. Roosevelt liked to drive around the Georgia countryside, and he witnessed firsthand the appalling poverty of the rural South. When he reached the White House, he was determined to direct federal monies to the South with the hope of alleviating that poverty. One of the first components of his New Deal was the Tennessee Valley Authority, signed into law on May 18, 1933, which put thousands of southerners to work building dams and levees in seven southern states, including the southwestern tip of Virginia. Roosevelt's Rural Electrification Project, Works Progress Administration (WPA), and Civilian Conservation Corps (CCC) also targeted the southern countryside, bringing immediate employment and long-term improvements to the local infrastructure. And of course, the establishment of Social Security and Unemployment Insurance helped millions of Americans nationwide.

Roosevelt's courting of the South was effective. Georgia writer Ferrol Sams Jr. recalls a popular story about a schoolteacher quizzing her class. She asks the students who paved the road in front of their house, and who brought electricity to their homes, and who got their uncle a job in the WPA and their granddaddy a pension. To each of her queries the students respond, "Roosevelt." Then the teacher asks, "All right, children. Now. Who made you?" One little boy stands and says, "God," at which a "gallused, barefoot, towhead leaped up in the back row and yelled, 'Throw that sorry Republican out of here.' " In 1940 Mississippi senator Theodore Bilbo celebrated the fact that his state had secured some $900 million "in good old Yankee money" since Roosevelt entered the White House.[12]

Roosevelt's motivation was not mere social progressivism or noblesse oblige. The "solid South" had awarded all of its electoral college votes to Roosevelt in 1932. He captured an astonishing 68 percent of the vote in Virginia, but that figure paled in comparison to the 91 percent of the vote in Georgia and 98 percent in South Carolina. But the southern Democratic senators were uniformly conservative, and to garner their support for his progressive policies Roosevelt had to make sure that plenty of federal largesse was distributed in their home states.

One of Roosevelt's southern critics was Lynchburg's most famous citizen in the 1930s, Sen. Carter Glass. He was the publisher of the local newspaper, a former U.S. secretary of the Treasury during the Wilson presidency, and, since 1920, a senator from the Old Dominion. Like Falwell's father, Glass loved automobiles and would have his own vehicle carried back and forth on the train from Washington so he was never without it. His mansion, on a knoll in front of Candler's Mountain, was the most elegant home in Lynchburg. Many years later Jerry Falwell bought the Glass mansion as part of his land purchases for Liberty Baptist College and converted it into offices. Falwell died there in 2007, and his body was buried in the garden.

Glass was originally a Roosevelt supporter and had urged his candidacy for the presidency as early as 1926. But his objections to the New Deal, along with the stalwart opposition of Virginia's other senator, Harry Byrd, whose political machine dominated the state's politics, placed him squarely among the anti-Roosevelt southern Democrats. They perceived in the New Deal a growth in federal power that worried them. These "states' rights" Democrats were anxious to maintain their local customs and independence from Washington's ways. "I hate the New Deal just as much as I ever did," Glass told Senator Byrd as they contemplated the 1936 election. They had lost the "War of Northern Aggression," as southerners still referred to the Civil War, and they were now leery of peacetime northern aggression as well. Glass was decidedly cool about supporting Roosevelt's reelection bid in 1936, but his concerns were not shared by his fellow Virginians. Roosevelt again won the state in a walk, taking more than 70 percent of the vote.[13]

Roosevelt paid a price for southern support of his program—or more accurately, he allowed black Americans to pay a price. He did not object when New Deal programs discriminated against blacks, and he even declined to put his political weight behind an anti-lynching bill, despite pressure from his wife and his own sense of decency. "If I come out for the anti-lynching bill now, they will block every bill I ask Congress to pass to keep America from collapsing," Roosevelt told Walter White of the NAACP. "I just can't take that risk."[14]

In his second term Roosevelt would pursue a distinctly more liberal course in the South, siding with southern liberals in internal party squabbles and appointing the foremost among them, Hugo Black, to the Supreme Court. Additionally, black Americans were included in certain New Deal programs, affording them a degree of economic independence they had not previously enjoyed. Wages rose for poor whites and blacks alike. Union organizing became more prevalent and more successful. And Eleanor Roosevelt lent her name and her presence to a variety of organizations and causes seeking civil rights for black Americans. Conservative southerners referred to the National Recovery Act, one of the New Deal's central programs, as the "Negro Relief Act." All these changes were threatening to the established order, and Roosevelt would never again achieve the over-whelming levels of support he had garnered in 1932 and 1936.[15]

World War II also had a profound effect on the South. Unem-ployment ceased throughout the country as America became first the "Arsenal of Democracy" and then a belligerent. Military bases and armaments factories were built up throughout the South. As more and more men enlisted, women went to work outside the home in large numbers for the first time. Black Americans enlisted in the armed forces and acquired skills unknown among their sharecropper parents. These developments would have been deeply shocking to traditionalists had they occurred in peacetime, and fiercely resisted, but the necessity of wartime conditions swept opposition away. Dur-ing four long years of war some women decided they liked having a job, and after the war they kept working. Some communities grew up that were economically dependent on federally managed military bases and industrial plants, not on local landlords and agriculture. On the surface, the South remained traditional and genteel, inexo-rable in its durability, but under the surface racial, sexual, economic, social, and political relationships were beginning to change in ways that would prove profoundly disturbing to many.

No issue so profoundly affected the history of the South as race. From the introduction of African slaves in the seventeenth century, the relationship between the races was the most distinctive thing about southern society. It shaped the South's patrician-dominated colonial culture. It hindered the region's economic growth in the new republic. The South's insistence on extending slavery brought on the Civil War, which decimated almost every city and every village south of the Mason-Dixon Line, leaving no family untouched by war casualties, marauding Yankee troops, postwar privation, or all three. After the war Reconstruction made whites feel powerless and deeply afraid. When Reconstruction came to an end in 1877, white south-erners erected structures of segregation that came to be known as Jim Crow—a series of legal, social, and cultural policies that kept blacks subjugated and the races separate.

"Almost as color defines vision itself, race shapes the cultural eye—what we do and do not notice, the reach of empathy and the alignment of response." That is the opening sentence in Taylor Branch's masterful three-volume biographical history of Martin Luther King Jr. and his times, and it captures the ubiquitous quality of racism in the segregated South. Racist cultural norms were like air. It was impossible not to breathe them in. Commenting on racial attitudes before the civil rights movement, Branch writes that "the notion of a drastic change for the benefit of Negroes struck the average American as about on a par with creating a world government, which is to say visionary, slightly dangerous, and extremely remote."[16]

Segregation dominated life in the Lynchburg of Falwell's formative years. Blacks went to their own churches, drank from separate water fountains, and had to sit in separate waiting rooms at the train station. White students went to all-white schools, and black students, if they went to school, went to poorly funded black schools. Blacks could not enter any of Carey Falwell's restaurants to enjoy a meal, although they could carry out.

The pervasive character of segregation during Falwell's early years might have inclined him to believe that the legal separation of the races was as permanent as it was pervasive. But already, in the late 1930s and early 1940s, the Supreme Court was beginning to chip away at Jim Crow: requiring Texas to admit a black man to the University of Texas law school because the black law school, though "separate," was not "equal"; forbidding segregation in dining and library facilities at the University of Oklahoma's school of education; and ruling that court injunctions employed to enforce racially restrictive residential covenants were unconstitutional. In a 1946 case that must have struck close to home, *Morgan v. Virginia*, the high court ruled that applying the state's bus segregation law to interstate passengers violated the interstate commerce clause. By 1950 the NAACP had won 90 percent of the cases it argued before the Supreme Court.[17]

Segregation was also being challenged outside the courts. In 1947 President Harry S. Truman addressed an NAACP rally at the Lincoln Memorial, delivering a forceful defense of civil rights. "We must make the Federal Government a friendly, vigilant defender of the rights and equalities of all Americans. And . . . I mean all Americans." The next year Truman ordered the desegregation of the armed forces, and that summer the Democratic Party adopted a strong civil rights plank in its platform, resulting in a walkout by several southern states. Also in 1948, the newly installed archbishop of Washington, D.C., Patrick O'Boyle, set about planning the desegregation of the Catholic schools and parishes of his jurisdiction. The process took several years, and O'Boyle met with stiff resistance in southern Maryland, which had long-standing cultural affinities with the South. When a group of laymen pleaded against the imminent desegregation order O'Boyle had given, arguing that it would take at least a decade for their communities to be ready to accept desegregated schools, O'Boyle replied, "Well, gentlemen, we're going to do it tomorrow." The changes were tremors, not earthquakes, and they did not portend any significant change in Falwell's teenage world in Lynchburg. There Jim Crow still reigned supreme. There Falwell understood that the separation of the races and the denigration of blacks were facts of public life, ordained by God, enacted into law, and practiced at the hospital, the lunch counter, the train station, the schools, and every other venue in the city beside the James River. Down the road at Appomattox, the War Between the States had ended, but not the hostility between the races.[18]

In addition to formal segregation, however, many white southern families actually experienced close, even intimate, personal relations with black southerners. Those relationships were always characterized by white dominance and black subjugation, to be sure, but this did not prevent whites and blacks from interacting in a host of ways. Young Jerry and Gene Falwell had a black nanny, David Brown, who had been hired to help Mrs. Falwell with the kids. "In the mornings he bathed and dressed us," Falwell wrote in his autobiography. "He held and rocked us at nap time. He fed and changed us. He helped us with our first faltering steps and he picked us up off the ground when we stumbled or fought and fell. He was practically a member of our family, but he ate alone on the back porch and sat in the shadows when he wasn't needed." Racial intimacy and segregation experienced simultaneously, and focused on the same person, extended into every nook and cranny of Falwell's young life.[19]

In subsequent years, Falwell's views on race, like the views of most southerners, would undergo an extraordinary transformation. He would come to regret segregation and would speak plainly and powerfully about the ways in which segregation had been wildly unfair to black Americans. But he would never examine the ways in which segregation had corrupted his own sense of human relations. The scars that segregation left on blacks were obvious, but the evil system scarred whites as well. The easy acceptance of the idea that one is superior to a fellow human being, reinforced in a million ways large and small, is as morally corrupting of those who perpetrate the idea as it is morally degrading to those who are unjustly discriminated against. In considering a different subject, the legacy of totalitarianism, historian Timothy Snyder observed, "The moral danger, after all, is never that one might become a victim, but that one might be a perpetrator or a bystander." Falwell never acknowledged this moral danger, and although he would eventually renounce the repugnant idea of racial superiority, it shows the strength of racism in the South that his embrace of the Christian faith, with its central doctrine of the common brotherhood of mankind, was not enough to bring Falwell to question Jim Crow.[20]

Jerry Falwell was unruly in his early years, and the family's relative affluence permitted the twins to be more unruly than most. Their father taught them to drive when they were about ten, permitting them to drive on the family property. When they were thirteen, Carey Falwell procured driver's licenses for the boys by lying about their age. Jerry was bright and excelled at school, and his second-grade teacher decided to skip him ahead one year, separating him from his brother Gene. Following in his father's footsteps, Jerry also developed a reputation as a prankster—for example, letting a snake loose in his fifth-grade classroom. He and his brother were driven to school and to Sunday services, but they skipped out of Sunday school, preferring to visit an uncle who lived nearby.[21]

Carey Falwell's business dealings had survived the Depression, but during World War II his failing health and the changing economic contours of a war economy proved too much. He sold his favorite restaurant and dance hall to his brother. With the rationing of oil and gasoline for the war effort, his oil distribution business shrank. The inn that Carey Falwell had built near an old fort was sold, as few Americans had the money or the inclination to vacation during World War II. A more vigorous man might have been able to weather the economic storm, but Carey Falwell was dying. His alcoholism had taken its toll, and he began a long, slow decline. In 1948 he died of liver failure. Again, there is some discrepancy about the state of the elder Falwell's soul. An early account relates that an old family friend named Josh Alvis "led Carey to Christ just before he died," but Jerry would later credit his father's salvation to the intervention of a business associate, Frank Burford, several weeks before his father's death. The loss of his father to alcohol-related illness would affect Jerry deeply.[22]

In high school Jerry continued to excel, and it became obvious that he had a near-photographic memory and a prodigious mind. He was especially good at math and science. Curiously, one teacher remarked that he seemed ill suited to public speaking. Falwell became heavily involved in extracurricular activities, writing for and later editing the school newspaper and playing baseball and football. On the athletic fields his natural competitiveness found an outlet and his leadership skills became apparent. He was the captain of his football team in both his junior and senior years.[23]

Falwell and his friends formed the "Wall Gang," named for the wall opposite the Pickeral Café where they gathered. Jerry was the nominal leader of the group, although this had as much to do with his possessing a red '34 Plymouth as with his leadership abilities. He was the only member of the gang to own a car. The Wall Gang would get into roughhousing and low-intensity fights with other "gangs," but Falwell insisted later that the violence never resulted in more than a few split lips, the occasional broken bone, and small-scale property damage now and then. Once, to punish a neighbor the gang thought had called the police on them, they grabbed some old tar-soaked railroad ties and lit them on fire in front of the offender's home. They did not anticipate that the asphalt on the street would catch fire, but it did, and soon the entire street was in flames.[24]

Falwell's skill as a prankster also took a darker turn. Like his dad, he could be cruel. Many years later he would recall taking on a teacher whom he described as "a mean little man who pranced about our physical ed classes" and who exhibited "prissy, falsetto ways." Falwell tackled him, took off his pants, locked him in a storage closet, and then pinned the man's pants to a bulletin board in another part of the school. Another time he placed a live rat in a teacher's drawer; when she opened the drawer, the rat jumped out and the teacher fell unconscious to the floor.[25]

Falwell would later recall that through such pranks, whether undertaken with his gang or carried out alone, he "began to understand the principle of cause and effect. Actions, responsible or irresponsible, lead to consequences." But the consequences were never severe. Falwell recalled that he was not punished by the principal for humiliating the physical education teacher. In fact, the principal had to keep himself from laughing. Falwell never acknowledged the need to pay for a broken window or the medical cost of repairing a broken leg. If the police had to intervene, as they did when the gang lit the street on fire, they knew the boys' families and sent them home with a warning. There were few repercussions.[26]

Falwell's last prank did have a consequence, and it affected him enough that he recalled it as a somewhat unfair punishment. Jerry and his football buddies acquired the combination to the school safe that contained lunch tickets. They would grab enough tickets for all of them each morning and distribute them in the locker room; they figured that eating for free this way was nothing more than a "harmless but embarrassing trick" on the school. However, when the school authorities eventually noticed the discrepancy between the money collected and the amount of food sold, they called in the police. The scheme was uncovered and the students brought before the principal. The students' parents paid back the money, which Falwell said amounted to "several thousand dollars." No charges were filed. But Falwell, the class valedictorian, was denied the privilege of giving the valedictory speech at the forthcoming graduation ceremony. Falwell would later write that "what I wanted most was being taken away from me as a consequence of my foolish indiscretion." Again, the punishment seems remarkably mild.[27]

After graduating from high school, Falwell enrolled at Lynchburg College, a small liberal arts school in town, intending to major in mechanical engineering. His studies included math and physics, English, history, and religion. His study of religion made "little or no impression" on him, though he did recall that his mother would tune the radio to Charles Fuller's *Old-Fashioned Revival Hour* every Sunday morning and turn up the volume so that the preaching carried upstairs to Jerry's bedroom. He held down a part-time job at a local paper mill and stayed at the small college for two years of study, living at home, continuing to fraternize mostly with his friends in the Wall Gang.

Our knowledge of Falwell's first two decades comes almost exclusively from his own accounts or from highly flattering biographies penned by others. There is no reason to discount them factually, but it is important to recognize that, by the time Falwell was recalling them, he was not interested in history but evangelization. Preachers rely on tales, including their own, to draw their listeners into a deeper truth than mere history affords. They want the listener to see the action of grace.

The prerequisite for grace is its absence, sin. So, in these accounts, Carey Falwell's drinking and young Jerry's misdeeds are discussed in the context of demonstrating what sin is like. In relating the stories, the tellers had to leave room for divine intervention. Jerry's misdeeds are never irredeemable. "Falwell's autobiographical corpus, both as he enacted and as he narrated it, bristled with misdeeds, bad characters, and an edge of zealotry," notes a cultural historian of Falwell and fundamentalist rhetoric. These tales reveal him as "a man distinctly protected and blessed, because he invariably gets away with things he ought not and gets what he wants at the expense of others."[28]

The childhood stories are not banal, and they are told with a view to leading the listener to faith, or deeper faith. But, by all accounts, faith played almost no role in Jerry Falwell's early years. He was his father's son: someone who played fast and loose with the world and his fellows, who was very bright, a bit hyperactive, and decidedly aggressive. He could have gone on to a successful life in business or, as he hoped, engineering. But his life was about to change. On January 20, 1952, Jerry Falwell decided to attend services at the Park Avenue Baptist Church, where he had been told some pretty girls could be found. That night, in the sanctuary, he met both the woman who would later become his wife and his destiny as a preacher.

Chapter Two

The Road to Damascus

Falwell's Conversion

Falwell's decision to go to the Park Avenue Baptist Church that January night in 1952 did not seem like a momentous decision at the time he made it. He might have gone to church with his mother the next Sunday. He might have decided to spend Sunday night as he did most Sundays—hanging at the Pickeral Café with his friends. But the consequences of that decision would shape the rest of his life and, eventually, the life of the nation. Not only did Falwell's conversion experience become a part of his personal narrative, but in its retelling his narrative became an effective way of reaching other potential converts. The fact that he chose a fundamentalist Baptist church might not have determined his eventual denominational affiliation, but it did. And of course, there was Macel, the young piano player at Park Avenue Baptist with whom Jerry Falwell would share the rest of his life.

Falwell's account of his conversion, like all such accounts, entails the unseen movements of grace. He would hold dear the third chapter of the Gospel of John, in which Jesus tells Nicodemus that he must be "born again," and evangelical Christians cite this passage as the most exact description of the conversion experience. That same chapter, however, has Jesus comparing the action of the Spirit to the wind: "The wind blows where it wills, and you hear the sound of it, but you do not know whence it comes or whither it goes; so it is with everyone who is born of the spirit." In recounting his conversion, Falwell would concentrate less on the uncertainty implied by this verse and more on the definite experience of being born again.

Unlike Augustine, who claimed to have heard a childlike voice saying "Tolle, lege" ("Take, read") as the immediate invitation to conversion, Falwell's conversion began with a different sound. He woke up that Sunday morning as he always did—in bed, with the radio blaring a sermon by Charles Fuller. He would later recall that this Sunday the radio sermon did not leave him indifferent, as it had in the past. He was restless and disquieted. Yet he did not go to church with his mother that morning. Later in the day, while hanging out with the Wall Gang, Falwell asked his confederates if any of them knew a church in Lynchburg that had the kind of preaching he heard on the radio. His friend Wilson Wright told him about Park Avenue Baptist Church. "It's kind of a holy-roller type church," Falwell recalled Wright telling him. "But they have good music and loads of pretty girls." Whether it was the likelihood of meeting pretty girls or the beckoning of the Holy Spirit, Falwell enticed Wilson's brother Otis and their friend Jim Moon to accompany him to the church that night.[1]

The trio arrived just as the service was starting, and the church was nearly full, so an usher directed them to seats in the front. The church's youth minister, Jack Dinsbeer, was leading the congregation in a hymn. The hymnbook had been printed and distributed by Fuller's *Old-Fashioned Revival Hour*, the same radio ministry Falwell had heard that morning. Playing the two pianos on either side of the pulpit were two attractive young women. Jim Moon pointed at Macel Pate and told Jerry he intended to ask her out on a date, so Falwell pointed at Delores Clark and said, "Then I'll ask that one." As luck would have it, the two men picked the wrong women that first night. Delores and Jim would be married five years later, and Macel would marry Jerry in six years' time.[2]

When the church's pastor, Paul Donnelson, walked to the pulpit and preached a sermon, Jerry was reminded of the sermons he had heard on the radio. Donnelson preached about "sin and its consequences, about Christ, his cross, and an empty tomb." At the conclusion of the sermon, Donnelson offered a prayer and the congregation resumed singing. One by one, a dozen or so young people made their way to the altar, where they were joined by members of the congregation who spoke softly to them as they knelt. An older man, Garland Carey, saw Falwell fidgeting and asked if he would like to come forward. He did, and Carey began to read from the Book of Romans, explaining the passage as he went along. "The wages of sin is death," the older man said, and Falwell would recall that his thoughts turned to his father. The older man asked Falwell to make a prayer of confession and then asked if he believed his sins were forgiven. Falwell said he believed his sins had been forgiven. "And that quickly I accepted the mystery of God's salvation," Falwell recalled. "In that simple act of confession and belief God forgave my sinfulness. I didn't doubt it then. I haven't doubted it to this day."[3]

As they left the church Jack Dinsbeer came up to invite them to a Bible class for young people he taught every Sunday morning as well as a youth meeting every Sunday evening. He told them to bring their friends. Falwell went home to share his news with his mother. But that first week after his conversion, he still went to school and to work. An early, authorized biography and his wife's posthumous biography both claim that Falwell rushed out on Monday to buy a Bible, a Bible dictionary, and *Strong's Exhaustive Concordance,* but Falwell's own subsequent accounts omit such immediate yearning for biblical knowledge. He did not encounter anyone from the church until Dinsbeer swung by the Pickeral Café to remind Falwell about the Bible class and youth meeting and to tell Jerry to bring his friends along. On Sunday half a dozen of the Wall Gang members joined Falwell and Moon at the morning Bible class at Park Avenue Baptist. Falwell sat next to Macel this time. That night he sat close to the piano that she was playing. He would later acknowledge that his motives were "mixed" in those early days after his conversion, his desire to get close to Macel intermingling with his desire to get close to God.[4]

In his first few months as a Christian, Falwell became more and more involved in the church's many activities. He went to youth group meetings, often held at Dinsbeer's house, and regularly attended Sunday services. Falwell also attended Bible study, for which his near-photographic memory was ideally suited. He learned to recite the five or six essential passages of scripture used by evangelicals to bring people to Christ, the same passages Deacon Carey had recited to Falwell at the altar the night of his conversion. These passages were to be used in their "soul-winning" efforts: Falwell and his newfound Christian friends would knock on doors every Monday night, telling perfect strangers about the change that had taken place in their lives because they had accepted Christ. The late-night poker games and hanging out at the Pickeral Café gave way to a life centered on the church. By the end of the spring, Falwell's habits had changed, and those changes would characterize his life until the day he died.[5]

At the heart of all these church-related activities was Falwell's desire to better understand precisely what conversion entailed. At the altar call the night of his conversion, he was introduced to the five key passages that fundamentalists use to explain salvation. In the Book of Romans, Paul writes, "Since all have sinned and fall short of the glory of God" (Rom 3:23), and later, "For the wages of sin is death" (Rom 6:23). These two passages lead the sinner to acknowledge his unworthiness, a necessary precursor to conversion and preparation for the acknowledgment of his need for a savior. "I am the resurrection and the life; he who believes in me, though he die, yet shall he live," from the Gospel of John (11:25), provides the remedy for sin, and that same Gospel describes the necessity of being born again: "Truly, truly, I say to you, unless one is born anew, he cannot see the kingdom of God" (Jn 3:3). Finally, Falwell learned the scriptural text that was at the heart of all Reformation theology, from Paul's Letter to the Ephesians: "For by grace you have been saved through faith; and this is not your own doing, it is the gift of God—not because of works, lest any man should boast" (Ep 2:8–9). These five scriptural passages represent foundational Christian doctrine, shared by all the churches, although different denominations understand them differently. For Donnelson, Dinsbeer, and their pupil Jerry Falwell, these texts were understood as the core of Christian belief, the primary explication of God's plan of salvation, the road map for the individual believer.[6]

It was during these early months as a Christian that Falwell learned how to pray. He had a long prayer list and a short one. The long list included the names of his family, ongoing needs, and generic prayers for the country and the world. His short list focused on daily issues. He learned to carve out time to pray. And Falwell recognized two essentials to biblical prayer. First, you must bring your requests to God confident that He will deliver them, and second, you must ask for those things that God, in the Bible, has already promised to give. Prayer rooted in the Bible means that it is "more likely God will listen to my request."[7]

When he recalled those early months after his conversion many years later, Falwell employed a mix of biblical and military metaphors. He saw his life as a "born-again" Christian as a journey, a common biblical metaphor for spiritual growth amid the dangers of temptation. He had learned that the "world of man" is run by Satan and the world of God is ruled by the Lord Jesus, and while the two overlap, only faith permits the soul to rest comfortably in the world of God while still living in the world of man. He saw his fellow parishioners at Park Avenue Baptist Church as "my fellow Christian soldiers marching as to war," with Christ as their Commander-in-Chief; the front porches where he and his fellow soul-winners witnessed were "scenes of battle" between God and Satan. Falwell learned that the principal task of the Christian is to evangelize, to spread the Good News. His decision to quit Lynchburg College and attend a Bible college was the final, decisive shift from his old life to his new one. At the recommendation of Pastor Donnelson and Jack Dinsbeer, Falwell decided to enroll at Baptist Bible College in Springfield, Missouri.[8]

Falwell could have wandered into any one of Lynchburg's many churches and had a conversion experience, but the church he did wander into was an evangelical Baptist church. The college he decided to attend on his pastor's recommendation was a fundamen-

talist Baptist college. Not only would the traditions of both the evangelical church and fundamentalist theology take root in Falwell, but
he would become the most visible face of fundamentalist, evangelical Christianity in a country that often misunderstood, sometimes
almost willfully, this kind of religious expression.

Falwell would be shaped just as profoundly by the history specific
to American evangelicalism. The great historian of religion George
Marsden highlights several characteristics of evangelical Christianity that reinforced or created aspects of the national character. The
"free individual" was a staple of evangelical calls for a spiritual decision to convert, as opposed to Calvin's doctrine of predestination,
and it amplified the growing democratic spirit of the age: Method-
ism, not Calvinism, was the largest denomination in the land by
1820, and it would shape, and be shaped by, Jacksonian democratic
ideals. As well, in the nineteenth century, science was seen as a means
for exploring God's creation, not as the source of a distinct, nonreligious worldview. Evangelicals also were unafraid of certain techniques that would later acquire secular power: the evangelist Charles
Finney, founder of Oberlin College, was a "proto-advertiser" who
carefully crafted his message to fit his listeners and advertised his
preaching with a view to attracting more listeners.[9]

Other characteristics of early evangelical Christianity in America would be especially prominent in Falwell's ministry. There was a
certain populism in the evangelical churches, a sense that they were
starting something new by getting back to the basics, which meant,
for them, back to the Bible. Evangelical Christians celebrated themselves as "primitive churches," free from the cultural encrustations of
the centuries, pristine and apostolic. This led them to emphasize also
the importance of mission work and preaching the Gospel as a way
of bringing about the millennial era. Some evangelicals advocated
social reforms as well, such as a ban on dueling, prostitution, alcohol, and Sabbath-breaking. Some of this social agenda overlapped
with anti-Catholic bias. Catholic immigrants, mostly from Germany
and Ireland in the late eighteenth and early nineteenth centuries,
considered alcohol a normal part of their culture. All these characteristics would manifest themselves in Falwell's ministry.[10]

One other aspect of religion's historical role in American culture warrants attention. The rise of the American Republic coincided with the advent of modern capitalism. Indeed, the religiously celebrated values of thrift and frugality were essential to the success of early capitalism. Nonetheless, the nascent capitalist economy stimulated the profit motive to an unprecedented degree, and "there were no other strong institutions or traditions to oppose the capitalist motive." Evangelical Christianity, especially in the North, approached the challenges of capitalism from a purely technical perspective, neglecting to address it as a moral or religious issue. In the South, where capitalism was less fully developed, the profiteering of the North was viewed suspiciously, especially when compared to the more traditional, genteel, and agrarian ways of the South—genteel, that is, for everyone but the slaves. In Falwell's later career, he would fully embrace capitalism, in part because of his intense anticommunism. For many evangelicals, including Falwell, communism was a possible harbinger of the End Times, and such evangelical opposition to communism would be one of the eventual bridges connecting him to conservative politics.[11]

The loose ecclesiological structures of the Baptist religion had been ideally suited to propagating that faith in the rural and frontier regions of antebellum America. Those same structures, however, were unable to keep the church in any kind of visible communion when the Civil War brought sectional loyalties to the fore. "Despite the fact that Baptists take it as creed that there is no defining creed— or perhaps because of that—their internal alliances have been fragile and fluctuating," notes one historian of religion. Among the Protestant denominations, only the Episcopalians escaped a permanent sectional separation. The ties of faith in most churches were snapped in two by the priority of the political divide that afflicted the nation, and not for the last time.[12]

Both sides in the Civil War invested their cause with crusading sensibilities. Both believed that God was on their side. "Religious commitments, rather than helping to unify the nation, now reinforced both sides' resolve to persevere in a tortuous civil war," writes Marsden. But the Civil War brought death and devastation to the entire South and only to the South. Apart from the physical devastation, southerners experienced in a way unique in American history what it is to lose, and to lose everything. Reconstruction, which compounded the sense of inferiority and insecurity, reached even into the pulpits. "All places of public worship in Norfolk and Portsmouth are hereby placed under the control of the provost marshals of Norfolk and Portsmouth respectively, who shall see the pulpits properly filled by displacing, when necessary, the present incumbents, and substituting men of known loyalty and the same sectarian denomination, either military or civil subject to the approval of the commanding general." These were the orders given in one Virginia area recently conquered by the Yankees. The certainties of Bible-believing churches provided the only antidote available to southerners who had seen their civilization crushed and extinguished.[13]

In the post–Civil War years, evangelical Christianity inspired a host of reform efforts that reinforced the Protestant character of the country. Prohibitionism was directed against Catholics. The Young Men's Christian Association (YMCA), brought to America in 1851, spread quickly throughout the country after the war and was understood as a form of protection against Catholic, immigrant influences. "Blue laws" forbidding the operation of public businesses on Sunday were directed against Jewish merchants. Progressive political reforms were presented not in terms of abstract, liberal constitutional theory but in the "ongoing Puritan spirit of civic responsibility," and liberal populists like William Jennings Bryan intertwined evangelical Christian and progressive themes at will. The "Manifest Destiny" of the United States to subdue the continent and spread the American Gospel combined Anglo-Saxon racialism with Protestant missionary sensibilities. When Theodore Roosevelt formed his "Bull Moose" Party as a progressive alternative to the Republican Party in 1912, the party's campaign song was "Onward, Christian Soldiers."[14]

Evangelicalism faced new challenges from within the Christian church at the turn of the century. The rise of biblical scholarship and the "Social Gospel" movement, which saw social justice as the heart of the Gospel, brought new understandings of what the Bible meant. The great Calvinist universities of the North—Harvard, Yale, and

Princeton—thoroughly lost their religious character, leaving only overly large, under-used chapels as testimony to their religious origins. Even North Carolina's Wake Forest University, founded to train Baptist clergy in 1834, had made attendance at chapel voluntary in the 1930s, and the last campus revival was held in 1934.[15]

Challenges came from outside the church too, even while church membership continued to grow. Popular writers such as Mark Twain criticized the Bible-believing culture, fashioning cartoonish characters like Senator Dilworthy in "The Gilded Age." Emerging alongside the evangelical liberalism of Bryan was the pragmatic and secular liberalism of men like John Dewey and Oliver Wendell Holmes, Jr. Charles Darwin's theory of evolution raised profound questions about the origin of man and encouraged a naturalistic, thoroughly mundane view of humankind. The leading Protestant denominations tripled their membership in the last four decades of the nineteenth century, but within each of these denominations questions were being asked about the historical roots of religious belief and the origin of mankind that shocked many Christians who were more conservative, especially those in the South.[16]

Southern evangelicals were slow to perceive the threats facing their faith. First, theirs was an essentially homogenous, mostly rural society, and so the social challenges posed by urbanization, industrialization, and immigration were not as great in the South as in the North and Midwest. Second, the evangelical focus on the conversion of the heart and spiritual rebirth insulated evangelicals from some of the intellectual challenges posed by biblical criticism and new scientific discoveries: rather than answer these challenges, evangelicals ignored and dismissed them as the work of evil—and not coincidentally northern—theologians. "It is better to trust the Rock of Ages than to know the ages of rocks," said Bryan confidently. And against the Social Gospel movement, southern evangelicals invoked the doctrine of the "spirituality of the church," which saw no role for the church as a vehicle for social or political agitation. They focused on preaching about sin and salvation and advocated daily spiritual reading and living a godly life. Of course, for southern whites this doctrine conveniently confirmed their cultural dominance within their own region. But the doctrinal challenge of modernist, liberal, critical theology would provoke a response from southern evangelicals of the kind who founded and attended Park Avenue Baptist Church, and fundamentalism would be born.[17]

Controversies surrounding biblical criticism and the Social Gospel movement were thoroughly opaque to Jerry Falwell as he drove his Plymouth to Missouri to attend Baptist Bible College. He knew he liked the fire-and-brimstone preaching of Charles Fuller that he had heard on the radio Sunday mornings before his conversion. He knew that he liked the similar preaching of Pastor Donnelson and Jack Dinsbeer at Park Avenue Baptist, and they were the ones who had recommended the school to him. Many of his nonfundamentalist contemporaries would not have even known of the existence of schools like Bible Baptist College. Fundamentalists were flying "under the radar screen" culturally, but Falwell was about to join them.

In the face of the modernist challenges to traditional Christian belief, Southern Baptists (and some other conservative Protestants) were able to build on aspects of their own tradition to resist the "acids of modernity," as Walter Lippman called the intellectual and social changes of the early twentieth century. The modernist challenge was principally a doctrinal one that used the tools of modern historical science to assess the scriptures, defined different literary genres, and openly questioned the historicity of certain biblical accounts. Some Baptists decided to ride the modernist tide, especially in the North. But among southern evangelical Baptists, the most characteristic response would become known as fundamentalism, a recommitment to the basic doctrinal teachings of the church as they had been popularly understood and as they would henceforth be even more rigidly enforced in seminaries and adhered to in the pulpits.

The term "fundamentalism" is taken from "The Fundamentals," a twelve-volume series of books containing essays on a variety of themes from the divinity of Christ to the virgin birth; these essays define and defend the "fundamentals" of the Christian faith as understood by conservative Protestants. The series was published between 1910 and 1915 by the Bible Institute of Los Angeles and paid for by Lyman Stewart, one of the cofounders of Union Oil. He wanted to have the books distributed for free to seminarians and pastors. Most important, the books attacked the efforts of biblical scholars to understand the books of the Bible in their historical context, an intellectual quest known as "higher criticism." For the fundamentalists, the Bible was the inerrant Word of God and every comma and preposition was placed there under the inspiration of the Holy Spirit. To question any part of the Bible was to question the whole structure of faith.[18]

The intellectuals who wrote the essays in "The Fundamentals" understood their project as a direct response to liberalizing trends in theology, and some of them were intellectual heavyweights themselves. J. Gresham Machen, professor of New Testament at Princeton University and one of the leading lights of the movement, denounced efforts to reach accommodation with science and modern historical scholarship. "In the intellectual battle of the present day there can be no 'peace without victory'; one side or the other must win." Dialogue with the mainstream culture was useless so long as it was corrupted by "unbelief" masquerading as science.[19]

For many less sophisticated Christians, the fundamentalist claims were unremarkable. In rural areas and especially among the unlettered, the Bible was often the only book a family owned, and many of these believers had never thought to question the account of Creation set forth in the Book of Genesis, although there are actually two separate and distinct accounts of Creation in that book of the Bible. They did not care to grapple with the differing accounts of such pivotal events as the Ascension of Jesus, which is placed in Galilee shortly after the Resurrection in the Gospel of Matthew, in Jerusalem immediately after the Resurrection in the Gospel of Mark, and in Bethany sometime after the Resurrection (tradition put the time at forty days) in the Gospel of Luke.

Immediately after the formation of a "fundamentalist party" within conservative Christianity, disaster struck. The Scopes trial brought scores of journalists to the small town of Dayton, Tennessee, where John Scopes stood accused of teaching evolution in the public schools in violation of state law. Some 165,000 words would be sent out by telegraph over wires especially installed to carry the news. Scopes was defended by one of the foremost trial lawyers of the day, Clarence Darrow, and the State of Tennessee had as its lawyer William Jennings Bryan. (The play and movie *Inherit the Wind* is based on the trial.) Although Scopes was convicted, the trial was seen as a complete defeat for fundamentalism in the court of public opinion. One of the most popular news writers of the day, H. L. Mencken, whose reports from the trial were syndicated through the *Baltimore Sun,* was merciless in his portrayal of fundamentalism and fundamentalists. "The Scopes Trial, from the start, has been carried on in a manner exactly fitted to the anti-evolution law and the simian imbecility under it," Mencken wrote. "The rustic judge, a candidate for re-election, has postured before the yokels like a clown in a ten-cent side show, and almost every word he has uttered has been an undisguised appeal to their prejudices and superstitions." On cross-examination by Darrow, Bryan did himself no favors, admitting that he was unable to resolve certain stories in the Bible with the demands of common sense.[20]

In the wake of the Scopes trial, fundamentalists went into exile, in part self-imposed. "They left their denominations and formed new organizations uncontaminated by modern theology; they declared social reform hopeless; and they disavowed all manner of modern sociability," writes one historian of fundamentalism.[21] By abandoning the culture and "separating out," conservative Christians were unable to combat the increasing secularization of the dominant culture. They created their own churches, their own schools, their own narratives. And they continued to grow. The Southern Baptist Convention doubled its membership between 1940 and 1960. Smaller, independent fundamentalist associations also grew rapidly. The Baptist Bible Fellowship, to which Baptist Bible College belonged, claimed 1,800 churches nationwide, with 750,000 members, within twenty years of its founding.[22]

All Americans, including southerners, got swept up in the patriotic fervor occasioned by World War II. Powerful southern senators ensured that military installations were built throughout the states of the old Confederacy. The sectional, separationist memories of the Civil War largely melted into the background as America fought the "good war" and as first radio and then television created a national culture. After the war, anticommunism kept the patriotic juices flowing and provided a religious, crusading temperament to U.S. foreign policy as America faced down "godless communism" around the globe. The horrifying specter of nuclear war added an apocalyptic hue to the Cold War. All this resulted in both unprecedentedly high rates of church membership and a fusion of Christian identity with Americanism. The words "under God" were added to the Pledge of Allegiance, the National Prayer Breakfast was begun, and William Randolph Hearst told his newspapers to "puff" an upstart evangelical preacher named Billy Graham.[23]

In the postwar era, increased prosperity brought the endemic poverty of the rural South and Midwest to an end. The Great Depression, coming on the heels of the Scopes Trial, had added to the sense of cultural and social isolation felt by many fundamentalists, but the postwar economy brought new wealth and the accoutrements of a technologically advanced culture into previously poor areas. Lynchburg had always had many wealthy families, but the postwar prosperity lifted middle-class families into the ranks of "the haves." Increased mobility accompanied the explosion of affordable automobiles and new highways.[24]

These great ideological struggles between fundamentalism and modernity were not Falwell's most immediate concern when he arrived in Springfield, Missouri. His roommate was, of all people, the fiancé of Falwell's own Lynchburg sweetheart Macel, Julius Blasz. Before leaving Lynchburg, Falwell had been courting Macel, who evidently did not take her engagement too seriously and later admitted to entertaining several suitors after putting Julius's ring on her finger. Falwell turned the situation to his romantic advantage, offering to carry Julius's letters to the post office and then destroying them and sending his own. He also neglected to pass on phone messages from Macel to Julius. Curiously, our knowledge of Falwell's acts of romantic sabotage comes from Macel herself, and she voices no concern about Falwell's violating her privacy.[25]

Baptist Bible College was only two years old when Falwell arrived in the autumn of 1952. He threw himself into the classes, which ran from 8:00 A.M. until noon, studying subjects like systematic theology, the Old and New Testaments, world missions, and church history. The central focus of the curriculum was on learning the Bible thoroughly, a task for which Falwell's photographic memory suited him well. The president of the college was a prominent midwestern fundamentalist, Rev. George Beauchamp Vick, pastor of the Temple Baptist Church in Detroit. Almost all of the professors were fundamentalist ministers, and their task was to train the next generation of preachers. In that very first year Falwell developed his lifelong approach to reading the Bible: by reading three chapters a day and five on Sunday, he could read the entire book every year.[26]

Falwell was not as coarse in his fundamentalism as were some of its earliest progenitors. Billy Sunday, a popular evangelist in the first decades of the century, had said, "When scholarship says one thing and the Bible says another, scholarship can go to hell." That was not Falwell's way. But his inquisitiveness about the meaning of scripture was strictly confined and easily satisfied. Later in life a fellow pastor asked him about an apparent discrepancy in the scriptures. The Gospels of Mark, Matthew, and Luke report that Jesus cleansed the Temple at the end of his public ministry, but the Gospel of John places the episode at the beginning of Jesus's ministry. Which was it? Falwell replied, "When I was a student at Baptist Bible College in Missouri, I had a professor who explained that all very well to my satisfaction." With that, he brought the discussion to a close.[27]

In the afternoon the students were required to work part-time. Falwell's mother had given him enough money that he did not need to earn a paycheck, so he offered his services to the school's faculty chairman, Rev. W. E. "Bill" Dowell, who pastored the High Street Baptist Church, one of Springfield's larger congregations. The church had two thousand students in the Sunday school, and Dowell sent Falwell to see Max Hawkins, who oversaw the classes for students aged nine through eleven. "I don't have much hope for you Bible student types," Hawkins told Falwell, deflating his enthusiasm while assigning him the custody of one eleven-year-old boy. Falwell and the boy were both unenthusiastic about their interactions, and Falwell could not see why the child couldn't be put into one of the other classrooms. When he went to Hawkins to complain, Hawkins told him to quit, which ignited Falwell's competitive streak. He began scouring the neighborhoods of Springfield for eleven-year-olds to join his class. He prayed daily for guidance and enthusiasm.[28]

Ever the prankster, Falwell devised a trick to impress young boys and entice them to attend his Sunday school class. He would drive around town in his Plymouth with some of the students he had already recruited. When he spotted a potential student, he would invite him to go for a ride. Falwell had loosened the steering wheel so that he could remove it while driving, using a set of pliers attached to the steering column to steer the automobile with his left hand. He would hand the steering wheel to the newcomer sitting in the passenger seat, who would be so fixated on the wheel that he did not notice Falwell's left hand clutching the pliers. The trick was enough to pass the "cool" sniff test of most eleven-year-olds. By the end of the school year Falwell had fifty-six students in his class.[29]

Between his junior and senior years, Falwell took a year off from Baptist Bible College to return to Lynchburg and help out at Park Avenue Baptist. Both Pastor Donnelson and Jack Dinsbeer had left to take new assignments, and Falwell thought he knew just the man to take the pulpit in Lynchburg. He drove Frank Wood, a fellow student at Baptist Bible College, all the way to Lynchburg, and Wood was hired on the spot. Falwell agreed to stay on for a year helping to get the youth ministry up and running. He worked closely with Billy and Iona Lynes, who taught key classes for the youth ministry, and they became close friends. Falwell used tactics similar to those that had worked in Springfield, driving around town inviting young people he encountered on playgrounds or at the market to join the group. He also made a concentrated, and mostly successful, effort to recruit one of Lynchburg's adolescent gangs. The yearlong sojourn also allowed Falwell to ramp up his courtship of Macel Pate, who had by then ended her engagement and appeared more receptive to Falwell's advances.[30]

Falwell returned to Baptist Bible College in the autumn of 1955 for his senior year. He took a weekend job at the Kansas City Baptist Temple, working as a youth minister. The Kansas City Bible Temple was a thriving church, pastored by Wendell Zimmerman, with more than seven hundred people at every worship service on Sunday. It was a three-hour drive from Springfield to Kansas City, and Falwell stayed with the pastor's parents each weekend. He worked with young adults, found many of the group's leaders too headstrong, and began forming new leadership within the group. Falwell claims that the old guard whom he replaced came around to appreciate him by the end of the year: they took him out for cheesecake at the end of his tenure and tearfully apologized—"confessed their shame"—for having resisted him at first. As with his accounts of his high school pranks, there was a happy, providential ending to this story of Falwell's, but there is no reason to doubt the basic facticity of his account, which paints him as a bit headstrong for a visiting, temporary weekend minister.[31]

As Falwell's tenure at the Kansas City Bible Temple came to a close, Pastor Zimmerman surprised him by insisting that he take the pulpit at the main service the following Sunday. Falwell prayed that he would be up to the task and that his sermon would not be a "flop." He fasted and prayed for three days, and when the time for him to enter the pulpit finally arrived, he was calm. He preached on sanctification, taking Hebrews 9 and 10 as his text. When he finished and made the call to the altar, nineteen people came forward, including an elderly woman who told Falwell she had been a charter member of the congregation but had only been truly "born-again" that morning as a result of his preaching.[32]

Falwell graduated at the top of his class in May 1956, and the graduation speaker was Dr. Bob Jones Sr., whose son would later challenge Falwell, calling him "the most dangerous man in America." Falwell's mother and sister surprised him by flying out to

Springfield for the graduation ceremony. He planned on returning briefly to Lynchburg before heading to Georgia: his friends Billy and Iona Lynes had moved there and were encouraging him to come and start a church. His conversion was now complete. Five years before, he had not bothered to darken the door of a church. Now he was a fully trained fundamentalist preacher.[33]

Chapter Three

The Preacher

Founding Thomas Road Baptist Church

Jerry Falwell returned to Lynchburg with the intention of enjoying a brief sojourn there before heading to Georgia to start a new church. But upon his return he discovered that his home church, Park Avenue Baptist, was in crisis, beset with divisions that threatened to tear it apart. In the end, this would lead Falwell to decide not to go to Georgia, but to stay in Lynchburg and plant a new church there. He would challenge head-on the biblical warning that no prophet is without honor except in his hometown. Once begun, his new church would be the foundation of his entire life.

Although the actions of divine grace are unseen, and to the believer transcendent in their origin and universal in their scope, they are received in a specific time and place. Transcendence is only half the equation; when the transcendent is made manifest in this life, the actions of grace are viewed as providential, as the divine having come down to earth to direct the footsteps and the minds of believers. These actions become attached to distinct memories, evoked by familiar faces or familiar surroundings. They become subject to the laws and the dynamics of enculturation.

Jerry Falwell had accepted the Lord Jesus as his savior at Park Avenue Baptist Church. The place and its people contained nothing but happy associations. Jack Dinsbeer had helped him take his first few steps along the path of Christian discipleship. Falwell had introduced the church to its new pastor, Frank Wood. He had built up the youth ministry only a year earlier. And of course, he had met his beloved Macel there. Park Avenue was his "spiritual family." But when Falwell made his way back to Lynchburg, Macel and her family were among thirty-five members of the church who had left, determined to start their own church. Macel recalled that they had been told to leave because they had voted against making Wood the permanent pastor. Falwell called the group the "dissenters," which had no negative connotations in the evangelical tradition.[1]

By prior arrangement, Falwell spent his first two Sundays back in Virginia preaching at churches in Richmond. On the second weekend the thirty-five dissenters traveled as a group to hear Falwell preach, and the former chairman of the deacon board at Park Avenue Baptist invited him to join them for lunch afterward at a restaurant in Richmond. There they invited Falwell to join them in their effort to found a new church. He was surprised by the request and promised to pray about it. On the subsequent two Sundays, Falwell again left town to fill the pulpits of nearby churches. During the week he prayed about what to do and discussed the situation with the dissenters. He liked being back home, surrounded by his family, close to Macel, but he was unsure of what to do.[2]

Falwell met with Frank Wood. He told the pastor that the dissenters were determined to start their own church and that they had pledged themselves to avoiding any sense of competition with Park Avenue Baptist Church. Falwell thought that Lynchburg was large enough for two churches belonging to the Baptist Bible Fellowship and that the two churches could work together; in fact, he pointed out, such divisions in other churches had often resulted in renewed growth for both churches. But the leadership of the Baptist Bible Fellowship disagreed and, through Pastor Wood, communicated their displeasure at the prospect of a second church in Lynchburg. Falwell, however, had made up his mind. He would stay in Lynchburg and pastor the dissenters, at least for a while. As a consequence, he found himself "excommunicated" from the Baptist Bible Fellowship, unable to preach in its pulpits or send seminarians to the college from which he himself had just graduated as valedictorian. The new church and its new pastor would be entirely on their own. "I felt terrible and alone and abandoned," Falwell would recall. Macel saw the conflict in biblical terms: "The enemy [Satan] designed this attack to either get Jerry out of God's will or leave him so hurt and bitter that he was no good to God. Because Jerry didn't let either of those things happen, God forged in him the kind of backbone required to change a nation."[3]

Falwell returned to his elementary school auditorium, where the dissenters gathered on June 21, 1956, for their first service. They prayed for God's guidance and, specifically, for a new home for their church. That week Falwell learned of a vacant building in the west end of town on Thomas Road. The area had been built up in the years since World War II, and the hills were dotted with small prefabricated homes. The building had once been the Donald Duck Bottling Company, and the floors were still covered with soda syrup. It was fifty feet long and thirty feet wide, and most important, it was available and affordable. They leased it for $300 a month and set about scrubbing the soda syrup off the floors, painting the walls, and hanging curtains over the cracked windows. They purchased seats from an old movie theater and an upright piano for Macel to play. On July 1, they held their first Sunday worship service in the newly christened Thomas Road Baptist Church. Until the day he died, Falwell kept one of the Donald Duck soda bottles in his study.[4]

The next day Falwell went to the church. They had walled in a little "pastor's study" that was six feet square, and Falwell put his small collection of books and a wooden desk in the room. He tacked a map of Lynchburg to the wall and drew concentric circles on it, with Thomas Road Baptist Church at the center. He prayed over the first chapter of the Acts of the Apostles: "And ye shall be witnesses unto me both in Jerusalem, and in all Judea, and in Samaria, and

unto the uttermost part of the earth." On the map he labeled the
ten-block radius surrounding the church "Jerusalem" and the next
twenty-block radius on the map "Judea"; the final circle he labeled
"Samaria." He would witness in each of these areas, recruiting new
church members. He later wrote that "that morning, I sat at my small
wooden desk feeling exactly like Eisenhower as he plotted D-Day
and the invasion of Europe."[5]

Falwell's method of evangelization and recruitment was a simple one. He visited one hundred homes per day. He left his pastor's
study each morning by nine o'clock, carrying his Bible and a yellow
legal pad for taking notes. If someone said they belonged to another
church, he would say that while he did not want to take them away
from their own church on Sunday mornings, he hoped they might
attend his Sunday evening service. Falwell also mentioned what the
subject of his sermon was going to be. Sometimes he was invited in
to speak at greater length, and other times he had dogs set on him.
He left each person with a card with two phone numbers, one at
the church and one at his home, promising that his mother would
take messages at the home phone. Upon leaving, Falwell would write
down everything he could remember: how many people lived in the
house, their names and ages, what church they attended, and any
problems they had shared with him.

The first week of his evangelization campaign a church volunteer helped Falwell put together a brief newspaper for the church,
listing activities such as the midweek Bible study, citing the number of children in the Sunday school, and including articles by the
young preacher in which he shared his dreams for the little church
in the Donald Duck Bottling Company. These newsletters would be
mailed to each of the homes Falwell had visited during the week,
and other church volunteers would make a follow-up phone call to
the home, encouraging the occupants to come for a visit. Falwell
referred to this method as the "triple whammy," and by the end of
the first week he awaited the results. On the second Sunday they
held services at the Thomas Road Baptist Church attendance had
doubled.[6]

Falwell was aware of the need for effective collaborators. He was never a "control freak" or a micromanager, and he quickly saw the need to delegate. He selected and trained two senior male members of the congregation to join in his door-knocking evangelization. At first Falwell accompanied them, his presence reassuring them, helping them overcome the predictable anxieties that come with knocking on strangers' doors. Once these two men became comfortable with the task, he had them train other men.

Falwell conveyed both his native enthusiasm and his beliefs about human nature to the men who went out on weeknights to spread the word. "I believe in ignoring the walls that people build," Falwell said. "Behind the facades that separate us, we are all alike. We all need to know that God loves us." Falwell would, in time, recognize that not everyone has a need to know that God loves them and that the differences among people are not entirely rooted in facades.[7]

Not everyone appreciated Falwell's efforts to spread the Gospel. Another minister called him in and said that Falwell and his people were encroaching on his part of town. Falwell asked if the minister was doing home visits, and the minister replied that he was not. Falwell said that he didn't care who brought people to Christ but that someone had to and as long as there were unchurched people in Lynchburg, his door-knocking would continue throughout the city.[8]

Not all of Falwell's efforts were uncontroversial. Church members and ministers at Thomas Road Baptist also made visits to hospital patients, as did ministers from many other churches. A nurse at one hospital noticed that the patients on her ward woke up bright and cheerful but were uniformly depressed and downcast later in the day. She hid behind a folding screen one day to see what was going on. Two ministers from Thomas Road Baptist Church entered the room and asked the patients if they were saved, then went on to provide vivid descriptions of the torments of hell. They offered to intervene with prayer for those who joined the church or made donations to it. One of the men offered to bring a lawyer should the patient want to change his will. "These scoundrels were scaring our patients into donating to their church!" the nurse told her own pastor. Stories such as this guaranteed that while his hard-hitting evangelizing strategies attracted many to Thomas Road Baptist Church, Falwell and his ministerial colleagues were also earning a reputation that turned off many people.[9]

One of the things Falwell noticed on his house calls was that most people had their radios on when he visited. This put him in mind of the radio broadcasts of Charles Fuller that his mother had played loudly every Sunday morning before his conversion. Other evangelists had been using the radio to evangelize since the 1920s, including such famous figures as Aimee Semple McPherson, who broadcast services from her Four Square Gospel Church in Los Angeles until her untimely, and apparently accidental, death from an overdose of sleeping pills. Billy Graham had briefly conducted a radio ministry in 1944–45 as well.

Falwell approached the owner of a recently started country-and-western music station in Lynchburg, WBRG, about carrying a religious program. "I had no doubts about whether to start a radio ministry," Falwell said. "I wanted to reach as many people as I could." Falwell suggested a weekly program on Sunday mornings, but the radio station owner wanted Falwell on first thing every morning. For seven dollars per show, Falwell could broadcast for a half-hour. The radio station went on the air with the sunrise, so in the autumn of 1956, when Falwell began his radio shows, he had to be at the station at 7:00 A.M. In the summertime, when the days grew longer, his broadcasts would go on at 6:30 A.M.[10]

The early morning programs began with a little musical interlude, followed by Falwell sharing news from the Thomas Road Baptist Church, especially tales of people whose lives were being "changed by God through our congregation's ministry." He would play some religious music, originally relying on records but eventually using tape recordings of the singers at his own church. He would then devote the rest of the time to a short sermon. Mindful that he would soon be knocking on doors, he began announcing what neighborhoods he would be visiting. And of course, the radio program reached far beyond the concentric circles drawn on the map in his pastor's study. Falwell's morning program could be heard throughout Lynchburg and in the surrounding counties.[11]

In August the church had so many members that they needed to expand their facilities. They purchased the Donald Duck building, enlarged the worship space, and added classrooms for the Sunday school students. Macel's father, Sam Pate, was paid $2 an hour as contractor to oversee the construction work of the team of volunteers he organized, the first of many contracts the church would extend to Pate. Falwell reached out to a former business colleague and drinking buddy of his father's to help get an unsecured loan of $5,000 from a local bank for the necessary building supplies. The next spring they would need to add another extension to the church building.[12]

By the end of 1956, Falwell had contracted with the local television station, WLVA, for one half-hour of television time every Sunday afternoon at 5:30. The format followed the same regimen as the radio show. Falwell began with news of the church, announcing the time of the services and, especially, that he would be preaching at the 7:00 P.M. service just after the television show. He hired a soloist from the local Methodist church to sing along while Macel played the piano on the set. Then he preached a short sermon. He would conclude with another invitation to join him at church: "Tonight, in just ninety minutes, I will be preaching from the prophet Jeremiah at our church on Thomas Road. You have plenty of time to eat a peanut butter sandwich, drink a glass of milk, grab your Bible, and come on over!" Falwell told his television audience: "I want to welcome you personally; so please stop me at the door and say hello!" The performance was vintage Falwell, folksy and welcoming, direct and filled with religious fervor.[13]

"No other preachers were on television," Falwell wrote. "Television made me a kind of instant celebrity. People were fascinated that they could see and hear me preach that same night in person." They were not the only ones fascinated by Falwell's "celebrity." He too enjoyed the spotlight and the increasing numbers it brought to his church.[14]

Broadcasting is different from ministering to a local community, and the opportunities it presented brought a different set of challenges as well. A pastor knows the people in his congregation and can tailor his message to his audience. To cast broadly is to lose that intimacy and enter the world of celebrity, with all of its unique temptations. Additionally, while every broadcast has the potential to reach a potential convert, it may also reach a potential enemy. The sanctuary of a church provides protection from criticism. The world of broadcast television offers exposure to criticism, which was not always welcomed by the upstart young preacher.

The greater danger, however, was the danger that attends becoming a celebrity. The life of the Spirit is a difficult thing to measure. How many parishioners were more loving and less judgmental, more kind and less vindictive, last week? How many people drew closer to God in prayer? A pastor can see the donations collected as an indicator of approval—but only the approval of men, not the approval of God. Television ratings are yet another way to determine approval, but Nielsen does not call Heaven. In short, the growth in the material aspects of ministry can distort a pastor's perspective. It is human nature to prefer that which is tangible and clear to that which is opaque, but when a pastor focuses overmuch on the material "evidence" of spiritual growth, he or she can easily end up admiring the leaf while forgetting the roots. This is a temptation that Falwell would face throughout his career as a television evangelist.

Such temptations were largely in the future. In these early years Falwell used his radio and television appearances primarily to advertise Thomas Road Baptist Church and recruit new members. Between his radio and television broadcasts and his aggressive door-knocking, the church continued to grow. As the church in the old Donald Duck building completed its first year in existence, Falwell predicted they would have 500 people in attendance at their anniversary service. When the day arrived, Falwell had the ushers count heads and then announced from the pulpit that 864 people had come to worship. His efforts were bearing fruit.[15]

Very few of Falwell's early sermons survive. But from various accounts, it is possible to ascertain the subjects upon which he preached. The vast majority of his sermons dealt with Christian doctrine and godly living. His first sermon, in Kansas City, had been on sanctification, taking the ninth and tenth chapters of Paul's Letter to the Hebrews as his text. The scriptural text for Falwell's first sermon at the Thomas Road Baptist Church was from the third chapter of Paul's Letter to the Philippians, verses 12–14: "Not that I have already obtained this or am already perfect; but I press on to make it my own because Christ Jesus has made me his own. Brethren, do not consider that I have made it my own; but one thing I do, forgetting what lies behind and straining forward to what lies ahead, I press on toward the goal for the prize of the upward call of God in Christ Jesus." We know from his radio and television announcements that at one Sunday evening service Falwell preached on forgiveness, at another on the theme "How to Pray and Get Your Prayers Answered," and that on a third Sunday evening he preached from the Book of Jeremiah.[16]

One early sermon, from 1958, has come down to us, printed in the newsletter that Falwell distributed to those who watched his television show. It is curious that he chose this sermon for the first installment of the newsletter, because it did not treat one of his usual topics. The sermon is entitled "Segregation or Integration, Which?" Unsurprisingly, given that the sermon was preached in 1958 in south-central Virginia, Falwell argued in favor of segregation.

Falwell's sermon begins by blaming the Supreme Court for the "chaos" and "racial tension" that was then on the rise. He also noted that the communist countries were using the racial tension as a propaganda tool throughout the world. Indeed, Falwell did not blame blacks for causing the trouble. "The true negro does not want integration. He realizes his potential is far better among his own." Falwell blamed the push for integration first on Moscow, second on politicians using the issue for their own ends, and finally on the Devil himself, who boxed God out of the Supreme Court's jurisprudence when it rendered its 1954 decision, in *Brown v. Board of Education,* ending legal segregation. "If Chief Justice Warren and his associates had known God's Word and had desired to do the Lord's will, I am quite confident that the 1954 decision would never have been made,"

Falwell said. "What could possibly have been worked out in a scriptural and orderly way, now has become a touchy problem."[17]

Falwell claimed that he had "no animosity in my heart" toward any race and that God was no respecter of persons. "The soul of the negro is just as valuable in the sight of God as the soul of a white man." He mentioned that the church supported a missionary family in Africa as evidence of his concern for "negro souls" and his willingness to engage a black person about the state of his soul. He also blamed those segregationists who did harbor hatred for blacks and proposed violence to defend segregation, and he expressed the hope that none of his congregants would engage in such "un-Christian tactics."

Turning to the Bible, Falwell preached that God had ordained segregation of the races, first by selecting the Jews as His chosen people. That was discrimination. He cited the Book of Deuteronomy and the Book of Genesis for his belief in segregation. In Deuteronomy, God ordains which land belongs to which people, thus separating them one from another. In Genesis, Falwell focused on the Curse of Ham, who had seen his father Noah naked and been sent away. Fundamentalists believed that Ham was the progenitor of the black race, Japheth the founder of the Gentiles, and Shem the ancestor of the Jews. Falwell urged his listeners to consult not only their Bibles but their Bible dictionary and concordance to see that what he was speaking was the truth. The biblical text is, after all, somewhat contradictory, and it conflates territorial with ethnic divisions.

The separation of the races had been God's doing. "If we persist in tearing down God's barriers, God must punish us for it. The theory of communism is social equality—but there is no such thing," Falwell concluded. "Souls are of equal value and importance, but that is as far as we can go." He warned that if blacks and whites mixed in schools and public places, soon there would be social mixing, "which can only lead to marital relationships." He told of a northern pastor he knew who had a mixed-race couple who "live next door to his church as man and wife." He finished with a call to pray for the nation's civil authorities, invoking Paul's Letter to Timothy in which he calls for prayers for the king and all who are in authority, "that we may lead a quiet and peaceful life in all godliness and honesty."

The sermon was not far different from what one might have encountered in any of the other white churches in Lynchburg in 1958. Even those pastors with more training in biblical scholarship and a higher commitment to it—those who could see that the Book of Genesis was more convoluted than Falwell and the segregationists made it seem—had to weigh the value of challenging the South's Jim Crow laws. Their arguments might have been less coarse and simplistic than Falwell's, but his opposition to integration was not uncommon at that time and in that place. There were exceptions, of course, most notably evangelist Billy Graham, who had called for the integration of Baptist colleges in 1952. The next year Graham forcibly integrated one of his revivals in Chattanooga, Tennessee, removing the barriers between the section for blacks and the section for whites erected by the local organizers. But Billy Graham was the exception.[18]

During these early years of his ministry, Falwell befriended R. B. Whittemore and his daughter Ann. They lived in nearby Campbell County on an old farm, and Falwell would drive out there two or three times a week to read the Bible and pray together. "There was something about those two Whittemores that drew me back to their home like a pair of magnets," Falwell recalled. "It didn't take many conversations with these two warm, loving, sensitive people to realize that they had 'something' that I needed and wanted very much." The "something" was a deeper spiritual life.[19]

The Whittemores, with their basic, searching questions, served as a perfect counterpoint to Falwell's hyperkinetic discipleship. He would tell them how many people had been converted in the previous week, or how many attended church services, and they would ask what God was doing "inside" his soul. While he read the Acts of the Apostles as an exciting tale of evangelism in the early church, they focused on how the Holy Spirit moved the disciples and the frequency with which those early church leaders "wasted" time in unfocused prayer. While he kept busy scribbling names and notes on his legal pad during his daily door-knockings, they urged him to simply praise God, stay close to Him in prayer, and let God accomplish His purposes through him.[20]

Falwell was introduced to a variety of contemporary spiritual and devotional authors under the tutelage of the Whittemores, as well as to some of history's great spiritual writers. But his education was uneven: Falwell would lump a genuine theological giant like Martin Luther with George Müller, a nineteenth-century German evangelist known for founding orphanages in England, not for his theological genius. Falwell's interest, and that of his teachers, was not in theology per se, but in prayer. The relationship between theology and prayer is intense, to be sure, but they are not the same thing, and Falwell's lack of interest in theology would be a constant throughout his career. For him, religion was a matter of the heart and the will, not a matter for the head. This did not diminish his effectiveness within the world of fundamentalist Baptists, but it would inhibit his eventual effort to reach out to more theologically informed contemporaries when he started the Moral Majority in 1979, and it would limit his capacity to develop religious rationales for the political positions he would espouse.[21]

Falwell records that the Whittemores criticized some of his tactics for growing Thomas Road Baptist Church. They chided him for publishing the number of people saved in his church, the number of people baptized, and the like. "It's not a game, you know," they told him. "You shouldn't be keeping score." Conversely, some of Falwell's parishioners warned him against spending so much time with the Whittemores. They wanted him engaged in the activist work of pavement-pounding evangelism and worried that the pious Whittemores would have him in a monastery. It is clear that Falwell was personally affected by the Whittemores and the spiritual writers to whom they introduced him, but any effects on his ministry were indirect.[22]

Falwell's ministry continued to grow, and not only by means of increased numbers attending services. Falwell had a knack for seeing in the events of his own life a cause for which to fight or a need to be filled. In the early years of his ministry, Thomas Road Baptist Church began a ministry to alcoholics and a youth camp in the summertime.

Carey Falwell's untimely death had been caused by alcoholism, and the tragic incident in which Carey killed his brother Garland had been caused, in part, by Garland's use of drugs. From the time of his conversion, Jerry Falwell considered alcohol one of Satan's tools to wreak havoc in people's lives, and as an adult he never took a drink of it himself. He credited the "deeper spirituality" he learned from the Whittemores with his decision to start a ministry to alcoholics: as he pondered his own life and the alcohol-related tragedies that had marked it, he "began to feel a burden toward the alcoholics in Lynchburg." To "feel a burden," in fundamentalist speech, is to sense an obligation placed by God upon the believer's heart.[23]

Falwell brought his "burden" to Macel, then to the deacons at Thomas Road Baptist Church, and finally to the entire congregation. He was aware of the activities of Alcoholics Anonymous, but he conceived of a different kind of program, an oasis far from the temptations of the city, designed for men in desperate shape. His brother Lewis owned a sixteen-acre farm in Stonewall, Virginia, not far from Lynchburg, and in January 1959 the church bought the property and a team of volunteers began fixing up the old farmhouse. They filled in the cracks in the walls, but they were not able to afford a hookup to the electrical lines, which were more than a mile away.[24]

They were still not finished with their repairs to the property when Rev. John Suttenfield, a pastor at another Lynchburg church, called with an emergency. He had a depressed alcoholic in his office and wondered if Jerry might be able to help him. The man's name was Earl Thompson, and he had once carried illegal alcohol for Falwell's father during Prohibition. Falwell brought him to his house so he could get sober and the next day drove him out to the farm. Thompson was joined by George Ragland, whom Falwell had known for a long time and who also suffered from alcoholism. Falwell named the farm the Elim Home for Alcoholics, after a biblical oasis where the Jews had found clean water. The church hired a full-time minister to oversee the home. The residents, who were expected to stay at least two months, were taught from the scriptures every morning, and in the afternoon they did household and farm chores, went fishing and hunting, or learned vocational skills. They also prayed together.[25]

Lynchburg's *Daily Advance* sent a reporter to the Elim Home to write an article about the program. When the story got picked up by the Associated Press, the home was flooded with applications. One reader, a wealthy utility executive named James Cooke, was so impressed with the new ministry that he flew out by helicopter to announce that an electrical line would be hooked up to the house shortly and that he had hired an electrician to do the wiring in the house. Cooke also arranged for a new septic system and new appliances. The Elim Home was up and running, and it continues to care for alcoholics to this day.[26]

Treasure Island is a small island located in the middle of the James River, just opposite the downtown section of Lynchburg and connected to the shore by an old bridge. The YMCA built a recreational facility on the island in 1912 and ran it until 1931, when, with the financial strains of the Depression, it could no longer afford to manage its programs. Still, the island was used by the citizens of Lynchburg every Fourth of July for a citywide picnic.[27]

In 1963 Falwell learned that the island was for sale. Elim, Inc., which was the nonprofit corporation Falwell had created to own the Elim Home for Alcoholics, purchased the island for $49,900, with the seller contributing the remaining $25,100 of the purchase price. A local lumberman and a wealthy woman who listened to Falwell's radio show contributed the lumber and materials for a youth camp, including a large chapel. James Moon Jr., who was the youth minister at Thomas Road Baptist Church, oversaw the camp, which was also used for church picnics and Sunday school outings. Every summer as many as two thousand children took part in the youth camp. "It was quite a thing," Moon recalled. "Treasure Island had become a very big part of the ministry." In the early 1970s, the island's cabins were winterized and turned into dormitories for students at Falwell's newly formed Liberty Baptist College. The island was used until

1985, when a massive flood damaged all the buildings and destroyed the bridge connecting the island to the mainland. Three years later vandals set fire to the buildings that remained standing.[28]

Falwell's last major building project in the early years of his ministry was the construction of a new sanctuary for Thomas Road Baptist Church. The congregation had outgrown its worship space in the old Donald Duck building. That original building had been added on to, and a new educational building had been built. But with his congregation continuing to grow, Falwell decided it was time to build a new structure. In that new space, he would deliver one of his most famous sermons.

As always, financing was a difficulty. Falwell's congregation was not affluent, and the contractor estimated that the building Falwell wanted to build would cost $195,000. He approached the head of the bank where Macel had worked to ask how he could go about securing the money for his new church building and was surprised when the bank's president offered him a loan for the entire amount on the spot.[29]

Construction began. The church was designed in classic colonial style, made of brick, with a columned portico in front. If it had had a steeple, which it did not, it would have looked at home on the village green of any New England township. Inside, white columns supported a balcony and heavy wooden pews lined the two aisles on the main floor. The pulpit was the central feature of the church, as it was in most Baptist churches, with seating for the choir behind. It was a handsome building, and more important, it held one thousand people.

The church was barely finished in 1964 when it was the scene of a desegregation protest. Four protesters from the Congress of Racial Equality (CORE) staged a "kneel-in" at Thomas Road Baptist Church. Three young white teenagers were joined by one black colleague as they stood on the steps of the church with a sign that read "Does God Discriminate?" Falwell told the ushers to let the students come in if they wanted to join the worship service, and when they did come inside, they were shown to seats in the balcony. They continued to be disruptive, however, and were arrested by police when they left the church because they threatened to return the next week. Falwell declined to press charges and told the press that there was nothing wrong with the boys that a good haircut couldn't cure.[30]

The CORE protest was not the first such antidiscrimination demonstration in Lynchburg. In 1960 two black students from Virginia Seminary joined white students from Randolph-Macon College and Lynchburg College in a lunch counter sit-in at a downtown drugstore. The next day more students staged another sit-in at a different drugstore. Both times the students were arrested and later released for "good behavior." Neither the sit-ins at the drugstores nor the kneel-in at the church resulted in violence. But the lack of violence did not portend a lessening of racial animus, and the race issue would shape Falwell's career even after he entered the political arena.[31]

Falwell did not yet believe that politics was a proper place for a preacher. It was from the pulpit of this second church sanctuary that Falwell preached one of his most famous sermons, "Ministers and Marches," delivered on March 21, 1965, at the evening service. The sermon was so popular that it was printed in pamphlet form. But its real fame came more than a decade later when it would be viewed ironically in light of its central theme: a call for preachers to stay out of politics.[32]

Falwell began "Ministers and Marches" by saying that he had no intention of questioning anyone's constitutional right to peacefully demonstrate for redress of grievances. Nor did he intend to focus on the issue of segregation itself. "It is my desire, in this sermon, to open the Bible and, from God's Word, answer the question—'Does the "CHURCH" have any command from God to involve itself in marches, demonstrations, or any other actions, such as many ministers and church leaders are doing so today in the name of civil rights reforms?'" Falwell answered this question firmly in the negative.

First, while acknowledging the sincerity of some civil rights protesters, he cast aspersions on Dr. Martin Luther King Jr., James

Farmer, "and others" whom Falwell claimed are "known to have left-wing associations." In the very next sentence, without actually calling King and Farmer communists, he pointed out that communists were calling attention to the civil rights demonstrations. He also asserted that the demonstrations were actually damaging race relations and generating more hate than help at solving the race problem.

"Preachers are not called to be politicians but to be soul winners," Falwell proclaimed to his Sunday night congregation. He claimed that he would "find it impossible" to fight communism or participate in civil rights reform because such tasks would take him away from the time needed to go out and win souls for Christ. He mentioned several of the church's ministries—the work at the Elim Home for Alcoholics, the youth camp on Treasure Island, the mission work in foreign lands—as the proper work of a church. "When the 2,000 members of Thomas Road Baptist Church attend our services, they do not hear sermons on communism, civil rights, or any other subject except the gospel of Christ," he declared. Indeed, he thought the civil rights ministers put the cart before the horse: "If as much effort could be put into winning people to Jesus Christ across the land as is being exerted in the present civil rights movement, America would be turned upside down by God."

Falwell explained the proper mission of the church by examining the Gospel of Matthew, chapter 28, verses 18–20, in which Jesus imparts the "Great Commission." He commands his disciples to do three things: make disciples, or as Falwell put it, "win souls"; baptize; and "teach them the Christ-life." Falwell noted that this same commission is found in the Gospels of Mark and Luke and in the Acts of the Apostles. "We have a message of redeeming grace through a crucified and risen Lord," Falwell told his listeners. "This message is designed to go right to the heart of man and there meet his deep spiritual need. Nowhere are we commissioned to reform the externals." He noted that many of his congregants had once lived sinful lives, but they did not become Christians because any human law forced them to abandon their sinful ways. "They received this Christ as their own personal Lord and Savior. When Christ came in, sin went out."

Countering the biblical example of Moses leading the Israelites out of bondage in Egypt as a metaphor for the civil rights struggle, Falwell pointed out that the Jews were God's chosen people and His dealings with them were "unique indeed." He also wondered why the preachers invoking the Exodus from Egypt did not point out to their followers that the deliverance from slavery was followed by forty years of wandering in the desert and only two of the Israelites who left Egypt, Joshua and Caleb, made it to the Promised Land. It did not occur to Falwell that King understood the Exodus story not only as history but as allegory.

Falwell also turned to the story of the Samaritan woman at the well as justification for his understanding of the proper mission of the church. She had asked Jesus why He, as a Jew, was asking anything of a Samaritan woman. Falwell saw the woman's position as an early example of discrimination and noted that Jesus ignores her question and invites her to address her spiritual needs and to seek the spiritual water He offers. "[Jesus] did not work from the outside in, but rather from the inside out. When she became a Christian, she forgot all about any racial differences."

Falwell then attacked the Social Gospel movement, which he labeled hypocritical because it was unbiblical. "When we as Christians see an existing evil, it is our responsibility to pray. It is also our responsibility to preach the message of a living Christ to those who are in bondage to such sin. But it is never our duty as servants of God to exert physical force or effort which constitutes striving."

The conclusion of the sermon was as clear and forceful as it could be. "Love cannot be legislated," Falwell proclaimed. "Education, medicine, social reform, and all the other external ministries cannot meet the needs of the human soul and spirit. . . . I feel we need to get off the streets and back into the pulpits and into the prayer rooms." He finished with a prayer—and pray well he might, because he would be explaining this sermon for the rest of his life.

Falwell's tireless efforts to expand his ministry—the door-knocking, the radio and television shows, the hospital visits—were all coming to fruition. His church was large and growing. He had become a household name in Lynchburg, and even those who were not members of Thomas Road Baptist Church were tuning in to his radio and television shows. He had begun his ministry to alcoholics and his youth camp on Treasure Island. And he had laid the groundwork for becoming a big player on the fundamentalist stage.

Chapter Four

Family of Faith

While beginning his new church, Falwell also spent the late 1950s and early 1960s building his new family. Falwell's ministry did not compete with his marriage because his wife, Macel, was an integral part of the church's life, and their children would share the ecclesial world into which they were born. And unlike many pastors, Falwell led a personal life that was beyond reproach, with not so much as a whiff of scandal. His wife and his family were his anchors, supportive and consoling, and Falwell was thoroughly devoted to them. Their involvement in his life would shape his ministry at Thomas Road Baptist Church.

Falwell had courted Macel Pate throughout his tenure at Baptist Bible College, driving back to Lynchburg from Missouri to visit both his mother and his intended. He had helped alienate whatever affections she had for her fiancé (and his roommate), and when she called off the engagement Falwell redoubled his efforts to win her. During his year off from school he had worked with the Park Avenue Baptist youth ministry, spending lots of time with Macel. Then, upon his return to Lynchburg, he had changed his plans and agreed to pastor the Park Avenue dissidents, among whom the Pates were prominent.

Macel's father liked Jerry, but her mother, Lucile, was less than enthusiastic. She had taken an instant dislike to all of Macel's suitors, not wanting to see her children leave her own nest. But Mrs. Pate

also disapproved of Falwell's family, with its reputation for bootlegging and fratricide. Macel's two sisters, Jean and Mary Ann, and her
brother Sonny also liked Jerry and helped cover for Macel when she
went on surreptitious dates with Jerry, before he had secured permission to call on Macel at her parents' home.[1]

When he was settled in Lynchburg, Falwell got into the habit each
evening of picking Macel up at the First National Bank, where she
worked. He would drive her home before returning to his work can-
vassing different neighborhoods, knocking on doors in search of converts. When he knocked off around 10:00 P.M., he would drive back
to the Pates' house and talk with Macel until her father knocked
on the wall from his bedroom, which was Jerry's cue to leave. Falwell played several pranks on Macel, such as putting a baby alliga-
tor in her bathtub and enticing a police officer he knew to pull her
over when she was driving without a license. On weekends the two
worked hand-in-glove at the church and the television studio, Jerry
doing the preaching and Macel playing the piano. His leadership of
the young congregation not only endeared him to Macel but wore
down her mother's opposition to the match, but Mrs. Pate still frustrated any effort to set a date for the wedding, and Macel was loath
to disappoint her mother.[2]

By the fall of 1957, Falwell had waited long enough. He noticed
that Macel's sister Jean had been engaged to a young man for years
and that there seemed to be no rush to plan a wedding date. (As
it turned out, Jean's engagement lasted thirty-six years while she
took care of her aging parents.) Macel recalled that Jerry gave her
an ultimatum and she immediately acquiesced, setting a date for
the next spring. In Jerry's account, she did not agree to his ultimatum and he walked out, spending a week apart from Macel, even
going on a date or two with one of the other young women from
the church. His account does not ring true: in the small world of
Thomas Road Baptist Church, going on a date with one or two
eligible young women from the church would have been quite risky
to his reputation.[3]

On April 12, 1958, Jerry and Macel were married before a packed
congregation at Thomas Road Baptist Church, which had only the

month before completed its expansion of the worship space. Rev. John Suttenfield, the minister from a neighboring Christian church, performed the ceremony assisted by a friend of Falwell's from Baptist Bible College, Rev. Vann Barringer. Macel wore a floor-length gown and veil and carried orchids, and Jerry wore a black tuxedo. Both Jerry and Macel recalled that her mother sobbed through the service in the front pew.[4]

After the reception, Macel's friends took her on a joy ride, which they said was part of the celebration. In fact, in an effort to pay back Falwell for his many pranks over the years, they "kidnapped" her, sending Jerry on a long search for his bride. When she finally came back, their car would not start: the spark plugs had been pulled and the wires crossed. When the car was finally fixed, they set out for Niagara Falls for their honeymoon, as they had planned. But then Macel decided that she would rather go to Miami, so Jerry turned the car around and headed south. Their strict moral code of behavior ruled out many of the indulgences of modern life, but spontaneity was something they both appreciated.[5]

The Falwells rented a small apartment in Lynchburg for $62.50 per month. Jerry's salary as minister was only $65 per week, and Macel made about the same at her job at the First National Bank, a job she was determined to keep. A few years later, in 1960, the Falwells bought a lot in a new subdivision after the owner gave them a 10 percent discount and they secured a mortgage. Macel's father built them a 2,000-square-foot home, big enough to start a family.[6]

Macel took over the family finances because, as both would say, Jerry was incapable of balancing his checkbook, which is strange given his aptitude for mathematics. Macel also made her best stab at cooking, but the results were disastrous by her own admission. Her sisters had done all the cooking when she was growing up, freeing her to practice the piano. Her first baked ham looked like a piece of charcoal after she neglected to cover it with tinfoil before baking it. She bought premade biscuits that needed only to be baked, but she forgot to remove the plastic. When she cooked her first turkey one Christmas, she forgot to remove the giblets, the sight of which spoiled her appetite.[7]

Not everything in Macel's life changed when she married. She kept her job at the bank and intended to keep working even when she started having children. She liked the independence and the responsibility her work entailed. Macel maintained a network of female friends with whom she continued to take trips, including a road trip to Montreal. Jerry appreciated Macel's independent streak, as well as her ability to give as good as she got with the practical jokes that became a family habit. Jerry also valued her opinion, asking her to critique his sermons; she took note of any words he mispronounced while preaching and helped him introduce greater inflection into his voice, which naturally tended to a monotone.[8]

Jerry and Macel were clearly devoted to each other, and their devotion was reinforced by their shared devotion to the church, which, in turn, reinforced their married commitment. "According to the Bible, God decreed just three institutions; the family, the church, and government," Falwell would write in a book about building Christian families. "The family is a God-ordained institution founded upon the marriage of one man and one woman, promising to remain faithful for life as husband and wife, and committed to one another for the purposes of mutual love and the raising of their biological or adopted children, should these come into their lives." Their marriage vows had taken place in front of the church, but not only in a physical sense. They believed that God Himself, and His church, was an integral part of their marriage.[9]

Evangelicals understood that in a Christian marriage the husband is "head of the household" and that if he fails to be the decision-maker, he is failing in his God-ordained duties, just as his wife and children fail if they disobey his decisions. "Scripture declares that God has called the father to be the spiritual leader in his family," Falwell would write. "Good husbands who are godly men are good leaders. Their wives and children want to follow them and be under their protection." Falwell also noted that there was a difference between being a leader and a dictator.[10]

Falwell was no dictator. He would often joke before his congregation that he and his wife had "a million fights, and she's won all of them." He also told his audience about his and Macel's decision at the time of their vows never to even contemplate divorce. "Macel and I have never considered divorce. Murder maybe, but never divorce." But in her description of their commitment to each other, Macel offers a revealing insight: "Jerry honored me and deferred to me. He hated confrontation and didn't want strife in our home." (His hatred of interpersonal confrontation may strike one as surprising given his later talent for political battle, but as his later career demonstrated, even in the political arena Falwell usually avoided any interpersonal confrontation.)

On Christmas Day 1961, the Falwell and Pate clans met at Jerry and Macel's home to celebrate the holiday dinner. As the guests prepared to leave, Macel asked them to wait a minute because she had one more gift for Jerry. She took him into the privacy of the bedroom and told him she was three months pregnant. He was thrilled and rushed out to tell the rest of the family. Macel continued working at the bank until just before her due date, and she intended to keep her job after giving birth. Jerry told her that whatever she wanted to do was fine with him.[11]

The Falwells' first child was born at 9:13 P.M. on Father's Day 1962. It was a long labor, beginning in the early hours of Sunday morning. Falwell would leave the hospital to run to the church and preach his sermons, first at the morning service and then, when the baby still had not appeared, at the evening service too. Macel was heavily sedated, as was the practice at the time, and quite groggy, and every time she gasped or cried Jerry sobbed. There was no doubt what the baby boy's name would be: Jerry Jr.[12]

After her maternity leave was completed, Macel went back to work at the bank. Jerry's mother, Helen, took care of the child during the day. But it only took two weeks for Macel to realize that her baby was changing in ways that she did not want to miss, even for the length of an eight-hour workday. She quit the job she loved at the bank and dedicated herself full-time to her home and her family.[13]

Two years to the day after their first child was born, Macel again surprised Jerry Sr. She had Jerry Jr. make a Father's Day card that read, "Dad, I'm going to have a baby sister." Once again, Macel had kept her pregnancy a surprise for the first three months. On November 7, 1964, which was also Sam Pate's birthday, Jean Ann Falwell was born. Their third child, Jonathan, was born September 7, 1966.[14]

Although Macel was the primary caregiver for the children, Jerry developed certain routines that guaranteed his children would not feel neglected by their father because of the many, and increasing, demands on his time. Falwell made it a point to have meetings over breakfast or lunch, but dinner found him back at home, dining with his family. At bedtime he would go to each child's room and pray over them when they were very young, and pray with them when they were a little older. Before they could read, Falwell read the Bible to them, and once they could read, they took turns reading from the Bible as a family. There were family devotions nightly. At his office the secretaries put through calls from Macel or the kids right away. When Falwell's travels kept him away overnight, he would always call as soon as he arrived at his destination with a phone number where he could be reached, and he would check in with his children every night, reciting a prayer over the phone with them. And when the children reached elementary school age, Jerry would frequently take one of them with him on his trips visiting other churches in Virginia and, eventually, around the country.[15]

Falwell's tastes were simple, but he liked to go first-class. He was not personally indulgent, and his salary was never excessive, although the ministry took care of most of his monetary needs. But where his family was concerned, he was always willing to move heaven and earth to satisfy them.

Falwell purchased a lake house at nearby Smith Mountain Lake, which had become a popular resort area for affluent Lynchburg families. During the summer months Macel would drive out to the house on Friday during the day, and Jerry would follow when he had completed wedding rehearsals and other church activities. He would return to Lynchburg Saturday for weddings or funerals, then come back to the lake house for Saturday evening. He would leave early Sunday morning to be at church, and the family would follow later, in time for the second service.[16]

Jerry and Macel had been to the Holy Land together, but on one trip he took Jeannie as his traveling companion while Macel stayed at home with Jerry Jr. and Jonathan. On the way back Jerry and Jeannie had a layover in Switzerland and decided to take a few days to visit the Alps. When he told Macel of the last-minute plans, she off-handedly remarked that she had always wanted to see Switzerland. Jerry told her to catch the next flight, but she demurred, not liking to fly alone. Soon Jerry Jr., Jonathan, and Macel were on their way to the Lynchburg airport for the flight to Switzerland. On another trip, after a stop in Rome, Macel said she had always wanted to drive across the Alps, and again, plans were changed at the last minute to accommodate her request. They ended the car trip in Paris and took the Concorde home.[17]

In 1967 Falwell founded the Lynchburg Christian Academy, an elementary school. Not coincidentally, the new school was begun just as his own children reached school age. If his family was his anchor amid all the challenges of pasturing a large, growing church, the church would help him in his parenting task.

The Christian school movement had begun throughout the South in response to two proximate developments and one more remote. First, court-ordered desegregation of the public schools began in earnest once the "massive resistance" to desegregation had failed. Rather than permit their white children to attend classes with black children, conservative whites established private academies, many of them with links to the churches, where the effects of *Brown v. Board of Education* could be ignored.[18]

The second spur to starting Christian academies came from the U.S. Supreme Court. In a pair of cases in 1962 (*Engel v. Vitale*) and 1963 (*Abington School District v. Schempp*), the high court ruled that prayer in the public schools was unconstitutional. Prominent conservative Christian leaders like Carl McIntire organized protests against the new law, and such diverse clerics as Billy Graham and Cardinal Francis Spellman of New York condemned the law. Efforts to pass a constitutional amendment permitting both school prayer and Bible reading in the public schools came to naught. Conservative Christians who had been content to absent themselves from mainstream culture began to wonder how long their self-imposed exile would be respected by outsiders trying to change their way of life.[19]

The third, and in some ways most basic, reason for the creation of a distinct Christian school was that the public school curriculum had become increasingly secular, aggressively so to conservative eyes. As mentioned previously, the progressive mantle had long since passed from William Jennings Bryan to John Dewey, especially in the area of education. New textbooks not only taught evolution but followed Dewey's principles on "values clarification," which encouraged children to reach their own judgments free from the authority of canonical texts or of their parents. It was unsurprising that some parents took this ill and that the secular curriculum was so much kindling for conservative Christian parents.

The cultural match was lit on the precise issue of sex education. In 1965, Anaheim, California, introduced a sex education curriculum with little controversy. But a homemaker named Eleanor Howe heard one of her sons make an offhand remark that caused her to investigate, and she was appalled by what she discovered. She organized a group of mothers who examined the materials and went to the school board to air their grievances. Howe began airing a film called *Pavlov's Children,* produced by right-wing extremists in California, the central thesis of which was that Soviet communists, working through the United Nations, had introduced Pavlovian techniques into American school curricula "to render American youth susceptible to totalitarianism." Howe mounted a successful campaign to elect anti–sex education candidates to the local school board, and the curriculum was scuttled. Similar efforts in Kanawha County, West Virginia, and the textbook evaluations produced by two Christian conservatives in Texas, Mel and Norma Gabler, helped stoke the Christian school movement.[20]

The anti–sex education crusades ignited a focus on what the right came to call the "secular humanism" of the public schools and, derivatively, the public square. The different attacks on the way of life of conservative Christians—from evolution to integration, from the ban on school prayer to the introduction of "filthy language" into school textbooks—were understood to emerge from a common source. Dewey's pragmatism had little in common with Soviet communism, but both attacked the values of Bible-believing Christians, and they became lumped together. Indeed, the linkage of American secular humanism with Soviet communism served a useful purpose: the conservative critics did not have to name names in their indictments of school officials. The "education experts" were seen as dupes of the Soviets. The effort to expunge the influences of secular humanism from the public schools was also "spiced with overtones of race and class," according to an Episcopal minister in Charleston, West Virginia, who watched "Sweet Alice" Moore and her conservative Christian colleagues literally shut down the city until the school board took actions to address their concerns. Emboldened by their successes, some Christian conservatives even tried to resurrect the possibility of teaching creationism in the public schools.[21]

Falwell's decision to start the Lynchburg Christian Academy was contemporaneous with the battles over sex education in the public schools. But it is more likely that his decision was influenced by the emergence of successful all-white Christian academies, his desire to turn Thomas Road Baptist Church into a full-service ministry, and the simple question of where he would send his own children for an education.

In turning his focus to education, Falwell solicited help and displayed a knack for hiring highly competent assistants that would characterize his future career. Falwell turned to A. Pierre Guillermin to help set up the school. Guillermin was a past president of Southern Methodist College in South Carolina. Falwell also hired an assistant pastor, Jim Soward, to help with both the Sunday school programs and the music ministry at Thomas Road Baptist.

When the school opened in 1967, it included only kindergarten through grade five, and it boasted eighty-one students. "Most of the successful Christian day schools in the nation today began with fewer than thirty-five students," Guillermin told the *Lynchburg Daily News*. "We at the academy are grateful to the hundreds of parents in the greater Lynchburg area who have expressed an interest in the academy." The next year saw the addition of sixth grade, and seventh and eighth grades were added in 1969. By 1971 Lynchburg Christian Academy had expanded to include all of the high school grades.[22]

The growth of both educational programs was remarkable, especially the Sunday school program. Seven hundred students attended Sunday school in 1967, but by 1971 that figure had grown to 6,400. At Soward's urging, Falwell had initiated a "bus ministry," hiring school buses that were not otherwise in use on a Sunday morning to drive to different parts of town to pick up children for Sunday school. He built a new, two-story educational building on the campus of the church to accommodate both the academy during the week and the burgeoning numbers on the weekends.[23]

While Falwell's own family grew, so too did his church family. He especially relished the fact that his decision to start a school allowed him more time to watch his own children, as his office at the church was just upstairs from the classrooms. Jonathan, in fact, developed an early habit of escaping his classroom to go sit in his dad's office, and Macel would come in to sit with Jonathan in his classroom to make him mind. But with time, both the family and the church adjusted to the growth. His family brought him joy, and he delighted in his children's intelligence and independence. Macel was the earthly anchor of his life, and his pastorate and prayers kept him convinced that he was rooted properly in the Lord's work.

There is no doubt that work was blossoming. Since opening in 1956, Falwell's church had added a vigorous and growing Sunday School program, a ministry to alcoholics and a youth camp, and now a Christian academy. Falwell never mentioned the similarity, but his addition of the school made the campus of Thomas Road Baptist Church look like an urban Catholic parish: church, school, and various ministries providing all the social and religious needs of the parishioners. Falwell also would not have used the term, coined decades later, but Thomas Road Baptist was becoming a megachurch. The church boasted 2,640 members in 1969, making it the ninth-largest church in the nation.[24] In 1969 he would begin construction on yet another new sanctuary, this one designed to seat 3,000.

The most stunning part of Falwell's recounting of the decade of the 1960s, as it pertained both to his own family and to the life of his church, is that it reflects none of the cultural turbulence that was going on all around. There was no sexual revolution, no rock music, no anti–Vietnam War protests in Falwell's world. His world was still centered in Lynchburg, a town sufficiently rooted in the Bible Belt culture of the South to keep the tectonic cultural shifts at bay. The wider world had little to entice him. Yet.[25]

Chapter Five

Building a Religious Empire

In July 1970, Thomas Road Baptist Church dedicated its new sanctuary, a visible symbol of the success of Jerry Falwell's ministry in his first fourteen years. In the years ahead Falwell would take his ministry nationwide, expanding the reach of his television ministry, beginning a Christian college, and accelerating his fund-raising methods. The entrepreneurial spirit he had inherited from his father would combine with his mother's dedication to old-time religion to produce a man perfectly suited to capitalizing on the growth industry of televangelism. At the same time as America was questioning its own most revered institutions in the wake of the Vietnam War and Watergate and the oil embargo and Jimmy Carter's malaise, Falwell was busy building up his own institutional strength, answering a felt need for certainty in a suddenly uncertain world.

Falwell's new church building was based on the plans Thomas Jefferson designed for his Lynchburg retreat, Poplar Forest. It was octagonal in shape, with a columned portico on the street facade and an enclosed hallway connecting it to the old sanctuary building next door. The inside was sleeker, with no columns cluttering the sightlines, and more modern than its predecessor. The design, however, was the only traditional thing about the church, which was designed to bring Thomas Road Baptist into the television age. It had special lighting and platforms for cameras so that Falwell's *Old-Time Gos-*

pel Hour could be televised live from the sanctuary. The space was a long way from the cramped studio at WLVA-TV, with its plywood cutout set. Also, in 1971, Falwell hired Don Norman, a man with television experience, to produce the *Old-Time Gospel Hour* broadcasts and make them more attractive to a television audience.[1]

The results of the changes were impressive. Throughout the 1960s, Falwell's radio and television shows could be heard in the Lynchburg area and a few other counties in south-central Virginia, airing on perhaps a dozen channels. Occasionally, he would make such an impression that Christians from as far away as Roanoke or Charlottesville would show up at Thomas Road Baptist to see in person the man they had first seen on television. Those visitors from close-in counties might become members of the church and therefore would be expected to tithe 10 percent of their income to the church. Visitors, too, would make contributions. With the new money, Falwell would buy more airtime, in more distant cities, which, in turn, would produce more donations to his ministry. Falwell would enliven his television program with guest appearances, including a Christian karate master who cracked a two-thousand-pound chunk of ice with his bare hands and the world's strongest man, Paul Anderson, who lifted a table carrying fifteen church deacons on it. After moving into the new sanctuary and sprucing up the *Old-Time Gospel Hour,* Falwell was on three hundred stations nationwide by 1971. Within a few more years the *Old-Time Gospel Hour* would be on nine hundred stations.[2]

Falwell would travel by car to preach at other Baptist churches and hold fund-raising events for the *Old-Time Gospel Hour*. Often Jerry Jr. would accompany him and help sell audiotapes of the Thomas Road Baptist Church choir or copies of Falwell's sermons. In 1971 the church purchased a small plane for Falwell so that he could travel farther afield to markets where *Old-Time Gospel Hour* was now airing. In the following year the church bought a still larger plane, allowing him to take longer trips and to bring along up to thirty-two choristers from the church for special programs and fund-raisers.

One thing did not change and that was Falwell's pulpit style, which remained the central focus of the *Old-Time Gospel Hour*. He was folksy, discussing the conversations he had with members of the church or encounters with the unchurched. He shared the stories of sin and redemption from his own life, illustrating the biblical tale of Cain and Abel by recalling his father's shooting of his own brother. He spoke about Christian marriage by discussing the family devotions he and Macel undertook with their children. And unlike some televangelists like Billy Graham, whom Falwell and others thought were insufficiently hostile to liberal Christians, Falwell was committed to pure, fundamentalist doctrine in his sermons. The most common refrain in a Falwell sermon was some variation of the words: "As it says right here in the Bible. . . ."[3]

Falwell followed Graham in one particular, however. Anticommunism became a frequent theme in his sermons, his admonition against preaching about communism in his "Ministers and Marches" sermon notwithstanding. For example, two of the four evening sermons he preached in August 1967 dealt with "Godless Communism." The anticommunist theme had entered the evangelical lexicon in the postwar era, with conservative pastors like Carl McIntire echoing the accusations of Sen. Joseph McCarthy about communist infiltration of the government. McIntire also believed that communism had sunk its teeth into liberal churches, a theme Falwell echoed. This anticommunist drumbeat would be a bridge to Falwell's political involvement later on in his career.[4]

The most frequent sermon topics that Falwell selected, however, were standard fundamentalist fare, from belief in the historical accuracy of the account of Creation in the Book of Genesis to an exegesis on the End Times found in the Book of Revelation. In the same month in which he preached twice on the communist menace he also delivered sermons with the titles "The End Is Near" and "Degrees of Punishment in Hell." Over the years he offered sermons as diverse as how to plant a church, world evangelization, and "Who Is Jesus?"[5]

A typical Falwell sermon—one for which we have a transcript— was preached on the *Old-Time Gospel Hour* on August 10, 1975. He took as his text Paul's Letter to the Ephesians, chapter 5, verses 14–25, specifically focusing on the sentence: "Redeeming the time, because the days are evil." Falwell quoted eleven other scriptural texts in the course of his sermon, from the Book of Job's observation that "Man that is born of a woman is of few days, and full of trouble" (14:1) to the psalmist's more upbeat song, "This is the day the Lord has made" (Ps 118:24). Falwell's ability to recall scriptural passages at will and work them into his sermons fluently was one of his finest qualities as a preacher.

"Redeeming the time" demonstrates how Falwell would work personal narratives into his sermons and use that narrative to make a point. In this sermon he recalled his conversion at age eighteen and his regret that it had not happened sooner. He mentioned that he once baptized a man who was more than one hundred years old, but he also emphasized his work with youth because no one is really alive until they are alive in Christ. He denounced "most of the magazines today" as "vulgar" and complained that "the Hollywood theater is not fit for Christians to attend." Rock music is "perverted and vulgar." He relished being called a teetotaler. Falwell exhorted his listeners to be filled with the Spirit of God—"When the Spirit of God is on you, everything you touch multiplies"—and recalled the biblical account of Jesus feeding five thousand people with five loaves of bread and two fish. He commended his flock to family prayer and called all to humility.[6]

Two weeks later Falwell gave another sermon on the *Old-Time Gospel Hour* for which a transcript survives. This time he chose as his text the Letter of James, chapter 5, verses 13–16, focusing on "Sins That Cause Sickness." Again, there are four additional scriptural quotes strewn throughout the sermon. He spoke of doctors and their work healing sickness, even saying that he knew some doctors who were as called to their medical work as preachers were to theirs. He also affirmed his belief in divine healing, in miracles. But he then moved to his central theme: that some sins are wrongly considered diseases because the culture does not want to label human failings as the sins they are. "We are hearing a great deal today about alcoholism being a disease. I do not believe that. . . . Alcoholism is what the Bible calls 'drunkenness.' We have coined the word 'alcoholic' to make drunkenness more respectable. No matter what it is called, it is still drunkenness. It is not a disease, it is sin. S-I-N." Falwell said that the only cure for alcoholism, as for all sins, "is the blood of Jesus Christ." He went on to discuss drug abuse in similar terms and noted that "children who have never been taught parental authority are sick." He concluded with a discourse on how bitterness is a sickness of the soul. All these sicknesses find their cure in conversion to Christ and conformity to His will.[7]

Another sermon dealt with the importance of tithing. Falwell began with six scriptural quotes that dealt with the topic, from Jesus standing near the entrance to the Temple treasury to see who gave and who didn't, to the passage in the Gospel of Luke in which Jesus says, "Give, and it will be given to you." Falwell cited Paul's Second Letter to the Corinthians in which Paul suggests that giving to God is the necessary proof of the sincerity of a disciple's love for the Lord: "God knows He doesn't have you till he gets your pocketbook. Why? Because Jesus said, where a man's treasure is, there will his heart be also." Tithing is one of the ways in which God shows His people how to live, setting before the congregation how to understand God's plan for their lives. Falwell exhorted his congregation to give, and to give cheerfully, and they responded accordingly. The revenues of the church continued to grow.[8]

These were the sermons that made Falwell's *Old-Time Gospel Hour* a nationwide hit. Rooted in scripture, they were filled with homey anecdotes and contemporary applications of biblical teachings, and they focused on the fundamentalist doctrines at the heart of his creed. He did not engage in faith healings as some other televangelists did. He did not preach a Gospel of Prosperity, as would also become popular in the pulpits of certain televangelists. The televised services of the 1970s may have been dressed up—broadcast from a larger, sleeker sanctuary and featuring bigger and betters choirs—but the content of his sermons was mostly what it had been when Falwell first preached to the thirty-five dissidents in the old Donald Duck building. The wages of sin is death. Christ died to take away our sins. The Christian has only to be born again to receive eternal redemption. Once saved, Christians should live godly lives lest the Enemy tempt them to unbelief. Week in and week out, these were Falwell's most common themes, running even through those sermons

that began to tiptoe into the political realm, such as his denunciations of communism.

In January 1971, Falwell announced to his congregation that he
intended to start a Christian college. He pointed to the Bible passage
in which Jesus chooses disciples to follow Him and to carry on His
ministry after His death. He recalled Paul's cultivation of Timothy to
be a missionary and his letters of instruction to Timothy in the ways
of Christian discipleship. He recalled the many blessings the Lord
had already shed on the various ministries of Thomas Road Baptist
Church. It was time to share their riches with the next generation
and build a Christian college "with the goal of seeing thousands of
young men and women, deeply in love with the Lord Jesus Christ,
who will go out in all walks of life to shake this world for God."[9]

It is one of the curiosities of the Protestant faith that, while it has
always held that human reason shares in the general depravity of sinful man, it was responsible for the building of the first great temples
of education in America. The first great Protestant theologian, Martin Luther, called human reason "Frau Jezebel." Calvin both condemned reason as affected by human depravity and commended it
as essential to the task of recognizing human depravity, the first and
necessary step toward acceptance of salvation; this tension was never
resolved in his writings. Lutheranism did not profoundly affect the
early American culture, but Harvard, Yale, and Princeton all began
as Calvinist colleges that were more like seminaries: institutions
designed not for the general advancement of human knowledge but
for the rigorous training of the clergy. The most learned men in most
colonial towns were the ministers, but their learning was in scripture,
in godly things, not in the liberal arts. Reason for its own sake was
a snare.[10]

Falwell, of course, was not a Lutheran or a Calvinist, and he
did not share the thoroughgoing suspicion of human culture that
orthodox Calvinism demanded. But he would not necessarily have
disagreed with Luther's warning, "Beware the whore Reason for she
will go with any man." For Falwell, as for other fundamentalists,

the purpose of a Christian education is to educate the student in the Bible, the one reliable source of truth, and a born-again soul no longer suffers from the depravity of the unsaved. Secondarily, and flowing from that knowledge of the truth, Christian education seeks to build the student's character. Lastly, education must prepare students with vocational training, but there is no doubt that they are being sent into the world to be Christian heralds within their chosen professions. Religion animates the whole of life. There are no dualisms separating a believer's Christian life, tucked into a busy Sunday morning, from the rest of his or her life. As Falwell told one of the school's first students at a chapel service, "Give everything you have and are to the Lord. Your time, your tithe, your talent—all are the Lord's. Satan, the world, and the flesh are all against you and want to keep you from being a champion."[11]

Falwell recruited Dr. Elmer Towns to help him found Lynchburg Baptist College. Towns had been president of Winnipeg Baptist College (now Providence College) in Canada and had taught at a divinity school in Chicago. He and Falwell were both of the same mind about the nature of Christian education and the relationship of the school to the church. They did not intend for their college to go the way of other Baptist colleges. The University of Chicago, Brown University, Spelman College, and the University of Richmond all had become thoroughly secular with little that attested to their Baptist origins. Their school would be owned and controlled by the church. Falwell and Towns would dictate the curriculum, hire only born-again professors, and enroll only those students who had been recommended by their pastors. As Falwell would later comment, "Anytime [the teachers at Liberty Baptist] start teaching something we don't like, we cut the money off. It's amazing how that changes philosophy." Books in the library that were not consistent with orthodox fundamentalist theology received warning notices:

> To the reader: This volume represents the wealth of knowledge that is present in the world today, and Liberty Baptist College accepts this knowledge in order to standardize the work and validate the credits of the college. However, use of this vol-

ume as a text for reference in Liberty Baptist College is not an endorsement of its contents from the standpoint of moral, philosophy, theology, or scientific hypotheses. It is necessary to use books whose content the college cannot wholly endorse. The position of Liberty Baptist College on the fundamentals of the faith and the separated Christian life is well known.

Falwell referred to the school as the "University of God" and expressed the hope that it would become for fundamentalist kids what Notre Dame was for Catholic kids—the school they all wanted to go to.[12]

There was one practical problem that confronted Falwell and Towns at the very outset: they had almost no students. Falwell's ambition had gotten out in front of him, not for the last time. He had advertised in local newspapers and spread the word on the *Old-Time Gospel Hour*, but by June, three months before the school was set to open, only eight students had enrolled. Falwell considered putting ads in every Christian newspaper and magazine, but it was too late for that. In 1971 ads had to be submitted at least two months in advance of publication. Falwell suggested that they offer a free trip to Israel to any pastor who sent five students to the school. Towns came back with an alternative suggestion. Why not offer a free trip to the kids themselves? Falwell liked the idea and began talking about it on the *Old-Time Gospel Hour* and on all of his trips to preach at other churches. By the end of the summer 154 students had applied to the school.[13]

Falwell and Towns were delighted with the results of their enrollment drive, but now they—and the incoming students—faced an additional hurdle: they had no campus. Classes were held in the hallways of Thomas Road Baptist Church. One student recalled Falwell saying that classes would have been taught in the bathrooms if only they had been a bit larger. They rented space in an abandoned elementary school that had been slated for demolition. When the furnace broke, the students sat in the classrooms, taking notes with their coats and gloves on. For dormitories, the church rented some homes in the area, putting as many as nine boys in a room. Other students lived in the cabins on Treasure Island, and some were soon housed in an old hotel downtown that the church bought. By the end of the first semester, the college's student body had declined to ninety-one students. Anyone coming to Lynchburg Baptist College expecting ivy-covered walls was in for a disappointment.[14]

What the school lacked in amenities, it made up for in rules. There was a strict code of conduct for the incoming students. Drinking and smoking were grounds for immediate dismissal, as was visiting the dormitory room of a member of the opposite sex. Dating was confined to weekends and had to be done in certain public venues on campus. Trips to the local movie theater were forbidden. Boys had to keep their hair cut above the ears and be clean-shaven. Girls were expected to dress modestly. Interracial dating was prohibited unless both sets of parents gave permission in writing. Most college students in 1971 would have rebelled against such a stern regimen, but the students attending Lynchburg Baptist College were mostly from fundamentalist homes where strict rules were common. In January those students who had braved the lack of housing and the rigid rules received their reward. They flew to Cyprus and boarded a cruise ship, the *Orpheus*, for a voyage to the Holy Land. They were joined by two hundred members of Thomas Road Baptist Church. As the ship approached Mount Carmel, Falwell asked for donations from the church members to help defray the cost of the trip. On the spot, he received almost twice what the trip had cost.[15]

In 1972 Falwell started the Thomas Road Bible Institute for those who wished to study at Lynchburg Baptist College but could not afford either the time or the money it took to attend a full-time, four-year school. The Bible Institute offered a "two-year crash course" in the Bible, all of it done from home. Falwell advertised the Institute on the *Old-Time Gospel Hour* and in the church's many mailings and newsletters, and soon he had enrolled hundreds of people in the program. By 1983 fifteen thousand families were enrolled. The following year Falwell launched the Lynchburg Baptist Seminary to train ministers, most of whom were drawn from the new college. He was creating in Lynchburg an educational nexus for virtually every conceivable need of his parishioners and television audience.[16]

The early years for Lynchburg Baptist College, the Bible Institute, and the seminary were difficult years for America. In 1971 the memory of the massacre at Ohio's Kent State University on May 4, 1970, was still fresh in the national consciousness, and anti–Vietnam War protests continued, as did the war itself. In the summer of 1972 a worldwide television audience tuned in to witness the Munich Olympic Games, a moment when all the enmities of the world usually gave way to the honest competition of the playing field, but terrorists interrupted the Munich Games, killing eleven Israeli athletes and coaches. The year 1973 witnessed the start of the Watergate scandal, which would culminate the following year in President Richard Nixon's resignation in disgrace. In response to American support for Israel during the 1973 Arab-Israeli War, the Arab nations would embargo oil from the United States, sending prices skyrocketing. There seemed to be uncertainty wherever one turned, but not at Thomas Road Baptist Church. There the certainties of the fundamentalist faith were drawing new adherents and providing them with the tools they would need to lead godly lives, provide their children with a Christian education, and keep the evil let loose in the world far away. The self-imposed cultural exile of the fundamentalist churches made more sense, not less, when the world was turned upside down.

The lack of a campus for Falwell's college and its offshoots seemed like an insoluble problem without an infusion of cash. At the same time, Falwell had commissioned a feasibility study about expanding the Old-Time Gospel Hour to yet more stations nationwide. Falwell killed two birds with one stone when he decided to make his first bond offering. This allowed him to raise $6.5 million in a short time to invest in the growth of both his ministry and his college. Falwell had already spotted the land he wanted to purchase: 2,100 acres on Candler's Mountain on the south side of Lynchburg. The land was owned by the company U.S. Gypsum, which was willing to sell it for $1.25 million. The bond offering allowed Falwell to buy the land, build something resembling a campus, and invest in new television markets for the *Old-Time Gospel Hour*. The bond offering would also cause the first crisis in Falwell's ministry.[17]

On July 3, 1973, the Securities and Exchange Commission (SEC) charged Thomas Road Baptist Church with "fraud and deceit" in the bond sale. The court papers also suggested that the church was insolvent, with no real prospect of paying back the borrowed money. Falwell was humiliated at the sight of the charges being spread on the headlines of the local newspapers, a source of shock and gossip around town and even among his congregants. But as it turned out, the SEC charges were the best thing that ever happened to Falwell's ministries.[18]

The bond issue had been sloppily done, to say the least. The SEC was unsure about whether there was even a prospectus, because it had never been properly filed. When Falwell produced it, the prospectus was a mess. It falsely claimed that the Lynchburg Christian Academy was accredited, which was not the case, and it overvalued the church's assets by including pledges as well as donations already received. Falwell had kept up with the payments to the bondholders, to be sure, so there were no disgruntled investors, but while the investigation failed to prove any intentional fraud on Falwell's part, it did demonstrate that the church's finances were a mess. Falwell saw the entire episode as the Devil's work. "The devil is after us," he told his congregation. He and Macel prayed throughout the SEC crisis that they would be delivered from the government Goliath.[19]

In August the federal court hearing the SEC charges agreed to dismiss them provided Falwell turned over control of the church's finances to an independent board of financial advisers. Five Lynchburg businessmen, none of whom were members of Thomas Road Baptist Church, agreed to serve on the board, and for the next three years they oversaw the finances of the ministry. Among the people they hired to help them make sense of the financial mess was a man named Jerry Huntsinger, an expert in fund-raising for nonprofit organizations. He was quick to recognize what Falwell had missed. Falwell was not only sitting on top of a financial mess. He was sitting on top of a gold mine.[20]

Huntsinger recognized that Falwell's newsletters did a good job of keeping the parishioners at Thomas Road Baptist Church informed and involved, but that a different approach was needed to raise donations from those who watched the *Old-Time Gospel Hour*. He suggested that the television show form "affinity clubs" that would make potential donors feel that they had an ownership stake in the ministry. There was the "Pastor's Team" and the "Ten Thousand Club" and the "Faith Partners," and membership in any of these clubs was rewarded for a small, but regular, donation. The key was not to get any one person to donate a lot of money. The key was to get large numbers of people sending $10 every month, as the Faith Partners did. The ministry's revenues grew from $3.5 million in 1973 to $12 million in 1976. Donations from the 110,000 Faith Partners would grow to an annual take of $13 million. The additional funds were plowed back into the ministry, buying more airtime so the *Old-Time Gospel Hour* could reach yet more people—and more potential donors.[21]

Falwell flew around the country to make the pitch in person. At each stop he would bring one of his favorite singers from the Thomas Road Baptist Church, usually Doug Oldham, to serenade the audience with religious music. Falwell would give a brief talk if the event was at a hall or hotel ballroom, a sermon if they were at a church. He would ask the assembled fans of his television show if they would join one of the affinity groups. He had bundles of membership forms and envelopes, with the postage already paid, for them to send in to the *Old-Time Gospel Hour*. Every Sunday morning, on the television show itself, Falwell would repeat his plea for people to join him in his great crusade. In 1975 Falwell inaugurated a second series of trips called "I Love America" rallies, which he held on the steps of state capitol buildings around the country, surrounded by flags. He contacted key pastors in each area in advance to guarantee a crowd and brought the Lynchburg Baptist College choir with him to perform. In 1978, on the steps of the state capitol in Little Rock, Falwell and his choir were joined by the state's young governor, Bill Clinton.[22]

*   *   *

The final piece of the fund-raising puzzle was put into place when Epsilon Corporation, a Massachusetts-based computer company, dispatched a staffer to see if the preacher wanted to use the company's services. Epsilon had been founded by a group of faculty members at the Harvard Business School who recognized that computers allowed companies and other organizations to automate their methods of communication with their members in ways that would produce a sense of brand loyalty. For example, Epsilon devised the first frequent-flyer programs for American Airlines. One of the company's founders, John Groman, recognized that televangelists were a prime target for the company's services. Falwell was the first televangelist to sign up for Epsilon's services.[23]

Groman recognized that the cultural isolation of the evangelical community was both a hurdle and an opportunity. He needed to persuade them to trust him. He found that in his initial interview with a preacher and his staff, someone would ask him when he had been saved. "I learned that if you answered with a general time period, like 'early fifties,' they'd know you were lying," Groman told *Forbes* reporter Dirk Smillie. "I always answered with the exact date and year." Conversely, once he signed on with a church, fund-raising from within the evangelical community was astoundingly easy. "They trust their own to a fault. If they could they'd build their own cars." At the time, if Falwell sent out a solicitation by mail, he did so by sending a certified letter. This was not only expensive but required the recipient to go to the post office. One might expect recipients to be resentful, and yet Falwell received virtually no complaints. Groman was stunned. Falwell's potential donors trusted him in a way that was truly remarkable in the orbit of professional fund-raisers.[24]

The 1970s witnessed the dawn of direct mail as a means of institution-building. Computer programs allowed a company to identify the "compulsive contributors" who responded to virtually every appeal. Other donors who gave more than $100 were targeted for specific appeals. For several years Falwell had bestowed gifts on donors, but Groman ramped up the giving program, every time aiming to create a sense of ownership on the part of the donors by offering them opportunities like the chance to purchase bricks for

Lynchburg Baptist College. Groman learned how to make the right
pitch for the evangelical community: he would ask potential donors
to pray about whether or not they could afford to contribute at this
time. Computers allowed the mailings to be personalized with "Dear
Fred" or "Dear Sally" at the top of the letter and to recall previous
donations later on in the text. Revenues soared.[25]

Lynchburg Baptist College got a new name, Liberty Baptist College,
in 1976 after a woman sent a check for $100,000 to "Lynchburg Col-
lege" and mailed it to the small liberal arts college across town. The
next year the school also got a new campus. In January 1977, after
the furnace at the high school they were using broke, Falwell assembled all the students on the property he had purchased from U.S.
Gypsum on Candler's Mountain. The school had grown to almost
2,500 students and faculty. They prayed for the funding to start construction on the site and sang the song "I Want That Mountain."
Whether it was the prayer or the singing or both—Saint Augustine
once claimed that "he who sings prays twice"—the ministry received
$2.5 million in February, and construction began the next month.
Falwell renamed Candler's Mountain "Liberty Mountain."[26]

Falwell's goals for the school may have been ambitious, and the
intellectual focus was decidedly spiritual in content, but the buildings were utilitarian in the extreme. The classroom buildings looked
as if they had been plucked from an office park. The dorms were even
worse, each building a long rectangle of brick without ornament or
architectural details. A pastor in town said that the campus looked
"more like a large, orderly prison than an educational institution."

The school's appearance was bound to impede recruitment, so the
college catalog was embellished to impress potential students. There
was a picture of a large, multistory building on the page marked
"School of Business," but the building in the picture was the Virginia
National Bank building in downtown Lynchburg. On the page labeled
"Division of Religion," there was a photograph of a small but beautiful
brick chapel—found on the campus of Washington and Lee University
in Lexington, not Lynchburg, Virginia. The chapel holds the tomb of

Robert E. Lee. When shown the Liberty Baptist catalog, the president of Washington and Lee exclaimed, "Isn't that the damnedest thing."[27]

The Liberty Baptist catalog also took liberties with the résumé of the college's president, Pierre Guillermin. He was routinely described as "Dr. Guillermin," and the catalog and other school literature claimed that he possessed a doctorate in psychology from the University of London. That claim was simply false. Guillermin did possess two doctorates, one from St. Andrew's College in North Carolina and the other from the Graduate School of Theology in California, but both of those were honorary doctorates. Most of the professors did not have doctorates, but many of those who did earned them at Bob Jones University or other evangelical universities.[28]

Building on Huntsinger's gift at writing appeals and Groman's computer programs, Falwell perfected the art of the desperate appeal: creating a sense of crisis that would cause people to open their wallets. In late August 1977, in an effort to raise money for Liberty Baptist College as the school began its new academic year, Falwell held a rally of his students on Liberty Mountain. He said they needed a fund-raising "miracle" to keep the college going. Labeling September 24 "Miracle Day," he said they needed to raise $5 million by then or else the school would close. For the next month every episode of the *Old-Time Gospel Hour* carried a plea for help. In imitation of the Prophet Joshua, he drove around Candler's Mountain every day—and seven times on Miracle Day—just as Joshua had circled the walls of Jericho. "We find ourselves looking up at a wall of bills and unfinished buildings," Falwell said. "A miracle is needed." When all the checks were in, Falwell had his miracle: he had surpassed his goal and raised $7 million for his college.[29]

Falwell was now a national presence within the evangelical world. His school began to attract students from all fifty states and several foreign countries. His *Old-Time Gospel Hour* was broadcast nationwide on a variety of channels. Falwell's donor list had expanded as he followed every opportunity to raise funds. His was not yet a household name outside the cultural universe of fundamentalist churches and families, but soon events would conspire to draw Falwell onto a larger cultural stage.

Chapter Six

Wading into the Religious-Political Estuary

Falwell had established himself as a national player in the evangelical world, but in the 1970s he and other evangelicals came to believe that their world was under attack. On a host of issues, their core beliefs were being challenged or repudiated by the mainstream culture. Their cultural isolation from that mainstream culture and efforts to evangelize had not been able to prevent what they viewed as cultural decline. On issue after issue, from abortion to the tax-exempt status of Christian schools, the political world seemed, at best, to be infringing on the moral universe of the fundamentalist community, or attacking it at worst. In response, Falwell found himself speaking out on issues that were equal parts morality and politics. He was not yet ready to jump into politics, but he was wading into an estuary where politics and religion mixed. The walls of the fundamentalist cultural ghetto were not pulled down in a flood of politico-religious activism. The water seeped in slowly, at ground level, weakening the foundation of cultural separation in ways that would prove irrevocable.

All the issues that would begin to engage Falwell had two things in common. They had a distinctively religious or moral quality to them, and Falwell's position on them would align him with the Republican Party and the conservative movement. Abortion, opposition to gay rights, race relations, the burden of taxes, and a commitment to a strong national defense capable of a robust response to the growth of atheistic communism—these were the issues that animated conservative politics and would increasingly preoccupy Falwell.

Many people had been toiling in the conservative trenches for years, and the 1964 Barry Goldwater campaign had organized them into a somewhat unified political movement come election time, but the conservative movement was never an ideologically cohesive whole. It included economic libertarians as well as Burkean conservatives, states' rights advocates and anticommunist crusaders, populists like Alabama governor George Wallace and plutocrats like *National Review* founder William F. Buckley. What it did not include was evangelicals. The conservative movement was largely opaque to the evangelical community. Even the religiously inflected language of Buckley was markedly different from the Bible-believing language of the world of fundamentalism. Falwell and many of his fundamentalist colleagues shared the concerns of political conservatives, but they viewed them differently, as issues of personal morality not public policy. What Falwell shared with all the different groups within the conservative movement was a disgust at contemporary liberal society, its libertinism and its renunciation not only of fundamentalist religious views but of all religious views, its willingness to challenge and even mock traditional moral values. Falwell, Wallace, Buckley, and other conservatives may not have seen eye to eye, but when they looked at contemporary American society they all saw red.

On January 22, 1973, the Supreme Court delivered its decision in *Roe v. Wade*, legalizing abortion nationwide in virtually all circumstances. The opposition to the decision was immediate and arose almost exclusively from Roman Catholics. Cardinal John Krol, the president of the U.S. Bishops' Conference, denounced the decision in the pages of the *New York Times* the next day. The bishops organized pro-life marches and adopted a pastoral plan to organize Catholic opposition to the decision. Conversely, several liberal Protestant churches applauded the decision. Feminists were exultant to the point of being offensive. "If men could get pregnant, abortion would be a sacrament," proclaimed feminist author Florynce Kennedy.[1]

There were many reasons the Catholic Church led the way in opposing *Roe*. First, its organizational structures permitted the kind of nationwide political efforts that Baptists, with their looser ecclesiological structures, completely lacked. Second, since World War I the nation's Catholic bishops had maintained a staff in Washington, D.C., the National Conference of Catholic Bishops (NCCB, now known as the United States Conference of Catholic Bishops, USCCB), which helped them understand the political process and also served as an avenue for the bishops to lobby on behalf of important causes. Most important perhaps, the Catholic Church had a long tradition of bioethical teaching on which it could rely. The secular philosopher Joseph Fletcher, no friend of Christianity, admitted that "Catholic literature on the morals of medical care is both extensive and painstaking in its technical detail, while Protestant and Jewish literature is practically non-existent." The disparity resulted both from the vast network of Catholic hospitals and from the case study method used in the moral manuals that instructed seminarians in hearing confessions. Years of doctors and nurses asking their confessors, "But what if . . ." had resulted in a comprehensive body of moral analysis on a range of bioethical issues, including abortion.[2]

To many observers, the Supreme Court's decision was yet another instance of the judiciary serving as an agent of social change that conservatives resented. First there was *Brown v. Board of Education,* which declared segregation unconstitutional. Then there were the decisions that banned prayer and Bible reading in the public schools. Now *Roe* challenged traditional ideas about the sanctity of human life. Secular liberals applauded the series of decisions as expanding the bounds of human freedom, while conservatives saw the same set of decisions as an assault on their values. Just as important, the decision short-circuited the political effort to liberalize abortion laws, which had been going on for years, and cast the debate in the absolute categories of legal discourse. Legislatures can find compromises that reflect popular ambivalence about complicated issues like abortion, but after *Roe* the debate pitted two absolute rights, life and privacy, against each other, and the categorical nature of that debate left little room for moderation.[3]

Furthermore, the differing reactions to *Roe* indicated differing understandings of the American Constitution. Falwell preached that while the Constitution was not inspired by God the way the Bible had been, it was nonetheless inspired and the work of godly men. For conservative Christians, all civil authority was ordained by God, which was no guarantee that the acts of particular governments would be godly. In the case of America, however, Falwell and other conservative Christians believed that the nation had been founded on religious principles, first in colonial times by the Pilgrims, but also at the time of the Revolutionary War and the drafting of the Constitution. Falwell did not recognize the Enlightenment influences on the Constitution on which the Supreme Court relied for its decision in *Roe*. These differing understandings of the Constitution and the American founding would characterize many of Falwell's future clashes with the culture.[4]

Falwell recalls reading about the *Roe v. Wade* decision in the morning newspaper with "horror and disbelief," but the news did not provoke him to take action. He had already preached against abortion on several occasions, but as an example of personal sinfulness. Now he began to refer to abortion as "America's national sin"; comparing the procedure to Hitler's murder of Jews, he labeled it a "biological holocaust." Falwell suggested later that the *Roe v. Wade* decision began an intellectual conversion, forcing him to confront his own bias against political involvement by the clergy, but that does not ring true: he did not form the Moral Majority until 1979, six years later. And as he would acknowledge, in the spring of 1973 his thoughts were mostly focused on the SEC investigation.[5]

Abortion is not directly mentioned in the Bible, although one of the earliest noncanonical Christian texts, the Didache, does explicitly condemn the act. Falwell would rely on those passages that speak of human life in the womb to support the thesis that abortion is murder and, consequently, a violation of the Commandment "thou shalt not kill." In the Book of Jeremiah, the "word of the Lord" came to the prophet and said, "Before I formed you in the womb I knew you, and before you were born I consecrated you" (Jer 1:5). In the Psalms, the Bible records: "For thou didst form my inward parts, thou didst knit me together in my mother's womb" (Ps 139:13). And of course, in the story of the Virgin Birth, one of the fundamental beliefs to which all fundamentalists subscribed, Mary is made aware of the divinity within her womb at the moment of conception.

Falwell preached against abortion, but he usually lumped it with other personal sins as evidence of the moral decline of the nation. The focus of most of his preaching was on lesser sins. He did not suspect that many members of his congregation were actually facing the prospect of an abortion, and so he preached at greater length about the temptations they did face. For example, in a sermon entitled "Conditions Corrupting America," preached May 16, 1976, Falwell spoke at length about the need for godly politicians. "First of all, we have politicians without principle," Falwell exhorted from the pulpit. "How long since a politician stood before a microphone and a camera and you believed exactly what he was saying?" He spoke about the pleasure principle that was corrupting the youth of America, blaming it for the rise in drug use and sex outside of marriage among the young. He spoke about profanity on television. Falwell condemned "wealth without work" and warned, "We are developing a socialistic state in these United States as surely as I am standing here right now." But he did not mention abortion.[6]

In 1974, Falwell would recall, he had a discussion with his family about abortion. He related that he was worried about the future of the country because of its "national sin," and he shared his fears with his children. Then his younger son, Jonathan, who was seven years old, asked his father, "Daddy, why don't you do something about it?" Falwell decided to learn more about the issue, and he read the writings of Dr. Francis Schaeffer, one of the leading evangelical thinkers, who had written about abortion. Schaeffer would prove critical to persuading Falwell to join forces with nonfundamentalists by the end of the decade. But in the short term Falwell did nothing specific to overturn *Roe* beyond preaching about the "national sin" on the *Old-Time Gospel Hour* and on his many trips to other churches and during his rallies with his Liberty Baptist College singers.[7]

*   *   *

The year 1973 would be a pivotal year for another issue that became central to Falwell's political beliefs. The 1973 Arab-Israeli War
placed America's commitment to the Jewish state in high relief, especially after the Arab states began an oil embargo that sent prices
soaring in America. In conservative circles, some extreme elements
harbored profoundly anti-Semitic attitudes, and others were generi-
cally isolationist. But mainstream conservatives resisted both biases,
and few Americans on the left or right questioned the strategic or
moral rationale for America's support for Israel.[8]

Falwell's views on Israel were not, strictly speaking, strategic or
moral. To him, America had to support Israel for three reasons, all of
them rooted in the Bible. First, the Jews are God's chosen people and
were given the land of Israel by God Himself, the Promised Land, to
which they were led by Moses. So no earthly authority can contest the
right of the Jews to the land of Israel. Second, in the Book of Genesis,
in the same passage in which God gives the land of Israel to Abraham
and his progeny, God also says, "I will bless those that bless you, and
him who curses you I will curse" (Gn 12:3). Thus, if America turns its
back on Israel, it risks being denied God's blessings. Finally, Falwell
believed that the Jews' return to the Holy Land is a fulfillment of biblical prophecy, a necessary step toward the Second Coming of Christ.[9]

In recounting the prejudices of his youth, Falwell recalled that he
did not know any Jews personally and that references to Jews were
always derogatory. "As a boy I never heard of Jews. If he was a Jew
he was always a 'damn' Jew." He compared his facile anti-Semitism
with the racism of the South. Falwell noted that his conversion came
only four years after the founding of the state of Israel, so that he
could honestly claim that throughout his life as a Christian he had
been a supporter of the state of Israel. And unlike other southern
racists who were as anti-Semitic as they were anti-black, Falwell shed
his anti-Semitism as soon as he became familiar with the teachings
of the Bible, although it occasionally poked through. In 1978, speaking to a Richmond congregation, Falwell joked that a Jew "can make
more money accidentally than you can on purpose," repeating one

of the oldest anti-Semitic tropes in the culture. He quickly apologized for the remark, saying he had spoken in jest.[10]

Early in his ministry, after vandals attacked the Thomas Road Baptist Church in 1957, breaking some windows in the old Donald Duck building, Falwell received a check to repair the damage from Abe Schewel, a prominent Lynchburg businessman. Schewel expressed his disgust at the vandalism and noted that such vandalism had preceded more catastrophic violence against the Jews. Over the years the Schewel Furniture Company would donate items for a variety of Falwell's ministries, and state senator Elliot Schewel would help move legislation on Falwell's behalf through the Virginia legislature. As well, Falwell's many trips to the Holy Land helped him come to appreciate the deep cultural and religious connections between Jews and Christians, and he became friendly with many leaders of the Jewish state. As he expanded his ministry nationwide he would frequently be called upon to speak at Jewish organizations or in synagogues about his support for Israel. In 1981 Israeli prime minister Menachem Begin bestowed the Jabotinky Award on Falwell, the highest honor given to friends of Israel by the Israeli government.[11]

It is one of the ironies of Falwell's commitment to Israel that he seems never to have commented upon the secular and socialist origins of the modern Jewish state, and he certainly did not wrestle intellectually with the conundrum presented by Israel's history. David Ben-Gurion, Levi Eshkol, Golda Meir, Yitzhak Rabin, and all the early leaders of the Jewish state were from the Jewish labor movement and the Mapai political party that belonged to the Socialist International. Indeed, Orthodox Jews were originally opposed to Zionism, believing that the Jews' return to Israel must be left to God's doing, not to the machinations of a group of central European, religiously non-observant socialists.

Falwell's loud and repeated commitment to Israel helped keep the residual anti-Semitism of extreme conservative groups at bay. It also helped put a nail in the coffin of the kind of provincial anti-Semitism of his youth. Students at Liberty, listeners to the *Old-Time Gospel Hour,* and his own parishioners at Thomas Road Baptist would be given frequent lectures about God's promises to Israel and the importance of America honoring its commitments to the Jewish state. Given the long, ugly history of Christian persecution of the Jews, Falwell's success in making pro-Israel views a centerpiece of contemporary fundamentalist Christianity was no small achievement.

Gay rights was a new issue in the 1970s, but to fundamentalists like Falwell, it was a very old issue, going all the way back to Sodom and Gomorrah. Fundamentalists had always considered the issue of homosexuality in terms of personal morality—that is, as an instance of personal sin, like abortion. There had never been a need to see the issue in political terms because there had never before been a push for civil rights for gays and lesbians, although in 1974 conservative activist Phyllis Schlafly's campaign against the Equal Rights Amendment had warned that the amendment would confer "special rights" on gays and lesbians. But as the decade progressed, gay men and women started protesting against discrimination based on sexual preference and insisting on their rights. The backlash from conservative politicians and fundamentalist preachers was quick and powerful.[12]

The fact that Falwell saw homosexuality as a sin was significant because it touched one of the central arguments about the legitimacy of gay rights. Those who argued that being gay was the result of nature, that men and women were born with same-sex attractions, saw their insistence on gay rights as little different from the insistence of blacks that it was unjust to discriminate against them for a condition over which they had no control. By seeing homosexuality as a sin, Falwell placed himself in the opposite camp that viewed homosexuality as the result of nurture, that is, homosexuality was caused by psychological influences, especially in youth. "I firmly believe one is not born a homosexual but learns this through environment," Falwell said. "We have a staff of Christian psychologists who deal with homosexuality and other moral problems. I am against the flaunting of a homosexual life-style before impressionable children. This is detrimental to the basic tenet of Christian society, the home." As in the case of abortion, gay rights was challenging fundamentalist values. Falwell did not see himself as looking for this fight; it was forced on him.[13]

In 1977 commissioners in Dade County, Florida, over the objections of conservative activists, enacted an ordinance barring employment discrimination against gays and lesbians. Anita Bryant, a Christian singer best known for her commercials promoting Florida oranges, began collecting signatures to force a popular referendum on the measure and to overturn the new ordinance. Her pastor was an admirer of Falwell's and suggested that she call him to enlist his support. Then she and her husband flew to Lynchburg, and over barbecue at the Falwell home Falwell pledged to come and help her campaign to overturn the gay rights ordinance. The next day Bryant spoke at all three morning services at Thomas Road Baptist, including the televised *Old-Time Gospel Hour*. Falwell shared with the congregation that he would be traveling to Miami to help Bryant. Falwell told Bryant to find the largest hall they could rent for his rally. Ten days later an overflow crowd of ten thousand people jammed the Miami Convention Center to hear Falwell and Bryant urge their supporters to call neighbors and friends to turn out for the special election. On June 7, 1977, 69.3 percent of the voters in Dade County voted to overturn the gay rights ordinance. It was Falwell's first real taste of electoral victory.[14]

The following year a similar referendum went before the voters in California. Proposition 6 specifically banned gay men and lesbians from being employed as teachers in the public schools. The effort put a national spotlight on a Southern California preacher, Tim LaHaye, as well as the campaign's manager, Lou Sheldon, who would go on to form the Traditional Values Coalition to carry on the work nationwide. Falwell flew out to lend his support, speaking at the San Diego Convention Center and at a rally held at a fairgrounds in Orange County. Falwell also went on the nationally televised *Tomorrow Show* with Tom Snyder to explain his position. Falwell told Snyder and his television audience that he thought homosexuals needed love and help, but "if we allow homosexuality to be presented as an alternate life-style, it will not only have a corrupting influence upon the next generation of boys and girls, but it will bring the wrath of God down upon our nation." Curiously, conservative hero and former governor Ronald Reagan opposed the anti-gay measure, fearing it would encourage false charges against teachers. Despite Falwell's effort, Proposition 6 failed at the ballot box, with 3.9 million voting against it to only 2.8 million in favor.[15]

Later that same year, on November 27, San Francisco mayor George Moscone and Harvey Milk, one of the city's supervisors, were assassinated by a disgruntled former supervisor. The murders shocked the nation, but Falwell took to his pulpit December 3, on the *Old-Time Gospel Hour,* to explain the assassinations. "Without question, San Francisco is undergoing a judgment from God today," Falwell said. By passing gay rights ordinances and becoming a haven for gays and lesbians, San Francisco's political leaders had said, in Falwell's view, "that it doesn't matter to us what God thinks about [homosexuality], we have endorsed what God has condemned whether He likes it or not." Falwell also called attention to the recent mass murder suicide in Guyana, where hundreds of members of Rev. Jim Jones's San Francisco–based "People's Temple" drank Kool-Aid laced with cyanide, as another example of disobedience to God wreaking havoc. "The people of San Francisco had better awaken to the fact that the judgment, the wrath that is falling upon the city, is of divine origin."[16]

Gay rights would become a popular theme in Falwell's sermons. Given the conservative nature of his congregation, Falwell did not engage the issue as a practical pastoral concern. Like abortion, in Falwell's view, homosexuality was evidence of the moral decline of the nation brought on by other people who were not Bible-believing Christians. In a 1976 sermon he fretted about the use of profanity on television, about a proposal to allow two-year "trial marriages," and about the possibility of same-sex marriage, "men with men, women with women, and State laws in many places . . . allowing it." Falwell's comments about homosexuality almost always came in a catalog of "threats" to the traditional family and godly values. Sometimes he would expand on the nature of the threat, and at other times he would discuss "conversions" among former gays, but usually homosexuality was simply thrown out like a red flag, which it was, to arouse the concern or ire of his audience. Falwell also learned that references to the "threat" posed by homosexuality in fundraising letters produced extraordinary results.[17]

*   *   *

Race stalked the politics of the last half of the twentieth century. Falwell, as we have seen, was devoted to segregation in his early years, but he would undergo a conversion on the issue, renouncing his former position and welcoming blacks into his church and school. If the word "conversion" suggests a perfect turn of 180 degrees, however, then it goes too far in describing what happened to Falwell and many others. Racial attitudes became inextricably linked with the cultural and political dynamics of the 1960s, the 1970s, and beyond. One would have to have been naive not to recognize how race was still used to manipulate prejudices and so divide the electorate. Falwell was many things, but naive was not among them.

Falwell's conversion from defender to opponent of segregation was not like the more famous conversion of Paul on the road to Damascus. There was no direct revelation, no falling from his horse, no one event or moment when the scales of bigotry fell from Falwell's eyes. He recalled instances when he had felt revulsion at the indignities to which blacks were regularly exposed in his youth, including a trip to the hospital after he and a black friend had been in an auto accident. Falwell was treated immediately, but his black friend received no attention from the doctors or nurses. While Jim Crow ruled, however, there was little to be done about such injustices. Falwell also recalled a 1963 visit to the Dominican Republic, where he was to speak at a missionary-run orphanage; the pastor asked him not to mention race because the children had no concept of racial differences, as Americans did. This experience did not, however, lead Falwell to change his views about segregation in America. That same year a black man who shined Falwell's shoes, Lewis, told Falwell he listened to his sermons on television and wondered when he would be able to join Falwell's church. Falwell admitted later that this was one of the few instances in his life when he found himself speechless.[18]

In the mid-1960s, Falwell hired Paul Tan, an Indonesian musician, to work in the music ministry at Thomas Road Baptist Church. Tan's dark complexion caused consternation among some of the parishioners, but Falwell kept him on staff. In 1968 Thomas Road Baptist Church accepted its first blacks as members, and in 1969 Falwell's Lynchburg Christian Academy welcomed its first black student. Falwell claimed that the civil rights movement did not bring him to reconsider his position, that his change of position was a more personal journey. "I realized that I was completely wrong, what I had been taught was completely wrong. For me it was a scriptural and personal realization that segregation was evil. I realized it was not taught in the Bible." This realization that he had been reading the Bible incorrectly, however, did not cause Falwell to reconsider his certainty about other areas of his biblical interpretation. He had simply been wrong in this matter.[19]

In this era when the South was adapting to legally enforced integration, race relations continued to have a profound effect on politics. The Democratic Party, long beholden to its powerful southern, segregationist senators, climbed out from under its racist past. After signing the landmark Civil Rights Act of 1964, President Lyndon Johnson told his aide Bill Moyers, "I think we just delivered the South to the Republican Party for a long time to come." But Johnson did not look back. Later that year, at a campaign rally in New Orleans, Johnson told the story of a senator speaking with a young Sam Rayburn about his regret that his constituents had not heard a real "Democratic speech in thirty years. All they ever hear at election time is 'Nigra, nigra, nigra.'" In the 1964 election, Johnson won in a landslide, losing only six states: Arizona—Sen. Barry Goldwater's home state—and the five southern states of Louisiana, Mississippi, Alabama, Georgia, and South Carolina. Johnson went on to push through the Voting Rights Act the following year, further alienating southerners, who flocked in 1968 to either Richard Nixon or Alabama governor George Wallace. Texas was the only southern state won by Democratic nominee Hubert Humphrey.[20]

In the 1970s, explicitly racist political speech disappeared from mainstream politics, but Republicans, conscious of the nearly ten million votes Wallace had won in 1968, adopted racially loaded language that achieved similar results. President Richard Nixon spoke out strongly against busing as a means of achieving racial integration in school districts, and his strong anticrime stance was laden with racial overtones. As well, the tax revolts of the 1970s included as a prominent subtext the contrast between white taxpayers and black recipients of government assistance. Black militants were lumped together with anti–Vietnam War protesters as "un-American." The politics of resentment that drove conservative populism was targeted equally at blacks and the elite liberals who championed programs, like affirmative action, that aimed to address the lingering effects of racism.[21]

Falwell's sermons adopted some of these coded racist tropes. One of the problems facing America, Falwell told his *Old-Time Gospel Hour* audience in 1976, was "wealth without work." He warned that "we are developing a socialistic state in these United States as surely as I am standing here right now. Our give-away programs, our welfarism at home and abroad, is developing a breed of bums and derilects [*sic*] who wouldn't work in a pie shop eating the holes out of donuts. And they will stand in line at an unemployment office rather than go look for a job." Falwell might merely have been intellectually lazy in adopting such racially laden words, repeating lines he had heard elsewhere uncritically. He apparently displayed no antiblack animus in his personal relations. Yet, while mainstream Republican politicians kept explicitly racist organizations like the John Birch Society at arm's length, Falwell ran ads for his college in the group's magazine *American Opinion*.[22]

Falwell's turn away from his segregationist past had another, less obvious consequence. Having been raised in a culture that accorded him racial superiority, Falwell acknowledged the degradation to which blacks had been exposed, but he never examined the psychological effects that Jim Crow had on himself. The sense of being superior to fellow human beings is not easily abandoned. "Already the law, and in part opinion, proclaim a natural and permanent inferiority between servant and master does not exist," Alexis de Tocqueville wrote when considering the situation of aristocrats who had lost their privileged status with the demise of the ancien régime. "But this new faith has not yet penetrated to the depth of the mind of the latter, or rather his heart rejects it. In the secrecy of his soul the master still deems himself to be of a particular, superior species; but he does not dare say it." For Falwell and other conservative southerners, the sense of racial superiority was transferred to a sense of national superiority. The New Deal had helped to reintegrate the South into the rest of the country, and World War II had increased national loyalty, although the South maintained a strong sense of its unique heritage. But as Jim Crow collapsed, the South became home to a fervent hyperpatriotism. White southerners might no longer be considered better than their racial inferiors, but as Americans, they were superior to the rest of the world. It was in 1975 that Falwell launched his "I Love America" rallies, the combination of patriotic singing and evangelical preaching that he took to state capitol buildings throughout the land. The rallies would continue through the rest of the decade.[23]

Falwell was capable of the most jingoistic of references. "That is the symbol of liberty for the greatest nation on earth—the United States of America," Falwell told his *Old-Time Gospel Hour* audience, pointing to the American flag.

> *I have many Canadian friends. I have many Australian friends who will be watching what you are saying right now on television. I know you think your Nation is the greatest, and you have the right to think that. I'm a citizen of my country, you of yours, and we ought to be willing to fight and die for these free countries. But if that flag comes down, Canada goes with us. Australia goes with us. The FREE WORLD goes with us, and so right now—and if you are here today and you don't like this, take a walk—we're going to do it anyhow. I want Robby Heiner to come and we're going to pledge allegiance to that flag. . . .*

Just as Falwell would soon be dressing politics in religious garb, he was just as comfortable dressing his religion in patriotic garb.[24]

There was one other motivation for Falwell's embrace of increasingly patriotic sermonizing. Some of the most prominent clergymen in America were liberal clerics who had risen to prominence in part on the strength of their denunciations of American involvement in the Vietnam War. William Sloane Coffin, the chaplain at Yale, had been very active in the anti-war movement. Father Robert Drinan, SJ, had won election to Congress as an antiwar candidate in 1970 and remained one of the most vocal critics of both the Vietnam War specifically and U.S. military spending more generally. When they strode into the public square as the face of Christianity in American culture, criticizing the government, it made Falwell cringe. His sermons had long criticized liberal theology, but this was something different and something worse. The only people presenting themselves as spokesmen for religion in the public square were liberal churchmen with liberal political goals. Like many conservatives, Falwell did not see how antiwar activism could be differentiated from anti-Americanism, and the idea that clerics were challenging Americanism in the name of the Christian church appalled him. In one sense, Falwell's subsequent political involvement can be seen as a reaction to the prominence of liberal clergymen on the national stage.[25]

The final straw that broke the back of evangelical isolation was a 1978 proposal from the Internal Revenue Service (IRS) to require Christian schools that had no black students to prove the segregation was not a result of their conscious efforts. The proposal was a central assault, not on anything amorphous like "values," but on the separatist institutions the Christian churches had erected, not only to avoid federal desegregation orders in the public schools but also to raise their children in schools with explicitly Christian teachings. As well, the anger at the IRS dovetailed nicely with the growing antitax fervor on the right, which would become the central, unifying theme of political conservatives from the 1980 Reagan presidential campaign until the present time.

In 1969 the Lawyers' Committee for Civil Rights first filed suit to strip a Mississippi Christian school of its tax-exempt designation because it was segregated. They won the suit, and the IRS during the Nixon administration issued regulations that were easy for the academies to circumvent by inserting a nondiscrimination clause in their incorporating documents. This caused more suits, which the IRS resisted. When the Carter administration took office in 1977, the new IRS commissioner agreed with those who were suing his agency, and he issued new regulations on August 22, 1978. The key change shifted the burden of proof from the IRS to the school: they would have to prove that they did not discriminate, not the other way around.[26]

The new regulations were the "precise trigger" for the rise of the religious right, and the response was overwhelming. Robert Billings, who would later be the first executive director of the Moral Majority, led the charge to see the rule rescinded; during this campaign, 126,000 letters of protest landed in the IRS mailbox, and calls to Congress were made. "It kicked the sleeping dog," said Richard Viguerie. "It galvanized the religious right." Within a matter of weeks, the IRS backed off and pulled the proposed regulations.[27]

The IRS assault confirmed the fear among evangelicals that their separationist stance vis-à-vis the ambient culture was no longer able to protect them from that culture. Legal abortion affronted their values. They believed that antiwar activism assaulted their patriotism. The welfare state threatened the economic values, and economic power, of white southerners. They tenaciously worried that the cultural acceptance of gay and lesbian "lifestyles" threatened their children, and the Equal Rights Amendment threatened their understanding of traditional family roles. Now one of the principal means they had built to keep the ambient culture at bay, their Christian schools, were not immune from attack by a government they no longer trusted. The fact that a born-again Christian, President Jimmy Carter, headed that government added a note of betrayal to their anxieties.[28]

Taxes were on the radar screen of political conservatives long before the controversy about the IRS regulations regarding Christian schools, but the two issues worked together in the face of a common enemy. In California, Proposition 13, a proposed constitutional amendment to limit property taxes, was passed by a popular referendum on June 6, 1978, with 64.8 percent of the vote. The vote also reflected how deeply views of government were affected by racial differences: only 29 percent of black voters in California supported Proposition 13. Thirty other states launched similar efforts to limit property taxes, although the tax revolt lost in as many states as it won as voters pondered the consequences of having to slash government programs. At the same time, at the federal level, conservative activists embraced "supply-side" economics that advocated drastically lower tax rates, in part to stimulate economic growth but also to starve the government of tax revenue and therefore restrain its growth.[29]

Other issues engaged Falwell's attention as they came and went during the 1970s. He worked with Phyllis Schlafly and Anita Bryant to help defeat the ratification of the Equal Rights Amendment. In 1977 he spoke out against the International Women's Year Conference, which was sponsored by the United Nations, an organization that frightened Falwell because of the biblical warnings against world government and because of the organization's growing hostility to Israel. The policy of détente with China and the Soviet Union was viewed with profound skepticism, if not outright hostility, by all conservatives, including Falwell. Few of these issues had "legs," but they did not do anything to cause Falwell to question his increasing allegiance to a conservative political platform. As the year 1979 dawned and the prospect of the 1980 election came into view, the key narrative for evangelical political involvement was set. Fundamentalists had withdrawn from the mainstream culture after the Scopes trial, to protect themselves from the "acids of modernity," as Walter Lippmann termed them. But separation was failing. Their country was increasingly repugnant to them, morally and politically. And the mainstream culture was, in any event, unwilling to let them alone and had embarked on an assault on their values and institutions. Falwell had grown accustomed to speaking out on issues that had political content, but he was not yet willing to enter the political arena beyond raising his voice. That was about to change.[30]

Chapter Seven

Starting the Moral Majority

The decision to start the Moral Majority in 1979 would catapult Jerry Falwell into the world of politics and onto a truly national stage. Already, his talents as a spokesman and his forceful personality had served to make him a leading figure in the world of evangelical religion, but when those same talents and personal energy were applied to the political stage, he became a ubiquitous presence in that field as well. His personal life would be disrupted by the need to travel hundreds of thousands of miles per year, organizing and enlivening the Moral Majority, giving interviews, attending rallies, speaking to meetings of pastors. The Moral Majority was a new trajectory for Falwell, and it was one that would not only make his a household name, but would also change forever the way he was viewed by his fellow Americans.

The impact of the Moral Majority would be felt in manifold ways. First and foremost, the Moral Majority registered millions of new voters. Conservative fundamentalists had shied away from political involvement because of the traditional belief that moral reformation and civic engagement were not proper tasks for the church, a belief that was especially prominent in the Baptist tradition. Falwell had to overcome a psychological barrier within himself and his community to generate political activism within the fundamentalist fold. He had been dabbling in issues that were both religious and political throughout the 1970s, but starting the Moral Majority would be an explicitly political act. He had to alter his previous understanding of the separation of church and state, and that of his followers, from both a theological perspective and a historical one. Once engaged, however, those new voters equaled political power for Falwell and his colleagues.

The Moral Majority changed the debate both within the Republican Party and across the nation. If, over time, America would acquiesce to such enormous previous changes in politics as the New Deal and the civil rights movement, the Moral Majority stood for the proposition that there would be no acquiescing to liberal abortion laws or the ready availability of pornography. They would resist efforts to enshrine gay rights into law. Conservative evangelicals and their political allies would fight on issues as diverse as support for the state of Israel, cutting taxes, and defeating the Equal Rights Amendment. Falwell did not ride the wave of political conservatism that characterized the 1980s; he helped generate it.

Falwell would become the face of Christian political involvement. In the middle years of the twentieth century, mainstream Protestantism had been the most public face of religion in American society. Serious theologians such as Reinhold Niebuhr and his brother, H. Richard Niebuhr, had profound influences on American intellectual life. The Reverend Martin Luther King Jr. and a host of black Baptist preachers led the civil rights movement in the 1950s and 1960s. Liberal pastors such as William Sloane Coffin joined hands with liberal Catholic priests like the Berrigan brothers to oppose the Vietnam War. In the 1980s, Falwell would eclipse these prominent Christian leaders and their followers as a political force. He would be reckoned one of the most admired men in America, but his prominence also created many enemies. Many of those enemies championed a different understanding of America's greatness, and many of them, displaying an antireligious bigotry that astounds, failed to acknowledge even the sincerity of Falwell's views. But whether he was loved or hated, Falwell was never again ignored.

Finally, Falwell changed not only what it meant to be a Christian for millions of conservative fundamentalists but also the perception of what it meant to be a Christian in the broader culture. In the more secular countries of western Europe, that might not have been such a consequential achievement. But in the United States, with its culture still frequently framed by values born in Protestantism, changing the image of the Christian church in the broader culture was an accomplishment of enormous significance. Non-Christians would think of Falwell when they thought of Christianity. Secular thinkers would think of fundamentalism when they considered what it meant to be an orthodox Christian. No longer did religion conjure up benign images of propriety in the American mind: Falwell's was a fighting faith, a muscular Christianity ready to do battle, not reach an accommodation, with the forces of secularization at work in the mainstream culture.

Falwell, ever the optimist, saw only the upside to his political involvement. There were abortions to be prevented. There were smut peddlers to be shut down. There was a nation to be recalled to its founding principles, as Falwell understood them. There was an evil Soviet empire to be fought. He did not see, as many still do not see, that by reducing religion to ethics in order to gain access to the public square, he was participating in the privatizing of religion and thereby aiding the very secularization he sought to defeat. Later on, in the late 1980s, Falwell would see the need to create a Christian culture and would focus his attentions on Liberty University, but all that was in the future. In 1979, launching the Moral Majority, he was convinced that if right-minded Christians—in both senses of the word "right"—would rise up and organize, they could save America from the moral licentiousness, political liberalism, and apathy toward communism that he thought endangered the nation he still believed had a unique role to play in God's plan of redemption.

Moral Majority Inc. was incorporated on June 6, 1979. The previous month, a group of conservative political leaders had come to Lynchburg to recruit Jerry Falwell for their project to "save America." The meeting was arranged by Robert Billings, who had previously directed the National Christian Action Coalition. They were joined by Ed McAteer, head of the Religious Roundtable, the direct-mail guru Richard Viguerie, Conservative Caucus chairman Howard Phillips, and Paul Weyrich, a conservative activist and strategist.[1]

Each man brought something unique to the table. McAteer, a former soap salesman, would prove especially useful to the group because his contacts extended beyond the evangelical churches. "Billings's outreach was mainly to the fundamental churches and some evangelical churches," Weyrich would later recall. "But McAteer's outreach was to Presbyterians and to conservative Methodists, and to Church of God people and the Seventh Day Adventists and all kinds of people who, as it turns out, for 20 years in his capacity as sales manager for this soap company, he had been going around visiting. . . . It was they who brought Howard Phillips and myself together with the Jerry Falwells, with the James Robisons, with the Charles Stanleys, you know, with all the different people who were doing stuff around the country." That "stuff" the ministers were doing was not politics, even though it frequently had political overtones. But the ministers had something the politicians lacked: millions of faithful television viewers.[2]

The group knew of Falwell's ambivalence about getting involved in politics. A historian of conservative religion in America writes that the idea of creating a hybrid organization that was half-religious and half-political "constituted a direct challenge to fundamentalist pietism, which traditionally manifested itself not only in disciplined devotional practice and strict standards of personal morality, but also in a general stance of separation from 'the world.'. . . That pietistic idea was predominant in the mind of the average person in the average pew in a fundamentalist church in America." Falwell would need to reshape the debate within the fundamentalist fold in order to change the debate in the country. He would need to find reasons to justify the abandonment of the traditional separationist principles that had shaped Baptists since the days when they were the object of persecution in the seventeenth and eighteenth centuries and, more recently, since the fallout from the Scopes trial had sidelined them from the dominant cultural and political debates in America.[3]

Falwell had been profoundly disturbed by the actions of the federal government—legalizing abortion, removing prayer from the public schools, sending the IRS after Christian academies. To him, this amounted to a political assault on his turf, the moral fiber of the nation, and he could begin to envision politics as the means for beating back the assault. If politics could bring ruin to the moral fiber of America, politics could also help to restore the moral fiber of America.

At an earlier meeting, Falwell had worried not only that getting involved in politics would take him and his energies away from his growing ministry, but that it would divide his congregation. Weyrich commissioned a nationwide poll that completely dispelled Falwell's worries. "It showed not only that people supported mixing politics with religion," Weyrich said, "but they were chomping at the bit to do so." Evangelicals shared Falwell's disgust at the liberalization of American society and held the same conservative stances on issues that Falwell did. They were prepared to get involved politically if someone would lead them.[4]

Phillips expressed his disgust with the moderate forces within the Republican Party, arguing that conservatives needed to imitate the 1960s radicals in their fervor, if not in their message. Falwell said that the GOP was "all we've got." Even though time was short, Phillips thought that if the group energized religious conservatives, they could have an impact on the 1980 Republican Party platform as well as the nominating process. The key for Phillips and his fellow conservatives was to use the abortion issue to divide the Catholic vote. Republicans who were mostly concerned about communism or high taxes would not leave the GOP over an issue like abortion, but the issue might strip off enough Catholics from the Democratic Party to win the 1980 election. Already, in 1978, conservative Catholics had played a crucial role in ousting liberal Iowa senator Richard Clark after conservative activists blanketed cars parked at Catholic churches the Sunday before election day with anti-abortion literature.

The appeal to the political efficacy of the abortion issue was designed to capture Falwell's imagination. He had been preaching against abortion in his pulpit ever since the Supreme Court's 1973 *Roe v. Wade* decision legalized the procedure. Abortion epitomized

for him the central cultural debate between licentiousness and morality. The fact that so many mainstream churches had supported the
decision galled him to the core. Most important, the issue showed
the necessity for fundamentalists to get politically engaged: they had
not sought this fight, the Supreme Court had started it. But the abortion issue also pointed to one of the lingering difficulties for Falwell in embarking on a political crusade, and the political strategy
outlined for him added to the conundrum. Abortion was seen as a
"Catholic issue." It was the hierarchy of the Catholic Church that
had been most vocal in its opposition to *Roe*. Could fundamentalists
join forces with Catholics in pursuit of a common political agenda?

The question touched a core principle of fundamentalist belief.
Fundamentalist Christians were warned against being "yoked" with
unbelievers. Evangelical churches had a long history of preaching
against Catholicism, even seeing the pope as the Antichrist. Weyrich was himself a Catholic, and Phillips was a Jew: he did not even
confess Jesus as his savior. "I didn't even get along very well with
other kinds of Baptists," Falwell observed, "let alone with Methodists, Presbyterians, or Catholics." In 1976 he had preached a sermon
at a midweek service at Thomas Road Baptist Church in which he
denounced other religions, even other evangelicals. "I turned on my
television the other night and there was Rex Humbard, Kathryn
Kuhlman, Pat Boone, Oral Roberts and a hodge-podge of charismat-
ics bringing disgrace to the cause of Christ," he told his congregation. He was withering on the Mormons because they denied Christ
was co-equal with the Father: "They struck out before they ever got
to first base." And he attacked Catholics for their devotion to Mary.[5]

Falwell, however, had been reading the works of Dr. Francis
Schaeffer, whom he had met for the first time the previous year.
Schaeffer developed the theory of "cobelligerents," an idea that
allowed evangelicals to work with Catholics, Jews, and non-
evangelical Protestants in the social and political arena provided
that they did not compromise their theological beliefs. Schaeffer
cited biblical accounts in which people of different beliefs worked
together to accomplish God's purposes. For example, it was Cyrus,
king of Persia, who ended Israel's exile and ordered the Temple in

Jerusalem to be rebuilt, and Simon, a Cyrenian, had helped Jesus carry his cross.

Additionally, Schaeffer had argued for Christian involvement in politics and society in dire, almost apocalyptic terms. "Evangelical accommodation to the world of our age," he wrote, "represents the removal of the last barrier against the breakdown of our culture." If Christians did not fight for the culture, who would? The politicians meeting in Lynchburg presented the exact same argument to Falwell: if he would not lead Christians into battle for the culture, who would? Schaeffer provided the intellectual justification that Falwell needed to "yoke" himself with unbelievers, create a political organization, and work together to restore America to the Judeo-Christian values that were held in common.[6]

The two problems—getting Baptists politically involved and working with nonfundamentalists—solved each other in a sense. The new group would not be religious but political, explicitly so, welcoming people of all creeds who shared the organization's political ambitions to restore America to values rooted in the "Judeo-Christian" tradition. That amorphous phrase lumped together a host of theological beliefs that nonetheless issued in common moral precepts, and these moral precepts were under attack from a common secular enemy. Nothing unites and galvanizes at the same time as efficaciously as a common enemy: what Falwell and his political friends saw as a deteriorating culture all around them was the common enemy that justified ending the separationist instincts of the fundamentalists and joining hands with those whose faith was not their own.

Once Falwell was won over to the idea of starting a new organization, the group turned to thinking about a name for the newborn. Several suggestions seemed too opaque, even boring, such as "People for a Stable America." Paul Weyrich did not like the names being suggested. "What we really need is a moral majority of Americans with a name like. . . ." He did not finish the sentence. McAteer asked him to repeat what he had just said. The phrase "moral majority" grabbed all of them. It conveyed their distinctiveness as a group: they would be dedicated to furthering an explicitly moral agenda. And the phrase also tapped into their hope that they would be speaking for a majority of Americans, not too different from Nixon's "silent majority." Indeed, the new organization would be the mouthpiece for that majority.[7]

The Moral Majority's first task was to determine its program. What issues would they focus on? The organization would be political, yes, but its distinctiveness was its emphasis on morality. Falwell and his colleagues had to create a platform that was both distinctly moral in focus and emphasis and wedded to a political agenda that would allow them to appeal to more than the fundamentalist base Falwell brought to the table.

Given the role of abortion in snaring Falwell's political attention and in the strategy that Weyrich and Viguerie had outlined, it was a foregone conclusion that the Moral Majority would be vigorously pro-life. They would argue that America needed a constitutional amendment to overturn *Roe,* or at least some mechanism to get the issue out of the courts and delivered back to state legislatures. Politically, the issue was a ready-made link to conservative Catholics, but it also would serve as the kind of extension from the pulpit to the polling place that seemed natural for evangelical Protestants.

Second, the group would be pro-family. Falwell had dipped his toe into the political waters of Florida when he helped Anita Bryant in her campaign against gay rights, and besides, the gay issue was already central to Falwell's fund-raising appeals. The pro-family label would also tap into the energy of those groups of conservatives who had already been organized to defeat the Equal Rights Amendment. Finally, the pro-family label would appeal to those who might not identify with the religious tenets of either Falwell or the Catholic Church but who were worried about the effects of libertine cultural influences on their own children.

Third, the Moral Majority would be "pro-moral." This plank overlapped with the first two but was intended to include opposition to pornography and the drug culture. It would be another link between the evangelical concern for personal righteousness and the law-and-order instincts of the conservative movement. And like the pro-family label, this plank of their platform would appeal to families worried about the potential effects of drugs and pornography on their children. It would reach beyond the confines of the churches to the concerns of the kitchen table.

Finally, the group would be pro-American, urging a strong defense posture in the face of communist aggression. Here was a necessary link to secular conservatives in the Republican Party, but Falwell also was deeply opposed to communism because of its persecution of religious believers and its denial of freedom. As an adjunct to being pro-American, the group would be pro-Israel, recognizing both Israel's special relationship with the United States and Falwell's belief, rooted in the Bible, that nations are judged by God based on how they treat Israel.

This fourfold platform was adeptly fashioned to achieve the Moral Majority's objective of becoming a bridge between the evangelical church and the Republican Party. It was more than that, however. It would reach into other denominations, banking on the proposition that there were ideological cleavages within those denominations that could be exploited for political gain. Not all Catholics were still wedded to the Democratic Party. Not all Protestants agreed with the National Council of Churches that *Roe* had been correctly decided. Many Jews were worried about the effects that drugs and violence had on their families. Denominational differences would give way, Falwell hoped, in the face of moral unity, and once united, the Moral Majority could reshape the political landscape.

Jerry Falwell was brilliant, but he was not a theoretician. He was a man of action. Once he had overcome the objections to political involvement in his own mind, he turned his relentless energies to the task of building the Moral Majority. He would hit the hustings, as it were, mounting his own campaign to galvanize the millions of Americans—the "majority" of Americans—whom he believed were ready to be educated on the issues, organized, registered to vote, and to begin taking their country back at the next election.

Moral Majority hired Billings to be the group's executive direc-

tor and Ronald Godwin to serve as vice president. Billings, with his
extensive network of friends within the fundamentalist churches,
would focus on the urgent goal of registering voters. Godwin would
be in charge of day-to-day operations, and his skills as a manager
would permit Falwell to serve mainly as the spokesman and cheerleader for Moral Majority. The board of directors included prominent religious leaders whom Falwell considered politically savvy:
Tim LaHaye, who would later become famous as the author of the
"Left Behind" series of books about the Rapture and was currently
the pastor at Scott Memorial Baptist Church in El Cajon, California; Rev. D. James Kennedy of the enormous Coral Ridge Presbyterian Church in Fort Lauderdale, Florida; Rev. Greg Dixon of the
Baptist Temple in Indianapolis, Indiana; and Charles Stanley, pastor
of the First Baptist Church in Atlanta, Georgia. The group brought
geographic diversity and ideological purity, as all were staunch conservatives. Falwell was chairman of the board. In addition to the lobbying organization, the board established a tax-exempt educational
organization, the Moral Majority Foundation, and a political action
committee (PAC) that could funnel money directly to candidates.[8]

Falwell built on his extant network of religious leaders as well
as on his own *Old-Time Gospel Hour* organization. He understood that he needed to get his fellow conservative pastors on board
because they held sway over their congregants. His colleague Ed
Dobson said that "Christians tended not to listen to or were suspicious of people who didn't bring the authority that a pastor would
bring." Falwell himself would later point out that while his degree of
political involvement had changed, his ecclesiology had not: "God's
plan is that his flock is to be led by shepherds, not by a board or committee." He had long traveled to preach at other churches at the invitation of the local pastors, and his contacts throughout the world of
fundamentalist churches were extensive. He had always asked how
many in the congregation were saved, but now he would also ask
how many were registered to vote.[9]

It did not require much to tweak certain efforts that Falwell had
already begun to propagate his new political gospel. The *Journal-
Champion,* which he had been publishing as part of the *Old-Time*

Gospel Hour's outreach, became the *Moral Majority Report*. He borrowed $25,000 from a Houston businessman to cover the costs of putting together their first mailing, but the lists he had already built up at the *Old-Time Gospel Hour* provided the most important asset for an effective mailing list: names and addresses of proven donors.[10]

Falwell started up his "I Love America" rallies again. As in 1976, when he had first held these demonstrations of patriotic fervor, he would fly to state capitals and hold a rally on the steps of the capitol building. Choristers from Liberty Baptist College would sing patriotic and religious songs, Falwell would give a speech, and legislators and local pastors would be invited to address the crowds. But now Falwell added a luncheon for local pastors, paid for by the Moral Majority, at which he would outline the group's goals and agenda. He would enlist the pastors' support and figure out who could provide leadership for the nascent organization at the state level.[11]

At an evening rally in Harrisburg, Pennsylvania, Falwell told his audience, "I am not a Republican! I am not a Democrat! I am a noisy Baptist!" After some patriotic music from the choir, he showed a ninety-minute $110,000 audio-video presentation entitled "America, You're Too Young to Die!" Falwell had begun using the "Too Young to Die" theme the year before when fund-raising for his school. The presentation was not shy in its graphic portrayal of the moral failings that Falwell believed were sapping the moral fiber of the nation. In addition to quotes from American Communist leader Gus Hall about his plans to take over the country, the video part of the presentation featured images of "Charles Manson, Times Square sex-film marquees, atom bombs exploding, young men with their arms around each other and unbreathing fetuses lying in bloody white ceramic hospital pans." Falwell knew how to excite his base, and he also knew something else. He knew that if he could get them to the polls, they could begin to roll back the filth he had just cataloged for them.[12]

Except for minor adjustments, the early literature from the Moral Majority would change little in the group's decade of existence. The

focus was on the four planks that were the center of the Moral Majority's political concerns, but the message would be tailored to appeal to
a broad audience and to place the organization's efforts in a context
that would be readily understood by conservative Christians.

At first, the Moral Majority literature, including its fund-raising
appeals, contained biblical quotes. Old habits die hard. Over time,
and in response to concern that these quotes muddied the image of
the Moral Majority as a nonreligious, political organization, the
Bible quotes were dropped. The literature, in fact, would create a
new style of political language that seamlessly blended unstated
religious motivations with a political hermeneutic. References to
the "Judeo-Christian" tradition would remain, and the role of that
Judeo-Christian tradition in influencing the thinking of the American Founders would be highlighted.

"This non-profit organization was created to give a voice to the
millions of decent, law abiding, God-fearing Americans who want
to do something about the moral decline of our country," began the
first brochure issued by the Moral Majority. The reference to "law-
abiding" may have derived from Richard Viguerie's prior work with
the George Wallace campaigns, which had tapped into middle- and
working-class resentment of the libertinism of those they deemed
"cultural elites." In the late 1960s and 1970s, images of wealthy college kids getting stoned on drugs and protesting the Vietnam War
had offended conservative sensibilities, especially in the South, where
the military was held in high esteem. "God-fearing," without further
theological specificity, spoke to the group's ecumenism.[13]

The Moral Majority's literature did not intend to mimic the "civic
religion" of America, about which sociologists Robert Bellah and
Martin Marty had written in the 1960s. The overlaps were obvious,
however, and a necessity of the new organization's goal of attracting
non-evangelicals. Falwell had to capture something of the comment
by President Dwight Eisenhower, who had once said, "Our form of
government has no sense unless it is founded in a deeply felt religious
faith, and I don't care what it is." They had to distinguish dogma
from morals, and the morality needed to be accessible to those who
did not share a Baptist's concerns about dancing and drinking.

That first Moral Majority brochure set out their ideological land-scape by listing eight symptoms of the "moral decline" that threat-ened the nation and against which the Moral Majority was called to do battle. The list fleshed out the four central planks of the Moral Majority platform:

1. "3 to 6 million babies legally murdered through abortion on demand;
2. creeping socialism, which is a first cousin to Commu-nism;
3. the philosophy of 'something for nothing'—give-away programs and welfarism;
4. vicious and determined attacks on the family, the public schools system and the ability to defend our nation;
5. unprecedented lack of leadership;
6. danger of capitulation to the Soviet Union a very pos-sible result;
7. the monogamous family—one man, for one woman, for one lifetime—may become extinct during the Decade of Destiny;
8. humanism, socialism, and moral permissiveness."

Item 3 seemed to be the only genuinely new addition to the Moral Majority program, demonstrating the influence of conserva-tive Republican ideology, as does item 5, an implied attack on Presi-dent Jimmy Carter. Socialism and communism were raised as threats that would be readily understood by conservatives, even though their power and influence were more remote than the excited verbiage sug-gested.[14]

The concern for the public schools had a demonstrable crossover appeal. Conservative Christians had long been worried about sex education in the public schools, the use of textbooks they deemed anti-Christian, and the judicially mandated removal of prayer from the public classroom. But many people who were not conservative Christians were also concerned about the public schools, which were experiencing higher dropout rates, lower test scores, and racial tensions. And as Falwell knew from the earlier fights over sex education and textbooks in the public schools—indeed, as he knew from his many years of active ministry—women were frequently the backbone of most religious organizations. Appealing to them on issues about their children's education was a surefire way to draw them in.

The brochure, for all its ungainly syntax, was effective. It included photographs of a gay rights parade, of a San Francisco heterosexual strip club, and of an anti-abortion protester carrying a large cross with a sculpted image of an unborn child affixed to it. Creating a sense of crisis was a key ingredient of all fund-raising, as Falwell had already learned when raising money for his ministries and his college. Soon enough money was raised to pay back the $25,000 loan, but the Moral Majority would never be a cash cow. It brought in enough to carry out its work, to publish its *Moral Majority Report,* and to provide voter registration materials to churches.[15]

Creating a sense of crisis in the literature of the Moral Majority was also effective because it fit with a recognizable pattern of evangelical preaching. Writing of Falwell's preaching style, Susan Friend Harding notes that "Falwell's speech is not like secular speech. He inhabits a world generated by Bible-based stories and, as a 'man of God,' his speech partakes of the generative quality of the Bible itself." America's moral decline had many analogies in the scriptural history of Israel, and each time God had sent a prophet to call His people back. Falwell was America's prophet, sent by God at this time of crisis. The sense of impending doom found in the literature of the Moral Majority was intended not only to open wallets but to open hearts—that is, to generate the kind of emotions, a mixture of fear and hope, that prompt people to action. The aim was to get people upset enough to get involved, but not despondent, lest they retreat back into their separationist posture. At the end of one of Falwell's sermons there would be a call for those who wished to be baptized to come forward. At the end of a piece of Moral Majority literature there was a call for political baptism.[16]

Falwell had a reputation for being an effective fund-raiser, and some of his friends even poked fun at the different ways he and other television preachers appealed for funds. At an event in Atlanta a fellow minister introduced Falwell by telling a joke. There are these three famous ministers and a reporter on a plane that's crashing. The reporter asks Billy Graham what his final words are: "Repent and be saved!" Then he asks Oral Roberts: "Something *good's* gonna happen to me today!" Then he asks Rev. Jerry Falwell: "Folks, this is absolutely the last chance you'll have to write in for the large-print Bible." Nonetheless, the Moral Majority, unable to sell large-print Bibles, never achieved great success with its fund-raising. Its annual budget would climb to $10 million, a pittance compared to the more than tens of millions Falwell's ministries brought in annually.[17]

The Moral Majority would not become a player in campaign fund-raising. Its political action committee, which was distinct from the main organization for legal reasons, never became a large conduit for campaign cash. What the Moral Majority hoped to bring to the table was organization and argument—specifically, the organizational means for registering and informing the "sleeping giant" of evangelical voters and the arguments that would appeal beyond the evangelical base to other religiously motivated conservative voters.

Early on the decision was made by Falwell and Godwin that it was vitally important to get Moral Majority chapters established in every state. They wanted to let each local chapter control itself. From Lynchburg and Washington, the national leadership could lend direction, disseminate ideas, sponsor training seminars for activists, and raise money. But it would be up to the people on the ground to do the organizing.

The decision to allow a great deal of local control had an immediate upside. Instead of the eighteen months Weyrich and Viguerie thought would be required to create a nationwide organization, Falwell, Billings, and Godwin had set up state chapters of the Moral Majority in every state of the Union by the end of the year. These local leaders would bring their already existing networks with them, and by reading Moral Majority literature and getting trained in the fundamentals of political organization, they could quickly have an impact. The downside, of course, was that the quality of the state-level organizations varied wildly, and whatever mistakes were made would tar the national organization and provide fodder to its critics.[18]

One of the Moral Majority's first successes came in Gaines-ville, Florida, where there were fifty-three vacancies on the Alachua County Democratic Committee. The pastor of the Southside Bap-tist Church, Rev. Gene Keith, attended a weeklong Moral Majority training seminar on political organizing in the autumn of 1979. Pas-tor Keith must have taken the lessons to heart. Forty-two members of his congregation won election to the Alachua County Democratic Committee. When the first Moral Majority organizational meeting was held in the state, more than four thousand people showed up, according to Dr. Rayburn Blair, who was selected as executive direc-tor of the Florida chapter.[19]

The Illinois state chapter of the Moral Majority had a mailing list of twenty thousand by the summer of 1980. They held a semi-nar in which they taught their members the dos and don'ts of giving interviews to the media. "Play hardball," Rev. George Zarris, head of the Illinois chapter, told his members. "Don't be nasty, but play hardball." The growth of the Moral Majority in the Midwest would prove decisive for many key House and Senate races in which Demo-crats and Republicans had been evenly split.[20]

In Alaska the Moral Majority had even greater success. Rev. Jerry Prevo of the Anchorage Baptist Temple had gotten involved in poli-tics in 1977 to fight a city proposal prohibiting discrimination against homosexuals in employment. He was also concerned about what he considered undue interference by the state Board of Education in his church's five-hundred-student private school. "In this country Chris-tianity has been discriminated against," Prevo told reporters.

The local Republican caucuses were held in February, and the Moral Majority's members ran as candidates to be delegates to the state convention. The state chapter of the Moral Majority, which had its first organizational meeting in December, distributed its own literature, which echoed that distributed by the national organiza-tion. "Our country is rapidly turning into a 20th century Sodom and Gomorrah because we have permitted a few amoral humanists to take over the most influential positions in our nation," one brochure written by Reverend Prevo read. "Humanism, with its moral emphasis on no absolutes and situation ethics, challenges every moral principal [sic] upon which America was originally founded." It called for overturning Roe v. Wade, attacked feminism as a threat to the traditional family, and voiced the worry that "the free enterprise system is endangered by the advent of socialism."

When the state convention met on April 18, the Moral Majority took control of the entire state party organization. They passed a series of resolutions that tracked with the Moral Majority agenda. The party went on record against legalized abortion and also voiced opposition to the White House's planned Conference on the Family, which Prevo thought was "stacked against family life." One resolution asserted the rights of parents to spank their children, while another criticized welfare for those able to work. As important as the resolutions was the state convention's delivery of all nineteen of its delegates to the GOP national convention to the candidacy of Ronald Reagan. Moral Majority's Alaska takeover became national news, and Prevo appeared on the ABC News program Nightline. "For the first time in my lifetime we're seeing the liberals scared to death," Prevo enthused. "We're doing something that neither the Democrats, Republicans nor Independents could do . . . that is, turn the country around."[21]

The Moral Majority scored another victory closer to home. In Alabama, Republican congressman John Buchanan, although a Baptist minister, had compiled a decidedly moderate voting record. He supported civil rights legislation and women's rights. In 1978 a more conservative Republican, Albert Lee Smith, ran against Buchanan in the primaries, but Buchanan fended off the challenge. In 1980, with strong support from the Moral Majority, Smith defeated Buchanan by ten points in the GOP primary and went on to win the seat in November. "They beat my brains out with Christian love," Buchanan opined after his defeat.[22]

With success came a greater degree of exposure and criticism. The Moral Majority's critics came in all shapes and sizes, from secular politicians to other preachers, armed with arguments drawn from a narrow understanding of the separation of church and state, from history, and from the scriptures and the traditions of the Baptist church. The criticisms forced Falwell to clarify his stances, often in ways that redounded to his credit and to his future political success, other times not. The criticism and response dynamic of the early years of the Moral Majority was to be expected. In addition to any of the particular issues involved, Falwell was renegotiating the social contract, charting a new course for Bible-believing Christians and overcoming "the array of cultural barriers that had quarantined them from other Americans for half a century."[23]

The most common charge, found frequently among liberal politicians and on the editorial pages of the major newspapers, was that Falwell was blurring the line separating church and state. Rabbi Marc Tannenbaum of the American Jewish Committee warned that the Moral Majority was establishing a "religious test" for public officeholders, in direct violation of the First Amendment's prohibition of such tests. Of course, the First Amendment says only that the government cannot establish a religious test for public office; moreover, people vote for politicians for a variety of reasons. Still, some thought the Moral Majority was crossing a line. "I don't think it is the province of the church to tell people how they should vote," said independent presidential candidate John Anderson.[24]

Sen. John Culver, a liberal incumbent from Iowa and former college roommate of Sen. Ted Kennedy, was targeted by the Moral Majority in 1980. He criticized the religious right groups for what he deemed their skewed moral sense. Culver noted that Florida congressman Richard Kelly had achieved a 100 percent voting record on morally significant votes conducted by the Christian Voice, a conservative evangelical organization, even though Kelly was indicted in the ABSCAM bribery scandal. Culver expressed his dismay that the issues raised by the Moral Majority and other groups failed to include such Christian concerns as helping the poor and the sick. The Jesuit weekly *America* echoed the charge, tagging the Moral Majority with exercising "moral fascism."[25]

Falwell and his allies thought such charges were evidence of nothing but liberal bias. He confronted the charge of imposing a religious test by arguing that none of the candidates the Moral Majority endorsed were strict fundamentalists. "I would feel comfortable voting for a Jew or a Catholic or an atheist, as long as he or she agrees with us on vital issues," Falwell told the press. Sen. Jesse Helms of North Carolina seconded Falwell's charge of bias. "Everybody says, 'Oh, gee whiz, you can't mix politics with religion.' Where were they when other religious leaders were hip deep in politics during the antiwar and civil rights movement?" Falwell was largely correct in perceiving a liberal bias, even animus, against his organization, rooted in opposition to his political agenda. Some of his critics would grab at whatever arguments might stoke the fires of opposition to his organization.[26]

In fact, Falwell had engaged in a searching reevaluation of his previous views on the relationship between church and state. "Somehow I thought the separation doctrine existed to keep the church out of politics. I was wrong," Falwell wrote. He came to the conclusion that the First Amendment was designed to keep government from "interfering" with religion. Most constitutional scholars would argue that the First Amendment was more of a two-edged sword than Falwell allowed, but his critics suffered from the same one-way view of the Constitution, albeit from a different direction. What was really at issue, however, was not so much the First Amendment as liberal disgust at Falwell's positions and the way he argued for them. His self-confident, fundamentalist certainty was different from the kinds of religiously motivated speech heard in the public square in the past fifty years.[27]

"Moral Majority strongly supports a pluralistic America," Falwell wrote in a signed editorial in the *Moral Majority Report*. "While we believe this nation was founded on the Judeo-Christian ethic by men and women who were strongly influenced by Biblical moral principles, we are committed to the separation of church and state." He thought it was entirely permissible to bring his moral concerns into the public square, just as Dr. King had brought his moral concerns into the public square in the 1950s and 1960s. Still, while Falwell would tip his rhetorical hat in the direction of pluralism, he could never quite get his head around the idea that pluralism was a value. It was a sociological and political fact with which Christians had to come to terms, especially in forging a political group intended to overlook theological divisions. But, in the end, Falwell thought most questions of politics and theology had one answer, not many answers, and that the root of the problem in American culture was to get back to where America, or at least Falwell's America, had been in the 1950s.[28]

The most difficult criticisms, and the most important for the Moral Majority to combat, came from within the Christian community. Falwell could breezily dismiss the National Council of Churches and other liberal Christians, but answering his critics from within the evangelical fold was more problematic. In bringing evangelicals back from their self-imposed exile of fifty years, Falwell was not only forcing liberals to adapt to his presence but forcing evangelicals to reexamine, as he had reexamined, their principles.

Falwell's rhetoric sometimes encouraged his opponents. "I have a divine mandate to go right into the halls of Congress and fight for laws that will save America," Falwell said, but the fight he proposed was an electoral fight. Many of his political enemies failed to appreciate the fact that Falwell's methods were never antidemocratic, even if his language was at times heavy-handed. And the concern about Falwell's self-righteousness rang truer coming from fellow evangelical pastors than it did coming from politicians.

Some of the criticism was not only immediate but close to home. Ed Dobson, one of Falwell's closest aides, recalled that one of Falwell's associates urged him not to launch the Moral Majority, saying that it was "the worst thing he could do" and that he would be "wandering off the path." Falwell replied that he appreciated his associate's concern, "but this is what I'm going to do." Dobson said that the decision to form the group was undertaken before Falwell had thought through all the implications. "It was kind of a 'ready, fire, aim' approach."[29]

Across town, at First Presbyterian Church, Rev. John Killinger delivered a sermon entitled "Would Jesus Have Appeared on the *Old-*

Time Gospel Hour?" Killinger actually answered his own question in the affirmative, but he suggested that Jesus would have some strong things to say to Falwell's congregation. By way of example, Killinger wondered if Jesus might not say, "You appear to be very religious, before your television audience. But, inside, you are rapacious, unconverted wolves, seeking only a greater share of the evangelical TV market, without really caring for the sheep you devour." Falwell responded the next week from his own pulpit: "I don't want you to hurt Dr. Killinger, but we don't need him in this town." Killinger claims that the incident was followed by his trash being searched and his phone being tapped.[30]

"There is an unnerving similarity between Jerry Falwell and the Ayatollah Khomeini," the Reverend William Howard, president of the National Council of Churches, exclaimed. The comment says more about Reverend Howard than it does about Reverend Falwell. Khomeini was at that time the leader of the revolutionary regime in Iran that had become complicit in the abduction of American embassy personnel, in violation of international law and all standards of civilized behavior. To compare Falwell to Khomeini was to completely ignore Falwell's commitment to American democracy, a commitment that was evidenced, not contradicted, by his formation of the Moral Majority. The right to petition the government is not denied to anyone by reason of his or her ordination. Falwell urged his followers to register to vote and to vote. He did not encourage them to kidnap foreign nationals. Nonetheless, the nastiness of Howard's comment shows the deeply felt emotions that the Moral Majority provoked.

More thoughtful concerns were raised by Falwell's fellow Baptists. Some were disturbed with the way Falwell equated God and country, an equation that was a staple of Falwell's and the Moral Majority's literature as well as the "I Love America" rallies. "All this [equating God and country] is quite alien to our traditions. Our Baptist forebears certainly did not hold these views," according to Glenn Hinson, a Baptist history professor at Southern Baptist Seminary in Lexington, Kentucky. Hinson gave no evidence to support his claim that the Moral Majority was seeking to "impose" its views, but his complaint that the group reduced Christianity to a prop for Americanism rings true. Falwell was not alone in doing so, but he was remarkably unalert to the danger of conflating patriotism with religious faith.[31]

William Elder of the Southern Baptist Christian Life Commission foresaw a different violation of Baptist principles. "We are precluded by the first amendment to the Constitution—absolutely restricted—from using the state to propagate our faith," Elder told a Baptist reporter. "And that's what we've got here. There are a good many people who see government as a good way to make this nation Christian, particularly the kind of Christianity they buy. And that's more than infringing on separation of church and state, that's using the state to propagate one's faith." This is not the same criticism as that leveled by secular critics. Elder held to the strict Baptist understanding of religious freedom once held by Falwell, the traditional Baptist teaching against the coercion of human conscience and the concurrent belief that all political involvement entails such coercion. The concern is not to protect government but to protect the purity of one's religious commitment to the sanctity of conscience.

The differences between Falwell's and Elder's approaches were sometimes stylistic. "We give the information and then allow you to make up your own mind—because we have respect for Baptist responsibility through the priesthood of the believer," Elder said, trying to contrast his approach with that of the Moral Majority. But Falwell was at pains to stress that he would never tell anyone for whom to vote from the pulpit, if only to make sure that he did not endanger his church's tax-exempt status. It is true that there was little doubt about where Falwell and his allies stood, both on the issues and on the candidates in any given election. And it is also true that Falwell's status as a preacher gave him a unique currency when he spoke on political matters on a TV talk show, and that there was only one Falwell playing different roles, a fact he would often try to elide. But there was nothing that could properly be called "coercion" in anything the Moral Majority undertook.

A different objection to the Moral Majority's methods was raised by William Hull, pastor of the First Baptist Church of Shreveport, Louisiana. Hull was concerned that the Moral Majority and the religious right had "set up a win-lose situation in which one group of our citizens battles another group in a fight to the finish." He understood that politics was all about winning and losing, and that fighting hard "may be alright in political warfare but I do not want my church, my denomination, and most especially, my Gospel, to become involved in that kind of bruising contest." Should a religion that proclaimed a universal call to salvation risk alienating those who found themselves on the other side of a political fight? Hull did not share the sense that all political enemies were necessarily enemies of the Gospel, and he worried that the credibility of religion would be sacrificed to political expediency. It was a fair concern, and one that Falwell never grasped. To Falwell, the "secular humanists" were the enemy, and they had already taken over large parts of the public square. The Christian obligation was to take it back, and if that required some political rough-and-tumble, so be it.[32]

What these discreet objections to the Moral Majority shared was a concern about the role of religion in the broader culture. While Falwell was aiming to affect politics, others were worried about how his political forays would affect Christianity. Interestingly, none of the contemporary critics warned that by reducing religion to ethics, the fundamentalist churches would sever their moral teachings from their roots in Christian doctrine. An appeal addressed to Christian and non-Christian alike must abandon its specifically Christian content. Fundamentalist Christians had always adhered to a strict moral code, to be sure, but the Moral Majority was putting the moral cart before the doctrinal horse. Over time the perception of others would shape the self-perception of fundamentalists, who came to see their distinctive contribution to society as defending a moral code shorn of its uniquely Christian dimensions, not as preaching the Gospel of Jesus Christ. In setting out to restore Judeo-Christian values to their proper place in an increasingly secular culture, the Moral Majority would unwittingly invite a secularization of the church itself.

Falwell's own statements in the first eighteen months of the Moral Majority's existence would continue to vacillate between the explicitly religious and the explicitly political. He, like his critics, had trouble defining the precise boundary between the two spheres. Falwell understood that the culture's moral underpinnings were at risk, and he understood, too, that the traditional values he thought America was shedding were Christian values. But he had difficulty in navigating his own role, and that of his new organization, between the religious and political worlds he was determined to bring together. Dobson had been right: he was firing first and then aiming.

A brochure for the Moral Majority noted that God had called forth Adam, Moses, John the Baptist, George Washington, and Abraham Lincoln and given each the task of providing leadership during troubled times. The brochure placed Falwell in this line of prestigious leaders, as a man called by God in troubled times. Falwell dismissed his inclusion in the group as the "excited verbiage of a PR director," but he did not concern himself with the makeup of the group. Among other differences, Washington and Lincoln had been elected to their high office, while Adam, so far as the record indicates, never stood for election. Falwell's self-effacing dismissal of his own inclusion on the list would not quiet the minds of those who recognized a difference between a religious leader like John the Baptist and a political leader like Lincoln.[33]

On May 2, 1980, Falwell sent a letter to all members of Congress. Taking his cue from Martin Luther's nailing ninety-five theses to the doors of a church in Germany, the act that would start the Reformation, Falwell outlined ninety-five theses for the 1980s in his congressional missive. The list included a mix of moral and political issues. Thesis 1, for example, stated: "That the concept of government itself, like that of marriage, is an institution divinely ordained by God." Thesis 2 stated, as boldly as possible, the triumphalistic Americanism to which Falwell was prone: "That America, unlike any other country in the world today, owes its origins to men of God who desired to build a nation for the glory of God." Some of the theses were banal restatements of constitutional principles, such as theses 7 ("That all its citizens have a right to religious freedom") and 8 ("That all its citizens have a right to peaceful assembly").

Some of Falwell's ninety-five theses touched on foreign policy. Thesis 24 urged "that this country cease aiding those unfriendly nations (Russia, China, etc.) through massive low interest loans, the selling of wheat below market costs, etc.," and it was followed by an appeal for aid to countries like Israel, Taiwan, South Korea, and South Africa, all of which were said "to support us." The last of the ninety-five theses also touched on foreign affairs, specifically America's commitment to Israel's geographic claims: "That America oppose any UN action which would pressure Israel to return to the 1967 geographical boundaries in the Middle East."

Many of the theses spoke to the areas of traditional moral concern that were the bulwark of the Moral Majority's appeal. Theses 38 through 49 listed those things that had to be opposed because they are "anti-family." The list included homosexuality, polygamy, "child or wife abuse," premarital sex, the Equal Rights Amendment, adultery, incest, pornography, and "communal living." One thesis asserted that "children belong to the parents," while another condemned certain IRS regulations that "permit unmarried couples living together to receive tax benefits unallowable to wedded couples." In a twelve-thesis section called "Concerning the Value of Life," most of the items concerned abortion.

Some items spoke to the evangelicals' concern not just with the moral tenor of the country but with what they believed were specific encroachments by secular society, especially the federal government, on the religious sphere. It should be remembered that the IRS's attempt to change the rules governing the tax-exempt status of certain religious schools had helped galvanize religious political involvement in the first place. Under the heading "Concerning the Separation of Church and State" was a thesis objecting to government "harassment" of churches and religious schools, while other entries called for those same churches and schools to be tax-exempt but also to subsist without state subsidies. Those churches and schools served as bulwarks against the secularizing forces in the culture, and Falwell believed that they should be valued as such. He also argued that the failure to do so infringed on the churches' First Amendment rights. "Rather than trying to 'take over' America," Dobson wrote, "the New Rightists were trying to protect themselves from being taken over by a secular society."[34]

The device of invoking ninety-five theses was strange enough. Luther's struggle was an explicitly theological struggle, and Falwell was writing to congressmen who probably could not tell an indulgence from an eggplant. The document displayed the kind of scattershot approach to politics that characterized Falwell's Moral Majority. Abortion was bad. Aid to South Africa was good. The sanctity of Israel's post-1967 borders was set alongside the sanctity of human life. The strange verb "belong" was used to describe the filial relationship between parent and child. It was becoming apparent that Falwell was not so much bringing a religiously motivated political agenda to the fore as he was seeking to baptize the Republican Party platform. There was no attempt to engage in the daunting task of devising anything like a coherent Christian philosophy for political engagement.

Still, Falwell tried to change the manner of his speech. He had dropped biblical quotations from the Moral Majority's literature. Now he also tried to stop using scripture when defending some of his political positions. "When I am talking to the press on El Salvador or the nuclear freeze," he told an interviewer, "I don't quote verses [of scripture] to them. The Bible says don't cast pearls before swine. Scripture is wasted on gainsayers. So I argue in secular terms entirely. But I use my scriptural understanding to form my opinions on issues." The Bible was expendable when it did not fit the necessary political strategy, but Falwell still needed a biblical justification for expending it.[35]

Falwell became a regular guest on many television shows. He made multiple appearances on ABC's new late-night news show *Nightline*, and he was a regular guest on *The Phil Donohue Show*. Often he would debate liberals. Other times he would be on a panel of religious leaders. At all times he was an articulate, lively voice for the conservative religious and political agenda he was advocating. There was a reason why he was asked back again and again: he was entertaining, pithy, and quick on his feet.

In all these speeches, appearances on television, and issues of *Moral Majority Report,* Falwell's message was recognized as distinctly new, which is why it garnered so much media attention.

At times he had trouble navigating between religious and secular speech, but when he hit his stride he spoke to a set of concerns about the direction the country had taken since the 1960s that resonated with many voters, not just evangelicals. His speeches were designed to galvanize evangelicals without offending others, and they largely succeeded. Large numbers of Americans may have been ambivalent about legalized abortion, but they were genuinely horrified by the explosion in the abortion rate since *Roe*. Many non-evangelicals were worried about their children being exposed to pornography, and many evangelicals felt that the government was encroaching on their rights. Thus, Falwell's central message was one that many voters could agree with: America was in a state of moral decline, and it was time to do something about it.

It was soon clear to Falwell and his followers that in order to arrest the moral decline of the nation, the most important thing to do was to elect Ronald Reagan as president. And Reagan, aware that newly energized evangelical voters might prove decisive in winning the South from the Democrats, was eager to enlist Falwell's support. For the next eight years the careers of both men would be intertwined, and together, more than any other two figures, they would define the contours of the modern Republican Party.

Reagan, at first blush, was an unlikely champion of the religious right. He would be the first divorced president in the nation's history. He had made his career in Hollywood, a den of iniquity to evangelical eyes, the place from which a poisonous libertinism had made its way onto the big screen and thence to movie houses nationwide. As governor of California, Reagan had signed one of the most liberal abortion laws in the country, under pressure from the Republicans in the state legislature, although he would soon come to regret his signature. Most seriously of all, Reagan was not a churchgoer. Although he fondly remembered his mother as a woman of notable piety and worshiped her memory throughout his life, he himself would rarely darken a church door. Moreover, Reagan's worldview was more Emersonian than evangelical. As one biographer noted,

"Redefining the nature of desire, Reagan's religion would deny nothing because life offered everything. Our beliefs about God no longer repress but liberate, as though Christ died on the Cross so that we might better pursue happiness, not the salvation of our souls." Such philosophical differences, however, remained opaque as Reagan's penchant for nostalgia and the platitudes that characterize political discourse masked the divides.[36]

What attracted Falwell to Reagan, however, was the latter's firm commitment to conservative principles. Reagan had all the conviction of a political convert. He had abandoned his earlier allegiance to the Democratic Party to embrace the candidacy of Barry Goldwater in 1964. Reagan's election eve speech on Goldwater's behalf made him a darling of the conservative movement and launched his own political career. Reagan articulated a virulent anticommunism, called for vastly increasing expenditures on the U.S. military, opposed the Panama Canal treaties, and evidenced a suspicion of domestic government programs; all of these positions appealed to Falwell. Reagan had challenged the moderate Gerald Ford for the Republican nomination in 1976 and came close to defeating the incumbent president. In 1980 Reagan was the undisputed heir of the conservative movement, and he dominated the GOP primaries, especially in the South.

More than any particular policy stances, Falwell and Reagan shared a common vision of America as a nation set apart by God and given a divine destiny. As early as 1952, when he was still a Democrat, Reagan had told the graduating class at William Woods College in Missouri, "I, in my own mind, have thought of America as a place in the divine scheme of things that was set aside as a promised land." Over the years Reagan refined his speech, first as a corporate spokesman and then as a politician, but his view of America as a nation ordained by God would never waver, and it dovetailed perfectly with Falwell's views. Nonetheless, the common language both used to describe America often covered over profound differences of opinion. Falwell had no sympathy for the libertarian aspect of Western conservatism, which Reagan embraced, and their relationship, both during the campaign and after Reagan was elected president, would fail to resolve the tensions within conservatism. These differences were rarely acknowledged and would be papered over when they arose. They are differences that continue to stalk the conservative movement in America.

Reagan and Falwell also spoke in similar idioms. Both believed in simple pieties. The free market economy, if freed of intrusive government regulations, would unleash the creative capacities of the American people and create wealth for everyone. The Soviet Union was evil. Welfare was an unwarranted government takeover of traditional, church-based charity for the downtrodden and a handout for the lazy. Reagan's political vision was cast in black and white. There was no gray. The similarities with Falwell's view of American politics were obvious.

Both Reagan and Falwell preferred a good anecdote to a logical argument. The preacher's craft is often built around the ability to use a personal story to dramatize a theological point. Falwell would repeat the sad story of his father's early death to illustrate the danger of alcohol abuse. He would illustrate his change of heart on segregation by telling a tale about a conversation he had with the black man who shined his shoes. Similarly, Reagan, in his 1964 speech for Goldwater, would illustrate his opposition to the welfare state by telling the story of a conversation he had with a judge. The judge told Reagan that a woman came seeking a divorce because her husband only made $250 a week but with her six children, and a seventh on the way, she would be entitled to $330 in welfare payments a week if she divorced her husband. The myth of the "welfare queen" was born and would be a staple of Reagan's three presidential campaigns. Reagan may not have spent much time at church, but he grasped the storytelling aspect of the preacher's craft intuitively, and indeed, his aides would recognize the need to present their preferred policy options with a good tale rather than detailed policy analysis.[37]

It was Falwell's ability to deliver his constituency, not his skill as a storyteller, that got him an invitation to join Governor Reagan in his Detroit hotel suite at the 1980 Republican National Convention, held in July. Phyllis Schlafly, Paul Weyrich, and Howard Phillips rode up the elevator in the world's tallest hotel with Falwell to meet Reagan and try to persuade him not to select George H. W. Bush as his running mate. Conservatives did not trust Bush, who could not be more different in style and substance from Reagan. The meeting was an indicator of the importance that Reagan and his campaign staff attached to the religious right. On this most important decision he had to make as a candidate, he wanted them to feel included even if he was unable to satisfy their desire. Falwell and the others were pleased to be consulted.

Falwell wanted Reagan to choose Sen. Jesse Helms, the conservative firebrand from North Carolina, but Helms was on no one's short list. A last-minute effort had been mounted to recruit former president Gerald Ford, but the negotiations got bogged down when Ford demanded special, extraconstitutional authority in foreign affairs and on budget matters. Even though Reagan did not care for Bush, he was the candidate most likely to unite the party. Reagan knew that he already had the support of conservatives. He needed to reach out to moderates with his vice presidential selection. The meeting helped the religious right leaders swallow a bitter pill: they did not trust Bush, but they accepted Reagan's assurances that his vice president would toe the conservative line. In the event, Bush would reach out to conservatives after he was put on the ticket, and he would thoroughly captivate Falwell. In addition, the Reagan campaign tapped Billings shortly after the convention to head its religious outreach.[38]

Ed McAteer's group, the Religious Roundtable, decided to organize a "summit" of conservative Christians in Dallas that would bring the politicians to court conservative Christian leaders. Invitations went out to 160,000 ministers and were signed by McAteer, Southern Baptist pastor Rev. James Robison, and Dallas Cowboys head coach Tom Landry. Although Falwell was not one of the principal organizers of the summit, he gave it his endorsement and used the Moral Majority network to advertise it. President Carter, Governor Reagan, and Congressman John Anderson, who was running as an independent, were invited to attend, but only Reagan accepted.[39]

Eighteen thousand delegates registered for the Dallas Summit, and 250 reporters covered the event. At a press conference before his speech to the assembly, Reagan was asked about his views on creationism. Reagan was a politician and he liked to tell people what they wanted to hear, so he gave a long reply in which he suggested that creationism might be taught in the public schools alongside evolution. His aides shifted nervously in their seats and figured out the best way to spin the response. "The only good news for us at this time is that we were making so many blunders that reporters had to pick and choose which ones they would write about," a campaign aide said. " 'Creationism' made Reagan look like an idiot, but he got away with it." The campaign aides were paid to worry about how such a remark would play among moderates, but Reagan's statement was music to the ears of the assembled evangelicals.[40]

Reagan gave a rousing speech to the eighteen thousand evangelicals gathered in Dallas's Reunion Hall. He pledged to keep the federal government out of local schools. He promised to oppose abortion. But what won the crowd over was Reagan's conclusion. "Now I know this is a nonpartisan gathering, and so I know that you can't endorse me," the candidate told the delegates. "But I only brought that up because I want you to know that I endorse you and what you are doing." After years of cultural exile, years of being snickered at, years of "Elmer Gantry" and jokes about the Scopes trial, here was a candidate for the presidency of the United States giving them his blessing.

The Dallas Summit was a milestone for evangelical political involvement, but it almost got overwhelmed by a controversy that overshadowed Reagan's secular blessing of the religious groups in attendance. Speaking to the delegates, the newly installed president of the Southern Baptist Convention, Rev. Bailey Smith, said, "It's interesting to me at great political battles how you have a Protestant to pray and a Catholic to pray and then you have a Jew to pray." Smith continued, "With all due respect to those dear people, my friends, God Almighty does not hear the prayer of a Jew. For how in the world can God hear the prayer of a man who says that Jesus Christ is not the true Messiah? It is blasphemy. It may be politically expedient, but no one can pray unless he prays through the name of Jesus Christ." Whatever one's theology, Reverend Smith was right about one thing: his words were not politically expedient.[41]

The press corps followed the candidate to the next stop on his campaign tour, but Smith's outrageous comments would come back when Falwell was asked at a press conference weeks later whether he agreed with Smith's view that God does not hear the prayers of Jews. He replied, "I believe that God answers the prayer of any redeemed Jew or Gentile and I do not believe that God answers the prayer of any unredeemed Gentile or Jew." The response was artful in that it shifted the discussion to a definition of redemption, an area of theology likely to be opaque to most reporters. But it failed to achieve what was politically needed at the moment: an end to the discussion. And when he did not repudiate Smith's remarks explicitly, some press accounts began attributing the original remark to Falwell. When Falwell appeared on *Meet the Press* on October 12, Marvin Kalb asked him: "I want to quote something that's been in the press. 'I believe God does not hear the prayers of unredeemed Gentiles or Jews.' Did you say that?" Falwell admitted that he had, but went on to assure Kalb and his television audience that he believed that "God answers the prayers of all people." Still, the issue did not die, and at an appearance before the National Press Club a questioner explicitly attributed Smith's remarks to Falwell, without the qualification about being redeemed or not. Falwell denied that he ever said any such thing.[42]

The controversy over Jewish prayers being heard was not the only time during the campaign that Falwell's words would come back to haunt him. The same month as the Dallas Summit the national press corps picked up a story that had been brewing under the radar for months. During a March speech in Alaska, Falwell had told his listeners about a breakfast meeting he attended at the White House in January. According to Falwell, "we had breakfast with the president about a month ago and we were discussing national defense and all these things and I asked the president, 'Sir, why do you have practicing homosexuals on your senior staff at the White House?'" Falwell told the crowd that Carter responded, "Well, I am president of all the American people and I believe I should represent everyone." Falwell replied, "Why don't you have some murderers and bank robbers and so forth to represent."

The difficulty was that the words Falwell attributed to the president, as well as his own comments, were never uttered at the January breakfast meeting. "I was present all the time the president was in the room and he [Falwell] did not ask that question," former Southern Baptist Convention president Rev. Jimmy Allen told the *Oklahoma Baptist Messenger*. "That simply was not said. . . . Anecdotes that do not tell the truth certainly ought to be avoided in any pulpit I know of," Allen added.[43]

Falwell tried to defend himself from imputations against his veracity. " 'I have stated as clearly and emphatically as I know how that my recent statement was not intended to be a verbatim report of our conversation with President Carter. Instead, my statement was intended to be, and was, an honest portrayal of President Carter's position on Gay Rights. It was an anecdote, intended to dramatically get the attention of the audience. It was an absolutely accurate statement of the president's record and position on Gay Rights. It was meant to be nothing else." For Falwell, the literal truth of a statement was less important than the intention to "dramatically get the attention of the audience." At face value, that was a strange posture for a fundamentalist to assume: the Bible was to be taken literally, but not every story a preacher tells. Falwell, like most preachers, understood this. Ronald Reagan, who had his own frequent use of inaccurate anecdotes thrown back at him, understood this. The press and the White House were less permissive.[44]

Rev. Robert Maddox, who served as President Carter's liaison to religious communities, released a transcript of the January meeting. The difficulty was not that Falwell had misquoted the president, but that the subjects of gays working at the White House had never even come up. At one point Falwell asked whether the White House Conference on the Family would include nontraditional families such as those of gays and lesbians. Carter gave no response, and the conversation went down a different path. Maddox went on the ABC news show *20/20* to push back against Falwell's "anecdote," but mostly the press had moved on. When Falwell formally apologized to Carter, the apology got scant attention.

In October the annual convention of the National Religious Broadcasters was held in Lynchburg. Reagan was invited to speak to the group. When he first arrived, Reagan was asked if he believed that God answers the prayers of Jews, and he answered that he was sure God hears all prayers. The press tried to parse Falwell's comments on the subject, questioning whether there was a difference between "hearing" prayers and "answering" them, but the controversy died down. Like the fabricated recollection of Carter's remarks on gays, this story was becoming old news.

Reagan did not need to go to Virginia to campaign, since the state was reliably Republican. The southerner Jimmy Carter had garnered almost 48 percent of the vote in 1976, losing Virginia narrowly to Gerald Ford, but in 1972 George McGovern had polled only 30 percent of the Virginia electorate, and in 1968 Richard Nixon had taken the state with 43 percent of the vote to 32 percent for Hubert Humphrey and 23 percent for George Wallace. Reagan did not go to Virginia; he went to Lynchburg. By this time Falwell was claiming to have registered four million new voters, scattered throughout the South and Midwest, through the Moral Majority. And just as important as the voter registration efforts of the Moral Majority was the even vaster reach of the television evangelists. "I will talk about the issues in my church," said Baptist minister Randy Stewart of Lexington, Kentucky. "I will recommend issues to the congregation, not candidates. But when I get through, they will know who I am voting for: Ronald Reagan."[45]

Falwell bused in students from both Lynchburg Academy and Liberty Baptist College for Reagan's speech, filling the auditorium with eight thousand devoted admirers. Reagan hit a home run, as he had in Dallas, but his Lynchburg speech stayed away from religious issues per se. Trying to counter Carter's accusations that he was trigger-happy, Reagan focused on the need for world peace and maintained that such peace could be achieved only through military strength. The former governor spoke about the scourge of inflation, not the scourge of secular humanism. But when he said, "I don't believe we should ever have expelled God from the classroom," the audience applauded wildly.

More than any words he spoke, it was Reagan's presence in Lynchburg that mattered. As in Dallas, the candidate was burying the idea that evangelicals, and especially fundamentalists, were outside the cultural mainstream. He had come to Lynchburg to court the religious right's support. He had spoken on an issue, school prayer, that might not have been at the top of the suburban voters' list, but it was an issue that confirmed the narrative of moral decline that Falwell had been articulating: without God, the country would be on the wrong track. And because it was the Supreme Court that had ruled against school prayer, Reagan's mention of the issue echoed Falwell's political analysis of the high court as the principal instrument of secularization in society. Reagan did not need to mention secular humanism to condemn the ruling. He condemned its purported champion, the Supreme Court. A code was developing inside the religio-political estuary: politicians spoke in ways that confirmed their commitment to the faithful without alienating those who did not understand the code.

Falwell had a different rhetorical challenge when he published his book *Listen, America* in October, just before the election. It was the same challenge he had been navigating all year: how to speak on moral and political issues in a nondenominational way without losing his preacher's voice, which was the voice of authority for the flock. The book was intended for his millions of television viewers but would be more widely read too. He needed to reach out to nonfundamentalists at the same time as he knew most of his readers would be fundamentalists.

Listen, America begins with a typical preacher's tale. Falwell is flying home from a speaking engagement in Oklahoma, accompanied only by his son, who dozes off to sleep. But Falwell's mind is not on the Oklahoma event just concluded, nor is he thinking about the next day's agenda. The previous week he had visited refugee camps in Thailand, filled with people who had fled the war and persecution in neighboring Cambodia. He recounts the harrowing images he had seen and catalogs the list of atrocities perpetrated by Pol Pot and the invading Vietnamese communists. "There in the darkness of the cabin of that plane, I looked intently at my son, who was asleep," Falwell writes. "I could not help but thank God that he has never gone hungry a day in his life. He knows little but what he has read about communism. As I looked at him while he slept, I prayed that God would turn America around so that he would know the America I have known. I vowed that I would never turn my back on the firm decision and sacred commitment I had made to myself and to God that I would preach and work and pray to stop the moral decay in America that is destroying our freedoms."[46]

Falwell does not, however, proceed immediately to address those instances of moral decay. Instead, he focuses on the communist threat. He quotes former Treasury secretary William Simon: "Our country today sits at the very crossroads between freedom and totalitarian rule." He quotes a bellicose general on the Soviet threat and details Soviet atrocities. With help from a quote from Milton Friedman, Falwell pivots to a denunciation of "welfarism" and a biblically based defense of capitalism, citing the Book of Proverbs. He contends that the nation suffers from a lack of leadership and treads dangerously close to violating his previously stated lack of concern about a politician's religion: "If a man is not a student of the Word of God and does not know what the Bible says, I question his ability to be an effective leader."[47]

The focus for most of the first chapter of Falwell's book is not traditional morality but America imperiled by the threat of communism abroad and socialistic thinking at home ("welfarism"). But the reason for these threats is that America has turned away from God, and turning back is the remedy. "We must, from the highest office in the land right down to the shoeshine boy in the airport, have a return to biblical basics," Falwell intones. He quotes a verse from scripture, 2 Chronicles 7:14, that encapsulates his view of the relationship between the moral and spiritual health of a people and their national success: "If my people, which are called by my name, shall humble themselves, and pray, and seek my face, and turn from their wicked ways; then will I hear from heaven, and will forgive their sin and will heal their land."[48]

Having established the link between national flourishing and moral righteousness, Falwell gives a pithy, and largely mistaken, interpretation of the rise and fall of empires. For example, he cites moral decay and the persecution of the church as the primary reasons for the fall of Rome, although this account overlooks the complicating fact that the persecutions had ceased and the empire had become Christian by the time it fell. He contrasts the fallen empires with America's providential founding. "Any diligent student of American history," Falwell writes, "finds that our great nation was founded by godly men upon godly principles to be a Christian nation." The phrase "Christian nation" directly contradicts what Falwell was writing in an editorial in the October issue of the *Moral Majority Report* entitled "Moral Majority Opposes 'Christian Republic.'" The phrase "Christian nation" would come back to haunt Falwell, for it did not sit well with his Jewish allies and with those who shared his moral concerns but were worried about sectarianism in politics. Moreover, this "diligent student of American history" had missed the complex influences on the Founders and the divergences among the Founders themselves, as we have already seen. Other mistakes dot the text. The settlers at Jamestown are described as "Puritans" but they were not, and Valley Forge and Cambridge are listed as Revolutionary War battles, although there were no battles at either location. If many contemporary histories mistakenly fail to acknowledge the role of religion in early American life, Falwell's account suffers from the opposite affliction—turning American history into a preacher's tale.[49]

Listen, America jumps around. Having started with the Soviet menace in the first chapter, Falwell devotes a subsequent chapter to that subject. He accuses liberals of pursuing a strategy of "détente," but evidently is unaware that the policy of détente was begun by Richard Nixon, no one's idea of a liberal. "Welfarism" has been attacked already, but it comes in for more abuse later when Falwell employs a truly horrifying metaphor. In an effort to show how recipients of welfare are coddled, Falwell discusses his two dogs. They had been given to him by the owner of a supermarket who explained the kinds of meat they ate. Falwell, saying he could not afford such a diet, gave them regular "brown nuggets" for dinner. "Sure enough, at first they wouldn't eat them, but four days later they did. They did not eat luxuriously, but they did eat." He seems unaware of how offensive the comparison is.[50]

In the second section of the book, Falwell considers more traditional moral issues. He has chapters on "Children's Rights" and "The Feminist Movement," which he opposes, and "The Right to Life," which he supports. Homosexuality, television, pornography, education, music, and drugs and alcohol all receive chapters, and in each case he warns of how these influences can harm our children. These chapters could have been drawn verbatim from his sermons, and they have the conversational tone Falwell adopted in the pulpit. He quotes from other conservative sources, such as Phyllis Schlafly, and recounts experiences from his pastoral ministry, telling of a letter he received from a woman who regretted having an abortion and voiced the hope that, now that she had repented and been saved, in heaven she would be a good mother to her aborted child. As we have seen, although Falwell labeled such practices as abortion and drug use as "national sins," he never recognized the social character of sin, seeing it only as an individual failing, nor did he acknowledge that the free enterprise system, conjoined with the sins of the flesh, inevitably made those practices more widely and indiscriminately available. One man's delight in drugs or pornography was another man's profit margin.

Listen, America evidences the blend of concerns that would characterize the ten years of the Moral Majority's existence, but the emphasis has changed from the original statements of the organization. Instead of leading with abortion, Falwell leads with the communist threat. Instead of starting with the scriptures, he starts with the Founders. He is trying both to appeal to new constituencies and to expand the range of moral concern for those already in the fold.

If the original four principles—pro-life, pro-family, pro-America, and pro-moral—were a kind of constitution for the Moral Majority, *Listen, America* was the religious right's equivalent of the Federalist Papers—a more detailed attempt to elucidate the four principles and demonstrate how they were linked.

As the election approached, Falwell also used his pulpit to convey a sense of political urgency. At this time the *Old-Time Gospel Hour* was being broadcast on 373 TV stations nationwide. The debate about the number of viewers continued, with some saying Falwell's show was viewed by as many as fifteen million people each week and others calculating the audience at closer to six million. Whatever the actual number, these were Falwell's most loyal supporters, and he wanted to make sure they were registered, informed, and energized.[51]

Falwell would touch on many of the themes found in the *Moral Majority Report* at this time, but speaking from the pulpit, he structured his sermons around a passage from the scriptures. In one, for instance, he used the first chapter of the Book of Nehemiah—"that's page 782 in your Faith Partners Study Bible," Falwell instructed his listeners.

"I beseech Thee, O Lord God of Heaven," the passage reads, "the great and terrible God that keepeth covenant and mercy from them that love Him and observe His commandments, let Thine ear now be attentive and Thine eyes open that Thou mayest hear the prayer of Thy servant which I pray before Thee now day and night for the children of Israel, Thy servants, and confess the sins of the children of Israel which we have sinned against Thee, both I and my father's house have sinned. We have dealt very corruptly against Thee and have not kept the commandments nor the statutes nor the judgments which Thoust commandest Thy Moses. Remember I beseech thee the word that thou commandest thy servant Moses saying if ye transgress I will scatter you abroad among the nations but if you turn unto me and keep my commandments and do them,

though there were of you cast out unto the uttermost part of heaven, yet will I gather them from thence and will bring them unto the place that I have chosen to set my name there."

From there Falwell launched into a dissertation on "national sin" and called upon his flock to repent not only for their own sins but, following Nehemiah, to repent for the nation's sins. He set the stage by recalling America's youth. "Our founding fathers were not all godly men," Falwell said. "They were influenced by godly principles. The pilgrims and the puritans left an indelible imprint upon the minds and hearts of the early Americans, the early colonists so that when they wrote the Declaration of Independence, the Constitution, the Bill of Rights and the various state charters and constitutions, you can find the philosophy of the pilgrims and the puritans in line after line of these very important documents." These were words he had spoken dozens of times in the past eighteen months at the "I Love America" rallies.

Falwell then recalled his own youth to show how the state of the nation had declined. He noted that when he was young, even before he was saved, he knew the moral law. "I couldn't quote John 3:16 when I became a Christian as a second year student in college preparing for a study of mechanical engineering but I knew right from wrong," Falwell told his congregation. "I knew the moral values. I knew the traditional values. I knew the family values. Because all Americans knew them." He used the example of homosexuality to drive home his point. "Homosexuality in my childhood was looked on as moral perversion. And although people did not hate homosexuals any more than they do now, they hated homosexuality—looked on it as moral perversion. It still is. Nothing has changed. God hasn't changed. But here in America our values are changing so that when one takes a position on a moral stand that is the traditional consensus of our nation for 204 years, he is looked upon as a bigot." The key to Falwell's preaching was to paint a dismal picture of decline, one that required the faithful to rescue the nation from the changes that were against God's law. He invoked Sodom and Gomorrah to illustrate how God dealt with homosexuality.

The Reverend Jerry Falwell, Bible in hand, stands in front of his Thomas Road Baptist Church where the marquee instructs congregants to "Register & Vote."

President Ronald Reagan meets with the Reverend Jerry Falwell in the Oval Office in 1983. Falwell made many visits to the White House during the Reagan and Bush presidencies.

The Reverend Jerry Falwell speaks at a 1983 rally in front of the U.S. Capitol in support of President Reagan's military buildup. Falwell and his allies mimicked Reagan's claim to be seeking "Peace Through Strength."

President Ronald Reagan and the Reverend Jerry Falwell share the dais at the Baptist Fundamentalism Convention in 1984, an event Falwell organized to highlight the growing political prominence of the religious right.

The Reverend Jerry Falwell and his wife, Macel, on the grounds of their home in Lynchburg in 1985. Unlike several prominent televangelists who got caught up in sex scandals, Falwell was devoted to his wife and family throughout his life.

Above: The Reverend Jerry Falwell plunges down a waterslide at Heritage USA on September 10, 1987. Falwell had promised to take the plunge as part of a fund-raising drive to salvage the beleaguered ministry of Jim and Tammy Faye Bakker.

Opposite, top: Moral Majority members at a 1985 protest in Dallas against 7-11's parent company for distributing pornographic magazines at its stores.

Opposite, bottom: Members of the gay rights group Queer Nation protest the Reverend Falwell's appearance at a 1992 meeting of fundamentalists in Houston, Texas.

President George H. W. Bush delivered the commencement address at Falwell's Liberty University on May 12, 1991. Despite Falwell's misgivings about Bush becoming Reagan's vice presidential pick in 1980, the two men became close political allies.

The Reverend Jerry Falwell and his wife, Macel, welcome President George H. W. Bush and First Lady Barbara Bush to the campus of Liberty University.

The Reverend Jerry Falwell with President George H. W. Bush at the White House on March 7, 1991, after a meeting between evangelical leaders and the president.

The Reverend Jerry Falwell joins *Hustler* publisher Larry Flynt on the set of the *Larry King Live* show for a joint interview on January 10, 1997. In the course of their legal battles over a satire in Flynt's magazine that poked fun at Falwell, the two men became improbable friends and were frequently scheduled to debate the First Amendment on television.

Israeli prime minister Benjamin Netanyahu speaks with conservative Christian leaders at a conference arranged by Falwell in Washington, D.C., on January 19, 1998. Falwell frequently met with Israeli leaders in Washington or Jerusalem in his effort to demonstrate evangelical support for Israel.

Karl Rove, senior advisor to President George W. Bush, is given an honorary degree at Liberty University in 2004, one of a long line of Republican officials to come to Lynchburg.

The rest of the list of national sins mirrored those found in *Listen, America*. Abortion topped the list, but here he began with his indictment of *Roe* by citing scriptural passages, such as Psalm 139, where David sings that God had written down his name when he was yet "imperfect" or, as Falwell explained, "unformed" in the womb. "We have ignored the dignity of human life in America, and we have murdered 7–8 million babies since 1973," Falwell exclaimed. "That's a national sin. That is a sin for which we must all repent." He went on to pornography and drug use. He spoke about how America's oil interests were distracting the nation from its commitment to Israel: "And we are allowing oil to muddle our thinking. We'd be better off to ride bicycles than to anger Almighty God. That is a national sin." He denounced the recent decision of the United States to abstain on a United Nations resolution condemning Israel for proclaiming Jerusalem its capital.

Invoking Nehemiah, Falwell pointed to the source of the problem as he saw it. "We're not going to get the smut peddlers and abortion clinicians to repent. We are not going to get the liberal politicians on the moral issues to repent," the preacher intoned, warming to his theme. "What's the real problem in America? . . . The real problem in America happens to be the churches in America. If we had not gone to sleep for the last 30 years, there could never have been a climate that would have allowed the existence of a Supreme Court that could legalize murder on demand. There could not have been legislation to allow pornography as it exists today. . . . The problem is we have been silent too long." The remedy to silence was obvious: the God-fearing churches had to rise up and take the country back. He called for a national day of prayer on the Sunday before the election.[52]

The following week Falwell used his sermon to announce a "Christian Bill of Rights." Falwell told his congregation that he usually did not preach from a text, but this text, this Christian Bill of Rights, was printed on the parchment he held in his hand. More important, it was also being printed in the current issue of *TV Guide* and other national publications. "We are sharing with 18,300,000 homes or about 75 million people what those Christian Bill of Rights are—exactly what I'm preaching on here today." And true to form, the ads included a coupon to cut out, sign, and send back to Falwell, pledging support for the Christian Bill of Rights and, wittingly or not, getting added to his mailing list.

The enumerated rights were unsurprising. "Amendment 1. We believe that from the time of conception within the womb, every human being has a scriptural right to life upon this earth." He cited Exodus 20:13 and Psalm 139:13–16 for his commitment to the unborn. "Amendment 2. We believe that every person has the right to pursue any and all scriptural goals that he or she feels are God directed during that life upon this earth." Here, Falwell grounded the link between freedom and faith: God was seen as the author of freedom, and freedom was fulfilled in following God's law. He cited the Book of Proverbs, chapter 3, verses 5 and 6: " 'Trust in the Lord with all thine heart, and lean not unto thine own understanding. In all thy ways acknowledge Him and He shall direct thy paths.' Yes, God loves freedom. God is for liberty." Amendment 4 urged that "traitorous, verbal or written attack on this beloved nation advocating overthrow by force [not] be permitted by any citizen or alien living within this country." Amendment 5 asserted the right of children in public schools to pray, and Amendment 6 claimed freedom for Christian schools from government interference. Amendment 8 asserted "the right to expect our national leaders to keep this country morally and militarily strong so that religious freedom and gospel preaching might continue unhindered." The laundry list was the same, even if the format was different.[53]

Falwell liked using devices such as his ninety-five political theses, and now he used his Christian Bill of Rights to bridge the perceived divide between religion and politics. But the bridge was a superficial one, as the Christian Bill of Rights showed. For Falwell, rights were established to direct people toward God. The righteous should be free from "attacks" on their beloved country. He could not see that such a stricture might circumscribe the rights of others to freedom of speech. Many Americans, and many of the Founders, conceived rights as guarantees of protection from government interference, as "freedoms from," as instances of what Sir Isaiah Berlin called "negative liberty," but Falwell's view of rights was more ambivalent. For him, the "freedom of the children of God" of which Paul writes was indistinguishable from the freedom guaranteed by the Constitution. He did not embrace the Enlightenment concept of freedom, the idea of negative liberty, except in economic matters—in that realm he always denounced government intrusion. Enlightenment freedoms were permitted in the boardroom but not in the bedroom. This ambivalence about the nature of rights, and Falwell's lack of appreciation for alternative understandings, would mark his entire career.

Falwell's sermons in the weeks before the election included a sales pitch for American flag pins. He spoke about his devotion to the flag in terms that were almost idolatrous. He acknowledged that those listening in other countries might disagree with him when he said that America was the greatest nation on earth, but "if that flag comes down," he asserted, "Canada goes with us. Australia goes with us." He called on one of his singers to lead the congregation in the Pledge of Allegiance. Falwell also made a pitch for prospective students to come and visit Liberty Baptist College. He spoke about his "I Love America" rallies and dedicated the service to "Our Constitution." It was Falwell at his most pumped-up patriotic best.[54]

As the election approached, Falwell did his best to use the tools at his command to motivate fundamentalists to register to vote, informed on the issues he thought were important. Without crossing the line into an explicit endorsement of Ronald Reagan, there could have been little doubt where his own allegiance lay and where he thought the allegiance of his flock should lie. He had not only used his pulpit but created the Moral Majority, enrolled members, collected money, and distributed literature about the importance of the issues he valued. He had gone on television shows, held rallies, hosted Reagan in Lynchburg. All that remained was the voting, the final test that would show if his efforts had come to fruition.

Chapter Eight

Proximity to Power

On November 4, 1980, Ronald Reagan was elected president of the United States. His victory was overwhelming, especially in the electoral college, where he garnered 489 votes to President Jimmy Carter's 49. Carter took only his home state of Georgia, Minnesota, Maryland, West Virginia, Rhode Island, and the District of Columbia. Reagan swept the rest, including almost the entire South. In the popular vote, Reagan took just under 51 percent of the vote to Carter's 43 percent and John Anderson's 7 percent. Reagan received almost 44 million votes.

In addition, the Republicans took back the U.S. Senate for the first time since 1954. Democratic incumbents lost in Georgia, Indiana, Iowa, Idaho, South Dakota, Oregon, Washington, North Carolina, and New Hampshire. Liberal stalwarts like Senators Frank Church, John Culver, and George McGovern were replaced by conservative Republicans Steve Symms, Charles Grassley, and James Abdnor, respectively. The Republicans also picked up thirty-five seats in the U.S. House of Representatives. Across the board, liberals had gone down to defeat at the hands of conservatives, riding Reagan's coattails, to be sure, but also riding a conservative wave that had begun in the 1978 congressional races.

Winning is not everything. Interpreting the win is just as important. Defeat is an orphan, victory is said to have a thousand fathers, and in the wake of the Reagan landslide many claimed credit. The evening of the election Reagan's pollster, Richard Wirthlin, credited his candidate and the Republican strategy with breaking into traditional Democratic groups. "We cracked the unions, blue collar voters, ethnics, Catholics, and the South, just as he had planned," Wirthlin told the *New York Times*. Curiously absent from his list was the religious right. Indeed, neither the *Washington Post* nor the *New York Times* mentioned the role of the Moral Majority in Reagan's victory in their coverage of the election results.[1]

As the results sank in, especially the Republican sweep in the South and Midwest, others did credit the religious right for achieving the landslide. Pollster Lou Harris said, "Reagan would have lost the election by one percentage point without the help of the Moral Majority." Evangelical Christians had backed Carter in 1976, but in the 1980 election they broke 56 percent for Reagan compared to only 34 percent for Carter. Harris believed that two-thirds of Reagan's margin in the popular vote came from those who watched television preachers. Another pollster had Reagan taking 61 percent of self-identified "born-again white Christians."

Just as important, Reagan took 48 percent of the Catholic vote compared to Carter's 43 percent, and most commentators believed that Reagan's position on abortion, which had been echoed by the Moral Majority throughout the campaign, was responsible. Falwell believed that as many as 30 percent of the Moral Majority's members were conservative Catholics and that the organization had given them the language and the logic to break from their traditional allegiance to the Democratic Party. "My proudest moment was when an article appeared that said right there—jumped out of the page—that Catholics in areas like Dubuque, Iowa, had helped elect the evangelical Grassley, and evangelicals in places like Mobile helped elect the Catholic [Sen. Jeremiah] Denton," said Weyrich.[2]

Not only had the Moral Majority made a difference, but it was seen to have made a difference. The election victory changed several dynamics for the organization. On the one hand, it is always easiest in a campaign to argue against something, and in 1980 it was enough to be against Carter to gain admittance to the Reagan bandwagon. "The Moral Majority was good at being against something. We never were good at being for something," Ed Dobson later recalled. Once in power, the coalition of interests that had backed Reagan jockeyed for influence as the different hopes they pinned on Reagan's election came to the fore. In addition, power brought increased scrutiny and increased opposition. So long as the Moral Majority's influence was unknown, opposition to it was scattered, but once the group had demonstrated its power at the polls, that opposition would become more organized. Still, the Moral Majority had helped evangelicals overcome the psychological hurdle of their many years in the cultural wilderness. At a post-election victory rally on the campus of Liberty Baptist College, Falwell entered to the strains of "Hail to the Chief." The hall erupted in applause. "We were no longer the backwoods yahoos who wore blue suits and white socks," commented Cal Thomas.[3]

Falwell may have been new to politics, but he had a keen sense of human psychology. He knew instinctively that victory invites hubris. He knew that in creating a sense of crisis to motivate evangelicals to go to the polls, he had raised their expectations about what a political victory would yield. Falwell knew that he had to be careful not to overplay his hand with the new president and the incoming administration. And he knew that Rome was not built in a day and that the expectations he had aroused to motivate his flock needed to be tempered by the hard realities of governance. Liberal Washington could not be unbuilt in a day.

"I had no illusions that when we had elected Ronald Reagan, we had changed America," Falwell said later. "We had only changed the direction America was taking; we had not saved the country." At the congressional prayer breakfast early in 1981, Falwell said that the damage "caused by secular humanism" would not be undone in thirty days. He predicted that the decade of the 1980s would produce the "greatest spiritual renewal" in the nation's history and set a goal of repealing legalized abortion by the end of the decade.[4]

The high point of the inaugural ceremonies for Falwell was when Reagan took the oath of office on a Bible opened to one of Falwell's favorite Bible verses, 2 Chronicles 7:14: "If my people, which are called by my name, shall humble themselves, and pray, and seek my face, and turn from their wicked ways; then I will hear from heaven, and will forgive their sin and will heal their land." Later, in his autobiography, Falwell would remember, incorrectly, that Reagan had spoken this passage of scripture, not that he had merely had the Bible open to it. Again, Reagan was showing his adroit skill at communicating with two groups simultaneously: most people in the crowd and watching on television were unaware that 2 Chronicles had been a part of the proceedings, but the ministers knew, and with a little embellishment, they viewed it as central to the drama.[5]

On the second day of the new administration, which marked the anniversary of the Supreme Court's *Roe v. Wade* decision, Health and Human Services' Secretary Richard Schweicker addressed the annual Right-to-Life March. A group of pastors, including Falwell, met with President Reagan at the White House. Their anti-abortion agenda was proving to be more than an election promise; Reagan's determination to end abortion seemed genuine at the time.[6]

This was heady stuff for Falwell and the ministers. Already some preachers were beginning to question their political involvement. Rev. James Robison, who had been the driving force behind the Dallas Summit, was one of the first to confess having second thoughts about the political process. "My motives started out pure, but power corrupts," Robison said. "I found myself saying hard things about Jimmy Carter—hard, mean, cruel things. I found myself caught up in that, but the closer I got to it, I was frightened of it. I watched what it did to people." Robison would not play a leading role in the marriage between evangelicals and President Reagan, even though he had played a significant role in the courtship of the election. Few of the newly empowered religious leaders shared Robison's worries. They had come into the political process "with a clear sense of moral vision. They were tired of the incipient encroachment of secularism in nearly every area of American life," and they were determined to do something about it.[7]

Every new administration faces two immediate tasks. It must appoint staff, and it must decide which issues it will prioritize. The religious right had little influence on either of these two tasks. They would need to be content with photo opportunities with the president for the first few months of the new administration.

The appointment of White House staff and principals at government agencies was an immediate source of contention. The members of the religious right were newcomers to politics, and no one in their ranks had the experience necessary to run a government agency. Indeed, this was a difficulty that many movement conservatives encountered, not just religious conservatives, but it was a difficulty they did not necessarily appreciate. In the February 1981 issue of *Conservative Digest,* JoAnn Gaspar criticized the lack of conservative women being appointed to the new administration. "They should be Reagan conservatives—not Ford women or Nixon women or Bush women, but the type of women who supported Reagan and who share his views on the role of government," Gaspar insisted. "These are the women whom the Republican platform wooed so eloquently: women who had not necessarily been active in the limousine-liberal GOP of old, but women who, by the droves, came out and worked for Reagan, supported Reagan and voted for Reagan." Any consideration of previous government experience as a requirement for a top-level appointment is notably absent from Gaspar's list.[8]

In the upper echelons of the Reagan White House, the principal actors had little or no affinities with the Moral Majority, although almost all top staffers were conservatives. The main divisions were between the Californians who had worked for Reagan previously and the politicians with White House experience. The struggle for power was not between religious and secular conservatives, but between former Nixon and Ford administration officials, such as incoming chief of staff James Baker, and longtime Reagan hands like Ed Meese. Falwell did not complain about such staffing issues: "I haven't asked for any of my friends to be put in the administration," he said at the time. "We simply want to be friendly supporters from the outside."[9]

Falwell understood and acquiesced in the decision by the incoming administration to lead with its economic agenda. The perceived need for lower taxes and budget cuts was something that both united all elements of the Reagan coalition and played well with the public.

Falwell and the Moral Majority supported the Reagan budget and tax cuts, even though this issue had not been a central theme of their campaign efforts. "It's a matter of realism that the budget issue is vital. . . . The pork barrel is empty, we're bankrupt," said Falwell during an appearance on *Face the Nation*. "The country is busted. We're broke. . . . We can't spend ourselves out of bankruptcy." Falwell did not fault the president for putting the social issues on the back burner. "I don't think the president is sidestepping the moral and the social issues. . . . I think he wants to give it [his economic program] the full shot."[10]

The proposed cuts to social programs also allowed Falwell to call on the churches to pick up any slack in help for the poor. "We must be sensitive to the fact that we cannot ignore the presence and the needs of the poor among us, and I think that is where the churches must quickly move in, particularly conservative churches of which I am a part, and fill the vacuum that no doubt the country can no longer fill," Falwell said. This call fit nicely with his belief that social programs aimed at justice actually inhibited church outreach aimed at charity. Falwell saw concern for the poor always as a matter of charity, not justice, for admitting any systemic failings in the nation's economy would require a critique of capitalism that he was not prepared to offer. As an add-on, there was a patriotic ring to his call for churches to step up and fill a need the government was no longer prepared to meet.[11]

The Moral Majority also embraced Reagan's early statements on foreign affairs. At a White House press conference on January 29, only eight days after taking office, Reagan said that détente with the Soviet Union had been a "one-way street" and that the Soviets had repeated their intentions, which had changed little over the years. "I know of no leaders of the Soviet Union since the revolution, and including the present leadership, that has not more than once repeated in the various Communist congresses they hold their determination that their goal must be the promotion of world revolution and a one-world Socialist or Communist state, whichever word you want to use." Not only did the Soviets recognize no morality, Reagan asserted, but they "reserve unto themselves the right to commit any crime, to lie, to cheat, in order to attain that." The mainstream press was alarmed by such language, and the *Washington Post* editorialized against a "good-vs.-evil approach," but the president's indictment of Soviet intentions resonated with what Falwell and his fellow preachers had been saying for years.[12]

While waiting for Congress to pass Reagan's domestic policies, the Moral Majority focused its efforts on the local level in early 1981. This yielded mixed results: some of the state organizations failed to grasp the political nature of the organization, others pursued activities of which Falwell did not approve, and some even embarrassed the organization.

In Indiana the local Moral Majority sought to have the state Senate permit the posting of the Ten Commandments in public schools and to allow creationism to be taught alongside evolution. This was the kind of activity that the national organization applauded unequivocally. In North Carolina the local Moral Majority chapter compiled a list of books that it thought should not be used in the public schools. This, too, was in accord with Falwell's long-standing belief that parents should have a say in what their children are exposed to in the public schools, but it fed the perception of the Moral Majority as favoring censorship, a charge that Falwell was at pains to beat back.[13]

New York, with its tradition of progressive politics and lack of a "Bible Belt," might not have been considered fertile ground for the Moral Majority, but the state backed Reagan in the election and also elected a conservative Republican senator, Alfonse D'Amato, who was the candidate of the Conservative and Right-to-Life Parties as well. The candidate questionnaire distributed by the local Moral Majority chapter the previous year had raised eyebrows. In addition to the usual requests for a candidate's position on abortion and the death penalty, the questionnaire also asked: "Have you ever been born again?" and "If you stood before Heaven's gate and were asked on what grounds you sought admission, how would you reply?" Such questions were at cross-purposes with Falwell's intention that the Moral Majority be seen as a political, not an evangelical, organization.

The Reverend Dan Fore, pastor of a Baptist church in the Bensonhurst neighborhood of Brooklyn, was the chairman of the local affiliate. He was, like Falwell, eminently quotable, and as also happened with Falwell, it was a comment he made about Jews that caused great controversy. "I love the Jewish people deeply," Mr. Fore told the *New York Times*. "God has given them talents He has not given to others. They are His chosen people. Jews have a God-given ability to make money, almost a supernatural ability to make money." Falwell distanced himself from Fore's remarks, saying, "I don't think you can stereotype any people."

Fore held a series of statewide "training seminars," and he set himself the ambitious goal of recruiting one hundred thousand members and sixty county chairmen within a year. Members would each pay $15 in dues in exchange for receipt of a planned monthly newsletter. "First you get a local chairman. Then you organize a moral action committee. Then you organize your telephone tree. You've got a woman who loves to talk?—and most of them do— you get a woman to be head of the telephone tree." But as of February 1981, Fore acknowledged, he had only one county chairman, although officials with both the Conservative and Right-to-Life Parties had pledged support. "I know that you've got to crawl before you walk," said Fore. But he knew where he was walking, even if the walk would be a long one. "We are not expecting to stop all the crime, all the homosexuality, all the lesbianism, all the harlotry," Fore told the *Times*. "We are simply here as a savoring influence, preaching what we believe is the truth, which is salvation by faith in Christ."[14]

In Maryland the Moral Majority chapter tried unsuccessfully to defeat a measure before the House Environmental Matters Committee that permitted guidance counselors in the public schools to distribute information about pregnancy and contraception. The committee acted on the measure with uncommon speed, and according to Torrey Brown, the committee chairman, the Moral Majority's campaign against the proposal had the effect of accelerating its passage. "Some of them [committee members] said they wanted to stop the phone calls. Others just said, 'Let's stop this hassle. It's foolish.'"[15]

Maryland's Moral Majority also got itself involved in a controversy that further tarnished the organization's image. A local bakery had begun selling anatomically correct gingerbread men. The Moral Majority first asked the state's attorney to take action, but he declined. Allowing that he found the gingerbread cookies "disgusting," assistant prosecutor Frederick Paone explained that the cookies did not violate a law that prohibited the sale of X-rated images to children. "All I saw was a visual representation of a gingerbread man, not a visual representation of a person," Paone said. Then the Department of Legislative Reference received a request to draft a bill that would ban the sale of sexually explicit bakery items. It recommended maximum penalties of ten years in prison and a $10,000 fine for anyone selling such products to those under eighteen years of age, and five years and $5,000 for selling such products to adults. The request to draft the bill came from the office of Republican delegate Robin Flicker, but he denied knowledge of the matter. The whole episode served only to paint the Moral Majority as unserious prudes.[16]

In Santa Clara, California, the Moral Majority chapter proposed a law that would impose the penalty of capital punishment on homosexuals. This earned a clear rebuke from Falwell. "I don't know this gentleman," Falwell told an interviewer. "I have never met him. I totally disagree with that concept. I don't know that he said it. I, like you, read it in the newspaper, but I would be very surprised and disappointed if, in fact, he does believe that." Falwell also pointed out that the national organization did not approve the activities or statements coming from local affiliates. "I have no control at all over the Santa Clara Moral Majority," Falwell said. "They organized without any technical connection with the national Moral Majority. In reality, it is a free-lance group. The statement regarding capital punishment for homosexual acts, to me, is out of the question."[17]

The local embarrassments were especially unwelcome because they came at a time when Falwell was trying to shape the Moral Majority's national image. In March the group ran full-page ads in both the

Washington Post and the *New York Times* entitled "They have labeled Moral Majority the Extreme Right because we speak out against Extreme Wrong!" The ad began by affirming the group's belief in the separation of church and state. It noted that some members opposed abortion on theological grounds, but that "other Moral Majority Inc. members believe this from a medical perspective." The ad restated the Moral Majority's opposition to pornography, but also insisted, "We do not advocate censorship." Perhaps in response to the incidents of local organizations straying from the message, the ad stated: "We encourage our Moral Majority state organizations to be autonomous and indigenous. Moral Majority state organizations may, from time to time, hold positions not held by Moral Majority Inc."

The full-page ad also listed "What the Moral Majority is Not": it was not a political party, it did not endorse candidates, it did not seek to elect only born-again candidates, and it did not oppose the extension of civil rights to homosexuals, only special rights. In a clear attempt to rebut the charge of self-righteousness that its very name seemed to suggest, the ad stated, "We do not believe that individuals or organizations which disagree with Moral Majority Inc. belong to an immoral minority." The entire text of the ad was sweet reasonableness, including its final call for fairness from the media and the public.

> *Millions of Americans have already joined Moral Majority Inc. and have pledged their time, talent and treasure to the rebuilding of the Republic. The pornographers are angry. The amoral secular humanists are livid. The abortionists are furious. Full-page ads, employing McCarthy-like fear tactics, are appearing in major newspapers. The sponsors of these ads, of course, are attempting by these means to raise funds for themselves. The opposition has every right to legally promote their goals and attack ours. But, certainly, we have the same right.*

Falwell was trying to convince a skeptical media that his organization was doing nothing different from what others were doing, without all the controversy. And he was willing to spend more than $50,000 on the ad to make the point.[18]

Falwell also addressed the differences between his religious ministry and his political activism in an appearance on *The Phil Donahue Show*. The host needled Falwell, saying, "You say it is not a religious effort, Moral Majority, but with you as its standard-bearer it is kind of hard to divorce this." Falwell blamed the confusion on the fact that he had to wear many hats, but Donahue persisted, asking, "Is it totally different, your message from the pulpit and your message on *Meet the Press*?" Falwell was just as persistent, answering, "Yes, it really is. In our church—I preached to 20,000 people Sunday in Thomas Road Church and we preached the Gospel of Christ, the death, burial, resurrection Easter message, and invited people to come to Christ. Moral Majority could never approach that because we have people there that don't believe that."

Later in the same program Donahue seemed to conflate the Moral Majority with the Reagan administration. "You are not cutting the Pentagon, you are cutting all those other—only the truly needy," Donahue said to Falwell, who replied with mock surprise, "I didn't know I had that authority." Falwell had developed his media skills, especially the ability to deflect an important question that overreached with a bit of humor, calling attention only to the overreaching, not to the underlying concern. Their exchange on possible exceptions to Falwell's hope to ban abortions again shows Falwell at his best:

PHIL DONAHUE: *Would there be an exception to that position?*

JERRY FALWELL: *Yes, I think if the mother's life is at stake, I certainly think that that again is a matter of self-defense and . . .*

PHIL DONAHUE: *How about rape or incest?*

JERRY FALWELL: *I don't think so. I think that we are committing two wrongs to correct one wrong, and I don't think it works that way.*

PHIL DONAHUE: *As you know, the IUD—I realize you are not an obstetrician . . .*

JERRY FALWELL: *I'm in favor of birth control, period.*

PHIL DONAHUE: *The IUD, however . . .*

JERRY FALWELL: *Just lost my Catholic friends; go ahead . . .*

This is vintage Falwell in his on-air interviews. He leavened the gravity of the issues—and the image many had of him as menacing—with humor and genuine friendliness. He would be one of Donahue's most frequent guests precisely because of these gifts he brought to the discussions.[19]

Reverend Fore in New York and other local Moral Majority leaders may not have been media-savvy, and they lacked the ability to deflect certain concerns with wit. And certainly Fore was dabbling in anti-Semitic tropes that were mere bigotry. But the confusion about how to address Christian concerns in the world of secular politics is understandable. After all, Falwell may have been insistent that he was merely trying to bring Christians into the political process, but what should they bring if not Christ? Falwell saw conservative moral principles as playing a mediating role, allowing believers to get involved without introducing sectarian, or dogmatic, concerns. He saw Christian moral principles not merely as conservative but as American because he understood the founding to have been a largely Christian event. There was a tautology at work, and Falwell's underlings understandably emphasized different aspects of it at different times, occasionally straying into the kind of sectarian, distinctly Christian statements that he was learning to eschew.

Falwell saw the necessity of the Reagan administration's desire to lead with its economic plans. And he saw that it was impossible to place key aides in the top echelons of the Reagan White House. But he also knew that his constituency wanted something for their efforts. While he stated that he was content to remain "outside," he needed to cultivate access, to show that the views of the Moral Majority would get at least a hearing within the counsels of the administration.

Most of the Reagan administration's top officials were not social

conservatives. Michael Deaver, who with Meese and Baker constituted the triumvirate of Reagan's top aides, had little time for the
concerns of evangelicals. "Mike Deaver probably couldn't spell
'abortion,'" Falwell said. In an interview, Deaver said that evangelicals were welcome in the Reagan White House, but that they needed
to come in through the back door. Falwell read the comment and
contacted Malcolm Blackwell, who was the administration's liaison with conservative groups, and said that he wanted to meet with
the president. A meeting was scheduled for two weeks later. Deaver
spoke with Falwell before the meeting and said that he had been misquoted. He asked Falwell not to mention it in his meeting with the
president. Falwell did not bring it up, but Reagan did, asking Falwell
if he had come in through the front door or the back. Falwell replied
that he had come in through the front door. "Feel free," Reagan told
the preacher. "That door is open." Falwell later recalled that while he
wasn't really mad over the Deaver comment, "I wanted to make sure
we weren't getting off on the wrong foot. We never had any more
problems with Deaver from that time on."[20]

Some thought that the only thing that interested the ministers was
access to the White House. "What overshadowed all their concerns
was simply the pleasure in being able to get in," declared Weyrich.
"They didn't want to do anything to jeopardize that." He called such
access "meaningless." Cal Thomas echoed Weyrich's assessment.
"As I'd travel around the country, I'd go into churches and I'd see featured prominently in the office or the hallway a picture of the pastor
with Ronald Reagan," Thomas recalled. "I think Christian people
were sucked into the political process so that it became primary in
their lives, and the moral and spiritual power that should have been
theirs, to speak truth to power, seemed to be put on the back burner,
because Ronald Reagan became the surrogate messiah."[21]

Ed Dobson held a similar view of the allure, but ultimate mean-
inglessness, of access. "This was heady stuff for people who, one or
two years earlier, had been unnoticed and unheard of, and nobody
cared about us. Now all of a sudden the gatekeepers of culture had
invited us in." Dobson saw that the Moral Majority's political influence was not inside but outside, in the fact that the group's issues

"have become points of discussion in every election." He worried that too much emphasis on the inside game would not only alter the spiritual focus of the religious leaders but rob them of their political capital over time. "We now have the votes to make the difference because we have concentrated on the basics of a spiritual ministry for over fifty years. We are not powerful because we sought power, but because we have sought the Lord."[22]

These criticisms did not deter Falwell at first. The *Moral Majority Report* did print some articles critical of the administration for not doing more for the social conservatives' agenda. The Reagan administration's decision to sell AWACS planes to Saudi Arabia was one of Falwell's major targets; his criticism of this decision would align him with the mostly liberal, pro-Israel lobby on Capitol Hill. But generally, Falwell was a cheerleader for the Reagan administration and remained sanguine that, with time, the social issues that really mattered to him and his organization, such as abortion and school prayer, would find their way onto the political agenda of the White House. It would take several years before Falwell realized that in order to shape the political world, he needed to focus on shaping the culture. Meanwhile, there was plenty of work to do, consolidating the organization and keeping the pressure on. If he wanted to be a "friendly supporter from the outside," he needed to make sure he had many friends outside, not just photo ops with the president.[23]

Falwell did not rest on his electoral laurels but used the early months of 1981 to recruit more members to the Moral Majority and expand its reach and influence. He continued his "I Love America" rallies, which had become recruiting tools. He continued to publish the *Moral Majority Report,* hoping it would get passed along to potential new members. The Moral Majority lobbied local officials on issues that were important to them, and unlike the effort to ban sexually explicit gingerbread men, sometimes they met with success. The Moral Majority had won an election, but now it needed to prove that it could become a full-fledged movement capable of winning future elections.

In Montana, the local branch of the Moral Majority was busy planning a "red, white and blue I Love America rally," set for May 14 at the Shriners' Auditorium. The group had already recruited 4,500 members by March and was hoping to reach its goal of 10,000 members by year's end. Rev. Don Jones, who headed up this Moral Majority chapter, also hoped to have one hundred pastors signed up by the summertime. "We believe the rally in May could put us over the top," Jones told a local newspaper.[24]

After Reagan appointed Rep. David Stockman, a congressman from Michigan, to his cabinet as budget director, the Moral Majority joined the effort to select his successor. Stockman endorsed a former aide, John Globensky, but he lost narrowly to the more conservative candidate, Mark Siljander. Michigan's Moral Majority chapter did not formally endorse Siljander, but in literature that it distributed it gave him a 100 percent rating on Moral Majority issues. Siljander resented the group's claiming credit for the win, noting that the Moral Majority had no offices in the district at the time of the primary and attributing his victory to "grass roots support." But in conservative primaries, especially in low-turnout contests like this one, the conservative Christian constituency *was* the grass roots, and the national media took note of the Moral Majority's role in Siljander's win.[25]

Even more fertile terrain for the Moral Majority could be found in Mississippi, where five thousand new members were signed up in the first four months of 1981. "As long as there's a battle against humanism here in Mississippi, we're going to be involved," said Karl Falster, executive director of the Mississippi Moral Majority. Falster said that he thought there were many "who would be glad to see Christians go back to sleep again," but predicted that the group would build on its electoral success. "Things that work have a tendency to stay around." Rev. Randall Hisaw led a campaign in Lauderdale County to require pornographic magazines to be covered in brown wrappers or not put on general display. At Meridian Junior College, Ron Godwin came from the national organization to address a group of ninety young people. Rev. Mike Wells, president of Mississippi Moral Majority, also addressed the students, telling them, "The voice of morality is beginning to be heard. It's the slaughterhouse for the liberals and they know it." Thirty county chapters of Moral Majority were organized in Mississippi by the beginning of June.[26]

The Moral Majority's national office also began new efforts to reach out and attract members. Harry Covert, editor of the *Moral Majority Report,* had a background in journalism and knew something about using newspapers to promote new products. In Martinsburg, West Virginia, the local newspaper, the *Martinsburg Evening Journal,* carried a copy of the *Moral Majority Report* as a supplement. Covert also negotiated an arrangement with the paper to print and distribute the *Moral Majority Report.* He announced plans to try to disseminate similar supplements in newspapers in Atlanta, South Carolina, upstate New York, and one newspaper in New England. An enthusiastic Covert announced that ten phone calls to the Moral Majority were received the day after the supplement ran from readers of the Martinsburg paper, all looking to sign up.[27]

The Moral Majority flexed its muscle not only at the ballot box but by lobbying key elected officials. In Virginia, Republican governor John Dalton vetoed three bills that had passed the state's legislature but were opposed by the Moral Majority and other conservative Christians. Two of the bills would have permitted the use of state Medicaid funds for abortions if the pregnant woman had been raped, her pregnancy was the result of incest, or the unborn child suffered from serious fetal abnormality. The third bill would have created a state holiday to honor Martin Luther King Jr. The abortion bills had passed when the state's lieutenant governor, Charles "Chuck" Robb, cast the tie-breaking vote in favor of them. The Moral Majority called Robb's vote "shocking and unexpected" and warned about its effect on his hopes of being elected governor later that year. They praised Dalton for resisting "the loud voices of special interest groups who seek to continue the slaughter of unborn babies on that altar of convenience."[28]

The Moral Majority's influence also manifested itself in more opaque ways. In northern Virginia, the Fairfax Christian Academy was started. The headmaster, Robert Thoburn, was deeply engaged in conservative politics. One of his sons worked as legislative affairs director for the Moral Majority's Washington office, and another worked for the Life Amendment Political Action Committee, a group seeking to overturn *Roe v. Wade* by means of a constitutional amendment. The school was "no frills." Students were crammed into classrooms, as many as thirty-five in one room; there were no sports teams and few extracurricular activities. There was no cafeteria, and students had to bring their own lunches. Tuition was a then-steep $1,350 per year, but parents were knocking down the doors to enroll their children. Among the prominent conservative politicians whose children attended the school were Sen. Strom Thurmond, Rep. Phillip Crane, Conservative Caucus chairman Howard Phillips, and conservative direct-mail guru Richard Viguerie.[29]

The Moral Majority also turned its attention to a congeries of issues that concerned what they believed were evil influences on children. Falwell had long been opposed to the general availability of pornography. He was in favor of parental rights in deciding what children in the schools should read. And he was generally opposed to sex education. In the spring and summer of 1981, all of these issues at the heart of the moral concerns articulated by Falwell and the Moral Majority would make news as he and his allies sought to combat the libertinism of the culture. In this quest, the Moral Majority would challenge not only entrenched economic interests—pornographers made a lot of money, and risqué television shows brought in millions in advertising revenue—but an opposing set of beliefs about the First Amendment, the content and purpose of public education, and the relative rights of children and parents.

On the last day of March the members of the Senate Human Resources Committee watched a sex education film, *About Sex,* designed for use in the public schools. The film, developed by Syracuse University, highlighted counselors talking with teenagers in "their vernacular." It had no explicit scenes, although it did contain some frontal nudity, and no obscenities were used. But Sen. Orrin Hatch of Utah labeled it "as disgusting a film as I have seen." Sen. Jeremiah Denton, from Alabama, whose election had been at the top of the Moral Majority's objectives the previous November, set the context for the viewing when he told the committee, "Increasingly, it appears that family-planning clinics are serving teen-agers in the absence of their parents' advice and counsel and in contradiction of laws concerning sexual conduct in many of their own states." Denton and other "Moral Majority senators," as the *Washington Post* dubbed them, wanted to gut federal funding for family planning efforts, such as those clinics and school programs that might use the film. The Moral Majority sent out a "legislative alert" urging supporters to write President Reagan to support Denton's effort to kill federal funding for such programs.[30]

In Peoria, Illinois, the local Moral Majority chapter weighed in to fight a sex education class taught at Limestone High School, arguing that the class was too liberal. Parents at all schools in the Peoria area had to give consent for their children to participate in the sex education programs, even at those schools that provided students with less information than Limestone did. The local newspaper praised the Moral Majority for raising the issue, but chided the organization for its stance. "We are inclined to think in most things, including sex education, more knowledge is better than less," wrote the editors of the paper. "We at the Journal Star are in the information business, and we think it is hard to overdose on facts."[31]

Other local chapters of the Moral Majority joined forces with conservative parents' groups to influence decisions about what materials were being taught, or even made available, to students. In Onida, South Dakota, all information about birth control was removed from the guidance counselor's office, and the books *Brave New World* and *Catcher in the Rye* were dropped from classes in literature. In Plano, Texas, teachers were instructed not to ask their students' opinions because doing so suggested that there was no absolute right or wrong. A high school production of the musical *Grease* was canceled in Des Moines, Iowa, and in Diablo, California, students needed the permission of both their parents and their teachers to gain access to *Ms.* magazine. In each of these cases, the religious right was seeking to restore the morality it believed was threatened by the secular humanism of the public schools. Sometimes these campaigns invoked "Judeo-Christian values" and sometimes they did not, but their effect was to paint the religious right, and the Moral Majority in particular, as latter-day book-burners in the eyes of their liberal critics.[32]

The teaching of creationism in the schools was another source of controversy for Falwell and his allies. The Moral Majority threw its support behind the efforts in fifteen states to pass legislation that would require that both creationism and evolution be taught in the public schools. Falwell tried to pull a card out of the liberal playbook and throw it back at his opponents. He argued that the academic freedom that liberals extolled required instruction in both theories of human origin. "We must leave situations like this open for children and their parents to arrive at their own conclusions," he said while filming a four-part special on creationism, the opening scenes of which were set in Dayton, Tennessee, site of the famous Scopes trial in 1925. Falwell supported a recent court decision that said both evolution and creationism had to be labeled as "theories" in public school textbooks. In that same interview in Dayton, Falwell also said something curious: "It is like comparing apples and oranges to bring science and religion against each other." This statement, taken at face value, was the ground for the broad acceptance of evolutionary theory by theological liberals. They believed that science tried to answer "how" questions while religion tried to answer "why" questions. When push came to shove, Falwell was always of the opinion that religion trumped science in any conflict between them.[33]

On June 7, Falwell broadcast the first of his shows on evolution. "This all boils down to the fact that the Evolutionists have to walk by faith, not by sight, just like the Bible Creationists!" Falwell told his television audience. "And, it requires much less faith to believe what God says in Genesis than to believe what Darwin said." The broadcast was officially sponsored not by the Moral Majority but by the *Old-Time Gospel Hour,* but the audience overlapped considerably. And the Falwell who stood on the steps of the courthouse in Dayton, Tennessee, was the same Falwell who sat chatting amiably with Phil Donahue.[34]

Falwell's efforts to control the content of public school teaching would raise the specter of censorship. According to Judith Krug of the American Library Association, complaints about censorship had increased dramatically since Reagan's election victory, from three to five calls per week to that many calls per day. "People are walking into school systems and libraries and maintaining that they have a mandate from the election to clean up America," said Edward Jenkinson, who monitored censorship for the National Council of Teachers of English. Jenkinson pointed the finger at the Moral Majority, and at Falwell in particular, but Ron Godwin and other Moral Majority officials tried valiantly to insist on their innocence. "We're against censorship and against it and against it," Godwin said, although he did acknowledge that the group encouraged parents to investigate what textbooks their children were using. He acknowledged, too, that the Moral Majority had recently sent a letter to four hundred thousand people warning about a new sex education textbook of which they did not approve. Dobson and Falwell would neither acknowledge that such warnings created a kind of "self-censorship" on the part of publishers nor recognize that their warnings might be creating the climate for such self-censorship, but others saw the linkage. Paula Hartz, an editor at Holt, Rinehart and Winston, told the *Washington Post*, "We're trying to second guess in advance what people are going to complain about. We certainly see the handwriting on the wall. Textbooks are becoming more conservative."[35]

In another effort to control what children were exposed to, directed not at the public schools but at the public airwaves, Falwell would again lead some to conclude that he did indeed favor censorship. In February a group called the Coalition for Better Television was formed, with the Moral Majority as one of its contributing members. The group, based in Tupelo, Mississippi, began drawing up a list of television shows that it found objectionable. Another participating group, the National Federation for Decency, had been tracking shows for four years. The new list of objectionable programs included such hits as *Soap* and *It's a Living*. In May the Coalition announced that it had begun contacting sponsors of these shows and alerting them to the group's intention to call for a boycott of the products advertised on the shows. They received a tepid response from some corporations. A spokesman for the Revlon Corporation said that the company had not changed its ad purchasing, but that they were keeping their "eyes and ears open." Dow Chemical Corporation said that it had been discussing the issues with the Coalition but had not yet made any changes to their ad purchases either. And the pharmaceutical company Warner-Lambert issued a statement saying, "We are sensitive to the issue. But we certainly cannot let special interest groups dictate where we advertise our products." In fact, Warner-Lambert had already pulled its advertising from the late-night hit *Saturday Night Live,* citing its inability to prescreen a live show for content.[36]

On June 15, 1981, Moral Majority members received a fund-raising letter from Reverend Falwell that urged contributions so that the group could counter the various nefarious influences in the culture, reminding potential donors that "right in your own home, the television screen is spewing out a massive volume of sex and violence." And that same month *Moral Majority Report* announced that the nation's largest purchaser of television advertising, Proctor & Gamble, was pulling its ads from fifty shows on the Coalition's list of objectionable shows. The company, which had bought $486.3 million of television advertising the previous year, applauded the efforts of the Coalition. Owen Butler, chairman of Proctor & Gamble, told a meeting of the Academy of Television Arts and Sciences that the Coalition "is expressing some very important and broadly held views about gratuitous sex, violence and profanity. I can assure you we are listening very carefully to what they say, and I urge you to do the same." In commenting on the decision, Falwell said that he hoped it would be the first of many such decisions. "When a $10 billion industry publicly indicates a real concern for the well-being of the American public, it is simply saying we're not too big to have compassion and concern," Falwell said. "I sincerely hope that other large industries will follow suit."[37]

Knowing that cries of censorship would be sure to follow the Coalition's success, the Moral Majority came up with a creative way to fight the charge. The group issued books of matches labeled "Moral Majority Book Burning Matches," and beneath that, on the cover, was the statement "See official book list inside." When you opened the book of matches, there was no list, only the additional statement, "That's right—there aren't any." These were distributed widely, especially at venues where Falwell was speaking.[38]

Parental rights over children were also at issue, not only in the classroom and on television but in the home. In Indiana, Rev. Greg Dixon, head of the state chapter of the Moral Majority, sent out a fund-raising letter that began: "Dear Friend: 'They've taken my son!' The father told me that his 9-year old son did not come home from school yesterday. You see, Tommy (not his real name) was taken away from his family by the State Welfare Department . . . because it was against Indiana law for the father to have spanked his own son for lying. That's right . . . the father lost custody rights for his son because he spanked him." In fact, according to a local newspaper report, the child was removed after the mother saw photos of the boy's buttocks after the father had given him a whipping. A judge ordered the child removed while the state Department of Child and Family investigated the case. Within a month a child advocate decided to return the child to his father's custody with a warning not to hit the child as hard in the future. "If you haven't left any marks," Reverend Dixon told a reporter, "you probably haven't whipped your children. . . . The Bible instructs parents to whip their children with a rod in their early years so they won't become a disciplinary problem as they grow older."[39]

In addition to efforts to change the law on spanking in Indiana and efforts to restrict funding for sex education at the federal level, the Moral Majority set about trying to get existing laws against the distribution of pornography enforced. The group planned a conference in the Bahamas ("It's cheaper to go there. . . . And it's a little nicer and that will help pull people in," a Moral Majority official said) on how to enforce existing laws against pornography. They invited prosecutors and mayors, all expenses paid. The leading speaker was to be Atlanta's solicitor general, Hinson McAuliffe, who had successfully closed down twenty-two of the city's forty-four establishments that sold pornography. "We're excited about the program and not at all apologetic about informing public officials how they can more aggressively enforce laws already on the books," Ron Godwin told the *Jackson News,* which ran a story about the Mississippi city's mayor who had declined the invitation.[40]

Conferences. Press conferences. Television appearances. Legislative battles. Boycotts. The Moral Majority was operating on all cylinders by the summer of 1981. The group was flexing its muscles at both the local and federal levels—sometimes to little effect beyond a photo op with the president, sometimes to great effect, such as getting Proctor & Gamble not to air commercials on racy television shows. In a little more than two years since he had started the Moral Majority, Falwell had gone from being a prominent figure in the world of Baptist fundamentalism to a household name throughout America. The goal of "restoring America" to a land where Christian values were respected seemed closer by the day.

With increased influence came increased opposition. Although Falwell and his advisers may have had their doubts about the extent of their influence within the Reagan administration, political opponents were certain that Falwell's influence was great and pernicious. Some of the criticisms were little different, albeit more urgent, from those made when the Moral Majority was founded. But the liberal voices that began denouncing the Moral Majority and Falwell personally in the spring of 1981 were sharper and more varied than those that had been leveled previously. Some of the objections to Falwell were specific and fair; others were vague and misrepresented not only his positions but even denied his right to assert those positions. The comfortable belief in certain secular circles that religion had been liberalized or tamed had vanished with the rise of the Moral Majority, replaced by an uncomfortable worry that a latter-day Elmer Gantry had taken over the country.

One of the first efforts to push back against the Moral Majority's newfound influence struck close to home. In early February the Virginia Senate passed a resolution encouraging public school students to study the Commonwealth's Statute on Religious Freedom, authored by Thomas Jefferson. Sen. Joseph Fitzpatrick introduced the measure by saying, "There are those in our midst today who seek to impose their religious opinions on others, including public officials." Falwell denounced the effort as a "juvenile and uninformed . . . grandstand act." Fitzpatrick displayed a letter he had received that threatened to place him on the "82 Hit List" and had been sent anonymously and signed "Friends of Dr. Falwell and the Moral Majority." There was no practical consequence from the Senate resolution, but it showed that not everyone in Virginia identified with the Moral Majority. The resolution also showed that not everyone agreed with Falwell's interpretation of the Founders and what they accomplished. For many Americans, the founding of the American Republic was a decidedly secular affair in which references to the "Creator" were either window-dressing or appeals to a Deist God who bore little resemblance to the God worshiped at the Thomas Road Baptist Church.[41]

Former senator George McGovern attacked "quasi-religious" groups such as Moral Majority in a March address at Holy Cross College in Worcester, Massachusetts. He warned that Moral Majority employed an "emotion-laden, single-issue type of politics" that threatened to cripple the American political system. Politics required negotiation and compromise, and McGovern suggested that religious groups were allergic to these necessary parts of the political process. McGovern also took exception to some of the religious right's tactics, citing specifically the "morality test" devised by Christian Voice, another conservative evangelical organization. McGovern, echoing the charge made by his former colleague Sen. John Culver, noted that former congressman Richard Kelly had received a 100 percent score on the morality test, despite the fact that he had been caught on camera in the ABSCAM scandal taking $25,000 in bribes from FBI agents posing as Arab sheiks, while the Reverend Robert Drinan, SJ, the only Jesuit member of Congress, had gotten a zero.[42]

Much of the press corps was similarly hostile to the Moral Majority. In an op-ed piece criticizing Governor Dalton's veto of bills allowing government funding of abortions in cases of fetal abnormality, *Washington Post* columnist Judy Mann discussed a couple, Jeff and Ellen Fleisher, whose son had been born with Tay-Sachs disease. Mann described the child's physical sufferings, and his parents' emotional sufferings, in the kind of lurid prose that, in another context, would have done Falwell's ghostwriters proud. The couple had urged the governor to sign the legislation. "Dalton's actions have made him a moral hero in the eyes of his buddy, the Rev. Jerry Falwell," wrote Mann, noting the prewritten thank-you notes that Falwell distributed to Moral Majority members to send to the governor. Mann accused Governor Dalton and Falwell of "ignoring human suffering."[43]

That same newspaper, however, also published an article that defended the Moral Majority's work with the Coalition for Better Television by columnist Richard Cohen. "Censorship is something the government does and at its most insidious it involves political ideas, not an attempt to boost ratings with a bit more smut," Cohen wrote. "We have a right not to buy what we don't want to buy." He compared the Moral Majority's boycott to the earlier boycott of table grapes and lettuce sponsored by the United Farm Workers. Cohen saw boycotts as a form of political speech, and whether or not one agreed with the content of such speech, it clearly was not outside the mainstream of American political discourse. "It is a way of expressing dissent, of putting your money where your mouth is," Cohen concluded. "That's all Jerry Falwell wants to do and there is nothing wrong with that."[44]

Cohen's article was the exception that proved the rule. The more usual scorn heaped on Falwell was not limited to the pages of the major newspapers. In rural Illinois, a columnist for a small local paper was equally disturbed by the Moral Majority. "Yes, Falwell and friends are claiming direction 'from on high' to announce the Christian position on each of the major issues of our time, suggesting that any other opinion on a given issue is 'un-Christian'. Not only un-Christian but unpatriotic. Pfui!" wrote Pat Bouchard in the *Palos Heights Regional*. "This bunch is dangerous. The danger of the Religious New Right is not that they are speaking out on political issues, which is their right if not their obligation; it is the way they attack the integrity and character of anyone who does not stand with them." Bouchard said that he disagreed with the religious right on a variety of issues, such as SALT II and the Panama Canal treaties, which he supported, but that he did agree with them on the abortion issue. He doubted that his stance on any issues put his soul, or the country, at risk, a proposition he labeled "Bunk!"[45]

The longest-lasting and most aggressive response to the rise of the religious right was the formation of a new liberal group, People For the American Way (PFAW). Spearheaded and funded by television producer Norman Lear, People For the American Way issued a mission statement that focused squarely on the perceived threat of the religious right. "We are alarmed that some of the current voices of stridency and division may replace those of reason and unity," the group announced. "If these voices continue unchallenged, the results will be predictable: a rise in 'demonology' and hostility, a breakdown in community and social spirit, a deterioration of free and open dialogue, and the temptation to grasp at simplistic solutions for complex problems." Among those joining the organization's founding board were former congresswoman Barbara Jordan of Texas; Andrew Heiskell, CEO of Time, Inc.; and Rev. Theodore Hesburgh, president of the University of Notre Dame. By September, the group had forty thousand members and was adding one thousand more each week. PFAW also began running television advertisements. One particularly effective ad showed a man in a hard hat saying, "There's gotta be something wrong when anyone, even if it's a preacher, tells you that you're a good Christian or a bad Christian depending on your political view. That's not the American way." In the years ahead, People For the American Way would monitor the activities of the religious right, engage in public debates with Moral Majority spokesmen, and issue its own voting guides, rating members of Congress based on their votes on issues important to the organization.[46]

Father Hesburgh's role in founding People For the American Way was but one example of the growing opposition to Falwell that had arisen within the religious community. Liberal religious voices were joining the chorus of secular critics, challenging not only the Moral Majority's positions on the issues, as some liberal religious leaders had done previously, but its methods as well; these challenges were made on political or religious grounds or both. The divisions between theological liberals and conservatives that had long been brewing beneath the surface within religious traditions broke into the open, and the political debate followed.

In Michigan one group gave the Moral Majority the highest form of flattery, albeit in opposition to Falwell's group. The Michigan Coalition for Human Rights imitated the organizational and educational model used by the Moral Majority. The Coalition was organized by religious leaders of a more liberal stripe precisely to confront the Moral Majority's claim to speak for those with religiously motivated political values. "They [the Moral Majority] have the right to speak out on social issues, but they wrap themselves in morality and righteousness and say this is what the Bible says," one of the group's founders, Rev. Rudolf Gelsey, told a local newspaper. "Others may interpret the Bible differently." State senator Gary Corbin was another founding member of the Coalition, which opened an office in the spring, enrolled new members, and began a speaker's bureau. Both the Episcopalian and Methodist bishops of Detroit joined the new organization too. The evangelical Baptist voice would not be the only religious voice in the public square.[47]

Some Protestant clergy traveled into the heart of the Bible Belt to denounce the religious right. Rev. William Sloane Coffin, senior minister at Riverside Church in New York and one of the leading lights of theological liberalism, gave a speech at an ecumenical lecture series sponsored by Christ the King Church in Little Rock, Arkansas. "It'd be nice to get away from the term 'liberal,'" Coffin told the audience. "I like to use 'generous.' Some policies seem generous; some strike me as ungenerous. And I score the right for being ungenerous, most of all—including the Moral Majority." He compared the Moral Majority to the children of Israel who wanted to go back to Egypt when they encountered challenges, accusing them of a similar nostalgia: "Everything is back—back to the time when we owned the Panama Canal, back to the time when we were the undisputed No. 1 military power in the world, back to the time when women were in the kitchen and gays were in the closet—back, back, back."

Coffin did agree that the Moral Majority was correct in believing that religion must be socially relevant or it becomes a "monument to irrelevance."

Coffin also voiced his objection to the Moral Majority's conflation of religion and patriotism, but not in the manner of his secular critics who resented the intrusion of conservative religious values into political debates. Coffin raised the concern that such a conflation did damage to religion, robbing it of its necessarily critical stance toward all societies and skating close to an idolatry of the nation. "I think, probably, the churches went out to religionize America and America took its revenge and Americanized religion," Coffin told the Little Rock audience. "So it's questionable whether the cross is higher than the flag or the flag is higher than the cross." Coffin was challenging, even mocking, Reverend Falwell about one his most central themes, the belief that America was a nation set apart by God. Falwell would not have been a fan of Coffin's theological liberalism, and there is no evidence that he responded. He certainly did not desist from selling American flag pins at the start of almost every sermon at Thomas Road Baptist Church.[48]

It was one thing to be attacked by William Sloane Coffin. It was more difficult to ignore challenges within the Baptist fold. Many Baptists resented the Moral Majority's politics and its theology, both in its particulars and in its methods. In March some four hundred moderate Baptists came to a meeting in Dallas to fight for what they believed was the true Baptist tradition of theological and political tolerance. Moderates accused the Moral Majority of threatening Baptist commitment to separation of church and state and with seeking to "coerce" fellow Christians into accepting only a rigid set of religious and political beliefs.

The Dallas meeting featured a debate between Gary Jarmin, head of the Christian Voice and a close ally of the Moral Majority, and John Buchanan, the ordained minister and congressman who had lost his GOP primary in Alabama to a more conservative challenger. Jarmin complained that "today we have a Government so secular, so dominated by a humanist mentality, that we've rejected the role of God in it." He also defended the "scorecards" on voting used by the Moral Majority and the Christian Voice to determine the moral acceptability of certain political candidates, noting that the score-card was not a personal attack. The morality scorecard "was not intended to pass judgment as to how righteous or unrighteous a Congressman may be," but only to evaluate candidates' stances on certain issues of special importance to religiously motivated voters.

In rebuttal, Buchanan argued that the scorecard approach con-centrated on a narrow set of moral issues and that any member of Congress had to be judged on a variety of moral concerns. He said that if he were to devise a "moral scorecard" it would include such issues as civil rights and women's rights. "I believe as a Christian," Buchanan countered, "that nothing is more important than to bring society to the place where every person, regardless of race, sex or geographical location, has the opportunity to be the most that that person can be." It is not difficult to see how Falwell would dismiss the moral agenda of promoting "the opportunity to be the most that that person can be" as "fuzzy."

Also addressing the group was Robert Bellah, the noted sociolo-gist from the University of California at Berkley, who spoke about the broader, nontheological context in which the theological debate was taking place. Bellah decried what he termed a "narrow and self-ish" mood in the electorate and called for a spiritual awakening to combat it. He thought that an "amoral majority" had linked forces with Christian fundamentalists in an effort to end the social experi-mentation in America that had begun with the New Deal. This linkage with the New Deal, as we have seen, spoke to sociocultural influences that were affecting religious attitudes.[49]

Bellah's linkage of the resurgence of fundamentalism with other social forces was echoed by other Baptists at the Dallas meeting. Dr. Glenn Hinson of the Southern Baptist Seminary in Louisville believed that a sense of social and economic instability made fun-damentalism attractive, both as a political and a religious creed. "People are ready for someone to come in with absolute answers," Hinson said. "It's being done with great effectiveness by television personalities like Mr. Falwell."

Baptists were not as uniform in their beliefs about either religion or politics as some thought in the wake of the Moral Majority's success at the polls. "We are not as monolithic as some think we are," said the Reverend Welton Gaddy, pastor of the Broadway Baptist Church in Fort Worth. "We are incredibly diverse." The recent reelection of Rev. Cecil Sherman as president of the North Carolina State Convention of Southern Baptists, after saying in his convention address that he could not accept the concept of an inerrant Bible, further illustrated the divergence among Baptists about this central theological issue. The issue of biblical inerrancy had no necessary connection with the Moral Majority's political agenda, but the overlap was obvious to all. And with its loose ecclesiological structure and lack of a central authoritative voice, the Baptist religion was unable to bridge any of the gaps that had opened up between liberal and conservative Baptists. "At present no single leader or agency has the respect, magnetism or platform to summon all divergent elements to a conference," Carl F. H. Henry, a renowned evangelical theologian, wrote in the magazine *The Christian Century*.[50]

If a person's views on biblical inerrancy served as a kind of template for determining their opinions on a host of other religious issues, abortion served a similar function in the political realm. Someone who supported abortion rights would, more often than not, hold a variety of more liberal views on any given "social issue." Someone who opposed abortion rights was likely also to be concerned about the teaching of sex education in the schools, cultural acceptance of homosexuality, and the proliferation of pornography. And abortion was about to take center stage in the national political debate. On June 18, 1981, the White House announced the retirement of Supreme Court justice Potter Stewart.

We have seen how the issue of abortion helped galvanize Falwell and others into political involvement. His horror and that of other fundamentalists at what they understood to be the murder of innocent babies was genuine, and Falwell's inability to appreciate those who argued for a woman's right to control her own body was complete. There was no greater example of sexual libertinism gone astray than the claim that a woman had a right to abortion. If Falwell did not share the Catholic view that human sexuality must always be open to conception, he certainly shared the view that, once conceived, a child was present, a child of God entitled to the same rights as other human beings.

The abortion issue was also central to conservative disgust with the American judiciary. The Supreme Court had dismantled segregation with its *Brown v. Board of Education* ruling, and while Falwell would come to view segregation as wrong, he never embraced the high court's right to decide the issue. Then, when the Supreme Court ruled that prayer in the public schools violated the Constitution, Falwell and other fundamentalists were even angrier. For them, the Constitution, far from proscribing prayer in the public schools, actually guaranteed their right to such prayer. Falwell could not understand how a normal practice of everyday life could be seen as opposed to the Constitution as he understood it. He may not have been a constitutional scholar, but he could recognize what he believed to be judicial usurpation of standard democratic practices: the Supreme Court, tainted by the secular humanism of the elite schools that produced most of its members, was exceeding its authority and trampling on the rights of Christians.

Roe v. Wade was the last straw. Falwell had not been involved in the pre-1973 struggles to preserve restrictive abortion laws. There is no record of him ever commenting on attempts by others to liberalize abortion laws, and there were no such attempts in Virginia. Then, at one stroke, the Supreme Court of the United States wiped away all of the state laws that limited or prohibited abortions. It was, for conservatives, a violation of states' rights as well as a violation of human rights, a gross usurpation of authority by unelected justices. The "liberal Supreme Court" became synonymous with all that was wrong with the direction in which the country had been headed before Reagan's election, despite the fact that most of the justices had been appointed by Republican presidents. Now Reagan had a chance to reverse that direction. This was why evangelicals had rallied to his candidacy. Now they had the chance to replace a justice who had concurred in *Roe* with a justice who would vote to overturn it.

Reagan had pledged during the campaign that he would appoint a woman to "one of the first openings" he had on the high court, and he let his advisers know that he wanted his first choice to be a woman. The four finalists presented to the president were all women, and of these, Arizona's Sandra Day O'Connor was at the top of the list. She would be the only candidate Reagan himself interviewed. She had the support not only of her own political mentor, Sen. Barry Goldwater, but of Reagan's best friend in the Senate, Sen. Paul Laxalt of Nevada, as well as the backing of Reagan's Attorney General William French Smith. She also enjoyed the endorsement of a fellow Stanford Law School alumnus, associate justice William Rehnquist. When Reagan met O'Connor, he liked her immediately and was quickly convinced that she was a genuine conservative, dedicated to the proposition of judicial restraint and deference to the political branches, even if it meant violating another conservative principle, *stare decisis,* the belief that prior decisions of the Supreme Court should not be lightly overturned. She was not a rabid ideologue and would probably be easily confirmed. And she was only fifty-one years old, guaranteeing a long tenure on the court. For Reagan, this most significant choice turned out to be a very easy one: O'Connor would not only be the first woman on the high court, assuring him a big historical footnote, but she could be counted on to bring a genuine conservative philosophy to the bench. On July 7, 1981, Reagan announced his nomination of O'Connor.[51]

Word of the appointment had leaked beforehand, and pro-life groups raised their concerns. President Reagan stepped in to quell the groundswell of opposition. He telephoned Falwell personally one hour before the public announcement was made. The president told Falwell repeatedly what he had said publicly—that he was satisfied with O'Connor's conservatism and with her position on abortion. He repeated the request that he had made of Falwell at the GOP convention in Detroit regarding the selection of George Bush as his running mate: "You've got to trust me, Jerry." Falwell responded as he had in Detroit. He could not bring himself to doubt his political ally and the president of the United States. He withdrew his opposition to O'Connor with the caveat that if O'Connor gave evidence that she was not "satisfactory" on abortion, either during the confirmation hearings or subsequently, he would remove his support.[52]

When Reagan announced the choice at a White House press conference, he mostly deflected questions about O'Connor's stance on abortion, saying that the attorney general would answer specific questions. Reagan did say he was "completely satisfied with her." The White House reiterated that there had been no "litmus test" on the abortion issue. In a press conference after the announcement, White House spokesman Larry Speakes said that during her July 1 interview at the White House, O'Connor had told President Reagan that "she is personally opposed to abortion and that it was especially abhorrent to her." Speakes also said that O'Connor "feels the subject of abortion is a legitimate subject for the legislative area." Speakes and other White House aides had been fielding calls from religious conservatives all weekend, after news that O'Connor was a leading candidate leaked to the press, so they knew they had to address the issue head on.[53]

Either the wires got crossed, however, or it was too late to retract the statement that Falwell had already prepared for the press. In the next morning's papers, Falwell and other pro-life groups sounded livid. "Either the president did not have sufficient information about Judge O'Connor's background in social issues or he chose to ignore that information," Falwell said in a statement released by the Moral Majority the day the appointment was made official. "Judge O'Connor also has been active in feminist causes and is a supporter of the Equal Rights Amendment, which Moral Majority believes would be a disaster for men and women and would further undermine the traditional family." It did not help calm Falwell to learn that the president of the National Organization for Women (NOW), Eleanor Smeal, announced her immediate support for O'Connor and called the nomination "a major victory for women's rights."[54]

At issue were votes that O'Connor had taken when she served in the Arizona state Senate. In one case she opposed an amendment to a bill authorizing a bond issue for a football stadium at the University of Arizona. The amendment would have prevented the hospital at the university from performing abortions. She also reportedly voted against a resolution calling on the U.S. Congress to pass a Human Life Amendment, and she sponsored a bill that allowed family planning clinics to distribute information about birth control without parental consent. These votes were heretical in the eyes of the pro-life community, and they were not offset by O'Connor's support for a bill that allowed doctors and nurses the right to refuse to participate in the performing of abortions.[55]

Others in the pro-life community were as withering in their criticisms of O'Connor—and Reagan—as Falwell had been in the statement he issued before he got the call from Reagan. "We feel betrayed by the President," Paul Brown of the Life Amendment Political Action Committee told the *New York Times*. "We've been sold out." The National Right-to-Life Committee pledged its efforts to defeat the nomination, even if it recognized that such an outcome was unlikely. "I'm not sure we'll defeat her," said the group's executive director, Peter Gemma, "but we want to send the President a clear signal at how much of an insult this is."[56]

The White House talking points on the issue did not help. The White House staff worried about any perception that there was a "litmus test" being applied to judicial nominations, even though the Republican Party platform had explicitly called for the nomination of only pro-life jurists. Falwell and his supporters absolutely did see abortion as a litmus test. To them, if someone could be wrong on something so obvious to them, and so foundational not only to their moral compass but to their views of the rights enshrined in the nation's founding documents, then it was impossible for that person to be a good judge.

Larry Speakes's reference to O'Connor's being "personally opposed to abortion" also did nothing to reassure conservative pro-lifers. That was language used by a host of Democratic Party office-holders, mostly Catholics, to justify their flip-flops on the abortion issue in the 1970s. Senators Edward Kennedy and Edmund Muskie and Gov. Mario Cuomo of New York, all prominent Catholic Democrats, repeated the mantra that they were personally opposed to abortion but did not want to force their views on others. To Falwell, personal opposition was not enough. He wanted legislators to legislate—and judges to decide cases—against abortion, which he thought was simply murder. No one, he would say, is "personally opposed" to murder but reluctant to force that view on others.[57]

In the exchange between the president and the preacher, the cards were stacked against the preacher. What to say to Reagan? That he had been duped? That he had willfully ignored the concerns of his most loyal supporters? That he was making the same mistake he had made in 1967 when he signed California's liberal abortion law? That the president of the United States had, intentionally or not, become complicit in what Falwell called "the biological holocaust" of abortion? Any of these questions would have ended their relationship when Falwell hung up the phone. The stakes were higher, as both men knew. A vice president might, if some misfortune occurred, rise to the Oval Office, and the job was a leg up in the eventual election that would pick Reagan's successor. But a Supreme Court position was for life. If O'Connor ended up valuing the conservative legal principle of *stare decisis* and voting to uphold *Roe v. Wade* over the conservative legal principle that such issues should be left to state legislatures, there would be nothing that Falwell—or Reagan for that matter—could do about it. The higher stakes, however, did not alter the fact that Reagan had all the chips.

Despite Falwell's decision not to actively oppose the nomination at this stage, other pro-life voices remained critical, and this conservative opposition to the O'Connor nomination earned a rebuke from one of their heroes. Sen. Barry Goldwater took to the Senate floor to deliver a speech calling on opponents to "back off" and labeling objections to O'Connor "a lot of foolish claptrap." Goldwater urged people to withhold judgment until after the confirmation hearings, a stance also taken by Falwell's close ally Sen. Jesse Helms. Falwell concurred, telling a reporter, "I still want to listen carefully to the [Senate confirmation] hearings. . . . If she is not committed to the same principles as the President, I hope that will come out and the Senate will respond accordingly."[58]

Falwell's acquiescence in the nomination did not prevent him from becoming the face of the opposition. He had succeeded so well in creating the aura of leadership within the religious right that he was seen as responsible for the statements of all of its members. Sen. Robert Packwood noted "a growing spirit of intolerance" that was "fueled by the Moral Majority." At a press conference, Senator Goldwater was blunter, saying, "Every good American ought to kick Jerry Falwell in the ass." As the confirmation vote neared, Goldwater again denounced those he thought were trying to "impose their views on him." Goldwater said he was "sick and tired of political preachers . . . telling me . . . that if I want to be a moral person, I must believe in A, B or C." He added that no nominee should be judged on only one issue, repeating the White House's opposition to a litmus test, a position that did nothing to convince pro-life groups that did view abortion as a deal-breaker.[59]

The press—and not just the elite press—was quick to join in the ass-kicking. "Most Americans are horrified by the events in Iran, where the revolution has attempted to put the state under the dictates of religious leaders," opined the editors of the *Grand Forks* (North Dakota) *Herald*. "Those same Americans apparently see little irony in the fact that very much the same thing is being attempted in this country by those who dub themselves the Moral Majority." The *News* in Greensboro, North Carolina, in an editorial entitled "Pope Falwell," worried that the line between church and state was getting blurred in the O'Connor nomination fight. And the *Hartford Courant* editorialized that the Moral Majority was too greedy in its quest for power: "Suffice it to say, adherents of the Moral Majority, the Conservative Caucus and other right-wing groups have been well served by the Reagan administration. To them however, one divergence is one too many. Their appetites have been whetted and they expect more and more from the White House."[60]

Falwell took these criticisms in stride, although the blast from Goldwater struck a nerve. He told the *New York Times,* "It appears that time has passed by Senator Goldwater." He suggested that Goldwater begin writing his memoirs rather than "kicking his friends in the posterior." It was ironic that the most prominent religious right leader who did not oppose the nomination of O'Connor nonetheless got tagged for leading the opposition mounted by many of his usual allies, using arguments he had first brought into the public square. In the end O'Connor was confirmed on a vote of 99–0. Falwell had correctly judged the way the winds were blowing, but he could not fail to see that those winds were increasingly chilly toward himself.

Less than a year had passed between the time when candidate Ronald Reagan came to Lynchburg to address the religious broadcasters and Falwell's students at Liberty Baptist College and the vote on the O'Connor nomination. In that time Falwell had emerged as the preeminent leader of the religious right. He was the man the television producers called for a quote or an interview. He was the man the president called to inform of his intent to nominate O'Connor. He was the man Senator Goldwater urged "every good American" to kick in the ass. Falwell's influence rested partly on his own gifts and partly on the army of evangelicals he represented. He needed to be mindful of the needs of his constituency, but he had also proven himself remarkably savvy about the political needs of the president he loved. He understood the need for the administration to lead with its economic agenda. He understood, even if he did not approve of, the need to appoint someone to the Supreme Court whose political philosophy was not so radical as to cause a major fight in Congress. Falwell was learning the ways of the world, even mastering the ways of the world, and he would spend the next several years wrestling with those ways.

Chapter Nine

The Moral Majority Matures

The separation of church and state is a cardinal principle of the U.S. Constitution, and despite the protestations to the contrary, Falwell's rise to political prominence did not seriously threaten that principle. The term "separation" suggests, however, that the founders anticipated a division between the secular realm and the divine, and indeed, ever since their time Americans have argued about where to draw that line. The relevant societal actors in the rise of a politically conservative, religiously motivated group of voters were not "church" and "state" but "religion" and "politics," and these two categories overlapped despite their many differences.

Furthermore, the Constitution is silent on where to draw the line between religion and the culture. As the 1980s progressed and Falwell grew accustomed to the possibilities and the limits of politics as he entered into discussions of issues that did not fit the usual paradigm of "moral concerns," increasingly culture would join politics as the venue for religious conservative activity. Sometimes Falwell brought religion into the culture and other times he fought against dominant cultural memes, but in all cases the image—and self-image—of Christianity in America was changed.

The separation of church and state is ordained by the First Amendment to the Constitution. "Congress shall make no law respecting an establishment of religion, or prohibiting the free exercise thereof," states the hallowed text. The Founders were well acquainted with "established" churches because most of the colonies and many of the states still had them when the Constitution was drafted. An established church received revenue from the government, and in some instances voting rights were restricted to those who belonged to the established church. In turn, the government tended to exercise varying degrees of authority regarding the appointment of clerics. After the First Amendment was adopted in 1791, some states continued to have established churches because the Bill of Rights applied only to the federal government until the passage of the Fourteenth Amendment.

Falwell certainly had no ambitions to establish a national or state church. His was an independent Baptist church, and he would not even join the Southern Baptist Convention, the largest Baptist organization in the country, because such associations were seen to threaten the independence of believers and congregations. Nor did he restrict his political support to born-again Christians: Sen. Jeremiah Denton, a Roman Catholic, was one of Falwell's favorite senators. And while Falwell thought children should be allowed to pray in schools, he thought the prayer needed to be voluntary; he did not want the government writing the prayers. To the extent that there were "church-state" issues for Falwell, it was his belief that the government was improperly encroaching on the rights of religion, in violation of the "free exercise" clause of the First Amendment, by trying to deny tax-exempt status to certain religious schools, forcing legal abortion on an unwilling populace, and allowing pornography and sex education to be available to children. As we saw in his "Christian Bill of Rights," Falwell did not have a highly developed familiarity with American jurisprudence. He read the First Amendment his way, and in his view the courts, for decades, had been reading something else.

The issues, then, were not church-state issues but religion-politics issues. Falwell believed that the government was improperly intervening in church and society, and it was this belief that had galvanized him and others to enter the political realm in the first place. But that belief was of a limited nature and provided insufficient grounds for full-scale political involvement. It was the moral climate of the nation, and religion's unique and historical role in shaping the moral values of the nation, that provided Falwell with the warrant for his more comprehensive political involvement. "Moral" issues such as abortion and family life resided clearly at the intersection of religious and political concerns.

Once he was knee-deep in politics, two things became apparent. First, he would be called on to support political positions that bore little relation to traditional Baptist moral concerns. Falwell's new political allies had other issues on their agendas besides the "moral" issues at the heart of the religious right's appeal to traditionally minded voters. Falwell would find himself embroiled in discussions of nuclear weapons and foreign policy as well as abortion as the 1980s unfolded. These positions would expand the reach of the Moral Majority but would also land the organization, and its leader, in unfamiliar territory.

Second, it became obvious that even the more expansive categories of "religion" and "politics" were insufficient to express the range of his concerns. Falwell began to realize that politics mattered, but it was not the only thing that mattered. Politics was a part of a society, and it was responsive to cultural norms, and the society often was being shaped by forces inimical to Falwell's views. Categories like "religious" or "moral" or "political" were porous, it turned out. An issue like confronting pornography involved moral norms, societal values, local, state, and federal legal frameworks, campaign pledges, religious organizations, and First Amendment zealots, to be sure. Falwell could try to influence the political climate to limit the spread of pornography, but pornography was also an industry, with vested interests, and he would take them on too. It wasn't easy to draw a neat line between politics, morality, and religion on such issues that touched many aspects of the society and its norms.

If it was clear that the political had to include the cultural, it also became clear that at some point the religious had to become theological. If few issues were properly seen as church-state issues and more properly considered as religious-societal, at an even deeper level Falwell's political activity raised concerns best characterized as belonging to the category of "faith-culture" issues. For all of his insistence that the Moral Majority was not a denominational or even Christian organization, at the end of the day Falwell's various stances required some measure of biblical warrant. He could not leave his fundamentalism aside, even if he wanted to. His approach to political issues continually betrayed a cast of mind that was steeped in the certainties of biblical fundamentalism, and in turn his politics came to alter the face of fundamentalism. His public image began to shape the self-image of evangelical Christians and the image that all Americans had of Christianity.

As had become habitual since he launched the Moral Majority, Falwell found his agenda crafted as often as not by his political and cultural opponents. Thus, he found himself in a battle of words with men like Yale president A. Bartlett Giamatti and Georgetown president Father Timothy Healy, SJ, over the proper place of religion in the culture and in the academy. Falwell found Moral Majority chapters pushing the legal envelope against previously uncontroversial sections of the law that governed religious organizations. Not all his encounters with the culture beyond Lynchburg were hostile: when the Moral Majority mistakenly sent a membership card to liberal champion Sen. Ted Kennedy, Falwell invited the senator to come to Lynchburg and address the students at his college. Kennedy came to dinner before the speech, and a lifelong friendship between the two political adversaries was born.

Despite the occasional bonhomie, in all of his conflicts—and Falwell's career was more marked by conflict than not—it became apparent that he was not challenging this policy or that. At issue were not just opposing points of view but often wildly different notions about the proper scope of the law, the central role of the family in society, the nature of patriotism, what constitutes an education, and so on. The fundamentalist was challenging the fundamentals of American culture. Falwell had set out to return American politics to the traditional moral vision he believed it had lost. In fact, he was igniting a culture war.

Falwell had shared in the bipartisan anticommunism that marked American politics through the 1960s. Although he and his conservative friends were loath to admit it, the American left had been as decidedly anticommunist as the American right. For example, organized labor in America, unlike its European counterpart, was exceedingly hostile to communism, in part because of the close alliance between the Catholic Church and the unions. Democrats like President Harry Truman had reached a consensus with Republicans like Sen. Arthur Vandenberg to craft a genuinely bipartisan foreign policy aimed at containing the Soviet Union. Only during the latter stages of the Vietnam War did the foreign policy consensus fall apart, with Democrats increasingly suspicious of anything that reeked of militarism and Republicans preferring a more robust American military.

President Reagan ran on a platform of rebuilding the American military and taking a more confrontational approach to the Soviet Union. Like Falwell, Reagan was willing to condemn communism in explicitly moral terms, and both men liked to use specific quotes from Marx or Lenin that were antithetical to American sensibilities. Falwell opened his chapter on "The Threat of Communism" in his book *Listen, America* with a quote from Lenin: "As long as capitalism and socialism exist, we cannot live in peace; in the end one or the other will triumph. A funeral dirge will be sung over either the Soviet Republics or over world-capitalism." Similarly, in his first press conference in the White House, Reagan had said that the Soviet leadership, both past and current, had reiterated "their determination that their goal must be the promotion of world revolution and a one-world Socialist or Communist state, whichever word you want to use." For Reagan and Falwell, the enemy was hiding in plain sight and only a fool would not take the Soviets at their word.[1]

Such general and shared abhorrence of communism was unremarkable, but once Reagan took office and decided on specific policies to confront communism, his ally Jerry Falwell backed him to the hilt. This led Falwell into discussions and debates on specifics for which there were no clear biblical citations. It was one thing to oppose communism generally, but it was something else to believe that Americans had a moral obligation to support the deployment of an MX missile or take sides in the civil wars raging in Central

America. Reagan, of course, had to endorse specific policies: that was his job. Falwell had a more difficult time: by casting himself as a defender of virtually every decision made by the Reagan administration, he found himself on unfamiliar terrain, making often superficial statements on subjects of enormous gravity.

The Reagan administration embarked on a series of ambitious military measures, from increasing and updating naval forces to deploying MX missiles—highly accurate land-based missiles that would greatly increase America's first-strike capability—to deploying medium-range missiles in Europe. Both the MX and medium-range missiles in Europe had been proposed during the Carter administration, but deployments had been delayed. There were debates within the Reagan White House about how the deployments fit in with the administration's negotiating strategies with the Soviet Union, but one thing was clear: the U.S. military was being turned into a more effective fighting force.[2]

This increase in military expenditures and readiness produced a counterreaction among those who believed that the Soviet Union's revolutionary fervor had dissipated and who saw Reagan's militarism as part of an unpredictable "cowboy" mentality that they considered a threat to world peace. Protests against the deployment of missiles erupted in Europe, where citizens feared that the new missiles would make their nations a target in any U.S.-Soviet nuclear exchange. The "nuclear freeze" movement, calling on both sides to suspend the further development and deployment of nuclear missiles, gained ground both in America and abroad.[3]

Falwell supported Reagan on all of his foreign policy initiatives, but he was especially outspoken on the subject of the nuclear freeze. He decided to embark on an eighteen-month nationwide campaign to support the president; directly echoing Reagan's language, he called it his "Peace Through Strength" campaign. Falwell told a meeting of the Baptist Bible Fellowship in Little Rock that most of those active in the peace movement were "good people with good intentions, but they've been duped," and that the movement was "spawned in Moscow." On the *Old-Time Gospel Hour,* Falwell again claimed that Moscow was behind the nuclear freeze movement. "I look at the nuclear freeze today," Falwell told his congregation. "In the Kremlin, Andropov or somebody decides that we need 300,000 to march in Stockholm or Berlin or New York, and the robots stand up and start marching for nuclear freeze." At a press conference in New Hampshire before giving an address at Dartmouth College, Falwell said that he had met with President Reagan to discuss the nuclear freeze and that the president agreed with him that a nuclear freeze was premature and should only be contemplated "once we reach parity with the Soviet Union." In short, Falwell thoroughly parroted the administration line. The White House did not want to seem too bellicose, so administration officials were suggesting that the United States already lagged behind the Soviet Union in nuclear weapons. And while not wanting to impugn the motives of the peace movement, they wanted nonetheless to tar it with the charge that it was doing the Kremlin's bidding, however unwittingly.[4]

In Savannah, Georgia, Falwell was invited to preach at the Bible Baptist Church, where his college classmate Rev. Cecil Hodges was pastor. After assuring the crowd that America was returning to the values that made it great, he urged that the United States continue to arm itself because the Soviets had not changed their intention of dominating the world. At a rally in Cincinnati, Falwell placed a Bible on top of a Soviet flag "to make clear his conviction that regardless of Yuri Andropov's plans for America God's sovereign plan will ultimately triumph." Against those who argued that he was spending too much time on defense issues at the expense of more traditional moral concerns, Falwell countered that he had never stopped preaching against abortion and pornography, but that "unless America survives as a free nation, all other issues will become historically moot."[5]

Falwell had the Moral Majority prepare a glossy booklet on the subject of nuclear weaponry and his support for the administration's policies. "The information in this booklet is based on briefing materials supplied by Reagan Administration staff members to Dr. Jerry Falwell at a White House briefing on March 22, 1983." Falwell had indeed gone to the White House and received a briefing from the national security staff on nonclassified information. The booklet was filled with charts and articles that sought to demonstrate how far advanced Soviet weaponry was compared to the U.S. arsenal. Again, Falwell attacked the peace movement: "If we don't succeed in winning the hearts and minds of ordinary Americans on this issue, then the propaganda of the 'freez-niks' and the 'better red than dead' crowd will soon come to dominate public thought," the booklet warned. "Once this happens the Soviets will take our freedom from us—it's that simple and that final!" The last page included a pledge card so that those receiving the booklet could contribute to the Moral Majority.[6]

In one interview, Falwell got himself into a kerfuffle with a Lutheran minister. Appearing on the television show *Morning Break,* the minister asked Falwell a question in which he suggested that President Reagan was a liar. Falwell blew up. "I am appalled that a minister of the Gospel would show disrespect for the President of the United States by calling him a liar," Falwell proclaimed. "I am appalled at the disrespect you would show to the leadership when you, as a minister, are told, by the Bible you teach and preach, to respect and honor the King and to obey the powers that be because they are ordained of God." The studio audience asked the obvious question: "Is Reagan a king?" Falwell replied that kings in the Old Testament were analogous to presidents in our time. Months later, on another television show, Falwell denied saying any such thing and promised to pay $100 to anyone who could prove that he had said it. Anthony Podesta, head of People For the American Way, produced the tape, but there is no record of Falwell paying up. Television host Maury Povich said that he had witnessed the wager.[7]

Falwell also let his verbosity get the best of him when he launched a broadside against Canadian prime minister Pierre Elliott Trudeau from the pulpit of his church. Falwell labeled Trudeau a "socialist" and spelled out the implications of that fact for his congregants. "If Moscow and [Cuban leader Fidel] Castro are successful in their campaign of world conquest and in what they're doing in Central America," Falwell said, "it's very clear that Canada is their next effort. And I have serious reservations as to whether Prime Minister Trudeau's loyalties to the U.S. are great enough to resist that kind of pressure." This outburst earned an understated rebuke from the prime minister's press secretary, who said, "[Trudeau] is not a communist, he's not a socialist and he's a friend of the United States." She termed Falwell's remarks "regrettable." The episode was innocuous enough, but it demonstrated to all that Falwell's penchant for shooting from the hip could be a liability.[8]

In an interview with *USA Today*, Falwell tried to modulate the ferocity of his pitch for more nuclear weapons deployments. He said he agreed with Reagan that eventually America should freeze its nuclear weapons deployment, as well as with Billy Graham, who equivocated on the merits of SALT II but said that the world needed a SALT 10 that would eliminate nuclear weapons from the face of the earth. But Falwell was insistent that the time was not yet ripe for such peaceful overtures. "Right now we have the Soviet Union participating in massive expansionism," Falwell said. "We have China to watch. We have a world where at least six, maybe eight, nations have the bomb. We must remain strong enough to deter hostile aggressors from robbing us of our freedoms." He called Reagan a "peacemaker" and warned that the issue was about "slavery for our children" if America did not have sufficient weapons to prevent the Soviets from achieving their goal of world conquest.[9]

In the fall of 1983, ABC prepared a docudrama about the effects of a nuclear explosion in the event of a nuclear exchange between the United States and the Soviet Union. The program portrayed, in full gruesome and graphic detail, what would happen if nuclear weapons hit missile silos near Lawrence, Kansas, and nearby Kansas City. Although Falwell acknowledged that the program was well done ("I was moved—no one can watch flesh peeling off human beings, millions of people destroyed, if they're human, without being wiped out themselves," he admitted), he accused the network of creating a "one-sided film" and announced his intention to ask for equal time under the Federal Communications Fairness Doctrine, which guaranteed equal time for divergent points of view. Falwell also indicated that he would be carefully monitoring which companies sponsored a program that "defames the President's Peace Through Strength Initiative." Few people in America grasped the power of television as well as Falwell did.[10]

Falwell's voice was not the only, or even the most influential, religious voice on the subject of nuclear weapons. In 1981 the Roman Catholic bishops began writing a pastoral letter on the nuclear arms race. The drafting committee met with scholars and experts of all stripes, as well as with moral theologians. They held public meetings around the country where ordinary Catholics could voice their opinions. The first two drafts of the text were released to the public, and another round of public hearings and consultations were conducted to improve the document. Finally, on May 3, 1983, the National Conference of Catholic Bishops adopted and promulgated *The Challenge of Peace: God's Promise and Our Response*. The final vote on the document was 238–9.

The document deeply reflected the Catholic moral tradition's dominant approach to issues of war and peace, known as just war theory. This theory, developed over sixteen centuries, beginning with Saint Augustine, states that in the conduct of nations there must be a presumption against the use of violence and that any recourse to violence must be proportionate to the evil it seeks to defeat. The bishops therefore condemned any "first use" of nuclear weapons in the belief that there could be no achievable good commensurate with risking the destruction of the planet. Just war theory also insists that noncombatants never be targeted, and so the bishops opposed any targeting strategy aimed at civilian populations. They also proscribed the deployment of tactical (small battlefield) nuclear weapons, believing that such weapons were more likely to be used.[11]

The bishops understood the partisan implications of their document. In a major address at Fordham University, Cardinal Joseph Bernardin of Chicago called for a "consistent life ethic" and invoked the metaphor of Jesus's seamless garment to describe the Church's approach to life issues. To Bernardin, no one who ignored the threat of nuclear war or supported capital punishment could claim the pro-life mantle, just as it made no sense to object to the death penalty on humanitarian grounds and also be indifferent to the fate of the unborn. Bernardin wanted both political parties to understand that they had no monopoly on the Gospel and that their respective positions both fell short of what the Church thought was an appropriate defense of human life.

Falwell was trying to reach out to Roman Catholics, who made up a substantial part of the Moral Majority's membership, so he had to be careful in criticizing the bishops. He contrasted their stance with the apparently more vigorous anticommunism of Pope John Paul II. "The Catholic bishops are very sincere men who want peace but, unlike the pontiff, approach the problem from a naive standpoint," he said during an address in Palm Beach, Florida. This was an even more dangerous tack, although Falwell did not see it as such. Bishops are understandably loath to acknowledge that there is a difference of opinion between them and the pope. Falwell also was quick to point out the double standard reflected in media coverage of his position and that of the bishops. "If a liberal clergyman gets involved, that's pluralism, that's investment and involvement in the electoral process," Falwell told an interviewer. "If a conservative minister gets involved, that's violating the separation of church and state." Falwell was partly right in noting the different media coverage of his stance compared with how they covered the bishops. The press praised the bishops for their consultations, the openness of the drafting process, and the reasonableness of their conclusions. The media did not hurl epithets at the bishops for getting involved in the political process.[12]

The differences between the bishops' pastoral letter and Falwell's eighteen-month-long "Peace Through Strength" campaign, however, were profound, and the two interventions were received differently not only because the bishops had consulted widely or because they ended up at opposite conclusions. The bishops had begun with traditional moral teachings and sought to apply them to current political realities. Falwell began with a White House briefing and then sought to find religious justifications for his stance. The bishops, who could scarcely be considered liberals, had not tried to "baptize" anyone else's political platform but had adhered to the centuries-long tradition of following just war theory where it led them.

Most important, however, the bishops' document specifically stated that while the bishops exercised a high degree of moral certainty at the level of moral principle, as their discussion moved to specific policies that reflected those principles the degree of moral certainty diminished. This point is key. Prudential judgment cannot be used to dodge moral calculi. Indeed, prudence is a moral principle itself. Prudential judgments must flow from moral principles and never contradict them, but there is room for disagreement at the practical level about how the moral principles upon which all agree should be enfleshed. Such distinctions were lost on Falwell, who jumped from his own intuition to an ontological claim in the twinkling of an eye. For him, the Soviets were evil and America was seized with a providential mission and purpose, so there was little need to examine the means and methods employed by the United States in its struggle with godless communism so long as they were effective.

In 1979 the Sandinista National Liberation Front, a Soviet-backed guerrilla group in Nicaragua, overthrew the corrupt Somoza regime and took control of the Central American nation. After immediately receiving material and political support from both the Soviet Union and Cuba, the Sandinistas, in turn, extended support to Marxist guerilla groups in neighboring El Salvador. Just so, they also became the object of fear among American conservatives, like Falwell, who were worried about the expansionism of communism. Falwell would throw his vocal support behind President Reagan's efforts to support the Nicaraguan opposition to the Sandinistas, known as the "contras," and this stance would again bring him into conflict with American Catholic leaders.

Falwell decided to make a fact-finding tour of El Salvador with a view to producing twin television documentaries on communist expansionism in Central America, one by the Moral Majority on the politics of the situation and one for the *Old-Time Gospel Hour* on the humanitarian crisis in the Central American country. "There is nobody on the conservative side," said his aide Cal Thomas, explaining Falwell's decision to make the trip, "who has [Falwell's] media access." Falwell asked for and received permission from the Reagan administration to make the trip.[13]

The trip to El Salvador took place in September 1983. Although Falwell spent only seven and a half hours on the ground, he came away convinced that the United States needed to do more for the government there. "I think they are fighting for their freedom and our freedom," he told his Wednesday night congregation at Thomas Road Baptist Church upon his return. He called the Sandinista leaders in Nicaragua "terrorists and killers" who were "the puppets of Fidel Castro, who is a surrogate of [Soviet president Yuri] Andropov." Falwell called for a massive lobbying campaign to urge Congress to support increased military aid to El Salvador and continued covert aid to the contras, stopping short of any suggestion that U.S. forces be used. He believed that the Salvadorean army was "capable" but that the United States needed to give it the tools to win.[14]

Falwell also told his congregation about the refugee crisis in El Salvador. He visited one of the eighty-nine refugee camps that were handling the 290,000 Salvadorans dislocated by the civil war. He warned that the ongoing conflict would lead to increased immigration to the United States, saying, "I can see millions of feet people crossing our borders," unless the insurgency was defeated. And he invoked the domino theory of communist expansion, arguing that if El Salvador was allowed to fall as Nicaragua had already fallen, the contagion of Marxism would spread throughout the hemisphere.[15]

The U.S. invasion of Grenada on October 25, 1983, earned high praise from Falwell. The small island country in the Caribbean had been ruled by a leftist government since 1979, but a revolutionary Marxist regime, led by Maurice Bishop, seized power in 1983. The army intervened, deposing and murdering Bishop, and the U.S. Marines landed to restore order and prevent Bishop's followers from mounting a counterattack. "Grenada rebuilt the image of America and its resolve to stop Soviet-Cuban expansionism in this hemisphere," he told an interviewer.[16]

In his support for the repressive regime in El Salvador and the contras in Nicaragua, Falwell again found himself on the opposite side of an issue from the Catholic Church. But unlike the more theoretical arguments about nuclear weaponry, the situation in El Salvador was anything but theoretical for the Catholic bishops, in both the United States and Latin America.

In 1980 El Salvador's Archbishop Oscar Romero was shot dead while celebrating Mass at a church in the capital. His assassination was the work of a paramilitary death squad operating under orders from the government, which also disrupted Romero's funeral, killing more than 30 people among the 250,000 who came to pay their respects. Later that year three nuns from the United States who had come to work with peasants affected by the civil war in El Salvador were also murdered, along with a laywoman. Two of the nuns had been sent by Cleveland's Bishop James Hickey, who had been promoted to the archbishopric of Washington, D.C., by the time of their murder. Hickey, a mild-mannered and soft-spoken man, became a vocal opponent of aid to the El Salvadoran regime and kept photos of the nuns on the wall of his private chapel for the rest of his life.

The Latin American bishops had a long history of denouncing the right-wing military regimes that had seized power in the 1970s and that advocated a doctrine of the national security state that was grossly at odds with traditional church teaching. "The ideology of national security placed above personal security is spreading throughout the Latin American continent, as has happened in the Soviet countries," the Brazilian bishops stated in a document issued in 1977, invoking an analogy to communist methods that was sure to anger those who claimed to be fighting communism. "This doctrine leads regimes to rule by force to incur the characteristics and practices of the communist regimes—the abuse of power by the state, arbitrary imprisonment, torture and suppression of freedom of thought." The bishops of other Latin American countries issued similar denunciations of the national security state.[17]

The appeals of the U.S. Catholic bishops fell on deaf ears, both with Falwell and, more important, with the Reagan administration. When Congress cut off aid to the contras in 1982 and reaffirmed the ban on aid two years later, members of Reagan's staff concocted an elaborate scheme—subsequently known as the "Iran-Contra Affair"—in which they sold arms to Iran in exchange for that country's assistance in gaining the release of American hostages held in

Lebanon. The proceeds from the sale of the arms were diverted to the contras. Col. Oliver North, a Marine serving on the National Security Council, was the principal actor in the clandestine arrangement. The scandal that ensued when this circumvention of the law came to light would give Reagan a black eye during his second term, but as we shall see, Falwell would consider North a hero even when his misdeeds were exposed.

Falwell had shown himself to be a loyal soldier in the Reagan revolution, both in pulling back from his frontal assault on the O'Connor nomination and in supporting the administration's military and foreign policies. "I think the Moral Majority moved from a prophetic role into more of an adviser role and lost some of its ability to speak against the administration," Dobson would say of this period in the organization's history. The Moral Majority, and with it the image of evangelical voters generally, was becoming intertwined thoroughly with the Republican Party.[18]

For Falwell, the excursion into areas where he lacked specific knowledge did not redound to his credit, especially when he also lacked an intellectual framework to use in assessing what knowledge he did have. His forays into foreign affairs appeared amateurish and got him into messes he could have avoided. What was to be gained by tangling with the prime minster of Canada or calling Catholic bishops naive? And whereas the moral aspect of the abortion issue or family-related policies was obvious, Falwell was unable to make the links between his moral beliefs and his commitment to a more aggressive nuclear posture or aid to the contras. He was an expert on Nehemiah, not Nicaragua, and unable to link the one to the other beyond generic invocations of evil communism. For Falwell, communism was evil, to be sure, but the question of how to confront it, asked since the end of World War II, was enormously complicated, and Falwell was not a man for complications. He shot from the hip and as often as not wounded himself as much as his intended targets.

At the same time that Falwell was getting involved in political issues more removed from his usual "moral" issues, his moral concerns led him to engage the society and the culture in new ways. Sometimes there was an overlap with his political agenda, as when his involvement in antipoverty programs served the useful political purpose of justifying the government's cutting back social programs. Other endeavors, such as his efforts to care for pregnant teenagers so that they would not have abortions, demonstrated that Falwell was unwilling to wait for political solutions and sought out more immediate remedies to social and cultural ills. Falwell had risen quickly to the pinnacle of political influence, real or imagined, but he also went hunting in other pastures in his effort to reclaim America for Christ.

In early 1981, Falwell joined forces with a conservative black pastor in Los Angeles, Rev. Edward Hill, to launch an antipoverty effort in fifteen U.S. cities. A member of Moral Majority and a prominent black Republican, Reverend Hill had begun pilot programs in Dallas and Cleveland the year before. The "Foundation for the Poor" program raised money from Dallas Cowboys' owner Clint Murchinson as well as Texas oilman and billionaire Nelson Bunker Hunt. Falwell served on the board of the organization.

The plan had several different components. One program worked with high school dropouts and ex-offenders, helping them to learn job skills and find employment. Another program worked with the judicial system, allowing judges to assign juveniles to structured community service rather than jail. "Operation Lookin' Good" was a community cleanup project that targeted a 110-block section of the Watts neighborhood in Los Angeles, planting one thousand trees and painting some two dozen houses. Speaking in Lynchburg, Falwell said that he wanted his congregation to join him in helping Reverend Hill, because these programs would "meet the legitimate needs of those who are poor." Falwell also took the occasion to contrast this effort with government welfare programs, which, he said, had created "a society of professional bums."[19]

In a joint appearance with Rev. Jesse Jackson on the late-night television news program *Nightline*, Falwell acknowledged that the evangelical churches had not always done enough to care for the poor. He said that their theological aversion to the liberal Social Gospel movement had resulted in evangelical churches throwing "the baby out with the wash. We were so against the social gospel that we did not believe that we should do anything but preach the gospel of Christ." He said that conservative Christian churches were changing, becoming more attentive to the needs of the poor, but that their primary concern would always be preaching "the gospel of Christ." Falwell defended Reagan from the charge of indifference to the poor, noting that the government budget was in the red, a concern that neither Falwell nor Reagan ever raised when the subject was military spending.[20]

Falwell was not just engaged in raising money for other groups and exhorting other congregations. His own Thomas Road Baptist Church ran a "Family Center" in Lynchburg that combined a supermarket and clothing store for needy families. Some of the members of his church tithed their time to the center, dentists and doctors provided free medical assistance to the poor, and plumbers and electricians offered their services. There were even lawyers from the congregation available to help. "We try to fill the gap that government leaves behind," Falwell said. "If there is one person in this town who is without food, it is simply because they haven't come forth, or someone hasn't told us."[21]

Helping young unwed mothers and keeping them from turning to abortion became an important goal of Falwell's in the early 1980s. He credited an exchange with a reporter in an airport for provoking his determination. The reporter had asked, "But what practical alternative do pregnant girls have when they are facing an unwanted pregnancy?" In Falwell's account, the reporter went on to ask what he was doing to help women in this situation; lacking an answer, Falwell said, he had escaped to the safety of his waiting airplane. This encounter led him to start the Liberty Godparent Home, located on Eldon Street in Lynchburg. Falwell entrusted the project to an ex-Marine, narcotics officer, and minister, Jim Savely, who was named director of family life services. The home, which was affiliated with the church, took in young women facing crisis pregnancies and helped them carry their child to term by offering classes at Liberty Academy so that they would not fall behind in school and providing adoption services to those who could not keep their child. Counselors were hired to help women who came from abusive situations, a not-uncommon occurrence. Falwell set up a toll-free phone number that women could call to get help. Within the first year of operation the home had assisted 2,500 women between the ages of fourteen and thirty-seven, according to Savely.[22]

The program was so successful that Falwell decided to take it nationwide, launching his "Save-A-Baby" campaign. He produced a booklet that explained to other congregations how they could go about setting up a crisis pregnancy center and maternity home. The plan called for the active engagement of the pastor but also for volunteer lawyers, doctors, and nurses who could help with legal and medical issues, as well as staff to work in the maternity home and volunteers to answer phones. The booklet warned that a young woman facing a crisis pregnancy had a lot on her mind and should not be further burdened: "REMEMBER: Although it may be tempting, this is not the appropriate time [for] theological or philosophical debate." Thomas Road's Jim Savely gave seminars to pastors on how to start such a ministry at their churches. The program also offered counseling to women who had already procured an abortion and needed healing for psychological or spiritual wounds they had incurred from that experience.[23]

In spite of Falwell's frequent denunciations of gratuitous sex and violence in the movies, he was willing to try to reach out to the film industry. In 1983 Pat Boone, a popular singer and actor who was active in religious organizations, held a dinner for Falwell at the Beverly Hills Hotel. The other guests represented an eclectic cross-section of Hollywood, including comedienne Joan Rivers and her husband Edgar Rosenberg; actors Pat and Dick Van Patten; actress Meredith MacRae, who had starred in the television series *Petticoat Junction; Mary Hartman, Mary Hartman* star Greg Mullavey; and actor Marty Ingels, who came without his more famous wife, actress Shirley Jones. Ingels was trying, unsuccessfully, to arrange a meeting between Falwell and Lear.[24]

Not all of Falwell's interactions with the culture were so benign as dinner at the Beverly Hills Hotel. In October 1981, Falwell learned that the next month's issue of *Penthouse,* a pornographic magazine, was going to feature an interview with him. He had given the interview to two freelance reporters who subsequently sold the article to *Penthouse*. "In my opinion, looking to *Penthouse* magazine for fair and objective reporting on a gospel ministry would be like purchasing your groceries in the middle of the city sanitation system," Falwell said, warning his congregation not to pay the interview any heed.[25]

Falwell had criticized Jimmy Carter in 1976 for granting an interview to *Playboy* magazine, and even though he himself had only spoken with freelancers, that was a distinction that might be lost on his flock and on the general public. He decided to sue, arguing that the magazine was "exploiting me financially and spiritually." The case was not a difficult one. Falwell had made no contract with the freelance journalists, but while he could protest that he did not want "a pornographer ever to make a dollar off Jerry Falwell," the judge correctly noted that there was no actionable claim. "The First Amendment freedoms of speech and press are too precious to be eroded or undermined by the likes and dislikes of persons who invite attention and publicity by their own voluntary actions," the judge declared in his ruling.[26]

The brief trial yielded some strange consequences. Of course, it was a great fund-raising device for both Falwell and *Penthouse*. Indeed, Falwell would later claim that several sinners read the interview and came to know Christ through it. One even made a $2 million donation to Liberty Baptist College. The lawsuit also strengthened his position with his followers—and his reputation with the general public—as someone willing to take on the pornography industry. If he had not challenged *Penthouse*, Falwell said after the trial was concluded, "that would have damaged me irreparably with my own constituency." Even more startling was the fact that, a few years later, when Falwell dueled in the courts with the even more ribald *Hustler* magazine, he would hire the same lawyer, Norman Roy Grutman, who had defended *Penthouse* against his earlier suit. Most important, Falwell learned that recourse to the courts could be used to call attention to his important efforts to fight for a more moral America, even if he lost. Later, when asked about the suit, Falwell told an interviewer, "The framers of that [First] amendment did not have modern day pornography in mind when they wrote it. Pornographers who are literally exploiting little children with child porn and moral garbage are not protected by the First Amendment."[27]

On December 18, 1981, Elizabeth Carr was born at the Norfolk General Hospital in Norfolk, Virginia, the first child born in the United States who had been conceived through means of in vitro fertilization. Falwell was ambivalent about the news, as evidenced by an op-ed he penned for the *Lynchburg News & Daily Advance*. "This entire in-vitro process is a modern technological miracle which allows conception to occur in otherwise hopeless cases," Falwell wrote. "I rejoice with the Carrs and the more than 20 couples worldwide who have received children by this means, but I see some problems connected with the process." He worried about the discarded embryos the process required, noting that he was "against the destruction of human life, no matter how small or insignificant it may appear to some." He also worried that those who were not married might avail themselves of the technology. "What is to prevent a judge from asserting that a lesbian has the 'right' to have an in-vitro daughter placed in her womb?" Falwell asked.

It was rare for Falwell to take to the middle ground on virtually any issue, but he did so here on the subject of in vitro fertilization. He was not endorsing the Catholic Church's opposition to any artificial interference with human procreation, an opposition that went back to 1930 when Pope Pius XI issued a papal encyclical, *Casti Cobnubii,* banning birth control for Catholics, a ban that had been restated by Pope Paul VI in 1968. But Falwell was also nervous about the possibility of technological advances running ahead of the moral framework needed to ensure that the technologies did not serve evil ends. He was the first evangelical to give voice to this fear and to link technological processes involving embryos to his opposition to abortion. Falwell's stance would blossom into a wholesale rejection of embryonic stem cell research on the part of most evangelicals in the last decade of the century. Although that position would be a minority position and would be denounced as "anti-science," for anyone living in the same century as Auschwitz, where science had been perverted to accomplish the most inhumane ends, the concern voiced by Falwell was not an alarmist one.[28]

In addition to his almost nonstop round of interviews, talk show appearances, and speeches and sermons around the country, Falwell initiated three new publicity efforts of his own in the early 1980s. In early 1982 he began penning a daily syndicated column, although the pen was largely wielded by his main speechwriter, Cal Thomas. Falwell said that the columns would be adaptations of his daily *Moral Majority Report* radio commentary and that they would be circulated to newspapers nationwide. On the same day he announced his new column, Falwell videotaped a "Moral State of the Union" message that he planned to air in May. Five thousand people packed his Thomas Road Baptist Church for the taping of the message, and they had to wait for over an hour as the television crew checked the lighting and sound systems before Falwell mounted the pulpit. The finished product included videotaped clips from President Ronald Reagan, First Lady Nancy Reagan, former president Gerald R. Ford, and interviews with Republican senators Jesse Helms and Jeremiah Denton and Rep. Bob Dornan.[29]

In the autumn of 1982, Falwell launched the *Fundamentalist Journal,* a new glossy magazine published by the *Old-Time Gospel Hour.* Falwell was listed as editor, but his assistant, Nelson Keener, was the point man for the project, which involved an initial publication of fifty thousand copies. The magazine was sent to a select list of contributors to either the *Old-Time Gospel Hour* or the Moral Majority. The annual subscription rate was set at $14.95, significantly less than the $21 per year subscription rate for *Christianity Today,* which was the aesthetic if not the editorial model for Falwell's journal.

The inaugural edition was sixty-six pages long and included an article on Jesus's resurrection, an article on the problems with the busing of Sunday school pupils, and a profile of Billy Sunday, the famous early-twentieth-century evangelist, as well as a reprint of a Billy Sunday sermon. Another article examined the issue "Why Christians Should Support Israel." The article on Israel was not listed as an editorial; citing his inexperience in the magazine publishing industry, Keener would acknowledge that it should have been. He promised many such editorial commentaries, saying, "We fundamentalists have been known to be opinionated in the past."

In introducing the new magazine, Keener also acknowledged that one of his principal editorial hurdles was the lack of scholarly work among fundamentalists, resulting in a shortage of gifted writers. "The field of scholarship isn't great. That's pretty well known," Kenner said. He also indicated that the magazine would not represent all conservative Christian points of view. In fact, Keener had been rebuffed when he solicited an article from a professor at Bob Jones University. "We received a reply that said in effect that they do not believe the same doctrine as Jerry Falwell does and would not be interested," Keener acknowledged. He also indicated that charismatic Christians such as those associated with Pat Robertson's school in Norfolk, Virginia, and Oral Roberts University in Tulsa would be "avoided."[30]

Falwell also tried to enlist his fellow pastors in his efforts to affect the culture. He denounced the "silent pulpits" of America. On September 24, 1981, Falwell traveled to Florida, where he addressed seven thousand people at the First Baptist Church of West Hollywood. "We're supposed to be the conscience of our country," Falwell said. "Every time our pulpits have been silent, our society has become sick. . . . You know why there's been a whole sexual revolution today? Because the preachers have been silent." A few days later he delivered the same message to an audience in suburban Philadelphia. "We cannot blame Democrats or Republicans for the moral decadence in this country," Falwell told a crowd of nine hundred at the Calvary Independent Baptist Church. "We must lay the blame on the doorsteps of our churches." He went on to instruct pastors not to be "sissies." Conversely, later that year, in an interview with the Catholic magazine *Our Sunday Visitor,* Falwell said that he praised Pope John Paul II "almost daily" for being such an outspoken "advocate of freedom."[31]

Evangelical Christian churches continued to grow. Falwell would tell an editorial board meeting that evangelical churches were "the only growing churches in America." In his travels around the country he would urge pastors to get involved in the Christian school movement, which, he claimed, was opening four new schools a day. "It is the most optimistic, encouraging thing that's happening today in the world of education, because all of these teachers and their school leaders and pastors are free enterprisers, they're strong national defense people and they're moralists according to the Judeo-Christian tradition," Falwell said, linking the school movement to his broader agenda of influencing the culture. Falwell also was excited by the growth in Christian broadcasting. "We are ready for the battle for the minds of the people of this country."[32]

"Freedom" is one of the most ambiguous words in the English language; beyond the sloganeering, it means many different things to many different people. Not once in his long career did Jerry Falwell ever acknowledge the differences between the Enlightenment notions of freedom that informed the American founding and the "freedom of the children of God" of which Saint Paul wrote in the Bible. Falwell was not philosophically inclined, and in this regard his thinking was characterized by traditional fundamentalist suspicions of philosophy as opposed to theology. He saw no contradiction between his calls for increased government involvement in prohibiting immorality regarding homosexuality, abortion, and even divorce and his opposition to government regulation of private business. The tension between the more libertarian elements within the Republican Party and the social conservatives had been covered over largely by Reagan's easy confidence in both.

One prominent libertarian, however, Prof. Murray Rothbard of the Brooklyn Polytechnic Institute, was willing to challenge the alliance with social conservatives. In the September 1981 issue of *Reason* magazine, Rothbard joined the social conservatives in heaping scorn on the "liberal secular humanists" and praising the Moral Majority for launching a parents' "uprising" against the public schools. He accused educators of "busily inculcating school children and our culture with their own secular humanist values: non-theism, skepticism, relativist ethics, 'if it feels good, do it' morality, sexual promiscuity, morbid literature, statist economics, and all the rest of the goodies of our current world." Parents not only objected to their children being taught "corrupt" values, Rothbard argued, but when those same parents realized that the public schools were also failing to teach their children basic reading and math skills, they rebelled.

Rothbard may have shared the Moral Majority's objections to the public schools, but he indicted their approach. In his telling, the Moral Majority sought "to return to the 'good old days' before 1900, before John Dewey and secular humanism appeared on the scene." Rothbard presented a short history lesson in the distinctly Protestantizing aims of the public school system, noting that in many jurisdictions teachers had to belong to a Protestant church, schools featured daily readings from the Protestant King James version of the Bible, and the curriculum aimed to inculcate pietist values. This, too, was an unacceptable solution for Rothbard, and he equated the Deweyites with the Falwellites. "One is trying to force a majority to accept hedonism and secular humanism; the other is trying to compel a majority to swallow the Protestant ethic," Rothbard wrote.

Rothbard's solution was to get the government out of the education business altogether: "Only when the public school system has been abandoned will we be free of any group of tyrants who might wish to force their values, whatever they may be, down the throats of the rest of us." The harsh language about "forcing their values" highlights the difference between the libertarian perspective and the socially conservative Christian worldview. For Falwell, values were not "forced" on anyone; the Word of God was the authoritative source of values, and human happiness resulted from adherence to those values. It is ironic that, at a practical level, Falwell had pursued the privatization of education for which Rothbard was calling. As an extension of his ministry, Falwell had opened his own network of Christian schools as his children reached school age. His reasons were parental and ministerial, not philosophical, and he never seriously examined the possibility of forging an alliance with libertarians around the issue of school privatization.[33]

Rothbard's critique illustrated a truth about some of Falwell's opponents. They could be as doctrinaire as Falwell, as committed to their secular view of American culture and education as Falwell was to his religiously motivated views. When Falwell became the target of an attack from some of the nation's most visible cultural figures in the fall of 1981, the battle would be fought on college campuses across the nation.

The president of Yale University, A. Bartlett Giamatti, was one of the best-known public intellectuals in America. Today, thirty years later, university presidents lack the kind of cultural role that Giamatti, Notre Dame's Father Theodore Hesburgh, and Georgetown's Father Timothy Healy, SJ, once occupied. In the age of the blogosphere and a zillion cable channels, no one really serves in the capacity of a universally acknowledged public intellectual as these men once did. In 1981, in different ways, all three began to train their fire on Jerry Falwell.

At the start of the 1981–82 academic year, Giamatti welcomed the students at Yale back to campus with a fierce denunciation of the Moral Majority as "peddlers of coercion." His criticisms were withering. He accused the group of using new technologies to advance old intimidation. "Angry at change, rigid in the application of chauvinistic slogans, absolutistic in morality, they threaten through political pressure or public denunciation whoever dares to disagree with their authoritarian positions," he told his incoming students. The Moral Majority was responsible for a "new meanness of spirit in our land" and "resurgent bigotry." Giamatti claimed that the Moral Majority exhibited "a racist and discriminatory posture" without providing any evidence of this highly inflammatory charge. He concluded that Moral Majority political positions were "dangerous, malicious nonsense." Such was Giamatti's standing in the culture that his speech was front-page news in the *New York Times,* and the two largest newsweeklies, *Time* and *Newsweek,* ran excerpts.[34]

Cal Thomas, vice president for communications at the Moral Majority, questioned Giamatti's facts as well as his opinions. "If I had been a student at Yale and turned in such a poorly researched document as Giamatti's speech, so full of error, bias and even bigotry, I would not only have failed the course, but been expelled from the university," he told the *Washington Post*. Falwell referred to the attack obliquely in a sermon he preached two weeks after the Giamatti broadside. He told his congregants at Thomas Road Baptist Church, "There are unreasonable and wicked men that you need to pray for us about! That they will not be able to do damage to the Gospel. Pick up your newspaper and they're clobbering us all the time. All we have to ask you is to believe that what we're doing is what we believe God wants us to do, and that when they start in on us you just have to take it with a grain of salt."[35]

Falwell did not have to do much in the way of offering a personal defense because many conservative intellectuals came to his defense. In the *Dallas News,* columnist William Murchison called Giamatti's speech a "mugging." Giamatti "hears, or professes to hear, in Falwell's tread the advance of storm troopers. *Seig heil!* Well, baloney," wrote Murchinson. In the *Wall Street Journal,* the editors accused Giamatti of hubris, noting that the Moral Majority was "one strain among many" in the political landscape and that there was scarcely any danger of the group taking over the country.[36]

The most prominent, and formidable, critique of Giamatti's speech came from William F. Buckley, whose powerful intellect could engage Giamatti in ways that Falwell did not. Buckley raised the question of secularism's claim to an exclusive and exhaustive approach to human knowledge. Buckley argued that Giamatti was a variety of intellectual hypocrite, too quick to set aside the intellectual questions posed by the Moral Majority's positions. "How is it that the president of a distinguished and cosmopolitan university tells us that God alone knows when human life begins?" Buckley asked. "If you penetrate this rhetorical formulation, you have a dimly obscured invitation to nescience. 'God alone knows' is the safest way to say, 'That is unknowable.' " Buckley jokingly added that Giamatti would remain stuck in his "nescience" because God was not slated to teach at Yale anytime soon.

Buckley was raising a very complicated issue that neither Giamatti nor Falwell was prepared to fully engage—the relationship of faith and reason—and arguing that the liberal monopoly on higher education left out alternative ways of knowing, such as those available to faith. Giamatti's religious skepticism kept him from examining the possibility that Buckley raised, and Falwell did not perceive fully the need for it yet. For the one, reason always trumped faith, and for the other, faith always trumped reason, but neither the Yale president nor the Lynchburg pastor considered whether or not the relationship between the two might be one of mutual enlightenment. As Falwell became more deeply engaged in the nonpolitical aspects of the culture, he would come to see the need to engage this relationship between faith and reason more closely, leading to his increased focus on the work of Liberty Baptist College.

Buckley also tweaked Giamatti for permitting a double standard in his judgment of religiously motivated Yalies. He noted that Giamatti accused the Moral Majority of being angry at change. "But anger was officially cultivated, by Yale among other institutions, quite recently in the matter of such things as civil rights and the Vietnam War," Buckley wrote. "Giamatti should lecture the kids against the dangers of gonorrhea and Gnosticism, and let the Moral Majority alone." He noted that liberal groups were often "very big on denunciation," so it was absurd to lay this charge only at the feet of Falwell.[37]

One month after Giamatti's attack, Father Timothy Healy, SJ, the president of Georgetown University, attacked the Moral Majority in similarly harsh terms at a convocation at the University of the District of Columbia and in a subsequent speech at the City University of New York. Healy argued that the Moral Majority and Reagan's budget cuts were both symptoms of a "bout of meanness" that he said was "souring" the nation. He condemned both Reagan's foreign and domestic policies, but especially the latter, which reflected a "bitter set of new national priorities [that] puts military hardware above the promises we made to the old, gulls children out of school lunches."

Healy also compared the Moral Majority to the earlier manifestations of intolerance in America's history, pointing to nineteenth-century nativism, McCarthyism, and the Ku Klux Klan. The Moral Majority's voice was "the voice of hatred," Healy said. "Its stand is against rather than for. It revels in a rhetoric of condemnation. Its master work is political assassination." He again drew the comparison between the Moral Majority and the Klan in the most striking metaphor of his speech: "Whether hatred comes wrapped in white sheets or the scripture, it is still a denial of man and his works." These were powerful words coming from any university president, but coming from someone who was a priest as well they were especially provocative.

Falwell dismissed Healy's charges as "simply another uninformed attack," and his assistant Cal Thomas noted that the Moral Majority was on record for its opposition to the Klan and that, furthermore, 18 percent of the members of Falwell's Thomas Road Baptist Church were black. "It is he [Healy] who is biased and bigoted," Thomas charged. Falwell would also subsequently combat the charge of racism by visiting secular campuses and inquiring as to the minority enrollment. Taking questions after a speech at Duke University, Falwell apologized for his former belief in segregation and further apologized for the fact that blacks constituted only 12 percent of the student body at Liberty Baptist College. He then asked the audience what percentage of students at Duke were black, and when no one knew the answer, he provided them with it. "Six percent!" Falwell told the astonished audience. "I struggled with whether the Lord wanted me to come here tonight to a school that, though you have been given great gifts, has such a poor record of minority enrollment."[38]

The autumn of 1981 also saw officials from the Moral Majority fan out to college campuses to engage in discussions and debates about the organization's positions and its public significance. They were realizing that the academy was both a critical influence on the attitudes of the press and public and a place where the evangelical voice had been so long absent that many misconceptions about fundamentalism had been flourishing. As well, the Moral Majority's decision to engage the culture more vigorously reflected a growing self-confidence about its role in society as well as its conviction that the bad manners of protesters, so frequently on display, might actually redound to its own credit.

At the University of Akron in Ohio, two hundred students and faculty turned out for a debate between Cal Thomas and Sam Brown, a former Carter administration official who attended the Akron event as a spokesman for People For the American Way. Brown agreed that the Moral Majority was neither racist nor anti-Semitic, but he maintained that members of the group were "narrow and mean-spirited." Brown warned that the Moral Majority's tendency to refer to its opponents as "ungodly" could lead to a deterioration of political discourse. Thomas countered that liberals were simply upset because conservative Americans were standing up and speaking their minds and, most especially, being successful at the polls. The liberals, he said, were "spoiled brats because the government has been their toy for many years." The debate was heavy on sarcasm from both protagonists, but it remained essentially civil.[39]

Civility broke down sometimes. At a debate on the campus of Kresge College, a former professor at the University of California at Santa Cruz, Rev. Lewis Keizer, accused Thomas and his organization of being "the real immoral ones" because of their intolerance. "Somewhere in the back recesses of my mind is this guy called Jesus," Keizer said. "He didn't take cheap shots at homosexuals and he sure as hell didn't teach that we have to be right-wing political activists to be good Christians." Thomas defended the organization, but he was met with hisses when he made a derogatory comment about women's rights. Uncharacteristically, Thomas lost his cool. "Pass gas; it's easier," he said to the audience in reply to the hissing. He then leaned into the microphone and made a "raspberry" sound.[40]

Sometimes Falwell himself hit the campus hustings to make the case, and unlike Thomas, the preacher never lost his cool. At the Harvard Divinity School, liberal theologian Harvey Cox introduced Falwell, ungraciously adding, "Please understand that my presence here tonight should in no way be understood as an endorsement of what Jerry Falwell recommends." Falwell stepped to the microphone and jocularly began, "Thank you for your kind introduction, Professor Cox. Students, please understand that my speaking here tonight should in no way be construed as an endorsement of the Harvard Divinity School."

The Harvard Divinity School audience was even more hostile than Cox. Falwell's speech was interrupted several times by chants of "Hitler rose, Hitler fell, racist Falwell, go to hell!" Two students shouted, "Racist, fascist pig," at the minister and had to be removed from the room by security. At Princeton, Falwell was met with a bomb threat. At Dartmouth and Yale, the reception accorded Falwell was similar. None of these protests achieved their objective of provoking him into displaying the bigotry of which he stood accused. In most cases, Falwell disarmed his critics even if he did not persuade them. In all cases, the publicity generated was invaluable. To those students attending the nation's most elite schools, and to those who read about all the controversy his appearances aroused, Falwell was becoming the face of Christianity in America.[41]

While Falwell was moving into the culture—and bumping into strong counterforces there—he continued to use the Moral Majority to affect the realm of politics. In the early 1980s, the Moral Majority would continue to raise money, promote its political agenda, register voters, and engage its critics. Sometimes the results were surprising, but the principal effect of Falwell's ongoing political activities was predictable, since it was precisely the same effect his nonpolitical ventures had produced. Falwell became the most prominent Christian in the country.

Organizations like Moral Majority are only as effective as their fund-raising operations. A fund-raising appeal sent to donors on April 15, 1981, contained all of the hot-button issues designed to get recipients to write a check. The letter cited the Moral Majority's successful efforts in defeating the ERA in Virginia. It warned about attacks on the organization from the "liberals and pornography kings." It called attention to the Moral Majority's efforts to secure passage of a Voluntary School Prayer Amendment to the U.S. Constitution. The fund-raising appeal promised to tell the readers of the *Moral Majority Report* about "what the gays were and still are doing to make homosexuality a legally accepted alternative lifestyle."[42]

Gays. School prayer. ERA. Liberals. Pornography kings. These hot buttons equaled higher returns, and when the Moral Majority's fiscal year ended in August the group had doubled its revenue over the previous year, taking in $5.77 million, according to an audit released to the press. Despite the increased revenue, the group also was carrying a $500,000 deficit. Executive director Rob Godwin said he was unconcerned about the deficit, noting that it reflected only one month's revenue. Godwin said that the increase in donations reflected the public's ongoing support for the Moral Majority's work. The audit showed that the organization spent $4.42 million on lobbying and publications and $942,906 on fund-raising expenses. The remainder was consumed by other administrative costs.[43]

Falwell had endorsed the Reagan administration's decision to pursue its economic agenda first, but after Reagan signed the centerpiece of that agenda, a massive tax cut, into law in August 1981, the Moral Majority clamored for attention to its social agenda. In September, Falwell held a press conference to announce the organization's support for an effort in Congress to overturn a new law passed by the District of Columbia's City Council that would decriminalize homosexual acts. (Congress exercises oversight of the District of Columbia and can overturn laws passed by the city's government.)

Falwell called the new law "a perverted act about perverted acts." Falwell said that the D.C. City Council and the mayor had backed the new law because of their "fear of the gay vote," and he expressed the worry that D.C. could become the "gay capital of the world" given its significance to the entire nation. The head of the D.C. Moral Majority chapter, Rev. Cleveland Sparrow, countered charges that Congress had no business interfering in the internal affairs of the District, saying, "This is not a matter of home rule—it's a matter of home ruin." In the end, after Congress declined to overturn the local measure, the next issue of the *Moral Majority Report* included a list of "Congressmen Who Voted for Sodomy."[44]

The Moral Majority also lobbied directly against certain proposed changes in the federal criminal code. In October, Ron Godwin penned a letter to the chairman of the Senate Judiciary Committee, Sen. Strom Thurmond, objecting to the fact that the new code removed all references to the death penalty and opposed the increased penalties for white-collar crimes. "Unfortunately, the stockholders and consumers who will suffer from this expanded use of criminal law against organizations will, by and large, not be the persons responsible for the criminal violation," Godwin wrote, echoing the line taken by corporations opposing the measure.

An "Urgent Legislative Alert" was sent to Moral Majority members in November, urging them to contact their senators to change or defeat the criminal code changes. The letter was sophisticated, beginning its objection with the concern that the new statutory provisions would be interpreted by liberal courts, unlike the current laws, which had years of more conservative legal interpretation behind them. In short, the new changes, no matter how well intended, were an invitation to the judiciary to put its own liberal stamp on the criminal code. Other objections tracked more closely to the organization's moral agenda. The bill reduced the penalty for rape from death or life imprisonment to twelve years' imprisonment and removed the "interspousal immunity from rape," permitting wives to charge their husbands with the crime. Finally, the Moral Majority objected to the reduction in penalties for those found guilty of violating laws restricting pornography.

The Moral Majority appeared to be fighting an uphill battle against the proposed changes in the federal criminal code. The bill built on a previous measure that had passed the Senate in 1978 and been painstakingly negotiated in 1981 by members of the Senate Judiciary Committee working with Reagan's attorney general, William French Smith. Not only did the president support the changes, but so did several conservative senators, including senators Strom Thurmond, Paul Laxalt, Orrin Hatch, and Robert Dole, all men who would normally find themselves fighting alongside Falwell. It was also backed by liberal stalwarts such as Sen. Edward Kennedy. Some of Falwell's closest allies in the Senate, such as Sen. Jeremiah Denton and Sen. John East, supported the Moral Majority's position but did not have the votes to overturn the carefully negotiated compromise. Moderate senator Charles "Mac" Mathias of Maryland also opposed the new law, but for different reasons. The politics of the bill was confusing, to say the least, but the Moral Majority's opposition was one reason why Congress lost interest in the reforms.[45]

The Moral Majority did not witness much activity on behalf of its two most important legislative goals. President Reagan honored his campaign promise in May 1982 when he sent Senator Thurmond's Judiciary Committee a proposed constitutional amendment permitting voluntary school prayer; the committee held hearings on the measure, but no action was taken before the midterm elections. The Human Life Amendment overturning *Roe v. Wade* was introduced by Sen. Orrin Hatch in September 1981; the Judiciary Committee held hearings on the measure and reported the measure to the full Senate in 1982, but the Republican leaders lacked the votes to overcome a filibuster and the measure died.

Falwell and the Moral Majority were not exceedingly active in the 1982 midterm elections. In fact, the weekend before the vote most of the organization's leaders were in the Bahamas hosting a conference on antipornography measures for law enforcement officials. The group's inattention to the significance of the midterms showed in the results: while the partisan breakdown in the Senate remained unchanged, the Democrats picked up twenty-seven seats in the House of Representatives. Falwell would not make that mistake a second time.[46]

The Moral Majority had been an educational and lobbying organization, not a political action committee. It did not endorse specific candidates, still less make financial contributions. In 1983, reflecting on the losses of the previous year, Falwell decided in February 1983 to form a PAC. "This will be new for us," Falwell told a fellow minister who wrote about their discussion in the religion column of his local newspaper. "We haven't announced it yet, but we're starting a PAC (political action committee) to support congressional candidates that are committed to the issues that are important to us. This is something we've never done before." The PAC would be able to give donations directly to candidates who supported the Moral Majority's issues.[47]

"We felt like in the 1982 elections, that we were not able to be as actively involved as we wanted to be in certain races where we felt it was important that the conservative candidate receive better support," Godwin told a press conference in Lynchburg a few days later. He mentioned the local congressional election in Lynchburg, in which the Democrat had won. Cal Thomas said that the new group would not share the name of its parent organization because some people had developed negative associations with the name. "We don't want to make Moral Majority the issue," Thomas said. "We want to make the issues we're addressing the issue." The March issue of the *Moral Majority Report* announced the formation of the new PAC, noting that it would be legally distinct from, but share much of the leadership with, the Moral Majority. "Dr. Falwell, in announcing the new PAC, said the organization would support candidates who oppose abortion and support Israel," the newsletter announced.[48]

The decision to form a PAC would not be consequential in terms of the electoral results it achieved. The 1980s witnessed an explosion of PACs, many of which had much larger war chests than Falwell could muster, not least because some of his donors might give money to promote morality but were less likely to make additional donations for purely political activities. This factor was what ultimately made the decision to form a PAC a bad one for Falwell. In the first few years of the Moral Majority's existence, he had been at pains to point out that the group was nonpartisan and that it was not in the business of supporting candidates or devising hit lists of enemies. But the ability to deliver $5,000 checks to candidates was pure politics. Just as the early years of the Reagan administration saw Falwell wade knee-deep into issues with only a tenuous connection to his moral agenda, the decision to form a PAC indicated that he was abandoning any pretense that his authority as a moral leader was "above" politics. Except for the fact that he was not running for public office himself, Falwell was now a fully engaged politician. Before the decision to form a PAC, he could say that there were political barriers he had not crossed, self-imposed limits on the extent of his political engagement. Once the

PAC was formed those barriers were gone, and with them went any pretense to being different from other politicians.

The Moral Majority continued its efforts to register voters. On July 6, 1983, Falwell made a five-stop visit to North Carolina, where, accompanied by that state's conservative senator Jesse Helms, he spoke to groups of ministers and laypeople, urging them to get involved. He set a goal of registering two hundred thousand new voters. Falwell told a press conference that his effort was not intended to counteract a voter registration drive being conducted by Rev. Jesse Jackson, the liberal firebrand, although he acknowledged that Jackson's efforts provided the Moral Majority with an incentive.

The North Carolina Moral Majority chairman, Rev. Lamarr Mooneyham, denounced Jackson's voter drive as racist. "Registering voting-age voters between now and October 1984 is the only way to keep a political blackmailer like the Reverend Jackson from acquiring the kind of political clout that he needs to implement his racist agenda," Mooneyham wrote in a letter sent to Moral Majority followers in the state. Falwell declined to call Jackson's efforts racist, but he did say, " 'I don't think the idea is to put blacks or whites in office." A spokesman for Jackson's organization, Operation PUSH, said that the voter registration effort targeted Latinos and poor whites as well as blacks because all three groups had been underrepresented in the electorate.[49]

In September, Falwell traveled to Alabama to promote the voter registration drive, and there he did label Jackson's efforts "racist." Falwell told an all-white audience of 150 religious and lay leaders in Montgomery, "We had hoped that we've gotten past such racist attitudes." He also voiced his "hope" that Jackson "will read these comments and clean up his act." Falwell called the Moral Majority's voter registration effort entirely nonpartisan. "I'm not a Republican," said Falwell. "I'm a Baptist. I could vote for a Republican or a Democrat. We're not trying to elect all white or all black congressmen—just those who best represent our views."[50]

Falwell's protestations notwithstanding, the Moral Majority's partisanship shone through when he rushed to the defense of Rep. Daniel Crane of Illinois, one of two brothers who served in the

U.S. House and were among its most conservative members. Representative Crane was caught up in a sex scandal in 1983 involving congressional pages, along with an openly gay congressman from Massachusetts, Rep. Gerry Studds. The House Ethics Committee voted to reprimand both men, but the full House upped the punishment to a formal censure. Ron Godwin spoke out on behalf of Crane, saying that the congressman had "repented after it was discovered he had had an affair with a teen-age congressional page in 1980." Godwin later denied making the remark, noting that the Moral Majority did not endorse candidates and was legally forbidden from doing so, although since they had earlier formed a PAC, they did in fact now endorse candidates. "We're not endorsing him and we're not condoning him and we're not condemning him," Godwin told a reporter. Crane was defeated the next year when he sought reelection.[51]

In addition to his voter drive, Falwell continued to speak at religious and Moral Majority events nationwide, intertwining his religious and political messages as the occasion warranted. He addressed a "Word of Life" conference in upstate New York where 1,400 religious conservatives heard him call Harvard University a "Godless and Marxist institution. Not only are they anti-Christ but they are anti-American." He praised Pope John Paul II as a man with backbone. He said that "public schools have made a commitment to mediocrity." And Falwell said of the times, "Historians will record the 1980s as the social and spiritual rebirth of this country."

At the same conference Falwell also condemned a recent Supreme Court decision that had ruled the government could deny the tax-exempt status of private schools that practiced racial discrimination. The case involved Bob Jones University. "They [the Supreme Court] let their hearts get in front of their minds and made a very bad decision," Falwell said, blaming the result on the high court's dislike for the school and its practice. He said he was opposed to racial discrimination and thought Bob Jones University was wrong to practice it, but he foresaw greater legal difficulties in the future. "Down the road, the ACLU will mount a legal challenge of the tax-exempt status of churches that do not ordain women—the fundamental Baptist and Roman Catholic churches, for example," Falwell warned. The Supreme Court justices "have dug themselves into a hole they will regret later."[52]

In July, Falwell went to the White House with a group of evangelical leaders to meet with President Reagan, hoping to revive the school prayer issue. There were several constitutional hurdles. Sen. Orrin Hatch had suggested that the prayer be silent, to avoid all or more of the hurdles, but Reagan rejected that approach. "Frankly, I don't believe we've been fighting this prayer battle for the right to remain silent," the president told the group. It was decided to insert new language specifying that any prayer used in a public school would not be written by any government official. Falwell endorsed the new language and praised the president for crafting it. "This is his amendment," Falwell told reporters after the White House meeting, adding that he hoped the Senate would begin hearings on the school prayer amendment that same week. The next year the measure would come before the full Senate, and Vice President George Bush would take the presider's chair to demonstrate the administration's commitment to the amendment. It would garner only fifty-six votes, however, eleven short of the two-thirds of the chamber needed for passage. When the measure failed, Falwell said he knew that they did not have the votes to pass the amendment but that he wanted to have the senators on record. He told an Arizona audience, "Fifty-six out of 100 were right; 44 were wrong; and two of them were your senators," referring to his recent nemesis, Senator Goldwater, and Arizona's Democratic senator, Dennis DeConcini. The inability of the Moral Majority to achieve any of its signature policy goals, even with the strong backing of President Reagan, was frustrating, and that frustration only galvanized the organization to redouble its efforts in 1984.[53]

One of the Moral Majority's outreach efforts went awry and led to a most improbable friendship. The group sent out membership cards to those who had signed up for the *Moral Majority Report*. One of these cards, number B0500878, was sent to Sen. Edward M. Kennedy, the liberal lion of the Democratic Party. The accompanying form letter from Reverend Falwell told of the "suffering, anguish and physical abuse inflicted on me by liberals." Kennedy's press secretary, Robert Shrum, commented, "I knew they were getting unhappy with Ronald Reagan, but this is ridiculous." The Moral Majority's Cal Thomas pointed out that all political groups frequently signed up for the literature coming from their opponents, but he impishly added that Kennedy's membership in the organization would not be revoked, even if the senator did not send a contribution. "I think we'll offer him an opportunity to atone for his past political sins," said Mr. Thomas. "No man is beyond redemption."[54]

Thomas, ever attuned to the possibility of stoking media attention, decided to phone the senator's office and invite him to speak at Liberty Baptist College. After all, Falwell had gone to Kennedy's alma mater, Harvard. Kennedy agreed to come to Liberty. When Senator Kennedy arrived in Lynchburg on October 3, 1983, he had dinner at the Falwells' home that evening, accompanied by his daughter Kara and his sister Jean Kennedy Smith, and Falwell's wife, Macel, recalled the evening as an enjoyable one.[55]

Kennedy's speech was a combination of soft praise for Falwell and a strong plea for tolerance. He spoke on behalf of the nuclear freeze, noting that the bishops of his church supported it, but he defended Falwell's right to oppose it. "There must be standards for the exercise of such leadership—so that the obligations of belief will not be debased into an opportunity for mere political advantage," Kennedy said. "But to take a stand at all, when a question is both properly public and truly moral, is to stand in a long and honored tradition." The senator also noted that Falwell had been criticized by some religious figures for "yoking" himself to nonfundamentalists to pursue his political agenda, a criticism that Kennedy did not share. "On this issue, he himself has become the target of narrow prejudice," Kennedy said. "When people agree on public policy, they ought to be able to work together even while they worship in diverse ways. For truly, we are yoked together as Americans." But, Kennedy also said, there were limits to religious assessment of political concerns. "I respectfully suggest that God has taken no position on the Department of Education—and that a balanced-budget constitutional amendment is a matter for economic analysis, not heavenly appeals."

When Kennedy called for tolerance of divergent opinions, Falwell and the five thousand people in the audience were less than enthusiastic. "In such cases—cases like prohibition and abortion—the proper role of religion is to appeal to the conscience of the individual, not the coercive power of the state," Kennedy told the crowd. He also instructed them that societal tolerance protected the rights of everyone amid the shifting tides of public opinion. "Let us never forget: Today's Moral Majority could become tomorrow's persecuted minority," Kennedy said, before finishing with a naked play for the students' affections: a promise to watch an entire episode of the *Old-Time Gospel Hour* if Falwell would, in his capacity as chancellor of the school, extend the students' curfew by one hour. This proposal was met with thunderous applause.[56]

"It was an excellent speech—of course, I disagreed with him on one or two points," Falwell said at a reception after the speech. "I liked his emphasis on religious freedom and pluralism." Falwell also indicated that he was thrilled with the effect of the speech on the school's reputation, telling a reporter that "I think it helps the image—particularly among everyone who thinks that we don't have anything here but robots." Kennedy returned the compliment, saying he was impressed by the gracious and attentive reception he had received from the students.[57]

The media, of course, ate up the entire episode, labeling Falwell and Kennedy "the odd couple." Kennedy's speech was excerpted on the editorial pages of the *Washington Post,* along with an article from Cal Thomas in which he said that the event helped to shatter stereotypes. "One man realized the other doesn't have horns," Thomas wrote. "The other man found that his frequent adversary isn't a demagogue trying to take over America. If nothing else was accomplished, a lot was accomplished." The newspaper also ran an editorial cartoon showing three devils in Hell, surrounded by snow, reading the "*Hades Gazette*" with a banner headline about the meeting of the reverend and the senator.[58]

Not all the media commentary was favorable, however, and Falwell was attacked from the right. The conservative journal *Human Events* published a hard-hitting article under the headline, "Kennedy *Is* a Threat to the Survival of the Republic." They not only objected to Kennedy's political positions but went after his character as well. "One does not have to dislike Kennedy on a personal basis, either, to realize that he is an exceptionally flawed human being, from his cheating in school to his despicable behavior at Chapaquiddick to his continued demagogic utterances in connection with public policy." The magazine also criticized Thomas's column in the *Washington Post.*[59]

With this criticism in mind, the next issue of the *Moral Majority Report,* which was sent to his most devoted supporters, contained an article by Reverend Falwell in which he pilloried Kennedy's speech. Falwell questioned why Kennedy had spoken so explicitly about censorship. "Even though no one has ever proved that a single Moral Majority member has ever burned a book or even called for one to be burned, Kennedy felt it necessary to preach against book burning," Falwell wrote. Given the wide circulation of Kennedy's speech, Falwell needed to defend his invitation to the senator. Falwell said that the school and church were not doing their job if "one liberal pied piper" could shake the students from their views. "If, on the other hand, we have done our job, then guest lecturers of any persuasion will only sharpen the defensive skills of our students," Falwell wrote to his supporters. Instead of calling the speech "excellent," as he had done when it was delivered, now Falwell said Kennedy "based his case on misinformation."[60]

Kennedy and Falwell were both astute public figures, but there is no reason to doubt the fact that they simply liked each other. In January 1984, when Falwell was speaking in south Florida, Kennedy phoned him and invited him to visit the Kennedy compound in Palm Beach, where Kennedy's ailing mother, Rose, was living. Falwell prayed with America's most famous political matriarch at the Kennedy mansion, and later the senator and Falwell walked on the lawns and spoke at length. A few days later, during the weekly chapel service at Liberty Baptist College, Falwell related the visit to the students. "I wish all of you young people could have heard what Sen. Kennedy said to his mother. He said, 'Mother, this is . . . this is Rev. Falwell, that I told you I spoke for his college in a day when colleges are going out of business. They have a college there that is a strictly Christian college,' and then he began to tell in glowing words descriptions of who you young people are."

Falwell, always aware of the value in cultivating powerful people, recognized that his friendship with Kennedy would help to defuse his image as a divisive figure, but the two men, both gregarious by nature, liked each other and would extend kindnesses to each other over the years. When Jerry Falwell Jr. applied to law school a few years later, Sen. Edward Kennedy wrote one of his letters of recommendation.[61]

Falwell's relationship with another liberal leader, Rev. Jesse Jackson, was decidedly frostier, as seen in Falwell's characterization of Jackson's voter registration drives as "racist." But the two men also explored the possibility of working together when a common cause might invite such cooperation. The November 1983 jailing of seven parents in Nebraska for operating a nonaccredited school seemed to offer just such an opportunity. In December, Jackson met with a group of conservative religious leaders in Chicago and spoke with Falwell on the phone about the Nebraska situation. Falwell told reporters that he and Jackson were in agreement that the arrest of the parents was akin to "some of the horrible civil rights violations" of the 1950s and 1960s. Falwell said the two planned to work together to secure the release of the parents. Jackson, however, said that he had only agreed to call for a Justice Department investigation.[62]

The two planned to meet, but confusion ensued, and it appeared that Falwell stood Jackson up for dinner. Falwell said that the dinner never made it onto his schedule, but he took the occasion to speak well of Jackson's bid for the presidency. "I'm glad he's running," said Falwell. "That says something good. It says that a black man can be a serious candidate for president. It says that an ordained minister can be a serious candidate for president." Falwell noted that the press seemed less concerned about a liberal minister running for office than about conservative evangelicals organizing to vote and called the disparate treatment a sign of the media's hypocrisy. He called Jackson "my good friend" and speculated that Jackson might be Walter Mondale's running mate in the next presidential election, but Falwell also said that he thought none of the Democrats had much of a shot at defeating President Reagan.[63]

By the end of the summer of 1983, all political activity became focused through the lens of the upcoming presidential election. Despite the fact that Reagan had been unable to deliver on any of the religious right's major goals, there was never any doubt that Christian conservatives would remain in the Republican camp. Some conservative activists were critical of Reagan for not doing more to advance their agenda, but Falwell was not among them. In 1984 Falwell was savvier than he had been during the 1980 election, but he remained as devoted to Reagan as ever.

At a September 1983 luncheon with the editorial board of the *Washington Times,* Falwell announced his unqualified support for Reagan's reelection. The support came at a critical time for the president, who had been attacked by some conservatives for not responding more robustly to the Soviet Union's recent downing of a Korean airliner. Falwell said that Reagan "still has his eyes on the goal that he was setting before us 20 years ago and that has caused me to be his disciple for at least 20 years of my life." Falwell said that he would be fighting for Reagan in 1984 because "I still believe in him," adding that Reagan was "as sincere as any human being I know." Falwell warned the Republicans not to take the evangelical vote for granted. He noted that while conservatives would never vote against Reagan, "they sure can go fishing on Election Day." At a prayer breakfast in Dallas in November, Falwell again reiterated his support for Reagan and predicted that Reagan would both run and win.[64]

Falwell's enthusiasm for Reagan was not shared by every conservative. Paul Weyrich, who had urged Falwell to form the Moral Majority five years earlier, was ambivalent about the Reagan administration. Speaking at the University of California at Santa Barbara in early 1984, Weyrich predicted that many conservative Christians would stay home. "The kind of fervor that was active in his [Reagan's] particular campaign in 1980 I do not think will be present again in 1984," Weyrich said. He believed that religious conservatives were more concerned about ensuring the reelection of Sen. Jesse Helms and other local candidates than they were about reelecting Reagan, although Reagan would still receive most of their votes.[65]

Reagan may have fallen out of favor with some conservative leaders within the Beltway, but he remained hugely popular with most religious conservatives. Falwell gave the president a platform to engage this part of the GOP base when he invited Reagan to address the "Baptist Fundamentalism '84" conference, held in Washington on April 11–13 and organized not by the Moral Majority but by a group of prominent fundamentalist ministers, such as Rev. John Rawlins of Cincinnati and Rev. Raymond Barer of Fort Worth, Texas. The official program included a letter of welcome from President Ronald Reagan as well as from the District's Mayor Marion Barry. The exhibition area at the convention center was filled with promotional literature for the Republican Party as well as for religious programs.

Reagan gave one of the twenty-three speeches and sermons at the event, which drew thousands of participants from across the country. When introducing the president, Falwell professed his impartiality in the election contest, but then added, "We are hopeful that during your second term. . . ." Laughter and cheers drowned out the rest of the sentence. Falwell said that Reagan was the finest president in his lifetime and then he added, looking out over the throng, "We're with you, Mr. President." Reagan was received with standing ovations when he arrived and when he concluded his speech.[66]

Later that month Falwell traveled to Philadelphia to speak at the University of Pennsylvania. At a press conference, he said that he hoped a second Reagan term would add more justices to the Supreme Court like Sandra Day O'Connor. "We would have into the 21st century a court committed in areas that we feel are vital to our country's health," Falwell said. He also expressed the hope that Walter Mondale would defeat his rivals for the Democratic nomination. "He's most beatable of the three [Democratic candidates], so I say nothing but good things about Mondale everywhere I go." The quip was funny, but it was also knowing, and while Falwell liked to be "in the know" and to be seen as such, that was precisely what worried many Americans. It was one thing for a pastor to speak on moral principles, but whenever Falwell portrayed himself as a political insider, it made some Americans squirm. Democrats would play on that uneasiness as the campaign progressed.[67]

Falwell still had an almost unparalleled ability to rouse the conservative faithful. His speech to the National Right to Life convention in Kansas City in June was a no-holds-barred, red meat exhortation that caused the delegates to interrupt his address with applause some two dozen times, including three standing ovations. "The traditional values—we call them Judeo-Christian ethics—are being assaulted like never before in our history," Falwell said, naming the National Organization for Women (NOW), the National Education Association (NEA), the American Civil Liberties Union (ACLU), and Planned Parenthood as some of the groups responsible for the "assault." He warned that if *Roe v. Wade* was not overturned soon, "then America will not survive. If there is no victory, America will not deserve to survive." This was vintage Falwell—focusing on the task at hand and swinging for the rhetorical fences with an over-the-top, needlessly divisive speech that was exactly what the delegates wanted to hear. At this point in his career Falwell's method was a political retelling of a morality play: he identified an enemy and warned that the survival of the country depended on defeating that enemy, all the while seemingly unaware of the corrosive effects that such divisiveness would have on both the body politic and the Christian churches. But if Falwell entertained any doubts about his method, they were drowned out easily by the thunderous applause.[68]

Falwell's humorous side continued to break through on some occasions, softening his public image. The same month that he addressed the National Right to Life convention, he went to Baltimore at the request of Democratic mayor William Schaeffer to speak at the mayor's prayer breakfast. Schaeffer was a large personality who was not afraid to stir up a bit of controversy. In addition, the City Council was considering a gay rights ordinance at the time, which made Falwell's appearance all the more likely to cause a stir. When the preacher from Lynchburg arrived at the podium in the hotel ballroom, he looked straight at the assembled press corps and observed that he knew that they had not come because of the controversy over the mayor's invitation, but because there was a rumor going around that he was going to announce his endorsement of Walter Mondale. "I'm not going to do it. I'm going to restrain myself," Falwell told the members of the press and the audience, provoking laughter from both groups. Falwell did not address the gay rights ordinance at all.[69]

In addition to humor, one of Falwell's favorite rhetorical tactics was to take a liberal phrase and turn it to his own purposes. In the July/August 1984 issue of his *Fundamentalist Journal*, Falwell noted that there were pacifists who conscientiously objected to war. He announced that he, too, was a conscientious objector. "I object to the United States becoming another Poland, Cuba, or Afghanistan," Falwell wrote. "Therefore, I conscientiously approve of a strong national defense as a deterrent to war and slavery. I conscientiously object to my children growing up under tyranny." Falwell related a humorous account of his appearance with a liberal clergyman on a talk show. "I once debated a liberal clergyman on this topic [the nuclear freeze] on a television talk show. Between commercial breaks I asked him where he lived and he replied, 'New York City.' I further asked him if he locked his doors at night and he said, 'I sure do.' I replied, 'Why do you lock your doors? If you can trust the Russians, why can't you trust your neighbors?'"[70]

In August, Falwell gave the benediction at the Republican National Convention in Dallas. He began by saying, "It is a great honor to ask our Lord's blessing upon a man that many of us believe, indeed, to be our greatest president since Lincoln and an equally prestigious and honorable vice president who have been God's instrument in rebuilding America. Let us pray." Falwell's prayer was an amalgam of political and religious themes: he asked God to bless the president, that he might have the wisdom to lead the nation and "the free world," and he gave thanks for "a party that has committed itself to compassion, outreach and love to all of its citizens and to all of the world." He thanked God for a president whose leadership had secured the privileges of being born in America for future generations. He linked the cause of America with the cause of religious freedom around the world, a freedom that would afford America "the privilege of giving your gospel, the message of your crucified son to every man

in our generation." He concluded the prayer "in Jesus' name." Falwell's prayer hit just the right notes for his audience, blending generic
civic religion with distinctly Christian themes and conveying the
clear understanding that God's agenda was making itself manifest
through the agency of the Republican Party.[71]

In addition to giving the benediction in the large arena before
the full convention, Falwell testified before the platform committee.
He recalled the decision in 1980 to include a pro-life plank in the
GOP platform and the howls from the media because of it. He noted
that in 1980 the platform plank's call for a Human Life Amendment
to the Constitution was considered the more important of the two
planks, but that now he thought, in light of the advanced age of
several Supreme Court justices, that the plank calling for pro-life
judges was of more critical importance. He warned the committee
not to backslide on its commitment. "Allow me to be blunt," Falwell
said. "If this platform backs down on either support for an amendment or that judicial promise, it will be seen as a Republican sell-
out." His plug for the creation of "pregnancy centers," along the
lines of his Save-A-Baby program, resulted in platform language that
praised such work. The committee voted to adopt virtually identical
language in support of both the Human Life Amendment and the
nomination of pro-life judges that it had taken in 1980.[72]

The Moral Majority's PAC launched a tirade, in a "Hotline
Report," against Democratic vice presidential nominee Geraldine
Ferraro in September. Ferraro had come under scrutiny because of
some of her husband's financial arrangements. "Will Geraldine Ferraro as Vice President continue to be as knowledgeable in the affairs
of state as she is in her own private affairs?" the report asked. "Will
she show the same inability to grasp the facts of foreign policy,
defense, and the traditional moral values of this country as she has
shown in her incredible naivete of her personal business dealings and
holdings?" This kind of hard-hitting, personal attack seemed inappropriate coming from a group organized by ministers. The report
also touted the influence of religious conservatives in achieving a
"pro-life, anti-pornography, pro-defense, pro-prayer, anti-ERA, pro–
free enterprise platform" at the recent GOP convention.[73]

On September 9, Falwell appeared on the Sunday talk show *This Week with David Brinkley,* where he predicted that Reagan would win easily, saying that Democratic nominee Walter Mondale "doesn't have a prayer—not even a voluntary one," a jocular reference to the recent debate over prayer in the schools. Falwell said that concerns raised by the Democrats about the separation of church and state were a "non-issue" because "no one wants to establish a Christian state. We want a nation under God." Falwell also defended a comment he had made at the Republican convention to the effect that President Reagan was "God's instrument." Falwell said that the Bible saw all political leaders as God's instruments, even the leaders of the Soviet Union, and he admitted that the same would be true of the Democrats were they to win.[74]

Falwell also took on those to his right who he thought were being foolish in their attempts to enforce conservative orthodoxy on all Republicans. In Illinois the National Conservative Political Action Committee, along with three other conservative organizations, refused to endorse moderate Republican incumbent Sen. Charles Percy, backing the Libertarian Party candidate in the race instead. Falwell acknowledged his differences with Percy but faulted his fellow conservatives for a lack of political pragmatism and a willingness to risk a Democratic victory. "These are all my friends, but I think they have suicidal tendencies," Falwell said of the conservatives. He said that no Republican or conservative should pursue a strategy that could hurt the president. In the event, the Democrat Paul Simon did defeat Percy in the election.[75]

In St. Louis at the end of September, Falwell addressed a smaller than expected crowd rallying at the Gateway Arch. "The Soviets would love to have Mondale as president," Falwell told the crowd. The rally was organized by Falwell, repeating the theme "Peace Through Strength" he first used in 1983, and indicating how far his political compass was straying from the bread-and-butter social issues that had driven his rise to political prominence in 1980. The small turnout was a warning to Falwell to stick to those issues about which Americans still turned to the churches for guidance. He would heed this warning eventually, but not for the next few years.[76]

The second presidential debate occurred on October 8. During one response, Mondale was asked about the role of religion in politics, and he singled out Falwell by name. "When the Republican platform says that . . . we're going to have a religious test for judges before they are selected for the federal court," Mondale asserted, "and then Jerry Falwell announces that means they get at least two justices of the Supreme Court—I think that's an abuse of faith in our country." Falwell undoubtedly relished the reference, but he also recognized that he needed to answer the charge. He told the press that Mondale was just "blowing smoke" and added, "I do not seek to be consulted for any appointment and I do not expect to be." But Falwell was smart enough to realize that perceptions of his influence skyrocketed as a result of being singled out by Mondale for abuse, that his stock had been raised with his own constituency, and that by protesting his lack of influence he was in fact making Reagan even more conscious of his influence.[77]

In the days after the debate Falwell enjoyed the spotlight and consistently refuted claims that he had any undue influence. At a press conference in Cleveland, Falwell explained that he did not have any more influence over the president than the average citizen. He mentioned that he had met with Reagan one-on-one for one hour a year before, that he had been to several meetings with the president at which other religious leaders were present, and that he spoke with members of the White House staff about once a month—but that was all. "I guess that is a little more contact than most Americans have with the president and the White House staff," Falwell allowed. He specifically denied any influence over Supreme Court nominations, the precise allegation Mondale had leveled.[78]

On October 11, 1984, the sole vice presidential debate took place in Philadelphia. Democratic candidate Geraldine Ferraro also singled out Falwell by name. "I also object when I am told that the Reverend Falwell has been told he will pick two of our Supreme Court justices," Ferraro said. "That's going a little bit far . . . and I think that is in violation of our Constitution." When questioned as to whether or not her characterization was fair, Ferraro's staff cited a remark by Falwell that "in Ronald Reagan's next five years in office we will get at least two more appointments to the Supreme Court." Cal Thomas, speaking for the Moral Majority, countered that when Falwell said "we" he was referring to conservatives as a whole, not to the Moral Majority specifically. Thomas said the Democrats clearly thought that Reverend Falwell was "an albatross" around the president's neck, but that no one could seriously believe Falwell would be picking the next Supreme Court justices. "It's ridiculous and inaccurate—but we hope they keep it up," Thomas said, noting that whenever Mondale or Ferraro attacked Falwell, the minister's supporters "sit down and write us out a check." Thomas also contended that the attacks had the perverse effect of motivating religious conservatives: "They think Jerry must be doing something right if he is being attacked by Mondale and Ferraro."[79]

Falwell called for a national day of prayer and fasting from sundown Sunday until sundown on the Monday immediately before the election. He called for a "spiritual awakening" and urged voters to support candidates who were opposed to the "national sin" of abortion. Meanwhile, the Moral Majority set up phone banks to get out the vote. The organization's PAC, however, was strangely inefficient. It raised $586,058 and spent more than that amount on publicity and fundraising expenses, but it distributed only $35,628 to federal candidates and another $24,792 to nonfederal candidates. The PAC was incapable of putting the Moral Majority's money where its mouth was.[80]

The mainstream media were clearly focused on Falwell's reaction to the election results. All three major networks and CNN set up cameras in his office in Lynchburg to record his views. "He [Falwell] has become part of the focus of the election," said a spokesman for NBC. Between 9:00 and 11:00 P.M. on election night, Falwell gave twenty interviews. His interview with the British Broadcasting Corporation was broadcast live to forty-two countries. "So far, this is a delightful evening," Falwell said. "I predicted Ronald Reagan would win 50 states and it looks like we may have a chance."[81]

Reagan did not win all fifty states, but he came close, losing only Mondale's home state of Minnesota and the District of Columbia. "I've been feeling this landslide for five months," Falwell enthused. Whatever doubts some conservatives had about the president, Falwell was still loyal to the cause, and he basked in the afterglow of Reagan's sweeping victory. Falwell also expressed his satisfaction with the victories of several Moral Majority–backed congressional candidates, especially Sen. Jesse Helms in North Carolina. The Moral Majority would continue to have access to the halls of power in Washington, and Falwell's prominence in the attacks coming from the Democrats were icing on the cake. By attacking him personally and warning against his "intrusion" into the world of politics, Mondale and Ferraro had done for Falwell something Reagan had not done: they anointed Falwell as the undoubted face of activist, involved Christianity in American culture.

Jerry Falwell was many things, but self-conscious was not among them. He was a bundle of energy, a man given to activity not reflection, a doer not a thinker. If he had been a Catholic priest, he might have been a missionary or an extraordinarily active pastor, but never a contemplative monk. His prominence within the culture required, however, that he assess his role and craft a self-image, if for no other reason than because journalists who interviewed him continually asked him questions that demanded such self-assessment. He could not escape evaluating his ministry, his political activity, and his very self.

Falwell had long understood the importance of self-promotion, and he was not afraid to brag about his successes. When he first formed the Thomas Road Baptist Church, he had advertised the church's growing numbers on virtually every early radio and television show, as well as in his sermons. When he began the Moral Majority in 1979, he knew that enrolling members was important not just for fund-raising but to add to the group's reputation as influential.

In a November 1981 press conference in Nashville, where Falwell was holding a fund-raiser for Liberty Baptist College, he claimed that his Thomas Road Baptist Church had more than nineteen thousand members, making it one of the largest churches in the country. He also said that the Moral Majority now boasted more than five million members. And his *Old-Time Gospel Hour* was carried on more than four hundred stations. "And that's two hundred more than Johnny Carson," Falwell said. His road trips, whether to attend fund-raisers like the event in Nashville or political rallies for Moral Majority, always included a press conference where he could repeat the mantra that his church and his political influence were growing.[82]

In April 1983, Falwell further inflated the numbers associated with his efforts. In asserting that "we have about 25 million people pledging allegiance to our flag," he acknowledged that the number included those who watched the *Old-Time Gospel Hour* as well as those who were members of Moral Majority. Even conflating the two groups, Falwell's estimate was on the generous side. The *Old-Time Gospel Hour* had only some 3.5 million donors in the early 1980s, and surveys from two television rating agencies, A. C. Nielsen and Arbitron, indicated that all television evangelists combined enjoyed an audience of only 7 to 10 million viewers.[83]

Falwell understood that his success, inflated or not, was creating a backlash; he also knew that many people who did not object to the Moral Majority's policy agenda might harbor concerns, "because nobody, conservative or liberal, wants any organization in this country to become so big and so powerful that they can dictate direction." Speaking in Colorado in April 1983, Falwell said that he thought his organization had to avoid appearing too dominant. "We've always got to be the underdog," Falwell said. He said that in 1980 it had been possible to be a bit "reckless," but that at that time "we had no negative rating to overcome"—a rating they had acquired by 1983.[84]

His worries about a backlash notwithstanding, he could not help relishing his role in fashioning a "spiritual awakening" in America. The 1970s and 1980s were a time when membership in mainline Protestant churches was declining, but evangelical churches continued to grow. Although Falwell said that fundamentalist churches were "the only growing churches in America," Pentecostal churches and the Roman Catholic church continued to experience growth as well. Falwell also touted the expansion of the Christian school movement, telling an interviewer for the *Washington Times* in the autumn of 1983, "It is the most optimistic, encouraging thing that's happening today in the world of education, because all of these teachers and their school leaders and pastors are free enterprisers, they're strong national defense people and they're moralists according to the Judeo-Christian tradition." It was one thing to extol the political consequences of the expansion of Christian schooling in an internal fund-raising letter or in a sermon at Thomas Road Baptist Church, but Falwell also felt confident in explaining the link to a newspaper reporter. This was quintessential Falwell. One month he worried about appearing too dominant, and the next month he was indicating how Christian schools were making the nation more capitalist and pro-defense.[85]

By year's end, in an interview with USA Today, Falwell claimed that there were 110,000 fundamentalist-evangelical churches in America, running 34,000 schools. He said that there were 1,600 Christian radio stations and 79 Christian television stations. The following spring he told an interviewer of the inroads being made by his Liberty Baptist College. "Our school of journalism," he said, "is a tremendous opportunity to do what the left has done to us—that is infiltrate the media." He was breaking through the culture in a variety of ways, he knew it, and he liked his prospects.

For all his self-confidence, in these same years Falwell was aware that his image was, in a sense, public property, and he took measures to avoid being defined by his critics. Typically, he often contradicted himself within a matter of months. For example, in a December 1981 interview, Falwell tried to distinguish himself from other "New Right" political operatives. "I'm a minister of the Gospel and I don't want to get polarized into endorsing candidates or opposing candidates," Falwell said, even though he was not shy about making his political preferences known and he would soon be forming a PAC that endorsed political candidates. In that same interview, Falwell admitted that he did not like having to send out such harsh fund-raising letters. "Everything we say is true but the approach is a very aggressive one," Falwell said, comparing his tactics to those of the ACLU. He said that his staff insisted on the fund-raising letters being over-the-top in their rhetoric because "people respond far better when the facts are laid before them in a very emotional appeal. I wish that wasn't true. But I realize that everyone is doing it." This is an alarming admission, so full of political sophistication and so seemingly unaware of the moral slipperiness of his argument.[86]

A few months later, visiting Dallas to speak at a Baptist Bible Fellowship convention, Falwell denied that he had moderated his views in order to become more acceptable to larger numbers of voters. Some conservatives had become increasingly critical of a perceived deviation from conservative orthodoxy on the part of the Reagan administration, and they turned their criticisms on Falwell too when he counseled patience with Reagan. Falwell also had an alternative explanation for the continuing growth of the Moral Majority: he believed that it was due to his ability to reclaim his image from his critics through multiple media appearances. "I think I've shown in the last year that I'm not an ayatollah trying to force what I believe down everyone else's throat," Falwell said.[87]

Falwell knew he was no ayatollah, and he rightly resented being painted as such. The double standard that was applied to him continued to reflect more poorly on his accusers than on him. When the National Council of Churches released a "non-sexist Bible," Falwell pointed out that there was no outcry from the media. "If conservatives had taken the Bible and said, 'We're going to rewrite it because we don't like the anti-racist position of the Bible and make it a racist book,' we would have been decried from every major magazine and media in the country," Falwell said. "The liberals do it, and not a blooming word is ever said about it, which shows the hypocrisy in the national media." His choice of analogy is arguably illustrative of the ongoing role that race played in conservative political calculations, but his argument about bias was a valid one.[88]

In addition to disassociating himself from the secular New Right, Falwell began to understand the importance of publicly distancing himself from those whose religious views were more extreme than his own. When asked in an interview if part of his task as head of the Moral Majority was "defining the limits of lunacy on the right," he answered that he was indeed playing that role. "Our most ardent enemies are not on the left. They are on the far right," Falwell told *Our Sunday Visitor* in December 1981. "We're looked on as compromisers. One person actually accused me of being the Anti-Christ and that with Moral Majority I was forming the one world Church right now merging Protestants, Catholics and Jews into a conglomerate to take over the world." He said that in undermining his base of support conservatives could cause harm that liberals could not.[89]

Facing critics on both the left and the right was a task that Falwell performed with facility, but it took him a longer time to understand that his brashness was off-putting to those who neither demonized him nor shared his views. In 1984 he even acknowledged that he might have been wrong to select the name "Moral Majority" for his organization. "It sounded right at the time, but looking back I would say it was wrong because it presumes everyone who does not agree with us to be immoral, which was not the intent," Falwell said in a rare moment of public self-correction. He did not repeat the correction, but he would change the name of the organization in a few years' time.[90]

Falwell also began to acknowledge that he and his organization had gone through a "maturing process" since Moral Majority was formed in 1979, and that they had "learned about mistakes we've made." But he reached a conclusion with which many of his critics would have disagreed. "We've looked carefully to see what it is that we are saying and doing that would leave the impression that we are very arbitrary, vindictive and that we have an ayatollah-type complex," Falwell said. "And, honestly, the only thing we were able to come up with is that we've stayed on the defensive too much. When you are defending, obviously, you have to be defensive." As with his pulpit tales, the admissions of wrongdoing only went so far.[91]

In fact, Falwell had matured considerably by the time the 1984 elections came around, and while that newfound maturity was not always or consistently on display, he did give hints of more nuanced views. We have already seen that he had no difficulty appreciating the complexity of the political process and that he had agreed to Reagan's decision to face economic issues first before taking up the conservative social agenda. And even though he had recognized that efforts to pass a constitutional amendment on school prayer would be unsuccessful, he saw as well the necessity of getting members of Congress on record on the issue. He was increasingly sophisticated about politics, even if he was rarely subtle.

Toward the end of 1983 and throughout the election year, Falwell also began to articulate a very interesting explanation for the social upheavals of the 1960s and 1970s, decades he called "the dark ages of the 20th century." He argued that in the post–World War II era, men and women who had survived the Depression and the war were determined that their own children would have every material advantage possible. "So they began to give them things—money, cars, luxuries, comforts—but without transferring to the children the moral and traditional values like the work ethics that make things have meaning. And this ushered in a period of unparalleled materialism." He said that the materialism without a robust values system had resulted in "rebellion," and he blamed the drug culture, the spread of sexual diseases, and the rising divorce rate on this rebellion. Falwell did not take this critique to the next level, and he would never qualify his endorsement of capitalism, which in the postwar era became characterized by a spread-eagle consumerism that undercut the very values that Falwell cherished.

One value, freedom, was central and ambiguous in Falwell's lexicon. The freedom of the children of God was never exactly the same thing as the freedom guaranteed by the Constitution or the freedom unleashed by capitalism. In one area, foreign policy, he realized that he had failed to make the connection between his moral compass and his political one, and he invoked the concept of religious freedom to justify his politics. In an article in his *Fundamentalist Journal* in the summer of 1984, Falwell provided a somewhat convoluted link between his forays into foreign policy and his pulpit values, but a link nonetheless. "As a minister of the gospel, my number-one priority must be world evangelism," Falwell wrote. "But as a citizen, I must also be concerned with maintaining personal and religious freedom in our nation so we will be free to proclaim the gospel. As a citizen I am concerned about abortion, pornography, and so forth. These are moral evils, to be sure, but they are not so great an issue as freedom. If we lose our freedoms, everything else is academic." He argued that the citizens of communist countries could not even fight against moral evils, because they were unfree, and this was why he supported Reagan's robust anticommunism. He did not elaborate a detailed theological analysis of his commitment to Reagan's foreign policy, but he had at least attempted to establish a link between those policies and his pulpit. Falwell's rationales always had a ring of certainty, a "QED" quality, as if his conclusions were essentially self-evident.[92]

Between the 1980 and 1984 elections, Falwell had indeed undergone a process of maturing. He had enlarged the scope of his activities, first to politics, then to the broader culture. He had shaped the image of his organization, trying to beat back the charge of extremism while still serving red meat to his base. He had stepped confidently along the divides between religion and society and between faith and culture, even if he sometimes put a foot wrong. Falwell would plead that he was acting only as a private citizen one moment and then tout the growth of the Moral Majority the next. He adopted essentially political arguments and tactics without ever abandoning his claim to be speaking with the moral authority that came with his pastorate.

Falwell emerged on the national stage as a man of contradictions, but he never experienced himself as such. It was not that he was shrewd about some things and naive about others. That is the human condition. Falwell could be shrewd and naive about the same thing at the same time—as in his frank admission that his fund-raising appeals were distasteful but necessary. It does not reflect well on his pastoral priorities at the time that, in that instance, he was shrewd about politics and naive about the moral implications of his crass, even hateful, fund-raising letters.

Falwell was all action—verbose action to be sure. He was always in motion, always moving forward toward his goal of fashioning a spiritual awakening that would produce a more robustly moral America, but moving via several roads simultaneously. His efforts led him to bump up against other dominant sociocultural forces that he often neither understood nor valued. And while many wrongly viewed Falwell's political activity as a threat to the First Amendment's guarantee of church-state separation, he was about to bump up against a different First Amendment guarantee—freedom of the press. That bump would change the legal landscape of the nation.

Chapter Ten

The First Amendment

Falwell v. Flynt

It is not hard to imagine the revulsion that Jerry Falwell felt when a reporter thrust a copy of *Hustler* magazine at him and asked what he thought of his inclusion in its pages. He did not take the time to look at it, but any association of his good name with that of a smut peddler was sure to rankle. He had sued *Penthouse* when they published an interview with him, submitted by two freelance writers who had not disclosed to Falwell that they might publish the interview in the notorious porn magazine. He had spent many years fighting to restrict the sale of pornographic magazines in convenience stores. Now the worst of the worst, Larry Flynt's *Hustler,* had seen fit to run a parody featuring him. "That is probably nothing new," Falwell said to the reporter, walking off and carrying his disgust with him.[1]

The November 1983 issue of *Hustler,* however, was something new. The vulgar parody suggesting that Falwell had lost his virginity to his mother in an outhouse embodied for Falwell all that was wrong with America culture. How could someone publish such evil? Surely there should be a punishment, not just in the next life but in this life, for such depravity. In filing suit against Flynt, Falwell would put the culture of sexual libertinism itself on trial and challenge the courts to defend his honor, and that of his mother, from such libelous attacks on God-fearing people.

At stake was more than a set of legal issues, although the fact that this struggle took place in the courts would shape both its content and its outcome. For Flynt and those who defended his right to publish the satire, the First Amendment was sacrosanct, designed to protect precisely the kind of vile, offensive speech that Flynt published. For Falwell, his suit was about protecting decency in society. Flynt's America was all about money and sex and doing whatever one wanted. Falwell's America was all about decorum and morals and doing God's will. The suit would go all the way to the U.S. Supreme Court. And of all the strange turns and twists the litigation took, the strangest was the friendship between Falwell and Flynt that grew out of the proceedings and that lasted until Falwell's death in 2007.

No one has to imagine what Falwell felt when, having thought better of his breezy dismissal of the *Hustler* issue the reporter had shown him, he asked an assistant to procure a copy of the magazine and he actually sat down to read the parody. At the subsequent trial, he told the court, "I think I have never been as angry as I was at that moment. . . . I somehow felt that in all of my life I had never believed that human beings could do something like this. I really felt like weeping. I am not a deeply emotional person; I don't show it. I think I felt like weeping."[2]

Well he might. The parody had become a regular feature at *Hustler*. At the time the Italian liqueur Campari was running a series of ads in which celebrities discussed the first time they had tried the aperitif. Using highly sensualized language to describe their experience of titillation when they had first imbibed Campari, the celebrities spoke in double entendres around the words "my first time," words that could easily be used to describe one's loss of virginity. It was a memorable ad campaign, and it proved an inviting target for the humorists at *Hustler*.

Like everything else about *Hustler*, the key to its parody was vulgarization—in this case the suggestion that Falwell had lost his virginity in an incestuous liaison with his mother in an outhouse. The ad parody showed Falwell with a bottle of Campari. The text was printed in interview format.

FALWELL: My first time was in an outhouse outside Lynchburg, Virginia.

INTERVIEWER: Wasn't it a bit cramped?

FALWELL: Not after I kicked the goat out.

INTERVIEWER: I see. You must tell me all about it.

FALWELL: I never really expected to make it with Mom, but then after she showed all the other guys in town such a good time, I figured, "What the hell!"

INTERVIEWER: But your Mom? Isn't that a bit odd?

FALWELL: I don't think so. Looks don't mean much to me in a woman.

INTERVIEWER: Go on.

FALWELL: Well, we were drunk off our God-fearing asses on Campari, ginger ale and soda—that's called a Fire and Brimstone—at the time. And Mom looked better than a Baptist whore with a $100 donation.

INTERVIEWER: Campari in the crapper with Mom . . . how interesting. Well, how was it?

FALWELL: The Campari was great, but Mom passed out before I could come.

INTERVIEWER: Did you ever try it again?

FALWELL: Sure . . . lots of times. But not in the outhouse. Between Mom and the shit, the flies were too much to bear.

INTERVIEWER: We meant the Campari.

FALWELL: Oh yeah. I always get sloshed before I go out to the

*pulpit. You don't think I could lay down all that bullshit sober,
do you?*

A disclaimer appeared at the bottom of the page, reading, "Ad
Parody—Not to Be Taken Seriously." The disclaimer, of course, was
small comfort to Falwell; he was genuinely shocked by the ad's vul-
garity and did not understand, still less appreciate, that "shock" was
the raison d'être of *Hustler*.[3]

Larry Flynt, the publisher of *Hustler*, and Reverend Falwell, despite
their obvious differences, shared certain characteristics. Both had
grown up in rural America, and each had been precocious in his
youth. Flynt enlisted in the Army at the age of fourteen, telling an
Army recruiter he was really eighteen. Both were successful entre-
preneurs who built their respective empires on the strength of their
forceful personalities. Both found themselves challenging the dominant culture, albeit from different ends of the ideological spectrum.
And both Flynt and Falwell were entirely, and sincerely, devoted to a
vision of what it meant to be an American, what the Constitution
meant, and what was good or bad for the nation.

Flynt had turned the newsletter for his strip clubs in Ohio into
a national magazine with more than two million monthly subscribers by 1983. *Hustler*, like its founder, was the "bad boy" of the porn
industry, eschewing the glamorization of sex seen in publications
like *Playboy* and *Penthouse*, reveling in grotesque images of dismem-
berment, excrement, and the like, lampooning its competitors for
their dandified approach, and, as often as not, lampooning itself
as well. Satire, parody, mockery, shocking images, these were what
made *Hustler* so offensive—and so successful. In addition to his
magazine, Flynt developed a distribution company that trafficked in
mainstream magazines as well. He was, by 1983, as successful in his
line of work as Falwell had become in the world of evangelism.

Flynt was as committed to his understanding of the First Amendment as Falwell was to the New Testament. Flynt led the legal fight
against the Reagan administration when reporters were forbidden

to go into Grenada with the U.S. Marines. He mailed copies of his magazine to all the members of Congress and successfully defended a suit brought against him for the effort, the courts ruling that Congress had no right to *not* receive mail and Flynt had a constitutional right to petition his government. The same month the Falwell ad parody came out Flynt had stood before the justices of the U.S. Supreme Court and delivered a vulgar rant of a kind never before heard in that august chamber—"Fuck this court!"—all in an attempt to prove his point: freedom of speech knew no limits. For his efforts, he was arrested on the spot for contempt of court, a charge that was later dropped. The Supreme Court ruled against him in the underlying case.

In 1978 Flynt was put on trial in Lawrenceville, Georgia, for publishing obscenity. It was there, returning to the courtroom after a lunch break, that Flynt was shot in the abdomen by an assailant who was never apprehended. Flynt thought that his investigations into the assassination of President Kennedy were the true cause of the attack. The gunshot wound left him paralyzed from the waist down, and he lived in chronic pain, alleviated only by massive amounts of the pain killer Dilaudid. A subsequent surgery to sever the nerves in his legs ended the pain, but in the meantime his wife Althea had become addicted to his painkillers. She died from an overdose in 1987.

Falwell responded to Flynt's parody with indignation. But he also consulted with his lawyers and decided to respond as well with a lawsuit. And true to form, Jerry Falwell recognized in this most vile attack an opportunity for fund-raising. Lawsuits are expensive, and Falwell knew that his followers would relish the opportunity not only to defend their hero's honor but to do battle against the porn industry.

Falwell sent out three different mailings in the next month regarding the *Hustler* parody. The first went to 500,000 members of the Moral Majority and asked for contributions to assist him to "defend his mother's memory." The second mailing went to a more exclusive list of almost 27,000 major donors to the Moral Majority. "As you know, legal matters are time consuming and expensive. . . . Will you help me defend my family and myself against the smears and slander of this major pornographic magazine—will you send a gift of $500 so that we may take up this important legal battle?" In this mailing, Falwell actually included a copy of the ad, blotting out the most offensive language. Finally, in a mailing to 750,000 people on the *Old-Time Gospel Hour* mailing list, Falwell asked for money, not to prosecute the lawsuit but to keep the show on the air. He told his viewers that this latest attack showed why it was necessary to keep the *Old-Time Gospel Hour* on as many channels as possible. "When I saw [the ad]—I decided that, in a society containing people like Larry Flynt, the Old Time Gospel Hour must remain on the air—on every station." He asked for donations in the amount of $150.[4]

In light of Falwell's future legal claim that the ad caused him emotional distress, it may seem odd that he would share a copy of it with 27,000 of his most loyal donors. "But it isn't irrational when you figure in the $50 contribution Falwell is seeking from each of the ad's recipients," opined Gene Owens, editorial page editor of the *Roanoke Times & World-News* on November 27. "Falwell and the nudie press enjoy a symbiotic relationship—he helping their circulation and they helping his cash flow." Indeed, the legal battle for which Falwell was ostensibly raising money would further raise the profile of both preacher and pornographer.[5]

Falwell filed suit in federal district court on October 31. He asked for $5 million in compensatory damages and $10 million in punitive damages in each of the three counts. The suit alleged, the *Washington Post* reported, that "the ad was an invasion of privacy, intentionally caused emotional distress and was libelous because it implied that Falwell committed a criminal offense involving moral turpitude." Falwell claimed that the ad was intended "merely to attract the attention of the public for the purpose of enhancing the sales of Hustler magazine." Although this is the purpose of most editorial content in a magazine, Falwell's claim revealed one of the deepest sources of his anger: his good name was being used to sell smut.[6]

The charges themselves were not remarkable given the circumstances, but Falwell's choice of a lawyer to handle the case raised more than a few eyebrows. Norman Roy Grutman had gone to Yale University and Columbia Law School. He was a partner at the prestigious New York firm Grutman, Miller, Greenspoon, Hendler and Levin. He was one of the most famous trial lawyers in America, a reputation that derived principally from his defense of his most famous client, Bob Guccione, the publisher of *Penthouse* magazine. It was Grutman who had defeated Falwell in court in 1981 when Falwell had sued to prevent *Penthouse* from publishing the interview he had given to the two freelance reporters. Throughout the trial Grutman had referred to Falwell as "Foulwell" in an effort to unnerve him, and Falwell appreciated the fact that similarly unnerving Flynt might be helpful at trial. Grutman said that there was nothing ironic in his now representing Falwell. To be hired by a former adversary, he said, "is the highest kind of compliment a lawyer can have."[7]

The choice of Grutman further compounded the sense that the reverend was developing a symbiotic relationship with the pornography industry. "There was more than a little irony in the fact that much of the money sent in to Falwell's coffers by all those faithful little old ladies from the Bible Belt and those Moral Majority donors was funneling its way in legal fees to a lawyer who had made his career working for Bob Guccione," observed a historian of the trial. Irony or no, the choice was Falwell's to make, and he chose well. Grutman was fearless in the courtroom, a man whose first, second, and third commitment was to winning. In the *Penthouse* case, he had been relentless in his attacks on Falwell. Now Falwell enlisted that same skill in his defense.[8]

Grutman grasped that to win his suit he had to do more than argue the legal merits of the case. This would be a jury trial, and so he needed to paint Falwell in the most glowing terms—as a pillar of Virginia society, a champion of a way of life shared by many of the jurors, a man devoted to educating the young and forming Christian consciences, a tireless minister of the Gospel. However controversial Falwell's views were outside the precincts of southwestern Virginia, this trial would be conducted in southwestern Virginia. The attitudes and biases of the region may have been foreign to Grutman, who was described in the local Lynchburg paper as "this plump, almost prissy, New York attorney," but they were not foreign to Falwell: these were his people, and Grutman knew his plaintiff would play well with the jurors.[9]

Every morality play needs a villain, so while Grutman was presenting Falwell as a paragon of virtue and decency he needed to portray Flynt as a veritable anti-Christ. Flynt was not only tailor-made for the role; he had made the clothes himself. He had denounced the Bible as the "biggest piece of shit ever written" in a recent interview with *Vanity Fair*. Despite his yearlong "conversion," under the guidance of Ruth Carter Stapleton, sister of the former president, in the 1970s, Flynt had no lingering respect for religious sensibilities. In the *Vanity Fair* interview, he had raised the prospect of Jesus being gay, but dismissed it on the grounds that He was having carnal relations with Mary Magdalene. His modus operandi, which had made him a multimillionaire, was to offend, but however effective this had proved as a marketing device, it would not play any better with a conservative jury than it had with the justices of the Supreme Court.[10]

The first decision facing Judge James C. Turk was determining the venue for the trial. Flynt's attorneys, citing his ill health, had asked that the trial be moved to Los Angeles. Falwell wanted the trial to be held right in Lynchburg, but Flynt's lawyers objected that it would be impossible to impanel an impartial jury in a town where Falwell was not only a neighbor but one of the city's largest employers. As a sort of compromise, Judge Turk decided to hold the trial in Roanoke, noting that the attorneys were from New York and Los Angeles so a neutral site seemed appropriate.

The local court expected a media frenzy on December 4, when the trial was to begin. The *Washington Post* said that the trial was "the best show in town," complete with "suspense, comedy, pathos, videotapes and dramatic speeches from a theatrical New York lawyer." Metal detectors were erected outside the courtroom, which held about eighty spectators. "We need more crowd control with Jerry

Falwell and his notoriety and Larry Flynt's notoriety in the opposite direction, just as a safety precaution," said Turk's law clerk Terri Dial. Although civil trials required a jury of only seven members, both sides had agreed to a full twelve-member jury. Instead of the usual twenty prospective jurors called for the process of *voir dire* by which the jury was selected, Judge Turk asked for fifty potential jurors, anticipating that the fireworks between the lawyers would begin early and that church membership or familiarity with Falwell's preaching (or Flynt's magazine) might be cause to disqualify potential jurors.[11]

The media frenzy did not immediately materialize. On the first day of the trial a local reporter went to the courtroom early, expecting to find long lines and a crush of fellow journalists. "I arrived early Tuesday morning half-expecting a howling mob outside the courthouse," Darrell Laurent wrote in the *Lynchburg News*. "Maybe ticket scalpers. What I found, instead, was a contingent of bored sheriff's deputies, a sheet of spectator ground rules taped to the outside glass and an almost eerie serenity. The howling mob must be up on the second floor, I thought. Nope. All I saw there was a sign that read 'Media Headquarters, Room 302.' I investigated. The room was empty."[12]

Media frenzy or not, the press was focused on the issues at the heart of the trial, and the attorneys for both sides were busy making their case to the press in advance of their presentations to the court. "The whole Flynt canon is gratuitous and malicious for sheer injury," Grutman told the *Washington Times*. "And if you can pick out a popular person to injure, so much greater the joy. He picked the Rev. [Mr.] Falwell because he is one of the most prominent people in America." Flynt's attorney, Alan Isaacman, was quick to go to the central argument of his defense. "Who cares how gleeful Larry was?" said Isaacman. "It's not defamatory, and it was not meant to be taken seriously. Only statements of fact, not parody, can be defamatory." Both sides understood that the libel charge would succeed or fail based on whether the jury thought that the disclaimer at the bottom of the ad parody was sufficient to remove any culpability for stating the clear untruths contained in the ad.

Grutman also told the press that Falwell's status as a public figure would not necessarily defeat the libel claim, since the law was not settled on this point. Here was an issue of great importance to all publishers of magazines and newspapers: did the fact that a public figure was a public figure automatically raise the bar for a libel claim? Grutman thought not, but his argument was a weak one. After all, if Reverend Falwell had never ventured beyond his pulpit, it was doubtful that anyone would have been doing a parody of him in the first place. Falwell had decided to venture into the public square of politics, where people need to know how to throw a punch and take a punch, but Grutman needed to insist that this did not warrant the kind of vile and personal attack that Flynt unleashed.

The jury was impaneled. Eight women and four men—Falwell would later describe the jurors as a "real church crowd"—would hear the testimony, which included an appearance by Sen. Jesse Helms as a character witness for Falwell. "In my judgment, there is no finer citizen than Jerry Falwell," the senator told the court. "He is easily one of the most dedicated men, not only to his noble profession, but to this country." The case would not be decided, however, by the comments of the friends of the principals. It was the testimony of Falwell and Flynt themselves that would be decisive.[13]

Falwell was the first to be questioned. Attorney Grutman led him through a long account of his life and good works. He was questioned about the start of his ministry and its subsequent growth. He was questioned about his work in the field of education and about starting an elementary school and then a high school and finally a college. He was asked to detail the various honorary degrees and awards he had received and asked about being named "Clergyman of the Year" by one group and "Humanitarian of the Year" by another. Methodically, the case was being made: Falwell was a model citizen whose entire life and work was being smeared by the contemptuous porn king who had libeled him and his mother.

It was Falwell's relationship with his mother, however, that provided the emotional punch of the case. Falwell spoke about her role in his conversion, about listening to the sermons of Dr. Fuller that she played on the radio. He spoke of going every week to his mother's home and of how she would cook breakfast for him: "She was a little better cook than my wife; my wife is better now, but she was better then. But she knew exactly what I liked. . . ." Falwell said that his mother had been a member of his church from the very beginning. When asked about her personal conduct as it pertained to the case, he replied, "I would stake my life on her purity." Grutman, after his opposite counsel interrupted several times to ask whether they were willing to stipulate to Mrs. Falwell's purity, reached the conclusion. "Mr. Falwell, specifically, did you and your mother ever commit incest?" Grutman asked. "Absolutely not," came the reply. The contrast could not have been lost on the jury: Falwell's life of good works and filial devotion to his mother, rudely interrupted by Flynt's disgusting charge, just as Grutman's question about incest interrupted the catalog of virtue that had gone before.

Grutman read from the ad parody and solicited comments from Falwell about it. Then, to offset the impression that Falwell could not take a joke, Grutman asked if he had been the object of satires and caricatures by others, to which Falwell rejoined that he enjoyed most of them. "But with respect to the materials that I have shown to you in this case, what is your reaction or response to it in terms of your feelings?" Grutman asked. Falwell's response epitomized the "emotional distress" that served as the basis for one of the legal claims against Flynt: "It is the most hurtful, damaging, despicable, low-type personal attack that I can imagine one human being can inflict upon another."

Flynt took the stand, and his burden was different from Falwell's. In a taped deposition that had been shown to the jury, Flynt had ranted and raved, screaming expletives and shouting down his own attorney when Isaacman tried to interrupt the relentless questioning from Grutman. The deposition was damning, showing with all the verisimilitude of videotape that Flynt was a man who delighted in spewing hatred and bile at others. At the time of the deposition Flynt was in a federal penitentiary on a contempt of court charge. He claimed that not only had he been suffering from bedsores, but he had been in the manic phase of his manic-depression and prison officials had not given him his medicine. More important than any particular answer to any particular question, it was necessary for Flynt to appear sane and calm in the courtroom, in the hope that the jurors would dismiss the taped deposition as the rantings of a man who had been suffering from acute mental illness at the time. "People don't like to admit it when they have a mental problem. I didn't want to admit it to myself. I was sick when I was in North Carolina. . . . I wasn't okay! You know I wasn't okay!" Flynt claimed. Despite Grutman's best efforts to unnerve him, Flynt remained calm throughout his testimony in court. The jury would have to decide which Flynt was the real one.

The other objective for Flynt was to show that the ad had been meant as a joke. He pointed out that his magazine made fun of many people, including the president of the United States. He noted that he had previously run other parodies of Falwell, who was "good copy." Flynt acknowledged that his magazine was not everyone's cup of tea, but he defended strenuously his right to publish and not be sued for his views. But his key theme was the nature of parody. "Well, you know, as far as making it with his mother," Flynt told the court, "I mean, that's so outrageous, I mean, that no one can find that believable."

Before sending the case to the jury, Judge Turk dismissed the charge that *Hustler* had used Falwell's name for commercial purposes without proper authorization. In fact, Flynt subsequently sued Falwell for copyright violations because the preacher had made copies of the ad parody and sent it out as part of a mailing to raise funds, all without getting proper authorization from *Hustler*. Falwell raised $717,000 from the mailing. In 1986 a court would rule that Falwell had not infringed *Hustler*'s copyrights.[14]

The jury therefore had only to rule on the libel charge and the claim that the ad parody had been intended to inflict emotional distress on Falwell. It returned a split verdict. It found that the ad was a parody and therefore did not involve facts, and that without a proven disregard for the facts, no libel could be alleged. But the jury also found that the ad had been written with the intention of inflicting emotional distress on Falwell and that it offended against generally accepted standards of decency. The jury awarded Falwell $100,000 in compensatory damages and the same amount in punitive damages.[15]

Despite the mixed verdict, Falwell claimed victory. "So far, so good," Falwell said after the preliminary verdict was announced. And when the final verdict was reached, he proclaimed, "We're very pleased. What has been proven here is that [neither] Mr. Flynt nor anyone else can prostitute the First Amendment. He felt that you can use the First Amendment to hurt anyone you want, and I think the jury decided that you can't do that." Later, speaking in front of his own congregation at Thomas Road Baptist Church, Falwell would interpret the verdict in the most expansive terms: "It says to Larry Flynt and his ilk that from here on out, there is a line. The First Amendment is not absolute. . . . You must pay the piper." He also expressed his lack of animosity toward Flynt personally. "I hope one day to hear that fellow really got saved," he said. "And I'd like to be the one to lead him to Christ. But I said when he does get saved, he'll shut his magazine down."[16]

The verdict also caught the attention of the press, not only as a news event but as a threat to their own First Amendment rights. The *Washington Post* editors called the jury's verdict "unusual and wrong" in finding for Falwell on the emotional distress claim.

They found that Mr. Flynt had purposely caused the Moral Majority leader "emotional distress" and they awarded him $200,000 in damages. Suits asking damages for emotional distress are rare and not generally filed by public figures. They require proof of outrageous conduct and do not involve the publication of words alone. In one reported case, for example, a woman suffered a mental collapse after being told by a malicious prankster to rush to a funeral home because her husband and children had been killed in an accident; in another, a man was put in fear of his life when a mob assembled and threatened to lynch him. The Falwell case does not fit this pattern, and if it is allowed to stand, there is a chance that people in

the public eye who cannot win libel suits will instead charge
that they have been embarrassed, or made uncomfortable or
ridiculed, and threaten to sue for particularly sharp or robust
criticism.

The editors were especially worried that making it easier for public officials to win libel suits would have a stifling effect on the lively
debate by which democracies flourish. "Discussion, debate and certainly satire and parody involving public figures are to be welcomed;
they cannot be penalized without diminishing and endangering free
speech."[17]

Whatever one thought of the jury verdict, it was clear that the
result was provisional. Flynt intended to appeal the ruling, and on
several previous occasions he had lost jury verdicts in the lower
courts only to have the verdicts overturned on appeal. Juries can
be swayed by their general disgust at pornographers, but courts of
appeal are more attuned to the constitutional guarantees of the First
Amendment. The case moved to the Fourth Circuit Court of Appeals
in Richmond, where there would be no jury.

A trial involves fitting the law to meet a set of facts. A jury determines
issues such as intent and injury. As the case *Falwell v. Flynt* moved to
the appellate level, the nature of the case changed. At the first trial
Flynt and Falwell were the principals, and their testimony and the
evidence presented were what decided the case. The lawyers—especially such flamboyant lawyers as Grutman and Isaacman—were key
actors in the drama, but juries tend to focus on the witnesses as much
as the arguments.

At the appellate level, neither Flynt nor Falwell would be called
on to testify. The issues before the three-judge panel in Richmond
were issues of law, not of fact, and thus the central player in the
drama would be not a person but a principle: the First Amendment.
Had the jury verdict gone too far? Did the relative weight of First
Amendment rights change when the jury shifted from considering
the charge of libel to considering the charge of intentionally inflict-

ing emotional distress? Should it change? As the editors of the *Washington Post* worried, if "emotional distress" is enough to create a tort against newspapers and magazines, wouldn't this have a chilling effect on public debate and discourse?

A key issue in applying the "emotional distress" tort was the fact that Jerry Falwell was a public figure. A private person would have lacked the resources to respond to the kind of personal invective that Flynt had directed at Falwell and, more important, could reasonably believe that his or her private position in life came with the right to be left alone. Public figures, by definition, lack such a clear right to be left alone. Cartoonists poke fun at public figures for a living, and some of the cartoons are doubtless distressing to those they target. Political figures have never been immune from such attacks, nor have they been able to recover damages because of the attacks on their views or their character, unless the attack was libelous.

Both attorneys could cite a string of opinions to back up their position. Isaacman could argue that the "emotional distress" charge amounted to allowing a "heckler's veto": someone who objected to another's expression of ideas could simply claim emotional distress, just as a person or group that did not like something they heard could start a riot and charge the speaker, not the mob, with the violence that ensued. This was the issue the Supreme Court had decided in 1949 in the case *Terminiello v. Chicago* when it ruled that unless the speaker intentionally tried to incite violence, he could not be held liable. Other rulings had held that just because language was objectionable did not mean it was unprotected by the First Amendment. Isaacman, freed now from the damning, emotionally fraught videotaped deposition and the effect it had had on the jury, had a strong case.[18]

Grutman, too, had a body of case law to which he could point. *Chaplinsky v. New Hampshire*, a decision by the Supreme Court in 1942, had set out a wide variety of speech that was deemed unworthy of First Amendment protections: "the lewd and obscene, the profane, the libelous, and the insulting or 'fighting' words" were all viewed as beyond the pale of First Amendment protections. A more recent set of rulings regarding the use of obscenities on television and radio—one as recent as 1978—had also demonstrated the high court's willingness to recognize values other than the free expression of ideas when deciding First Amendment cases. The First Amendment did not guarantee a license to say or publish whatever one wanted, even if Larry Flynt thought it should. Grutman, too, had a strong case.[19]

On August 6, 1986, a three-judge panel of the Court of Appeals upheld the jury's verdict. Flynt's attorney asked for the entire circuit, all eleven judges, to rehear the case *en banc*. In December that request was denied by a vote of 6–5. But in an unusual, although not unprecedented, move, Judge J. Harvie Wilkinson III filed a dissent from the decision not to hear the case *en banc*. Wilkinson had once been an editor at the *Norfolk-Virginian Pilot,* and so he shared the concern that Isaacman had expressed that the ruling would dampen the freedom of the press to pillory public figures if it saw fit. He recognized, too, that the more outrageous the satire the more likely it was to inflict emotional distress—but at the same time it was less likely to be taken at face value, as an assertion of fact. Wilkinson could not persuade enough of his colleagues to retry the case before the entire circuit, but by filing a formal dissent, his opinions became part of the formal record of the trial, should Flynt decide to appeal to the Supreme Court of the United States.

Flynt, unsurprisingly, appealed his case to the Supreme Court. The "emotional distress" tort simply did not seem to fit well when applied to the press, especially when applied to a satire or parody. No one had the right to tell someone their child was gravely ill when the child was fine. No one had the right to harass an employee in ways that made his or her job a torture. These were cases in which a victim should be able to recover on grounds of emotional distress. But after entering the public square, publicly condemning pornography and the "porn kings" who produced it, and encouraging boycotts of stores that sold pornographic magazines, did Reverend Falwell really have the right to expect that the porn kings would not strike back? Was not a thick hide part of the requirement for entering into public debate?

The mainstream press found itself in a bit of a quandary. It did not want to be associated with someone like Larry Flynt, but it most definitely understood that the issues in the case would affect them and their work. Curiously, Falwell would adopt precisely the opposite tactic: he befriended Flynt the man while continuing to object to his "abuse" of the First Amendment. The *New York Times,* the American Newspaper Publishers Association, and other mainstream media organizations joined an *amicus curiae* brief initiated by John Stewart Bryan III, the publisher of the *Richmond Times-Dispatch* and the *Richmond News Leader.* One of the more powerful briefs was filed by the Association of Editorial Cartoonists. It included an appendix with examples of the use of satire through American political history, much of it quite vicious, if not as vulgar as Flynt's parody of Falwell in the outhouse.[20]

On March 20, 1987, the U.S. Supreme Court agreed. Oral arguments were set for December 2. That summer Justice Lewis Powell had resigned from the Court, and the vacancy had not yet been filled. Indeed, the nomination of Judge Robert Bork to the high court had, in the very different circumstance of a Senate confirmation, dealt with some of the same conflicting worldviews at issue in *Flynt v. Falwell,* as the case was now known, the names having been reversed because Flynt was the petitioner seeking to overturn the lower court ruling.

Of the eight justices who would hear the case, several, including Chief Justice William Rehnquist, had shown no inclination to side with the press in First Amendment cases. Twenty such cases had come before the Supreme Court since Rehnquist joined the bench, and twenty times he had ruled against the press. Others, such as Justices Thurgood Marshall and William Brennan, were reliably liberal votes. Still, Falwell could like his chances. The summer before, when President Reagan had raised Rehnquist to the chief justice seat and nominated Antonin Scalia to the Court, Falwell had said that Rehnquist was "our finest judge" and that if Scalia was opposed by the National Organization for Women, he was all right by Falwell.[21]

Therefore, the Supreme Court that would hear Falwell's case was decidedly more to his liking than it had been even six years earlier, when Ronald Reagan appointed his first justice. A Court led by Chief Justice Rehnquist had greater promise for Falwell than the Court that had ruled in favor of abortion rights in 1973 and against prayer and Bible reading in the public schools in 1962 and 1963. The Supreme Court, according to Falwell, was one of the villains in the decline of morality in America, but that was a Court that did not include the likes of Antonin Scalia and did not have Rehnquist sitting in the chief justice's chair.

There was no doubt that Rev. Falwell would attend the oral arguments in the grandiose Supreme Court chamber. The question was whether Flynt would. His last appearance in that chamber had been a disaster: he had shouted personal insults and expletives at the justices, had to be removed from the courtroom, and was charged with contempt of court. Nonetheless, just before the arguments began Flynt was rolled into the hall in his gold-plated wheelchair. This time he behaved and left the talking to his lawyer.

Isaacman did his client proud. He answered the questions posed by the justices with vigor, and his answers were on point. When Justice Byron White seemed to question whether the Court could revisit the jury's verdict that the ad was not libel, Isaacman pushed back, knowing that the jury's determination that the ad contained "no statement of fact" was central to his contention that no one could take the ad seriously and therefore Falwell was simply unable to take a joke—a vulgar joke, to be sure, but a joke nonetheless.

In reply to a question from Justice John Paul Stevens, Isaacman defended the right of the press to engage in satire, to "deflate this stuffed shirt," and in the course of his reply he said that satirists should be able to "bring him down to our level." The use of the pronoun "our" in such a setting provoked gales of laughter in the room, including among the justices. It may have been one of Isaacman's best moments: if the justices of the Supreme Court could laugh at the idea that anyone could be brought down to their level, why couldn't Falwell? When Isaacman cited a cartoon that referred to George Washington as an "ass" and compared that cartoon to Flynt's parody of Falwell, Justice Scalia again brought forth fits of laughter from the courtroom: "I think George could handle that. But that's a far cry from committing incest with your mother in an out-house." The philosophical point of Scalia's intervention may have told in Falwell's interest, but the laughter did not.

Still, Isaacman needed to show that this case was about impor-tant first principles, not just about a bad joke. The case "affects everything that goes on in our national life," Isaacman said in his closing peroration. "And we have a long tradition, as Judge Wilkin-son said, of satiric commentary, and you can't pick up a newspaper in this country without seeing cartoons or editorials that have criti-cal comments about people. And if Jerry Falwell can sue because he suffered emotional distress, anybody else who is in the public would be able to sue because they suffered emotional distress. And the stan-dard that was used in this case—does it offend generally accepted standards of decency and morality?—is no standard at all. All it does is allow punishment of unpopular speech."

Grutman knew that Isaacman had performed brilliantly as he approached the lectern in front of the justices. He had to change the focus abruptly, reminding the justices of what had provoked the jury in the first place. "Mr. Chief Justice, may it please the Court. Delib-erate, malicious character assassination is not protected by the First Amendment to the Constitution. Deliberate, malicious character assassination is what was proven in this case." Indeed, it was Larry Flynt himself, in his manic deposition while in prison, who had said that he wanted to assassinate Falwell's character. Just as Isaacman had tried to keep the justices focused on the jury's not-guilty verdict on the libel charge, Grutman needed to keep the justices focused on the guilty verdict the jury did render on the emotional distress charge.

After his strong start, Grutman's performance was more uneven. At one point, in reply to a biting question from Justice Stevens on the relationship between the libel charge and the emotional dis-tress charge, Grutman was forced to acknowledge the difficulty in sustaining the latter charge without appealing the former: "Justice Stevens, I admit that maybe I should have done something differ-ent, but I thought at the time that the damages we were seeking to recover were equally recoverable under the intentional infliction of emotional distress." It was "the lowest moment of the argument for Grutman." He made up some ground in his closing moments, rebutting the idea that the freedom of the press was the central concern in this case: "This case is no threat to the media. It will be the rare case indeed where this kind of behavior will ever be replicated, but where it occurs, it deserves the condemnation the jury gave it, which the Fourth Circuit found, and which I respectfully submit this Court should affirm."[22]

The Court did not affirm. On February 24, 1988, in an opinion written by the chief justice, the Supreme Court ruled that Reverend Falwell was not entitled to any damages from Flynt arising from the ad parody, and it reversed the lower court rulings. "Court, 8–0, Extends Right to Criticize Those in Public Eye; Falwell Rebuffed," read the headline in the *New York Times*.

In its ruling, the Court held that the First Amendment did protect the kind of satire that Flynt published in his magazine and that the fact that such satire was outrageous could not obscure the right of the press to undertake satires that poked fun at public figures. "The art of the cartoonist is often not reasoned or even-handed, but slashing and one-sided," the ruling stated. Quoting a 1971 ruling in *Monitor Patriot Company v. Roy*, the Court seemed to chide Falwell, and others who entered the public arena, for not expecting to be called to account when he led with his chin: "The candidate who vaunts his spotless record or sterling integrity cannot convincingly cry 'Foul' when an opponent or industrious reporter attempts to demonstrate the contrary." Falwell was not a "candidate," but the rule applied to all public figures, and certainly to a man who had made condemnation of porn kings a part of his regular repertoire.

The Court also held that while libel was still grounds for recovery by a public figure, the emotional distress claim could not be advanced by a public figure as the basis of his or her claim to damages. The Court acknowledged that this was a new issue. "This case presents us with a novel question involving First Amendment limitations upon a state's authority to protect its citizens from the intentional infliction of emotional distress." The lower courts were free from the charge that they had misapplied the law; the law was unclear.

There was nothing unclear about the Court's willingness to maintain its most forceful endorsements of a broad interpretation of the First Amendment. "The freedom to speak one's mind is not only an aspect of individual liberty—and thus a good unto itself—but also is essential to the common quest for truth and the vitality of society as a whole," the ruling stated, quoting from its 1984 ruling in *Bose Corp. v. Consumers Union of the United States.* Quoting from a different prior ruling, the Court insisted that the right to speak freely was especially in need of protection when such speech was controversial. Just because "society may find speech offensive is not a sufficient reason for suppressing it," the Court stated. "Indeed, if it is the speaker's opinion that gives offense, that consequence is a reason for according it constitutional protection . . . government must remain neutral in the marketplace of ideas." There would be no retrenchment on First Amendment protections in this instance, despite the willingness of Rehnquist and others to vote against the press on prior occasions.[23]

Champions of free speech exulted in the victory. "It is an essential win because the lower court had found a way to end-run and potentially abort all the protections that the Supreme Court previously had accorded to the media in libel cases," Henry Kaufman of the Libel Defense Resource Center in New York said. The editors at the *Times* were equally fulsome in their praise. The ruling furthered a "thrilling principle of liberty," they wrote in an editorial two days after the decision. "But who is to decide what is too gross or too repugnant?" the editors asked, pointing to the difficulty facing would-be censors, such as Falwell, who might object to government overreach in other areas of public life but here sought the long arm of the state to intervene on behalf of his reputation. The *Times* editors kept their distance from Flynt—whom they should have been applauding, if not for his editorial policies, then for his tenacity in fighting his battles for the First Amendment—while embracing Rehnquist: "The Larry Flynts are left to paddle in their own mire. Out of it, the Rehnquist Court has fashioned a sparkling vindication of free speech."[24]

*   *   *

The high court's ruling was a complete defeat for Falwell. The Court, he complained, had given a "green light" to Flynt and others to run vile satires and to attack him and those like him (and even their mothers) with satire and parody. "I fully appreciate the deep concerns the Court has shown for the sacredness of the First Amendment," Falwell said after the ruling was announced. "However, I respectfully disagree with their ruling. Just as no person may scream 'Fire!' in a crowded theater when there is no fire . . . likewise, no sleaze merchant like Larry Flynt should be able to use the First Amendment as an excuse for maliciously and dishonestly attacking public figures as he has done so often."

Falwell had gone up against the mainstream culture and lost again. His vision of an America where people did not publish attacks on preachers, still less their mothers, was trumped by an alternative vision of America in which the free expression of ideas reigned supreme. The "free marketplace of ideas" to which the Court had alluded was not the kind of free market he and his fellow evangelicals embraced. Much of his ministry was devoted to suppressing base instincts, and he could not grasp that others reveled—and made fortunes—cultivating such instincts. The man who had a reputation as a practical jokester could not see the humor in the ad parody that Flynt had published. In the end, Falwell's ideas about freedom were Christian ideas about freedom, and his view of freedom was no more American—and no less so—than the more expansive Enlightenment view of freedom that he could not grasp. For Falwell, the Court's decision endorsed not freedom, but licentiousness.

There may have been some myopia in Falwell's vision of an America where decency was as important as the free expression of ideas, if not more so. He was genuinely shocked that the Supreme Court—the Rehnquist Court no less—did not see the issues through his own lens. They did not see what he saw: that a freedom that permitted such evil to flourish and granted it the protection of law was a freedom that itself threatened a moral chaos far different from the ideas of ordered liberty he championed. The twelve jurors in Lynchburg had weighed the need to protect the First Amendment against his right to his reputation, and their split verdict had reflected the conflicting values at issue in the case to Falwell's satisfaction. He had not anticipated that the Supreme Court would overturn both that verdict and the lower court ruling.

There was certainly a sense of nostalgia for the days when preachers were respected, when his status as pastor of the Thomas Road Baptist Church had immunized him from such attacks as the one Flynt had launched. Falwell did not see how he had set himself up for such attacks by his public and political involvements. Had he not realized that his constant effort to restrict the sale of pornography might produce a backlash? After all, his antipornography campaign was just a different kind of attack—an economic attack on Flynt's pocketbook. But Falwell was never one to calculate the cost of his decisions in advance, and he often failed to understand that others—in this case the Supreme Court—operating from motives as altruistic as his own, could reach such different conclusions.

There was one final chapter in the *Falwell v. Flynt* saga. Nearly ten years passed before the two men met again. In 1997, Larry Flynt published his autobiography, and a new film was released about the trial, *The People vs. Larry Flynt*. Larry King invited both men to appear on his show. "I'd do anything to sell the book and the film," Flynt wrote of the encounter, "and Falwell would do anything to preach, so King's audience of 8 million viewers was all the incentive either of us needed to bring us together." When Falwell arrived on the set, he gave Flynt an embrace, which startled the pornographer, who had spent $3 million fighting Falwell in court. Shortly after their appearance on *Larry King Live*, Flynt was in his office in Los Angeles when Falwell showed up unannounced to pay a visit. They talked for two hours and agreed to do a "dog-and-pony" show, going to colleges to debate morality and First Amendment rights.[25]

After a joint address to the National Newspaper Association convention meeting in Boca Raton, Florida, Flynt offered Falwell and his son a ride home on his Gulfstream IV jet. On the flight back to Lynchburg, Jonathan watched as the two men left morality and the First Amendment on the tarmac to discuss football and politics instead. Falwell would visit Flynt whenever he was in Los Angeles for the rest of his life. Once, after he complained about his weight, Flynt told Falwell about a new diet that had worked for him, and when Flynt got back to Los Angeles he faxed Macel a copy of the diet.[26]

Over the years they would call each other to voice their vigorously held sentiments. Flynt recalled objecting when Falwell referred to lesbian actress Ellen DeGeneres as "Ellen Degenerate." Flynt told Falwell, "What are you doing? You don't need to poison the whole lake with your venom." Falwell responded that "these lesbians just drive me crazy." The two men would never see eye to eye, but when Falwell died in 2007 Flynt wrote a moving tribute to him in the *Los Angeles Times* that concluded with these words: "I'll never admire him for his views or his opinions. To this day, I'm not sure if his television embrace [on *Larry King Live*] was meant to mend fences, to show himself to the public as a generous and forgiving preacher or merely to make me uneasy, but the ultimate result was one I never expected and was just as shocking a turn to me as was winning that famous Supreme Court case: We became friends." Commenting on Flynt's tribute to her husband and his calling Falwell a friend, Macel wrote, "nothing would have pleased Jerry more."[27]

Chapter Eleven

The Perils of Power

Political Missteps

Ronald Reagan's second term was dominated, and tarnished, by a self-inflicted wound, the Iran-contra scandal. Members of the Reagan administration violated the law by secretly selling arms to the radical regime in Iran in exchange for Iran's assistance securing the freedom of American hostages held in Lebanon. The proceeds from the arms sales were used to fund the contras in South America, in direct violation of a congressional ban on such aid. The scandal was bad in itself, but it also played to a long-standing caricature of President Reagan as out of the loop, divorced from key decisions, and incapable of effective oversight.

Similarly, the four years of Reagan's second term witnessed Rev. Jerry Falwell being embroiled in a host of missteps and self-inflicted difficulties. From renewed concern about his handling of finances to his shoot-from-the-hip verbal style that provoked controversies with friend and foe alike, Falwell's leadership of the Moral Majority and of Thomas Road Baptist Church was beset by criticisms. And like his political hero Reagan, Falwell's mistakes fed a caricature of him as a reckless, media-hungry pastor more concerned with winning political points than the pastoral care of souls.

There was another similarity between the president and the preacher. Beneath the controversies, both continued to prosper in fundamental ways that may not have garnered headlines but would continue to shape their place in the culture. Reagan presided over times of peace and prosperity, winning political converts to his cause of smaller government and lower taxes. And in Lynchburg, Falwell's ministries, both the televised *Old-Time Gospel Hour* and the Thomas Road Baptist Church, achieved their largest measure of growth in the mid-1980s, when his church-planting and church-growing techniques would be widely adopted. Both Reagan and Falwell were winning young minds and hearts, persuading the next generation to view the world as they did, and the effects are still being felt today.

Ministers are afforded a great deal of trust by their congregations, and the extent of that trust had shocked veteran direct-mail fundraisers like John Groman. Conversely, any hint of financial impropriety could spell doom for a growing ministry like Falwell's. The unscrupulous and money-hungry Elmer Gantry was an iconic type that nonfictional evangelists had to avoid. Falwell's clumsiness about money made him a target not only for critics but for charlatans who wanted to ride his gravy train.

In 1984 the *Old-Time Gospel Hour* sued one such charlatan, a former associate named Paul Greiner. Greiner had solicited $177,000 from a woman in Utah, Naomi Burch, to be placed in an annuity that the *Old-Time Gospel Hour* would hold, paying her an annual sum. But Greiner pocketed the money. Falwell reimbursed Mrs. Burch for the full $177,000 and then sued Greiner. In December 1984, a court ordered Greiner to repay the money to the *Old-Time Gospel Hour*. Falwell used the incident to demonstrate his probity, but how Greiner came into possession of the funds in the first place shows how easy it was to abuse the trust of devoted viewers and parishioners.[1]

Another incident in Milwaukee demonstrated the way Falwell's need to rely on local officials sometimes landed him in the crosshairs of media attention. He was slated to speak at a prayer breakfast sponsored by the local Jaycees. The organizer had compiled a list of "sponsors" from among those who had sponsored the breakfast in previous years, and the list read like a who's who of Milwaukee's business establishment. Unfortunately, the organizer had not realized Falwell's polarizing potential, and many of those listed as sponsors would disassociate themselves from the event. "I never lent my name for this," one public relations executive said. "People have been calling me to say they're startled. Well, I'm startled too. Falwell and I certainly don't agree politically. I'm one who feels religion has no place in government activity." The Jaycees withdrew their sponsorship as well. None of this was Falwell's fault, but it was his name in the headline of the *Milwaukee Journal,* "Falwell List Misleading, Many Claim."[2]

The following year a fund-raising appeal for Liberty University raised eyebrows. Falwell warned that cuts in federal funding from the Department of Education could cost the school $8 million. To avoid this, Falwell asked his donors to send $3 million by June 30. But a spokesman for the Department of Education said that there was no real possibility of the school losing the money. "Theoretically, yes, they're in danger of losing funds," the spokesman told the *Lynchburg News.* "For all practical matters they are not."[3]

Another source of controversy concerned Falwell's raising money for famine relief in Africa. In 1985, Falwell accompanied Vice President George Bush on a trip to Africa, where he was so moved by the suffering he witnessed that he decided to send missionaries from Liberty University to the Sudan. In the following years Falwell raised $3.2 million for the mission to Africa, but a report by the *Roanoke Times & World-News* showed that only 10 percent of the funds ever reached the continent. One of Falwell's spokesmen noted that the original ten-year plan had to be cut short because of political turmoil in the Sudan, but that did not really answer the charge the critics were leveling. Falwell himself was indignant about the charges, saying, "Every penny raised for our mercy mission in Sudan, and in 65 other nations, has been and continues to be applied exactly as represented in our fund-raising efforts." This was not entirely true, as the report made clear, and the newspaper stood by its reporting. Still, Falwell insisted that his donors trusted him to spend money wisely, even if funds did not always go for the designated purpose of a specific fund drive.[4]

None of these incidents became national news. Only Falwell's full-time critics took note of them beyond the occasional news item. But the person who most needed to take notice of them, Falwell himself, was oblivious to the danger they portended. In 1972 his sloppy bookkeeping had landed him in court facing the Securities and Exchange Commission. Continued sloppiness and overeager, untruthful fund-raising could ruin him again. Falwell was unalert to the small danger signs, and so he was unprepared when a real financial crisis hit.

Falwell's fund-raising appeals often relied on antigay rhetoric to catch attention. On a couple of occasions, however, Falwell's antigay sentiments landed him in hot water with the media and even in court. These incidents did not necessarily hurt him with his base, but they did contribute to his image as someone who was reckless with his words, a serious moral deficit in a pastor.

In March 1984, Falwell made a trip to Dayton, Ohio, to raise money for his college. He spoke to an audience of eight hundred people, dining on chicken and broccoli, about what was wrong with America. He relayed a story about a "Jewish, liberal, feminist lesbian" who had approached him recently and told him that she objected to his position on abortion. "She looked like the Lord made her as ugly as he could . . . and then scared her," Falwell told the crowd. "She was so big she could have played linebacker for Ohio State. I told her, 'Of all the people in the room, you have no reason to worry about abortion.'" The tale may have earned him a laugh from the crowd in Dayton, but it also earned him the scorn of the local and national press.[5]

A more serious wisecrack would end up costing Falwell $5,000. In 1984 he appeared on a television talk show in Sacramento, California. A gay man in the audience, Jerry Sloan, who had once been a student with Falwell at Baptist Bible College before becoming a gay activist, accused Falwell of saying hateful things about the Metropolitan Community Church (MCC), a gay-oriented denomination. Falwell denied saying any such thing and said that he would pay $5,000 to anyone who could produce a tape of him condemning the gay church. In a Sacramento courtroom, Sloan produced a videotape of a Falwell sermon in which he said of the MCC, "Thank God, this vile and satanic system will one day be utterly annihilated and there will be a celebration in heaven." The judge told Falwell that he had to pay up, tacking 7 percent interest onto the $5,000. Sloan was exultant. "The man called me a liar," he told a local newspaper. "I felt maligned in a vicious manner. I needed some personal vindication."[6]

Falwell was unrepentant. He told the *Lynchburg News,* "The situation is only one more example of the harassment by a militant homosexual group in Sacramento. I believe homosexuality is moral perversion and I have preached that for years." He accused Sloan of distorting the tape and twisting his remarks out of context, although the context spoke for itself.[7]

The mid-1980s also witnessed the onset of the AIDS epidemic. Falwell appeared on ABC's *Nightline* with Thomas Stoddard of the ACLU. Falwell urged mandatory testing of food service employees and others to defend public health, dismissing concerns about the civil liberties of gays. "And as far as it revealing—you know, the smoke-screen of saying Haitians and drug users; that's a smokescreen," he said. "It is clearly a male homosexual disease that sometimes, by contaminated blood or by the use of a dirty needle in a drug user's arm, is communicated." Stoddard asked if Falwell thought people should lose their jobs if they had AIDS, and Falwell said it was better to lose a job than one's life.[8]

Stoddard also accused Falwell of advocating the quarantining of AIDS victims. "You made that up," Falwell said; he would deny the charge a total of six times on the show. But the host, Ted Koppel, produced a news article that quoted a fund-raising letter from Falwell in which the preacher called for legislation to "give the health department of each state the authority to quarantine or isolate individuals with AIDS who, by continued irresponsible behavior, pose a threat to our public safety." Falwell denied the veracity of the news article.[9]

That autumn Falwell traveled to Antioch, Tennessee, to help dedicate a new sanctuary for a church founded by an alumnus of Falwell's Liberty Baptist Seminary. Before the service he told reporters that America needed more churches like his, and he blamed liberal churches for the rise in abortions and tolerance for homosexuality. "All these things have happened because our preachers are getting respectable. Our good orthodox preachers are afraid to tell people to stop the behavior that spreads AIDS," Falwell said. "They're afraid of a bad headline. There's nothing deader than dead orthodoxy and liberalism. They smell different but they're both dead." He said that AIDS was not a punishment against gays, but against their behavior. "[AIDS is] judgment against homosexuality, which is unhealthy, unclean. God loves the homosexual . . . but he's violating his body and will pay the consequences." Falwell also urged churches to provide pastoral counseling to those afflicted with the disease.[10]

In a subsequent appearance on *Nightline,* Falwell reiterated his position that homosexuality was a chosen behavior that could be cured. In stating his opposition to granting any special recognition of gays for antidiscrimination purposes, he compared homosexuality to adultery and wondered if adulterers should be guaranteed antidiscrimination protections. Falwell said that he "regularly" worked with men who had "a homosexual background and practice, [who] have come to know Christ and have not only found God's forgiveness through the death, burial and resurrection of the Savior, but have found deliverance from that lifestyle." He said that he knew some pastors who had similarly been converted from being gay.[11]

Falwell's statements on gay issues were not entirely uncommon in religious circles. Pat Robertson embraced the theory that gays could be cured, as did James Dobson's Family Research Council. In 1986 the Vatican issued a document that, while avoiding speculation on whether or not homosexuality was the result of nature or nurture, argued that even though only homosexual behavior was sinful, the disposition to be gay was itself "disordered." In the face of AIDS, however, most mainline Protestant churches and the Catholic Church declined to follow Falwell in calling attention to the means of acquiring the disease and focused instead on alleviating the suffering of those afflicted by the disease. Mother Teresa of Calcutta opened an AIDS hospice in Washington, D.C., in 1986, and in New York City Cardinal John O'Connor, a leading conservative prelate who had spoken out against homosexuality on countless occasions, nonetheless established a clinic for AIDS patients at a Catholic hospital. Cardinal O'Connor frequently volunteered at the clinic, where he changed bedpans and nursed the dying.[12]

Falwell's intemperate remarks about gays on a Sacramento talk show had already cost him $5,000. His effort to overturn that decision in 1986 put him at odds with one of his usual allies as his lawyer's tactics provoked charges of anti-Semitism. It was the second time in as many years that he was in trouble with Jewish groups, having earlier angered them with a comment about America being a "Christian nation." Unlike his verbal jousting with gays, however, Falwell quickly moved to repair his relationship with Jewish organizations.

In February 1985, Falwell purchased thousands of copies of a book about his views on Israel and the Jews and sent them to rabbis across the country. The book was fawning in its praise of Falwell's commitment to Israel. Falwell said that he was sending the copies to dispel the charge that his commitment to Israel was founded on his dispensational beliefs about the Second Coming. He mentioned that he was bringing one thousand evangelicals to Israel later that year and that they "will stay at Jewish hotels and use Jewish guides in order to truly experience the national rebirth of the Jewish people." Falwell also noted that this trip would be his fifteenth visit to Israel.[13]

The next month Falwell traveled to Miami to address the eighty-fifth annual convention of the Rabbinical Council. He did not try to deny that he, and other evangelicals, had spoken of America as a Christian nation. "We were wrong and we are sorry. What more can I say?" he told the 1,200 rabbis. He also declined any effort to proselytize Jews: "I am not here to convert you, and I can tell you're not going to convert me. . . . I am with you. I am for you whether you want me to be or not."[14]

Falwell told the assembled rabbis that twenty-five years earlier many preachers had spoken of a "Christian nation," but that through his efforts and those of others, conservative Christians had come to exhibit a "spirit of pluralism." He drew a distinction between a religious nation and a denominational one. "We most certainly do feel with all our hearts that this is a pluralistic nation and a nation under God, but it is not a Christian nation nor has it been nor do we want it to be a Christian state with a state church." He noted that Baptists had a long tradition of arguing for church-state separation; on this occasion and in front of this audience, he kept his reservations about First Amendment jurisprudence to himself.[15]

Rabbi Marc Tannenbaum of the American Jewish Committee applauded Falwell's comments. "It was thrilling to watch Jerry Falwell become a born-again American," Tannenbaum said. Not everyone was as fulsome in their praise. Henry Seigman, executive director of Tannenbaum's organization, acknowledged that Falwell was not an anti-Semite, but argued that the First Amendment was not just about tolerating unorthodox beliefs, as Falwell allowed, but also about not identifying the nation with any one group. Seigman said that Falwell "misses the point completely." A Jewish adviser to the Reagan administration told the *Washington Post* that Falwell's speech helped lower anxiety levels among Jews, who had begun to place the issue of church-state separation alongside support for Israel at the top of their concerns.[16]

For all of the sensitivity he demonstrated in Miami, the next year, when appealing the Sacramento verdict, Falwell made a huge misstep. His attorney, Weldon Ray Reeves, claimed that opposing counsel had tried to unfairly affect the trial by comparing the case to one involving a Holocaust denier who was ordered to pay a Holocaust survivor $50,000. Reeves argued that this comparison was not on point and in fact was a blatant appeal to the racial sensibilities of the judge, who was Jewish. Rabbi David Saperstein, a leader of the Union of American Hebrew Congregations in Washington, D.C., condemned Falwell's lawyer. "The contention that a Jewish judge will be swayed by a precedent of law based on a case that involved Jews or Jewish concerns is an irresponsible legal assertion and an outrageous moral affront to our judiciary system and the Jewish people," Saperstein said. The opposing counsel called the incident "insulting and disrespectful" to the judge. Falwell lost his appeal.[17]

Falwell's missteps on Jewish issues were easily repaired because he had built up relationships with leading members of the Jewish community, both in Israel and in the United States. They knew he was not an anti-Semite. But Falwell did not apply this lesson in the value of relationships to other groups, and so when he said something offensive or outrageous about other issues, his efforts to repair the damage were not always successful. That lack of a prior long-standing relationship with the black community became apparent as Falwell turned his attention to Africa.

Increasingly during Reagan's second term, Falwell turned his attention to foreign policy issues. At a speech to the National Religious Broadcasters in February 1985, Falwell touched on his bread-and-butter issues of abortion, gay rights, and pornography, but the principal focus of his speech was on deficit spending, communist incursions in Central America, and the nuclear arms race. He also raised the issue of South Africa's fight against communism.[18]

In the spring of 1985, religious leaders began protesting the South African government's policy of racial apartheid with a series of demonstrations in front of that government's embassy in Washington. The protesters called for American disinvestment in South Africa until apartheid ended. Falwell denounced the protests and attacked the religious credentials of those leading them. He compared liberal evangelical Jim Wallis to the Baptist modernist Henry Emerson Fosdick, and he suggested that the Baptist Joint Committee on Public Affairs should fire its executive director, James Dunn, because of his participation in the protests. "If they really meant what they were doing they should go down to the Soviet embassy and do their demonstrating," Falwell said, noting that in Marxist countries no one was free, no matter what race they were. Falwell said that the Republic of South Africa was only 24 years old and that America had been 180 years old before it tackled civil rights.[19]

The South Africa disinvestment issue was bitter in every regard

and reopened racial issues that Falwell had tried to quell by forth-
rightly denouncing his previous views on segregation. In other ways,
however, the issue did not fit the usual right-left divisions in American
political life. Conservative rising stars Rep. Jack Kemp of New York
and Rep. Vin Weber of Minnesota both supported disinvestment, a
rare break with the Reagan administration. The White House dispatched an anonymous source to accuse the congressmen of being
"politically naive." Howard Phillips of the Conservative Caucus was
unusually harsh in criticizing Kemp and Weber. "They're operating
from a large base of ignorance," Phillips told the *Washington Post*.
He accused them of "acute moral cowardice." Falwell, true to form,
backed the Reagan administration.[20]

Falwell held a press conference in May with an interracial delegation of South African community leaders to denounce what he characterized as Soviet efforts to destabilize South Africa. "We accuse
the international media, of which the American media is a part, of
a conspiracy of silence on the real problems in South Africa—that
the Soviets are working aggressively to capture this jewel on the African continent for themselves," Falwell told the assembled members
of the press corps. He said that he did not approve of the policy
of apartheid, calling it a "cancer," but he warned that unless it was
removed carefully, South Africa could be overrun by Marxists, as had
happened in some other African countries. These sentiments were
echoed by the delegation of South Africans, most of whom worked
for the government in some capacity.[21]

In August, Falwell led a delegation of nine American clergymen
to South Africa on a fact-finding mission. While there, he met with
South African president P. W. Botha. Falwell said Botha had explained
that apartheid was not so much a policy as a "social reality." Botha
was committed to reform, he said, and South Africa was "a friend of
the West." Subsequently, Falwell fine-tuned his warning about communist influence in Africa: "It is not a black and white issue, it is a
red and white issue, communism versus freedom." Falwell said that
none of the South Africans with whom he had met supported the
policy of disinvestment, and that he intended to return to the United
States and urge "millions of Christians to buy Krugerrands," refer-

ring to the South African currency. Falwell also promised to lobby Congress to oppose disinvestment.[22]

In a brilliant public relations maneuver, Botha used the occasion of Falwell's visit to meet separately with several South African clergymen who were calling for an end to apartheid. Rev. Peter Storey, a Methodist leader who was among those meeting with Botha, challenged Falwell. "He has not the slightest notion of what is happening in the minds and lives of the people of this land," Storey told a press conference in Pretoria. The frustration the leaders expressed with Botha's intransigence, which their meeting had reaffirmed, made Falwell's praise seem nonsensical. But in news reports the competing news conferences by the clerics gave the story a "he said–she said" quality that served the South African regime's purposes.[23]

The press conference in South Africa might have passed into obscurity, and Falwell might have moved on to other issues, if he had not held another press conference at John F. Kennedy Airport upon his return to the United States. There he made his most outrageous statement yet. He attacked the Anglican bishop of Johannesburg, Desmond Tutu, a leader in the anti-apartheid movement who had received the Nobel Peace Prize the previous year and who would become the archbishop of Cape Town in 1986. "I think he's a phony, period, as far as representing the black people of South Africa," Falwell said. He tried to dial back the statement in subsequent interviews, acknowledging that "phony" was "an unfortunate word choice." He said that he had not intended to impugn Tutu's character as a person or as a minister, but only to suggest that Tutu did not speak for all South Africans any more than he, Falwell, spoke for all Americans. As an apology, it was unconvincing. For his part, Bishop Tutu said, "When he calls me a phony, I don't think I should give him the pleasure of even responding. I mean, one has just to treat it with the contempt it deserves." Tutu called Falwell "ridiculous."[24]

The controversy made for great television. Falwell and Rev. Jesse Jackson appeared jointly on ABC's *Good Morning America* a few days after Falwell's "phony" remark. Falwell reiterated his position that the South African government was bent on reform but worried about communist efforts to destabilize the country and take over the government. He portrayed Botha as a moderate who could be toppled and replaced by a still more draconian racist regime. And Falwell again said that all the people he had met in South Africa were opposed to the disinvestment campaign in the United States.

Jackson questioned Falwell's account of the situation in South Africa and then went even further, contrasting Falwell's support for the white minority in South Africa with his unwillingness to support minorities in the United States. Jackson said, "For you to identify with Botha over Tutu and [Rev. Allan] Boezak is to identify with [former Birmingham, Alabama, sheriff] Bull Connor over Dr. King . . . to identify with . . . Hitler over the Jews and Herrod over Jesus."[25]

Jackson decided to take his case to Lynchburg, where he appeared at an anti-apartheid rally. Falwell, unafraid to engage, showed up at the rally as well. He said that he had been told there was going to be a fake funeral for him. "I assumed I should be attending my own funeral," he quipped. After listening to several speakers excoriate him for his praise of the South African government, Falwell was given ten minutes to make a rebuttal. He would come away from the encounter convinced that Jackson understood his opposition to apartheid, even if they disagreed on how to end it. "We developed a mutual respect, but agree on nothing but motherhood," Falwell said. The following week they debated the issue on ABC's *Nightline* and the show got 650 calls rather than the usual 100.[26]

In between the two television debates with Jackson, Falwell made the cover of *Time* magazine. The accompanying article discussed the different branches of evangelicalism and the issues on which fundamentalists were most engaged. It discussed their lobbying efforts in Washington and their ability to generate grassroots political protests through their ecclesiastical networks. The article featured photos of fellow evangelists Pat Robertson, Tim LaHaye, and W. A. Criswell. But it was Falwell who was on the cover and who received a separate three-page spread inside.[27]

Falwell's defense of South Africa earned him both abuse at home in Lynchburg and ridicule nationally, both of which sometimes interfered with his efforts to address other issues and caused organizations to hold him at arm's length. In Virginia Beach, the organizers of the Neptune Festival, sponsored by the Chamber of Commerce, rescinded an invitation to Falwell to speak at the festival's prayer breakfast, citing his controversial statements. The following week, when Falwell joined a planned protest at the Dallas headquarters of the Southland Corporation, the parent company of 7-11 convenience stores, to urge Southland to stop selling *Penthouse* and *Playboy* at its stores, the antipornography protesters were confronted by counterprotesters objecting to Falwell's comments on South Africa. And when Lenoir-Rhyne College, a Lutheran college in North Carolina, canceled a football game with Liberty University later that autumn, it cited Falwell's defense of the Botha government and the campus-wide opposition to the game.[28]

Lynchburg was equally inhospitable to Falwell's pro–South Africa campaign. "Well, first of all I was surprised," said fellow Lynchburg pastor Donald Johnson of the Court Street Baptist Church. "Then after being surprised I was ashamed." M. W. Thornhill Jr., Lynchburg's vice mayor, also expressed his surprise that Falwell called Tutu a phony. "It came as a surprise to me that he would refer to another internationally known religious leader as such." The local newspaper also conducted "man on the street" interviews about the issue, and responses were uniformly negative. "I think he ought to mind his own business," said Jeff Nelson, twenty-three, of Madison Heights. "He sticks his nose in a lot of things he has no business." Even closer to home, contributions to Falwell's ministries dropped by $1 million in the six weeks after the South Africa controversy began.[29]

Further afield, the nation's cartoonists had a field day. The *Baltimore Sun* ran two editorial cartoons on the subject. One shows Falwell at the foot of a cross, with a crucified black man on it. Falwell, dressed as a centurion, looks up and says, "Phony." The other cartoon has Falwell sitting at a desk, counting out Krugerrands. The caption reads: ". . . Twenty-eight, twenty-nine, thirty!" a not-so-subtle reference to Judas's betrayal of Jesus. The *Los Angeles Times* portrayed Falwell in a Ku Klux Klan hood and robe, saying, "I, too, am a man of the cloth. . . ." The comic strip *Doonesbury* ran a weeklong series showing Falwell organizing an "Aparth-Aid" concert, a spoof of the "Live-Aid" concert sponsored by several prominent musicians that summer to raise money for famine relief in Africa. In one panel, Falwell instructs the chorus to support a solo by President Reagan, who sings: "Okay black folks gonna confide, rappin' Ron Reagan is on your side! Gotta believe if apartheid goes, it sure ain't more skin off my nose!" Falwell urges the president to watch his tempo.[30]

Whether it was the drop in contributions or sheer stubbornness, Falwell decided it was time to preach to the choir. The next issue of his *Fundamentalist Journal* included a "Special Report" focusing on the issue of South Africa. Falwell's article reiterated his case that the greatest danger facing South Africans was not the perpetuation of an abominable racist policy like apartheid but the danger of a communist takeover. Cal Thomas explained that, for him, one of the trip's highlights was meeting Nelson Mandela. Thomas and an accompanying journalist from the *Washington Times,* John Lofton, were the first journalists to meet with Mandela in eight years. Thomas called Mandela a "terrorist" and said he was pleased to be able "to identify him and some of his followers for what they clearly are—Marxists." Ron Godwin wrote that "to the national media, racism has become far more abhorrent than Communist terrorism." The *Fundamentalist Journal* also included comments from black leaders who worked with or for the Botha government, all of whom parroted the party line.[31]

Falwell's efforts to support South Africa did not meet with success. In 1986 Congress voted to override a presidential veto of the Comprehensive Anti-Apartheid Act. It was the first time in the entire twentieth century that a presidential veto on a foreign policy matter had not been sustained, indicating how far out of touch both Reagan and Falwell were on the issue. Nor could either man be credited with reading the signs of the times. Before the end of the decade, with Botha sidelined by a stroke, the South African government led by F. W. de Klerk would free Nelson Mandela and begin negotiations to end apartheid. The Berlin Wall would fall, ending fears of communist takeovers around the globe. And in 1994 Mandela would be elected president of South Africa.

The South Africa kerfuffle cost Falwell, but he did not learn his lesson. In November 1985, he reprised his foreign policy fumbles over

donations to his ministries was temporary. The Reagan White House had been grateful for Falwell's support. But one man was unhappy—or should have been—to see all the attention focused on the Lynchburg preacher. Wyatt Durette was the Falwell-endorsed Republican candidate for governor of the Commonwealth of Virginia in the autumn of 1985, and he was about to get creamed.

In April, Falwell had spoken to a group of Lynchburg-area Republicans about his support for Durette. Falwell described the candidate as "a genuine Christian and conservative," adding that Durette was "everything I believe in." Falwell said that he might not campaign personally for Durette but that he and his family would be supporting the candidate financially, and he urged the assembled Republican activists to do the same. Durette was the only "acceptable" candidate.[35]

In the late summer and early fall, the Moral Majority in Virginia marshaled its organization to support Durette. At a candidate forum in Henrico County, Rev. Donnie Cantwell, head of the Virginia chapter of Moral Majority, praised Durette for his opposition to abortion and his support for "the God-given right of our children" to pray in school. Durette returned the compliment, promising an "agenda that reflects the values that Donnie [Cantwell] has outlined and you and I share." He said that candidates and voters alike were called to translate their values into public policy. The forum was sponsored by the Virginia Association of Independent Baptists, which represented 500 churches and 150,000 members. And although Falwell was not in attendance, Cantwell was his man on the spot; everyone knew that Cantwell would not have made the endorsement without Falwell's approval. The Moral Majority endorsement made headlines in most of the state's newspapers. Weeks before the election, Falwell's PAC sent out a mailing urging support for Durette.[36]

There was evidence, however, that Falwell's embrace was a mixed blessing. A poll conducted by the *Richmond Times-Dispatch* reported that 51 percent of Virginia voters were less likely to vote for a candidate whom Falwell had endorsed compared to only 8 percent who said they would be more likely to support a Falwell-backed candidate. Thirty-three percent said that it would make no difference.[37]

The Democratic candidate, Gerald Baliles, recognized that Falwell had become a divisive figure. Even the Republican mayor of Norfolk had agreed with the decision to cancel Falwell's appearance at the Neptune Festival prayer breakfast. The Democrats ran a commercial that mentioned the Moral Majority endorsement, and while a picture of Falwell filled the screen it finished with the voice-over statement, "So when you think about Durette, think about the people behind him." On election day, Baliles crushed Durette with more than 55 percent of the vote. Additionally, Falwell aide Henry Covert received only 22 percent of the vote in his quest to win a seat in the Virginia Senate from Lynchburg.[38]

"I think a lot of people are averse to Jerry because Jerry gets a lot of adverse publicity," said Flo Traywick, a Republican National Committeewoman and Lynchburg resident, after the election. Another Republican official spoke anonymously to a reporter for the *New York Times,* saying, "I think the thinking among most candidates, and I have worked with 86 candidates, is that they want his support, but they want it quiet. But that can't really be done." Larry Sabato, a politics professor and pollster at the University of Virginia, echoed the changing views of Falwell's influence. He warned that attachment to Falwell came with a price: "I think the basic element of Falwell's unpopularity is his projection of intolerance." Falwell countered that he had not been involved in the election at all and that he and Pat Robertson still had the influence to deliver the Virginia Governor's Mansion to the candidate of his choice "if we had chosen to do so."[39]

Democrats in Washington took note of the results in Virginia and decided to make Falwell a campaign issue in the next year's mid-term elections. Democrats sensed a backlash against the influence of the religious right in politics. "When Falwell is very active, it offends them [voters]," said Mark Johnson, the communications director of the Democratic Congressional Campaign Committee (DCCC). "His mere involvement is a negative." In March the DCCC made Falwell the centerpiece of a fund-raising letter to Democratic donors. "These religious extremists have learned how to change the outcome of elections," wrote DCCC chairman Tony Coelho (D-Calif.) in the fund-raising appeal. The committee also began producing ads that focused on Falwell's influence within the GOP for use by its candidates in the upcoming elections. Falwell labeled the effort "anti-Christian bigotry."[40]

Falwell denied that his influence was waning, but he also took steps to change his public stance. He could have made the argument that his opposition to the spread of communism grew out of a coherent moral view of the world, rooted in his faith. Indeed, that argument was being made at the time by Pope John Paul II. But Falwell's fundamentalism, which had been formed in opposition to the modernists' attempts to craft a "Social Gospel," saw morality in terms of personal behavior. Instead of making an argument based in his faith, he took steps to separate his moral views from his political views. These steps, however, actually undermined the distinctive contribution that the Moral Majority made to public discourse: its explicitly moral language against the often dispassionate, technocratic, and promethean worldview of contemporary liberalism.

In January 1986, Falwell announced the formation of a new organization that would subsume the Moral Majority—the Liberty Federation. "We want to continue to be the standard bearer for traditional American values. But it's time to broaden our horizons as well," Falwell wrote in the *Liberty Report,* which replaced the *Moral Majority Report.* He noted that some had objected to the Moral Majority's focus on national defense, not seeing national defense as a "moral" issue. Falwell disagreed with that assessment but nonetheless admitted the need for a change. "And even though we disagree, to deal with that accusation—and also to make us more international in our effectiveness—we have created a new organization to enlarge our goals. We are taking on new horizons, enlarging our camp, becoming more international, not just American." Falwell insisted that this move was an expansion, not a retrenchment. The *Liberty Report* also indicated that the new organization would permit Falwell to become more involved in advocating for a balanced budget amendment, tax reform, education reform, and President Reagan's Strategic Defense

Initiative (SDI), which was better known by its pejorative nickname "Star Wars."[41]

Two days after the announcement, Falwell made an appearance at the National Press Club in Washington to explain the new organization. He noted that in just seven years 6.5 million people had joined the Moral Majority and that organizations such as the American Coalition for Traditional Values and Concerned Women of America had been "spawned or generated by our lead." Cataloging the many and varied issues on which the Moral Majority had weighed in, he explained that he was forming the new group because "many persons have felt that the Moral Majority name and charter are not broad enough to cover many of these domestic and international issues." The Moral Majority would continue as a subsidiary of the new group, continuing to focus on the "strictly moral" issues. Falwell announced a "national summit" later that month for the new organization, revealing that Vice President George Bush would be giving the keynote address.[42]

"We are not disbanding or retreating," Falwell told the *Washington Post,* but the change was seen as a response to Falwell's increasingly negative image. A poll done by Republican pollster Robert Teeter showed that Falwell no longer enjoyed widespread popularity. Among twenty-one well-known Americans, he ranked near the bottom of the approval ratings. "On a ranking of zero (unfavorable) to 100 (favorable), Reagan received a 68.3; Kennedy, a 54; Fonda, a 43, and Falwell, a 33.1," according to the news report. Even onetime ally Paul Weyrich wondered if the change would do much good. "Survey data shows that the name [Moral Majority] has a significant number of negatives. I'm not sure that it will do them a lot of good. The organization will still be known by its founder." Falwell's erstwhile nemesis, former congressman John Buchanan, said that the name change confirmed what many had long believed—that Falwell was admitting "that he is in the political arena. . . . He should stop pretending to be chairman of the Lord's political action committee and stop suggesting that to disagree with Jerry Falwell is to side with Satan against God."[43]

Conservative direct-mail fund-raisers for other organizations noted that the more traditional concerns about school prayer and abortion had lost some of their fund-raising cachet and that issues like SDI and aid to the contras were "hot" and more likely to produce contributions. "Issues like the balanced-budget amendment, aid to the freedom fighters in Nicaragua will be on the front burners in the coming year or two," said Richard Viguerie. "Consequently, social issues will be generating less interest than these other issues." This was a damning admission that the Reagan administration had failed to deliver on the issues at the heart of the religious right's agenda.[44]

An editorial in *The Christian Century* saw the change as further testimony of Falwell's brilliance as a political strategist. "So Falwell has it both ways. He can tell cynical journalists that he has political reasons for some of the things he says and theological reasons for others, including the 'moral' issues of abortion and pornography. At the same time, his fund-raising letters will brush aside that linguistic nuance and continue asking for money to defend the world against immorality and communism." The editors also noted that the change had been forced by the orthodoxies of the left as much as those of the right—hostility to religious leaders in the public square had forced Falwell to differentiate his "religious" issues from other "secular" issues. They argued, however, that religious leaders possessed a "vision for America that is rooted in a reading of history and a belief in God" and that this vision, rooted in the ways of a "mysterious God," must always be characterized by "a tentativeness born of the awareness that all human action is ambiguous." Of course, Falwell was allergic to ambiguity and tentativeness was not his forte.[45]

No one was fooled by the name change, and it did little to expand Falwell's base of support or to allay the charges of critics that as a minister he had no business getting involved in explicitly political issues. Most important, Larry Sabato's polling showed that Falwell was not polling well among Republicans under the age of thirty. "The under 30s are the most Republican group in the population— overwhelmingly pro-Reagan," Sabato reported. But, he warned, if the Republican Party sought a "realignment, fueled by young people,

Falwell and fundamentalist Christians threaten the GOP gains."
Here, in September 1986, was the first evidence of a generational
rebuff of the kind of conservative religiosity embodied by Falwell,
and it was discernible even among those who, like Falwell, shared
Reagan's conservative political agenda.[46]

It was also in the autumn of 1986 that Falwell first gave an indication that he might be tiring of politics. "I think I can now, with thousands of conservative pastors and Christian leaders involved, share
this leadership and stop neglecting my primary calling—which is the
ministry of the gospel," Falwell said in an interview. He said that he
was tired of the travel; he had traveled over four hundred thousand
miles the previous year. "I'm not backing away from the fray, I am
creating a new emphasis in my life," he said. "My emphasis will be
more recognizable in the pulpit and in spiritual matters." He promised to continue speaking on issues through the Moral Majority and
the Liberty Federation.[47]

Falwell's announcement that he was backing off from politics was
met with skepticism. "He loves it, and I think it will be very hard for
him to stay out," said University of Virginia professor Jeffrey Hadden, who studied contemporary evangelicalism. Professor Sabato
seconded Hadden's doubt. "Jerry says a lot of things," said Sabato.
"The proof is in the pudding. We'll see if he is able to stay out of it.
He has a tendency to say things, to make headlines. He doesn't have
the ability to resist making those headlines." In the event, the skep-
tics were right: although Falwell cut back on his travel schedule, his
presence on the national political stage was undiminished.[48]

For all the criticism he had received for his excursions into foreign
affairs, his anchor in the storms remained his domestic arrangements.
His children were now in college or had graduated. They had often
accompanied Falwell on his trips at home or abroad, and most of his
travels did not take him so far away from Lynchburg that he could
not be home for dinner. In the 1980s, Macel, with prodding from her
children and husband, decided to enroll at Liberty Baptist College,
her long-held desire for further education having been deferred when
she started a family. The Falwell family was intensely close, and by
all accounts Jerry Falwell remained an attentive father and deeply

devoted husband throughout his life. Falwell would experience none of the personal scandals that damaged other televangelists.[49]

Falwell may have seen the need to try to change his public image, but he was certainly not without influence in the political realm. His new organization was a force to be reckoned with in the Republican Party, not least because he continued to receive lavish praise and support from the White House and conservative members of Congress. And he was still considered personally powerful: a *U.S. News & World Report* survey ranked him as the third most powerful American outside Washington, after Lee Iacocca and Dan Rather and just ahead of *New York Times* publisher Arthur Sulzburger. And behind Falwell stood not only his army of religiously motivated voters but the means to communicate with them, which was especially useful for those aspiring to public office.[50]

The Reagan administration did not run from Falwell, whose loyal support they had been able to count on time and time again. In the spring of 1986, Education Secretary William Bennett traveled to Lynchburg to speak at Liberty University. "What's a nice Catholic boy from New York doing at a fundamentalist university in Virginia?" Bennett joked to the seven thousand students and Thomas Road Baptist Church members gathered for the speech. He praised the school for teaching traditional values, echoing Falwell's belief that such values, along with parental love and support, not government-run social programs, were the secret to educational success. In May, Interior Secretary Donald Hodel gave the commencement address at Liberty's graduation ceremony.[51]

Falwell's influence achieved more than speaking engagements at his school. For example, Jerry Combee, dean of the School of Business and Government at Liberty University, was hired as general editor for a project to produce educational materials about the U.S. Constitution suitable for high school students. The Department of Justice awarded $186,710 for the project through a program designed to attack juvenile delinquency. Falwell's PAC distributed funds to a variety of congressional candidates in 1986, including future House

Majority Leader Richard Armey. Falwell got into a public spat
with Illinois Sen. Paul Simon when Simon questioned the hiring of
Combee to administer the grant on the Constitution curriculum; Falwell would make headlines with his accusation that the Illinois Democrat was an antireligious "bigot." In short, Falwell continued to
possess all the attributes of a political heavyweight—he could raise
money, pull strings, and make headlines. Any one of these attributes
would have made Falwell a player, but possessing them all made him
a heavyweight in GOP circles.[52]

No one was more solicitous of the preacher in Lynchburg than Vice
President Bush. Falwell and other religious conservatives had fought
unsuccessfully to keep Bush off the ticket in 1980. By 1985 Bush
understood that if he hoped to move up to the top job after Reagan's two terms, he needed to appease the suspicions of conservatives in general and religious conservatives in particular. Falwell, for
his part, developed a genuine fondness for Bush. In February 1985,
when Bush addressed the National Religious Broadcasters, Falwell's
warm introduction of the vice president sounded to many like an
early endorsement.[53]

In early 1986, Bush and Falwell were both headed to the Sudan at
the same time, although the two men had planned their trips inde-
pendently of each other. Nonetheless, when they realized that they
would be there at the same time, the vice president arranged for Falwell to be invited to the state dinner hosted by Sudanese president
Nimiery. That autumn, when Falwell's remarks about Bishop Tutu
got him in hot water, Bush rushed to his defense, saying that the
minister shouldn't be given a "bum rap" over the comment and trying to change the subject by pointing to Falwell's efforts on behalf of
famine relief.[54]

When Falwell launched his Liberty Federation in January 1986,
Vice President Bush delivered the keynote address. "America is in
crying need of the moral vision you have brought to our political
life," the vice president told the delegates to the "Liberty Summit" at
the convention center in Washington. "What great goals you have!"

A few months later Falwell returned the compliment. In a survey of leading conservatives regarding their preferred candidates for the 1988 Republican presidential nomination, published by *Policy Review*, Falwell came out strongly for Bush. Falwell noted that he had opposed Bush's selection by Reagan in 1980, but that he had gotten to know Bush during the intervening years. "At this point, I do not know of one major area where the religious right disagrees with what George Bush says," Falwell told the magazine. He said that he liked conservative darling Rep. Jack Kemp and thought that Kemp would be president someday, but that he was still a "rising" star, lacking in experience. Falwell considered senators Robert Dole and Howard Baker "lukewarm" on social issues.[55]

The greatest service that Falwell provided to Bush was his vocal ambivalence about the prospect of a presidential campaign by fellow Virginia televangelist Pat Robertson. Falwell shared many of Robertson's views, but not his theology. Robertson was a charismatic, and the fundamentalist Falwell did not believe in such charismatic practices as speaking in tongues. And of course, both men competed on the airwaves for viewers and supporters.

Robertson was the son of a former U.S. senator and an alumnus of Yale Law School, and his candidacy was not entirely far-fetched. Like Falwell, he had experience running a media empire. Falwell had a stock answer when asked about Robertson's candidacy for the presidency: "I think Pat Robertson would make an excellent president. I just think George Bush would make a better one." But when pushed, Falwell would admit publicly that he worried that a bid for office by Robertson could harm the evangelical cause. "I hoped that none of our pastors, preachers, would run," Falwell said. "But I have always said everyone has the right to run." At a breakfast meeting at the Robertson home, Falwell reiterated his support for Bush, but said he could support Robertson if he won the nomination.[56]

Falwell's relationships with Bush and with Robertson illustrated both his influence and his instincts. Bush had cultivated his relationship with Falwell and sought his support actively. Robertson saw the need to limit the extent of that support as much as possible, recognizing that he needed the overwhelming support of evangelicals in the Republican primaries if he was to defeat a sitting vice president. Falwell, in the final analysis, was unlikely to support anyone other than Bush: he respected Bush's loyalty to Reagan. Falwell not only valued loyalty per se but was impressed by, and attracted to, power, and Bush could help Falwell navigate the political waters within the Reagan White House. He was also the most likely victor for the GOP nomination, and Falwell liked to back a winner.

The events of 1985 and 1986 raised questions about Falwell's political heft, but these years also witnessed continued growth in his ministry. Fund-raising totals reached record levels. Church membership grew at Thomas Road Baptist Church, and Falwell was active in planting more fundamentalist churches. He expanded programs like his Save-A-Baby ministry, and fund-raising for Liberty University (Liberty Baptist College became Liberty University in 1984) went into high gear. Falwell did curtail some of his political trips, but he continued to travel the nation speaking at churches and preaching his brand of Christianity.

Fund-raising not only kept the ministries afloat but served as an indicator of approval from his base. We have already seen how Falwell's legal battle with Larry Flynt aroused conservative Christians to send him money to lead the charge against one of the nation's leading "porn kings," a fight that was sure to enflame the passions of his followers. And there was always a project he was pitching to donors. "Fundamentalism appealed to my father because of the entrepreneurial nature of it," Jerry Falwell Jr., then a law student at the University of Virginia, told a newspaper interviewer. "The idea is to build a big church, build a big school, start a TV ministry. Most religions are not like that."[57]

In fiscal year 1985–86, Falwell took in $84 million in contributions, his highest total ever. The Moral Majority had a separate $7 million budget that year. The strong fund-raising numbers were achieved despite the five-week downturn that resulted from the fallout over his remarks about Bishop Tutu. "That was over a five-week period when we were called bigots and everything else in the media, but that money has long since come back," Falwell said. He plowed the money back into the ministry, buying television time in more expensive media markets.[58]

Liberty University became a major focus of Falwell's fund-raising effort. As with all his ministries, he appealed for small-scale contributions from his millions of viewers and followers. But the school also attracted a different kind of donor—the super-rich. Nelson Bunker Hunt, a Texas oil baron, had given millions of dollars to the Moral Majority, and he now became a major donor to Liberty. Arthur Williams and Art DeMoss, who had both made millions in the insurance business, gave large contributions; the school's largest scholastic building was named for DeMoss, and Williams's name now graces the school's football stadium after his foundation donated $4.5 million for its construction.[59]

At least one of Falwell's critics turned to underhanded means to disrupt the flow of money to the Lynchburg preacher. Edward Johnson was a computer-savvy man who had come close to losing the family farm when his sixty-eight-year-old mother almost signed over the deed to a televangelist after hearing an especially provocative sermon. Johnson began calling Falwell's toll-free number to tie up the operators, but he felt guilty about it because the operators were so nice. So he rigged a computer to call the number repeatedly, clogging the system. Falwell reported the calls to AT&T, which tracked the calls to Johnson's Georgia home and ordered him to desist or lose his phone service. The "Demon Dialer" desisted.[60]

Falwell was no better at handling large sums of money than he had been at handling smaller amounts. In early 1986, he had to lay off some 225 employees at Liberty University—almost one-tenth of the staff—cut back on scholarships, and increase fees when the school faced a financial crunch. Falwell noted that the school had embarked on $14 million worth of construction projects in the past two years, in anticipation of a visit from a college accreditation agency. He also nixed the Old-Time Gospel Hour's toll-free number and increased tuition at the Lynchburg Christian Academy. After Falwell purchased a historic old theater in downtown Lynchburg, intending to renovate it, he discovered that the costs were too high and had to sell the

property at a loss. And after a court battle, Falwell had to turn over
control of a trust given to his ministries to a bank after the donor
charged him with mismanagement. Despite the huge increases in
donations to the ministries, Falwell's eagerness to do more, and to
do it faster, kept the whole enterprise mired in a series of boom-and-
bust cycles—hiring and building one year, cutting back the next.[61]

In January 1986, Falwell purchased a satellite television network in Florida for more than $2 million, not including leasing the
equipment, and moved it to Lynchburg. He was broadcasting fifteen
hours of television weekly by later that year. The network carried
programs from Liberty University, such as football and basketball
games, as well as the talk show *Jerry Falwell Live,* which Falwell
planned to expand to ninety minutes. The network broadcast the
Old-Time Gospel Hour, Sunday evening services at Thomas Road
Baptist Church, and the midweek chapel services at the school. The
programming could be viewed only by people with satellite dishes,
but in rural parts of the South and Midwest these were becoming
increasingly common.[62]

Falwell was also busy planting other churches around the country
and helping those he had already planted. He had gone to Antioch,
Tennessee, to help inaugurate a new sanctuary for a church begun
by an alumnus of his seminary. In Huntington, West Virginia, the
Gateway Church had been founded by another alumnus of the seminary, and Falwell was seen as "instrumental" in the church's success.
He gave a keynote address on world evangelization at a conference
on missions held by the Baptist Bible Fellowship and often preached
on church planting, saying that he hoped the graduates of Liberty
University could help American fundamentalists plant five thousand
new churches: "We have a burden on our heart to go out to the four
and a half billion souls of our world today and plant churches all
over the planet."[63]

The Christian school movement continued to receive encourage-
ment from Falwell. Addressing a convention of Christian educators,
he likened the Christian school movement to the biblical figure of
Nehemiah, who rebuilt Jerusalem in the face of God's enemies. Falwell recounted a recent conversation he had with a public school

board member, telling her, "Your idea of passing out birth control pills to junior high school students to limit sexual permissiveness is like passing out cookbooks at a fat farm. It takes a bureaucrat . . . dumb enough to think of that."[64]

Falwell also expanded his Save-A-Baby program in the 1980s. By 1986, 260 churches were participating in the program, establishing homes for unwed mothers who had nowhere to turn in the hope of keeping them from having an abortion. "I realized that while we were cursing the darkness, we were lighting very few candles," Falwell told the *Wall Street Journal*. "I saw we had to conduct a massive education campaign about what abortion is and to provide without cost an unlimited alternative for women." He renamed the program in Lynchburg "Liberty Godparent Home," and it had a two-month waiting list to get into one of its eighteen rooms.[65]

Falwell was going in many different directions during the mid-1980s. Alongside the missteps like his needless defense of the South African government, he could point to successes, such as the continued growth of his ministries. He recovered from his difficulties and retained an influence that, though controversial, continued to gain him powerful suitors like the vice president of the United States. He continued to exert profound influence on the culture as well, through his speeches, his political organizations, and his ministries. It was Falwell after all, not the other televangelists, who had made the cover of *Time*. He would need all of his assets in 1987 when the biggest crisis of his career befell him.

Chapter Twelve

Scandal and Retrenchment

Jerry Falwell could take great satisfaction in the progress he had made toward his many and varied goals as the springtime came to the hills of Lynchburg in the spring of 1987. His ministries were growing and had just posted their best fund-raising year to date. His political influence had been challenged, but he still had the ear of the president of the United States. Abortion was still legal, but Reagan's Supreme Court appointments were diminishing the Court's pro-choice majority. He had challenged one of the nation's leading pornographers in court, and though he had eventually lost the court battle, he had called attention to what he considered a cancer in society. If fundamentalists had lived in self-imposed cultural exile through most of the twentieth century, in less than ten years Falwell had led them boldly onto the cultural battlefield.

He could not know that 1987 would bring the greatest crisis in the history of his ministry and that he would shut down the Moral Majority by the end of the decade. The turmoil caused by Jim and Tammy Faye Bakker's "PTL" scandal, and Falwell's involvement in it, nearly brought his religious empire crashing down. The scandal would cause Falwell to reassess his priorities, and in 1989 he would leave the political stage to return to Lynchburg and concentrate on his church and his university. It was a startling turnaround for the once high-flying preacher.

*   *   *

Falwell was in Florida at a convention at the end of February in 1987 when another minister, Dr. D. James Kennedy, first approached him about rumors surrounding a fellow televangelist. There were others present, so Kennedy did not go into details, but he did say that the situation was urgent. A few days later Falwell phoned Kennedy and learned that reporters were investigating charges of sexual and financial impropriety on the part of Jim Bakker, the founder of "Praise the Lord" (PTL) ministries. The rumors were news to Falwell, who barely knew Bakker.[1]

Jim and Tammy Faye Bakker belonged to the Assemblies of God, a Pentecostal denomination that believes in faith healings, speaking in tongues, and other practices that did not cohere with Falwell's fundamentalism. Their television show, *The PTL Club,* combined Pentecostal confidence with the Gospel of Prosperity, the belief that if the viewer gave to God, in the person of the PTL ministries, God would richly reward him or her financially. The Gospel of Prosperity certainly rewarded the Bakkers. They built up a huge empire, the centerpiece of which was Heritage USA, a sprawling Christian theme park in South Carolina that brought in $126 million in 1986. The Bakkers also used time-share marketing to raise an additional $158 million, promising lifetime vacations at the park. This last fund-raising device turned out to be a Ponzi scheme: the lifetime memberships were turned into operating cash, and no funds were set aside against the members' eventual redemption of their claims to the time-shares.[2]

True to form, Falwell consulted the scripture, specifically the eighteenth chapter of the Gospel of Matthew, in which Jesus says: "If your brother sins against you, go and tell him his fault, between you and him alone. If he listens to you, you have gained your brother. But, if he does not listen, take one or two others along with you, that every word may be confirmed by the evidence of two or three witnesses." Falwell, on Kennedy's recommendation, consulted another minister, Rev. John Ankerberg, who had originally told Kennedy of the impending charges. Ankerberg sent Falwell a draft letter to Bakker, with the suggestion that it be sent under the signature of himself, Falwell, and Rev. Jimmy Swaggert, who, like

Bakker, belonged to the Assemblies of God. The letter asked Bakker to meet with the ministers in the spirit of Matthew 18 to discuss the charges.[3]

Swaggert refused to sign. He wrote to Ankerberg stating that he had already tried to confront Bakker about the allegations, to no avail. He warned that Bakker would use the letter to suggest that he was the object of a witch hunt by other ministers intent on taking over his profitable ministry. "As far as I am concerned, Matthew 18 has been satisfied with these people," Swaggert wrote. He predicted, accurately, that the Bakkers would try to lie their way out of the scandal and that they would try to turn the confrontation to their advantage, seeking yet more money from their followers to fight the charges. It was clear that there was bad blood between Swaggert and Bakker. Falwell dispatched three aides to meet with Rev. Richard Dortch, who worked with the Bakkers, and they presented the unsigned letter to him. The next day Dortch told one of Falwell's aides that Bakker wanted to meet with Falwell alone.[4]

Falwell flew to Palm Springs to meet with the Bakkers. Tammy Faye was receiving treatment there for a drug dependency at the famous Betty Ford Clinic. Bakker admitted having had an improper sexual encounter with a church secretary, Jessica Hahn, but he claimed that there had been no intercourse because he had been temporarily impotent. He denied that any "hush money" had been given to Hahn. Bakker told Falwell that he had confessed the entire episode to Tammy Faye, she had forgiven him, and the two were receiving Christian marriage counseling. Falwell thought that if Bakker confessed his sin to his church and accepted his denomination's requirement that he leave the ministry for two years of "restoration and renewal," he might be able to reclaim his ministry eventually.[5]

Falwell and Bakker left the room in which they had been speaking privately and joined Reverend Dortch, Falwell's associates Mark DeMoss and Jerry Nims, and PTL's attorney, the omnipresent Norman Roy Grutman. Then Bakker delivered his bombshell. "I want you to take over PTL," he told Falwell. He said that the PTL Board would meet the next day to transfer authority to a new board that

Falwell would name. He asked only that Dortch and fellow televangelist Rex Humbard be appointed to the new board. Falwell agreed to assume temporary control of PTL.[6]

It is a testimony to Falwell's reputation for probity that Bakker turned to him. It did not hurt that Falwell would guarantee that Swaggert could not swoop down and claim any share in Bakker's ministry. Still, Falwell and Bakker did not share theologies. They knew each other very little, having met only a few times in passing at conventions. In a sense, they were competitors for the viewership of those who turned to televangelists. But Falwell knew that a public scandal would harm all such ministries; confident as always in his own abilities, he thought he could forestall or limit whatever firestorms were about to rage. In this last calculation, he was supremely wrong.

Bakker's decision to turn to Falwell was not the first time a fellow pastor had turned to the preacher from Lynchburg at a time of crisis. In January 1986, Falwell had flown to Bangor, Maine, to temporarily assume control of the Bangor Baptist Church after its minister, Rev. Herman "Buddy" Frankland, publicly confessed the sin of adultery. Frankland continued to preach at the church, causing some members to break off and start a new congregation. Then Frankland resigned, and the church's board of deacons turned to Falwell for help.[7]

"Bangor Baptist Church is going to make it," Falwell told 650 congregants gathered at the church to welcome him. He brought accountants with him from Lynchburg to conduct an audit of the church's finances, but told the congregation that they were hurting financially and behind on their bills, so they needed to give more money if the church was to survive. He told them that he was not being paid for his work on the church's behalf and that he was even covering his own traveling expenses. Falwell promised that his tenure as interim pastor would be a short one and that he had told Macel as much, eliciting laughter from the congregation. He promised to help them find a permanent pastor. Several parishioners told the press that they felt Falwell's leadership was precisely what was needed to save the church.[8]

Falwell put one condition, however, on his involvement in the effort to rescue Bangor Baptist, and it was one that should have gotten Jim Bakker's attention. Falwell insisted that Reverend Frankland agree to leave the area and that the church help his family relocate. Frankland was to be barred from further dealings with the church he had almost ruined. Falwell correctly understood that after such a searing wound in the life of a church, a clean break was needed.

Back in Lynchburg, Falwell set about figuring out how to approach his new task. Grutman had already contacted the *Charlotte Observer* and asked the paper to delay printing its exposé for a week in exchange for an interview with Bakker. They agreed. On March 18, the PTL board met with Falwell, connected by speakerphone from his office in Lynchburg. They agreed to his nominees for a new board: Ben Armstrong, head of the National Religious Broadcasters; former Interior secretary James Watt; the former president of the Southern Baptist Convention, Charles Stanley; and other similarly prominent members of the evangelical community.[9]

On March 19, Bakker called the editorial board of the *Charlotte Observer*, as promised, for his interview. He began by reading a statement that was filled, not with the sense of remorse Falwell had expected, but with indignation and blame-casting. Bakker said that he was "appalled at the baseness of this present campaign to defame and vilify me." He announced that he had also resigned from the Assemblies of God, though he neglected to mention that his resignation freed him from any penalties that the denomination might impose as a result of its own investigation into his improprieties. He even blamed others for his tryst with Jessica Hahn, calling her a "confederate" of "treacherous former friends." Contradicting what he had told Falwell just a few days earlier, he admitted to having paid money to those he now called "blackmailers." It was Falwell's first indication that the repentant sinner he had met with in Palm Springs was only one of the many faces Jim Bakker chose to display to the world, and that there was more to this scandal than a sexual encounter now seven years in the past.[10]

When it was announced that Falwell was taking over the PTL ministries, the media rushed to Lynchburg. Falwell was interviewed on
all three major networks the day of the announcement. He received
warnings from many of his friends and colleagues and promises of
support from others. Vice President George Bush, evangelist Billy
Graham, and Sen. Jesse Helms all called to offer their support for
him as he began the arduous task. Some longtime admirers were
appalled that he was working to salvage a Pentecostal ministry. "You
have become a traitor to every Bible-believing Baptist, to the true
Baptist church (which is by the way, The New Testament church),
and to every major Bible doctrine," wrote a North Carolina pastor
who had been raised in Lynchburg in a column that ran in the *Lynchburg News*.[11]

The media frenzy wasn't pretty, but it was certainly comprehensive. The next week, when the new PTL board met for the first
time at the organization's headquarters at Heritage USA, three hundred journalists gathered for the press conference. The *Charlotte
Observer* had begun publishing the results of its investigations, and
those results were far more damning than Bakker had led Falwell to
believe. Tales of lavish bonuses for the Bakkers and other top executives were published around the world. The sordid story around
Jessica Hahn, and the efforts to hush her up with money from the
ministry, contained everything a good tabloid story could want:
clergy, sex, and money.[12]

It soon became apparent that the Bakkers were having second
thoughts about their decision to turn the ministry over to Falwell.
Requests for documents from members of the PTL staff were met
with stonewalling tactics, and Falwell heard that the Bakkers were
urging their people not to cooperate. He received anonymous phone
calls from people identifying themselves as PTL staffers, who told
him that documents were being shredded at the PTL headquarters
and more money was being paid out to top executives, even though it
was clear that the ministry was desperately strapped for cash. Then
Falwell learned that the Bakkers were intending to demand his resignation and reclaim their leadership of PTL.[13]

The deeper Falwell dug, the uglier the scandal grew. Early reports from the accountants showed that the PTL ministries were more than $60 million in debt. (They would soon realize that the number was closer to $70 million.) In April a $601 million class action lawsuit was filed against PTL on behalf of those who had bought lifetime time-shares at Heritage USA. Sworn affidavits were produced in which witnesses charged Jim Bakker with making sexual advances against men and engaging in homosexual liaisons. Falwell learned that other charges, of both a financial and sexual nature, were swirling around the PTL organization. Nor was there any way to keep the charges quiet: Reverend Ankerberg, learning of the Bakkers' desire to take back their ministry, went on *Larry King Live* to bring these revelations to light.[14]

Ever alert to potential fund-raising opportunities, Falwell sent out a letter to his own supporters. He asked them to let him know if they thought his decision to help save PTL was the right decision. And recognizing that contributions to his ministry had already begun to drop off—they would fall short of projections by $4 million in the first six months of the year—he asked his donor base to send $25 to the *Old-Time Gospel Hour*.[15]

It was not the lurid sexual details about Jessica Hahn and the hotel room in Florida, however, that most captivated the public. It was the evidence of the Bakkers' lavish lifestyle that truly shocked the conscience of the evangelical world. The Bakkers had built a $5 million lakeside home for themselves, paid for with ministry funds. Their salary in 1986 was $1.9 million. They had an air-conditioned doghouse constructed. They owned his and hers Rolls-Royces. They had once ordered $100 worth of cinnamon buns to be delivered to their hotel room, not to eat, but because they liked the aroma. Tammy Faye was fond of telling her television audience that shopping was better therapy than seeing a psychiatrist. She wasn't kidding.[16]

The Bakkers fought back. In April they sent Falwell a telex asking him to turn over the ministry to a new board, composed entirely of Pentecostals, with James Watt as chairman. Bakker said that he was keeping track of all the documentation in the case. "I will not fight you if you ignore my wishes but I must let you know that what you are embarking on will truly start what the press has labeled a 'holy war,'" Bakker wrote. In May the Bakkers went on ABC's *Nightline* show on two consecutive nights to plead their case to the public. They denied all the charges of wrongdoing, admitting only that they had been "a tad flamboyant." They accused Falwell of trying to steal their ministry.[17]

Falwell was incredulous. While the Bakkers had told a nationally televised audience that their avarice was nothing more than "flamboyance," Falwell had received requests from the Bakkers for $400,000 annually for life in severance pay. Falwell called a press conference to discuss the Bakkers' appearance on *Nightline*. "I don't see any repentance there," Falwell told the press corps. "I see the same self-centeredness. I see the avarice that brought them down." He denied that he had "tricked" the Bakkers into turning over their ministry to him, saying of Jim Bakker that he "either has a terrible memory or is very dishonest or is emotionally ill." Falwell said that he did not need the headache and had not taken the assignment with a view toward adding to his own religious empire.[18]

Falwell also, however, voiced his belief that there should be no criminal prosecution of the Bakkers. He worried that a trial or imprisonment of "a major minister of the Gospel in this country would hurt the entire cause of Christ across the world." He urged repentance on the Bakkers and forgiveness on everyone else, and he was not worried, he said, that the PTL scandal would hurt the cause of evangelicalism more generally. "You have human frailties, and you have failures. You don't throw out the system with the person. You hopefully learn from it and, hopefully, down the road, you do a better job," Falwell told a National Press Club luncheon. When asked if there was anything in his own past that might cause a similar embarrassment, Falwell joked, "Yes, I was raised a Democrat."[19]

Beating back the assaults from the Bakkers was only part of Falwell's efforts to keep PTL afloat. He also launched a $22 million fund-raising drive. Fulfilling a promise he made as part of the pitch, Falwell, wearing his trademark dark suit and tie, rode down the waterslide at Heritage USA on September 10. But the gimmick wasn't enough to salvage the fund-raising drive. In June 1987, the

PTL board decided to file for Chapter 11 bankruptcy protection. That autumn, convinced that there was nothing more they could do to salvage the PTL ministries, the entire board resigned to the bankruptcy court. Despite Falwell's urgings, criminal charges were brought against Bakker, who was found guilty of twenty-four counts of fraud and conspiracy and sentenced to forty-five years in prison, a sentence that was later reduced. The entire episode had lasted only six months, but it would reverberate through Falwell's life and through the evangelical community for years.[20]

The PTL scandal affected Falwell personally. Both Falwell and his wife would recall the six months he was involved with PTL as among the most sleepless and painful times in their lives. Macel recalled an especially long, sleepless night before one of the PTL board meetings, while Falwell was debating whether to resign as the new chairman of the board. Falwell's account of the episode is littered with references to "a knot growing in my stomach," to how he "dreaded the board meeting," and to his constant questioning as to whether he should resign his post. Falwell rarely confessed to stress in his life, except in this episode. Shortly after resigning from the PTL board, Falwell told the congregation of Thomas Road Baptist Church that "if Pope John Paul II, and Billy Graham and Pat Robertson all collectively got in trouble at the same time, they need not call Lynchburg for any help." He was getting out of the church-rescuing business.[21]

There were spiritual ramifications to be considered as well, and for Falwell this was perhaps the most important aspect of his wrestling with the scandal. Falwell recognized why the scandal had happened: the lurid excesses of the Bakkers and the lack of accountability throughout their organization had allowed it to unfold. But he also had to answer a different question: why had God let the scandal happen? Falwell concluded that PTL had become "the Mecca of the 'Prosperity Gospel' movement" and that "God wanted it terminated." Heritage USA had become a "modern Sodom and Gomorrah," and Falwell had been given the task of stamping it out.[22]

Falwell may have been able to catch up on his rest and find solace after he discerned the will of God in the scandal. But he could not repair the damage the scandal had done to televangelists nationwide. Contributions began to plummet. He had already seen his revenues fall $4 million short of projections by the end of the fiscal year on June 30. The new fiscal year was no better: donations to the *Old-Time Gospel Hour* dropped $10 million between July 1, 1987, and June 30, 1988, lower than any annual levels since 1982. "We have made a conscious effort in the past year to look for other sources of income, realizing that contributions can and will drop depending on the climate of the country," said Falwell spokesman Mark DeMoss. The ministry sold some land, put some projects on hold, increased fees at the schools, and hoped that tuition at the new "School of Life Long Learning" might make up some of the difference.[23]

The drop in donations required severe cutbacks. In October the *Old-Time Gospel Hour* was pulled from 50 stations nationwide, and plans were made to cut back from some of the remaining 340 stations airing the weekly show in the months ahead. Falwell hoped the cutbacks would be temporary. In February 1988, two television stations in Pittsburgh reported that Falwell owed them $50,000 for television time. "He's flying around in his private plane and he hasn't paid us since October," said one of the station managers. A ministry spokesman said the check was in the mail.[24]

Other ministries reported similar drop-offs in contributions, and this began a downward spiral. With fewer contributions, televangelists had to pull their shows off more stations. Donors who could no longer see the televangelists' shows understandably were not inclined to donate to their ministries. Falwell's *Old-Time Gospel Hour* slipped in the Nielsen and Arbitron ratings, dropping from the sixth most popular religious program to the number-eight slot. Sales of Bibles and other religious books fell off. Bonds used to finance ministry expansion were coming due, but ministries were not expanding. Only Billy Graham reported an uptick in contributions, undoubtedly because his was a reassuring presence compared with his counterparts among the newer, more flamboyant televangelists.[25]

In an effort to keep his ministries afloat, Falwell launched his largest bond offering to date. He worked with Willard May, a Texas financier who had developed a thriving business in the church bond market, issuing some $400 million in such bonds by the end of the decade. In 1988, Falwell promoted the new bond offer in mailings and on air, and within a matter of months 2,200 investors had purchased $32 million in *Old-Time Gospel Hour* bonds. The next year, however, May's company was shut down by Texas insurance commissioners, and shortly thereafter banking regulators moved in. The Securities and Exchange Commission deemed the company insolvent and acquired all of its assets, including the title to properties used as collateral. It was galling to Falwell to discover that the same SEC that had nearly ruined his ministry back in 1973 now owned the deed to Thomas Road Baptist Church.[26]

As Falwell tried to set his sinking ship aright, he turned to a variety of short-term and long-term financial arrangements. He acquired loans where he could, restructured debts when possible, and pleaded for more money, both from his large base of small donors and from large individual donors. When he was unable to pay back a $6 million loan to the Stephens Investment Group, Stevens turned the matter over to its counsel, the Little Rock–based Rose law firm, which promptly foreclosed on the Liberty University building that had been named as collateral. Falwell would never forget the indignity of being foreclosed upon—and of having to move his office—and he would remember that indignity when a member of the Rose law firm, Hillary Rodham Clinton, became first lady of the United States.[27]

The ministry embarked on a range of cost-saving and revenue-generating measures. At a meeting with his top aides—now joined by his son Jerry Jr., who had recently graduated from law school and who would begin demonstrating the business acumen his father lacked—Falwell agreed to sell his jet for $2 million. They put some additional land on the market. They cut the wrestling program at Liberty University, which saved $70,000. Another, and most unfortunate, casualty was the *Fundamentalist Journal*; even with its occasional hurriedly ghostwritten pitches from Falwell, the journal had aspired to bring fundamentalist theology into mainstream academic discourse. Most important, the *Old-Time Gospel Hour* was pulled from all but a few local television stations. These were bitter pills to

swallow, but there was no alternative. The PTL scandal had brought
an end to the projections of constant financial growth upon which
Falwell had based his plans for expanding the ministry. It would be
years before his ministries were completely solvent again.[28]

Falwell's financial situation was not improved by a series of articles
in the latter half of 1987 about how monies donated to his political organizations ended up in the coffers of his religious organizations. One of the problems with wearing many hats is that it is close
to impossible to keep track of all the different enterprises one has
going. This problem is exacerbated when one of the organizations is
governed by campaign finance rules and another is governed by rules
that apply to tax-exempt religious organizations. But Falwell was
chairman of the board of all of his organizations, and he was ultimately responsible for making sure that all the rules were followed.
If something was not kosher, he was held accountable.

"Falwell Political Funds Shifted to Religious Arms," read the
New York Times headline. Over three years, $6.7 million raised
from political contributors had gone to Falwell's religious ministries.
These funds were in addition to payments to ministries for such
activities as direct-mail processing and the use of television facilities.
Falwell claimed that the fund-raising letters were clear about where
and how the monies could be spent. "In these fund-raising letters we
clearly stipulated that the funds were to be used exactly as they were
used by the ministries which received them," Falwell claimed. "There
was no diversion or duplicity."[29]

Critics admitted that the transfer of funds would not be illegal
if there was no effort to intentionally mislead donors. But, as University of Virginia professor Jeffrey Hadden noted, Falwell had consistently maintained that his political organizations and religious
ministries would be kept entirely separate. Falwell countered, "I
think that most people are giving because I signed the letter. They
could care less if the project was being administered by whatever
arms of the Jerry Falwell ministry enterprise." He recalled an indus-
trialist, whom he declined to name, who had given him a check for

his religious ministries but who, for whatever reason, did not want it known that he had donated to a religious organization. He wrote the check to the Moral Majority, and Falwell transferred the funds.[30]

In addition to the direct contributions, it became known that Falwell's religious ministries and political organizations had made loans to each other, totaling $2 million, over the previous four years. Again, Falwell defended the practice, saying that the separate boards of the organizations "have through the years agreed when funds were available to make loans available in an arm's-length, businesslike manner. These loans are always paid in full as approved by the directors and management. This is both legal and ethical," Falwell asserted. "Any criticism of such aboveboard practices is pure and simple nitpicking."[31]

Had these revelations not come on the heels of the PTL scandal, they might have garnered less attention and generated less controversy. As it was, they undercut Falwell's efforts at the time to appear more accountable about the ministry's finances. Indeed, the newspaper reports were the result not only of the press's investigative efforts but of Falwell's own disclosure statements issued in the wake of the PTL scandal to demonstrate greater openness about his church finances. "We believe that full disclosure is a necessity for all Christian ministries if in fact credibility is to be reestablished since the PTL scandal," he said at the time. But the news accounts only further muddied the waters and damaged his reputation. When, in October 1987, the Federal Elections Commission fined both the *Old-Time Gospel Hour* and the "I Love America" PAC for commingling funds by transferring Bibles that were subsequently used as gifts to donors, Falwell's claims that he followed only "aboveboard practices" rang hollow.

In the autumn of 1986, Falwell had expressed his desire to spend less time on politics and more time on his ministries in Lynchburg, but he had not really backed off from political involvement when the PTL scandal kept him again focused on something other than his home base in Lynchburg. Now, one year later, Falwell again affirmed his intention to spend less time on politics and more time on ministry. Whether he was motivated by the fallout from the PTL scandal or the bad publicity surrounding the commingling of funds between his political organizations and his religious ministries, on November 3, 1987, Falwell resigned as president of the Liberty Federation and Moral Majority. "There's no need now for Jerry Falwell to walk point and be the lightning rod," he said in a prepared statement. "Sometimes you get tired of being the lightning rod."[32]

Falwell turned to one of his most trusted aides, Jerry Nims, to take over the Liberty Federation and Moral Majority. Nims had been one of the aides first dispatched to speak to Dortch about the rumors swirling around Jim Bakker. "Our plans for Moral Majority are going to be on the aggressive side," Nims told the press conference at which his appointment was announced. He said that they intended to work on developing the grassroots network of evangelicals to get them more involved in the organization's work. He also promised that the groups would be active within the legal community to advocate for a better understanding of the First Amendment. "We don't believe today that the First Amendment is there to protect the state from the church," Nims said. "We believe it is there to protect the church from the state."[33]

Cal Thomas, who had worked for Moral Majority in its early years and who now wrote a syndicated newspaper column, predicted that Falwell's political organizations would be closed within a year. He thought that the organization had had its priorities wrong for some time. "They found the window of opportunity of media attention and squandered it on short-term fundraising, rather than building a real political organization," Thomas said at a forum in Spartanburg, South Carolina. He said that most state chapters of the organization were little more than a chairman and a phone. But Thomas commended the Moral Majority for getting many conservative Christians involved in the political process, and he predicted that they would stay involved even if the organizations of the religious right folded. At the same forum, conservative activist Phyllis Schlafly said that the religious right had helped elect and reelect President Reagan and that its continued importance was demonstrated by the fact that the current candidates for the presidency were "all trying to out-Reagan Reagan."[34]

If people had thought that the Moral Majority's capacity for polarization would dim with Falwell no longer in the driver's seat, Nims quickly dispelled the possibility. In January 1988, when Democratic presidential candidate Sen. Gary Hart was caught up in a sex scandal, Nims sent out a fund-raising letter that condemned Hart and urged donors to help keep him out of office. "Have the basic standards of morality sunk so low that a man like Gary Hart would even think he has a chance to become President of the United States?" Nims wrote in the letter. When asked about the fund-raising appeal, Nims said that he had watched Hart, with his wife standing by his side, at the press conference. "I had a sense of deja vu. . . . It looked like he'd been taking lessons from Jim and Tammy."[35]

Nims also proved true to his word regarding the organization's focus on the legal culture. In the spring of 1988, Congress passed a law known as the Civil Rights Restoration Act, the object of which was to overturn the Supreme Court's 1984 *Grove City v. Bell* decision. In that case, the Court had limited the degree to which civil rights protections extended to recipients of federal monies, specifically colleges and universities. After an appeal from the nation's Catholic bishops, an amendment was passed stating that the new law would not affect abortion policy. The amendment had been opposed by women's rights groups, and the National Organization for Women refused to support the final bill because of the abortion amendment. But once the abortion provision was added, the Catholic bishops and most religious groups supported the new law.[36]

Two prominent people did not approve of the law, even with the abortion amendment. Ronald Reagan and Jerry Falwell both thought the law placed unnecessary restrictions on private schools. Ranged against them were not only the Catholic bishops and most other religious leaders but most of the nation's civil rights organizations, as well as advocates for the handicapped and the elderly. Nonetheless, Reagan vetoed the law, and Falwell and Nims doubled-down in their opposition. The Moral Majority sent out a mailing to 32,000 pastors that said the new law would force churches "to hire a prac-

ticing homosexual drug addict with AIDS to be a teacher or a youth
pastor." Nims warned that the override vote would be a central focus
for evangelical voters that year. The congressional switchboard was
overwhelmed with calls.[37]

The Moral Majority's claims earned it strong rebukes, even from
some of the group's usual allies. Conservative congressman Tommy
Robinson from Arkansas penned an op-ed in which he noted that
he usually agreed with the Moral Majority, but not on the issue of
the civil rights bill. Robinson said, "I also resent his [Falwell's] tactics." Sen. George Mitchell of Maine accused Falwell of "spreading
outrageous untruths." Father Brian Hehir of the U.S. Conference of
Catholic Bishops said, "We are deeply disappointed this legislation is
being subjected to such significant distortion." Falwell's effort failed,
and Congress overrode Reagan's veto.[38]

The March 1988 issue of the *Liberty Report* also caused controversy for the organization. The cover depicted House Democratic
congressional leader Jim Wright as a vampire. Falwell's article in
the newsletter began, "As Adolf Hitler manipulated Chamberlain to
achieve his objectives in the 1930s, the Sandinistas are manipulating
Jim Wright to achieve their objectives in the 1980s." Wright's press
secretary alluded to Falwell's fight with Larry Flynt in crafting his
reply. "I would think that Jerry Falwell would be more sensitive to
scurrilous pictures since he's had experience with them and he sued
about that," the spokesman said.[39]

Falwell used Liberty University's commencement exercises that
spring to gin up yet more controversy. He selected Lt. Col. Oliver
North to give the commencement address. A former national security aide to President Reagan, North had been at the center of the
Iran-contra scandal. His televised congressional testimony on the
subject in 1987 had made him a hero to conservatives, but his activities were demonstrably illegal. Two days before the ceremony, North
had resigned his commission in the U.S. Marines. His legal status at
the time was up in the air because his testimony before Congress had
entailed a grant of limited immunity. There was a campaign afoot in
conservative circles to seek a presidential pardon for North.

North was received as a conquering hero at Liberty's commencement ceremony. Falwell introduced him as "a true American hero" and compared his situation to that of Jesus Christ. "We serve a savior who was indicted and convicted and crucified," the preacher told the nine hundred graduating seniors and nine thousand guests. North's address was a call to arms. Claiming that the charges against him were "not a brand, they are a badge of honor," North said that he had merely gotten caught up in a political struggle between the White House and Congress and that he was being "vilified" for trying to help the Nicaraguan people throw off their communist government. He said the principal lesson from the scandal was that "even a strong, right-minded, God-fearing president" could not keep America safe by himself and that America needed a better Congress, stoking speculation that he intended to run for the U.S. Senate from Virginia, which he did in 1994.[40]

Falwell was still trying to generate more attention for his university, and the device of selecting a controversial speaker like North had the desired effect. North's speech was carried live by Falwell's new satellite network, and CNN picked up the feed. Along the bottom of the screen, Falwell's network ran a toll-free number where people could make donations to North's legal defense fund. The CNN technicians tried to blot out the announcement with their own graphic, but because of the broadcast delay the number flashed several times to a worldwide audience. CNN could not recall another such instance and made a statement that CNN in no way supported the effort. Professor Hadden commented that Falwell's support for North's effort to win a pardon was a "no-lose maneuver." Hadden anticipated that Reagan would eventually grant the pardon and that Falwell would be able to take credit. In the event, no pardon was forthcoming, North was convicted on three felony counts, all relating to obstruction of justice, and his conviction was eventually overturned on a legal technicality.[41]

Falwell's decision to stay away from politics so that he could concentrate on ministry was honored as much in the breach as in the observance for the rest of the year. In June, after giving the sermon at a church in Alabama, Falwell spoke to the press about his support for Vice President Bush: "Everybody knows I'm supporting George

Bush. . . . Bush is the best person to carry on the work of Reagan."
He said he thought that electing Democratic candidate Gov. Michael
Dukakis of Massachusetts would be a "step backward." Falwell said
that he did not plan on doing as much campaigning as he had in the
past, but that he would do whatever Bush asked him to do. Later that
month, in Tennessee, Falwell reiterated his opposition to Dukakis,
noting his support for abortion rights. He said, "There is very little
the country can do worse than elect Dukakis and capitulate to Jesse
Jackson."[42]

During the August Republican National Convention in New
Orleans, Falwell made a round of interviews at the skyboxes set up
by the networks, praising Bush's selection of Sen. Dan Quayle of Indiana to be his running mate and citing Quayle's conservative position
on social issues. Falwell went across town to address a group of conservative Christian students at Tulane University and encourage them
to get involved in the election to preserve Reagan's legacy, specifically,
the remaking of the federal judiciary. Speaking of the change that
had come to the country under Reagan, Falwell told the students, "I
think the country was that close to a wipeout. Ronald Reagan saved
the country." Several commentators noted that Falwell's "retirement"
from politics had been, albeit unsurprisingly, short-lived.[43]

When George Bush won the presidency, Falwell was given a seat
on the main dais at the inauguration as a reward for his steadfast
support. The invocation and benedictions were both offered, however, by Rev. Billy Graham. Falwell could be onstage, but he was still
too controversial to be at center stage. Falwell took some credit for
Bush's victory, telling the press, "It has taken fully five years to bring
the religious right into George Bush's column." He pronounced himself "gratified" by Bush's election and predicted that he and his fellow religious conservatives would have as much access to Bush as
they did to Reagan. "We don't make it a practice to over-use the welcome," Falwell said.[44]

The Moral Majority, however, had overstayed its welcome on the
national stage. New conservative religious groups had come to the

fore and were eager to grab their share of the spotlight. And as Cal Thomas had indicated, because the Moral Majority had never engaged in the grunt work of political organizing, the group could not deliver new blocs of voters. Falwell made the decision to shut the organization down. He would concentrate on his church and his school, and this time he meant it.

On June 11, 1989, Falwell announced that the Moral Majority was closing up shop because it had attained its original goals. "The religious right is solidly in place, and, like the galvanizing of the black church as a political force a generation ago, the religious conservatives in America are now in for the duration," Falwell told the press. "We don't feel in 10 years we've solved the nation's problems, but we've laid the groundwork," he added.[45]

In its ten years of existence, the Moral Majority had failed to achieve many of its goals. Abortion was still legal, and despite Reagan's appointments to the Supreme Court, overturning *Roe* seemed unlikely. Falwell's push for an amendment to the Constitution to allow prayer in the public schools had never made it out of Congress. Gay rights were still severely circumscribed within the law, but in the broader culture there was an increasing measure of toleration for gays and lesbians who wished to live openly. Support for a robust military had grown throughout the 1980s, but it is likely that such support would have grown regardless of the support of religious conservatives given Reagan's commitment to increased military spending and the willingness of Congress to go along with any project that created more jobs. Neither Falwell nor anyone else could have predicted it in June 1989, but by the year's end the Berlin Wall would come crashing down and his longtime nemesis, communism, would be largely consigned to history.

Nonetheless, Falwell was right to take credit for the Moral Majority role in helping elect Reagan twice and Bush once. As Falwell said, the group had helped "train, mobilize and electrify" conservative Christian voters who had previously shied away from political involvement. "Now the mind-set of the country is that activism is everybody's job," Falwell correctly stated. New conservative religious organizations had grown out of the Moral Majority, while other older or contemporaneous organizations, such as Concerned Women for America, received new attention, energy, and recruits from Falwell's prominence.[46]

Just as important, Falwell had forced the nation's political class to focus on issues important to conservative Christians. As he had said many times during the Moral Majority's ten years, it was now impossible to get elected dog catcher without stating one's position on abortion. Not only had the Moral Majority brought voters to the polls, but it had brought issues—their issues, moral issues—to the politicians. And the national Republican Party recognized that conservative Christians were integral to its electoral strategies and endorsed Falwell's positions on these issues. If no one could get elected dog catcher without stating his or her position on abortion, it was also true that no one could get nominated for national office in the Republican Party without sharing the religious right's positions on social issues.

Perhaps the most significant change in the political landscape that Falwell wrought was the introduction into political discourse of the language and logic of orthodoxy. American politics is most often concerned with the adjudication of interests. Government regulations require action on the part of producers in order to protect consumers. An increase in the minimum wage decreases the profits of owners and adds to the wages of workers. Compromise is relatively attainable in such debates. If a politician advocates raising the minimum wage to $8 per hour and an opponent wants to keep it at $7 per hour, they can compromise at $7.50. Abortion and gay rights, however, involved categorical debates, and Falwell supplied positions on these issues that were literally doctrinaire, that is, rooted in doctrinal positions about which a religious believer could not compromise. Doctrinal differences were not so easily adjudicated by the political class, and indeed, the principal political effect of the rise in prominence of such issues was to increase political polarization within the electorate.[47]

The Moral Majority, of course, also occasioned a backlash. Norman Lear's People For the American Way was the one group specifically founded in response to Moral Majority, but the developments that Falwell promoted on the right were now mirrored by various organizations on the left. For example, abortion rights groups applied litmus tests to Democratic candidates, demanding liberal orthodoxy to gain their support. The support of the National Organization for Women (NOW) and the National Association for the Repeal of Abortion Laws (NARAL) was never as essential to Democratic candidates for the party's presidential nomination, but the lack of such support made winning a Democratic nomination very difficult. Outside the South and certain conservative areas of the Midwest, only pro-choice candidates had a shot at winning Democratic nods for other political offices. Liberal groups embraced their own orthodoxies as fully as Falwell embraced his.

Falwell did not entirely foreclose the possibility that the Moral Majority could be restarted. He warned that if the Democrats were to nominate a "liberal" like Rev. Jesse Jackson, he would be inclined to get the organization going again. But Falwell also called attention to Dr. James Dobson, whom he labeled "a rising star" for the work he was doing with his radio ministry. Dobson was the founder of the Family Research Council, an organization that, as Falwell predicted, would become one of the major shapers of conservative opinion in the coming decades.[48]

The demise of the Moral Majority occasioned a lively debate about the group's significance. Nancy Ammerman, a professor at Emory University in Atlanta, noted the Moral Majority's emblematic role "as a kind of cultural symbol that they [evangelicals] were gaining a place in the American political scene." She also emphasized that the group's demise was typical of such social movements, which need a charismatic leader like Falwell to get started but must cultivate troops on the ground to keep going. Writing in the *Atlanta Journal Constitution,* analyst Tom Baxter wrote: "What made [Moral Majority] a potent force is that for the first time, one political party appears to be gaining a significant edge among church-goers. The Reverend Falwell did not engineer that shift, but his decision to back Mr. Reagan over a born-again incumbent in 1980 has become a symbol of that much larger development." Baxter perceived the opening of what would become known as the "God gap": religiously motivated voters leaning heavily toward the Republicans and secular voters backing the Democrats.[49]

Editorial opinion about the Moral Majority's demise was mixed, and predictable. The editors of the *New York Times* denied the political significance of the Moral Majority, arguing that abortion was still legal, school prayer was still unconstitutional, and, in a reference to his fight with Larry Flynt, pornography, "even that specifically targeting Mr. Falwell," still enjoyed First Amendment protection. The *Times* editors took note of Falwell's claim that he had replaced the image of fundamentalists as "yelling, screaming, foaming at the mouth" fanatics with that of "informed, respected and well-behaved" believers and allowed that Falwell had not descended to the depravity of Jim and Tammy Faye Bakker, but even here they refused to give him too much credit. "Nor does this Falwell claim take into account the fact that some of his predecessors—Billy Graham comes immediately to mind—did much more than he to create an image of responsible fundamentalism than the Moral Majority ever did," they wrote, failing to recognize that Graham was not a fundamentalist. The *Times* editors' ignorance of the diverse theological positions within the evangelical church was shocking, but not nearly as shocking as the claim that "Americans, even the most religious, are uncomfortable when their leaders and their movements turn to politics," a claim that would have difficulty explaining the career of the Reverend Dr. Martin Luther King Jr.[50]

More thoughtful analysis came from smaller newspapers in the South, where religion was not such an alien phenomenon. The editors of the *Virginian-Pilot* in Norfolk wrote that "millions of Americans did perceive, often correctly, political apathy among Christians and an anti-Christian bias among political activists. And millions more didn't mind a voice raised in opposition to 'liberal' tenets that collapsed traditional morals and mores under '60s permissiveness." The *Roanoke Times & World-News* editors noted that the religious right "depends for its vitality on the fervor of evangelistic superstars, who are by nature lone rangers with little taste for sharing the limelight in cooperative political ventures." They might also have noted the loose ecclesiological structures of evangelical churches. The

News & Observer editors in Raleigh, North Carolina, gave thanks for the group's departure. "Jerry Falwell, the grinning cherub from Mount Lynchburg, is closing down one of this decade's monuments to intolerance, the Moral Majority," they wrote in an editorial.[51]

Whether it was the organization itself or Falwell's frequent speaking engagements and television appearances, the Moral Majority's ten years of activity had altered the political landscape profoundly. Most remarkable is the fact that a correlation between church attendance and party affiliation emerged for the first time. Dwight Eisenhower had garnered the same percentage of votes from those who attended church frequently as he did among those who never attended. But the "God gap" emerged in the last decades of the twentieth century, largely as a consequence of Falwell's efforts. By 1990, approximately 60 percent of all college-educated white churchgoers voted for Republican presidential candidates, while the GOP never gained a majority among college-educated white voters who rarely attended church. Those numbers would continue to grow as the seeds that Falwell planted took root. In the first decade of the twenty-first century, the percentage of college-educated white churchgoers voting Republican neared 70 percent.[52]

Falwell had also succeeded in changing the issue landscape for both parties. When Ronald Reagan had signed California's liberal abortion law in 1967, he noted that his advisers were divided, not along partisan lines, but by denomination. The Catholics on his staff opposed abortion, and the non-Catholics supported the law. By the time Falwell shut down the Moral Majority, no pro-choice Republican could aspire to the party's presidential nomination. Social attitudes toward sex before marriage may have changed. Societal tolerance of alternative lifestyles, from divorce to homosexuality, was growing. But opposition to abortion, now linked to party identification, stayed relatively stable in public opinion polls, and those who opposed abortion continued to put far more weight on the issue than did those who favored liberal abortion laws. Not only had Falwell preached to his choir, but he had kept his choir singing, and singing effectively.[53]

Another consequence that flowed from Falwell's years of political activity was one that he did not intend—the emergence of the "nones." The word refers to those people who, when asked to specify their religion, reply "none." By 1990, fully 30 percent of the population said that they "strongly agreed" that religious leaders should not try to exert influence on how people vote. More important, in surveys of religious affiliation up until that time, only 5 to 7 percent of Americans had indicated that they had no religious affiliation, but as the 1980s came to a close, and then throughout the 1990s, that figure grew substantially. By 2000, the number had grown to almost 15 percent and was especially pronounced among young people. Of those reaching adulthood in the 1980s, the number of "nones" began to grow in the late 1980s, and it has not stopped. (In the latest Pew survey of religious affiliation, conducted in 2008, more than 16 percent of respondents professed no religious affiliation.) Just as Falwell's rise to political prominence had been in part a reaction to the liberal clergy of the 1960s and 1970s, the rise of the "nones" was clearly attributable—again in part—to the Moral Majority. If conservative politics was the new face of Christianity, many young Americans decided to opt out.[54]

Religious and political behavior follow complex patterns, and it is silly to think that if Jerry Falwell had never been a preacher, or if he had never formed the Moral Majority, some of the conservative changes that came upon America in the last quarter of the twentieth century would not have happened. There were other Baptist preachers who could have fit the bill. Had Falwell not listened to Paul Weyrich and Howard Phillips and the others who urged him to form the Moral Majority, they would have sought out another evangelical preacher. But Falwell did become a preacher, he did listen to Weyrich and the other conservative political activists urging him to get involved, and he did start the Moral Majority. There are many ways in which American culture might have responded to the counterculture of the 1960s, but one of the principal and most consequential responses was the Moral Majority.

It had been almost two years since Falwell announced his intention to spend less time in politics and more time in Lynchburg, an intention that he had so far not been very good at keeping. He had reduced the hours he spent on the road doing political events, but he was still a vocal lightning rod when he wanted to be. Now he really did intend to focus on his church and, especially, his university. For the rest of his life, even though he would occasionally dabble in politics, he mostly left politics to others. Lynchburg was home, and as he grew closer to sixty than fifty, he wanted to spend more time there. He wanted to focus on a different legacy from that afforded by sound bites and press interviews. He was looking to the future, a future without Jerry Falwell, and he wanted to build something more lasting than political influence.

Chapter Thirteen

Liberty University

The Next Generation of Culture Warriors

Throughout Falwell's time leading the Moral Majority, his Liberty Baptist College continued to grow and, in its way, to flourish. After it achieved university status in 1985, enrollments continued to grow. The school kept close to its founder's vision as an orthodox, fundamentalist school where students would become "champions for Christ," trained to bring the fundamentalist Gospel to the world with the aim of transforming that world, just as the Moral Majority had been an attempt to change the political landscape.

The world also had things that Falwell needed for his school, from accreditation to financial aid. As much as Falwell wanted to use the university to transform the world, the outside world would have profound effects on the shaping of the university. As in Falwell's suit against Larry Flynt, a series of legal squabbles would define, in part, the terms of the relationship between Liberty University and the secular world in which it was required to operate. Falwell's crusade against liberalism could not, in the end, fully overcome the demands placed on his school by the cultural expectations and requirements of a college education. To change the world, Falwell and his school had to enter the world, and the world had its own demands.

*   *   *

Jerry Falwell was always explicit and forthright about his ambitions for Liberty University: he wanted it to become the evangelical equivalent of Notre Dame. Liberty had posted impressive growth since its humble beginnings: by 1985, when it achieved university status, it had more than 5,000 students and had become the largest private university in Virginia. Liberty expected 1,600 freshmen that year. Falwell also decided to drop the word "Baptist" from the school's title when it became a university, given the fact that many of the school's students were not Baptists. But school officials guaranteed that Liberty's doctrinal position would not change.[1]

The school was still owned by the *Old-Time Gospel Hour* to ensure that it would never stray into liberal theology. Armed with orthodoxy, Falwell had a large goal for the school. "Liberty University is my way of carrying out the dream and vision God has given me. That vision is to give the gospel to the world in my generation," Falwell told an interviewer. "Television and radio are effective; the local church here is effective; our speaking tours are effective. But my hope for making an impact on the world with this generation and generations to come is to train young people in the things that are vital to the cause of world evangelization."[2]

Liberty University exercised a great deal more discipline over its student body than did most schools. As early as 1976, Falwell had preached on the importance of discipline to a Christian education. "You can attend most of the colleges and universities in America today dressed in overalls and barefooted and an American flag attached to the seat of your pants," Falwell told a midweek service at Thomas Road Baptist Church. "You can walk in smoking a cigarette and your hair down in your face and over your ears, and dirty face and all is well. No discipline. . . . But when you go to God's school, He immediately puts you into a program of discipline. He teaches you what's right and what's wrong and what to do and what not to do and how to do it." Liberty had strict rules prohibiting students from smoking or drinking alcohol, restricting dating, and requiring proper attire, and all of them remained in force, teaching students not just what to know but how to live. "Unwed motherhood is an almost negligible problem at Liberty Baptist College here, because we teach the students properly," Falwell explained in an article.[3]

Even the student newspaper was not beyond Falwell's attention. In 1986, when the ministry was going through a round of cutbacks due to financial constraints, he and university president Pierre Guillermin pulled three stories from the student newspaper. "We felt that they should not continue to harp on the cutback," Falwell said about the censorship. "It was not because of any disagreement: we just felt this horse was ridden far enough." However much he downplayed the incident, according to one of the student editors, at a meeting with Falwell and Guillermin the school's administrators had questioned if any of the students had leaked the story to the local paper and a threat was made to defund the school newspaper.[4]

In another incident, school officials stopped students who belonged to the archconservative Young Americans for Freedom chapter on campus from distributing literature critical of Vice President George Bush on the day before he was to appear on campus. The students appealed to Falwell's aide, Cal Thomas, who said, "A lower level official made a decision he did not have the authority to make"; after consulting with Falwell, he gave the students permission to distribute the literature. Thomas suggested that the decision showed the growing spirit of tolerance on the campus. "For a school of this type, this is a new avenue to drive down, and I think it is a tremendous thing for Dr. Falwell to have allowed, and it demonstrates his commitment to First Amendment freedoms," Thomas told the local newspaper. The next month the Young Americans for Freedom criticized Education secretary Terrell Bell in advance of his visit to the campus, again on grounds of being insufficiently conservative. There was at least a variety of pluralism on the Lynchburg campus.[5]

Falwell's insistence on doctrinal orthodoxy was not negotiable, even when it cost him. In the early 1980s, it was brought to Falwell's attention that Lynn Ridenhour, an English professor on Liberty's faculty, was conducting charismatic prayer meetings at his home. He was fired. Falwell also charged that Ridenhour was working on a profile of the school for *Penthouse* magazine and thereby discrediting the school. When Ridenhour sued, Falwell reached an out-of-court settlement with him for an undisclosed amount, and the court also placed a gag order on all involved.[6]

Falwell used his *Old-Time Gospel Hour* network to promote the school. At the beginning of a videocassette with tapes of his sermons, Falwell included a promotional segment for the school. He asked parents and grandparents to send in the name of a high school junior or senior whom they thought might be interested in Liberty. In return, they would receive two "Jesus First" lapel pins. Falwell told the viewers that at Liberty University you could tell the boys from the girls "without a medical examination." He noted that there were no beer parties and no coed dorms at the school, and almost the entire message focused on how the culture of the counterculture was kept firmly at bay at Liberty. He mentioned the school's growing number of course offerings in passing.[7]

The quality of the student body, however, was improving in the 1980s. Falwell initiated a scholarship program for high school valedictorians and salutatorians as a way of attracting smarter students to the school. Another scholarship program was extended for children of pastors, a way of promoting the school within the evangelical community and broadening the pool of applicants. He also initiated an effort to recruit more professors with doctoral degrees.[8]

Falwell's commitment to athletics also continued to exercise a dominant influence on campus life. In his sermons, he urged congregants to attend the university games, especially football games, and sought donors to provide funds for better athletic facilities. Falwell practiced a kind of "muscular Christianity" in the pulpit, and he wanted the same from his players. "Our goal is to be the hardest-hitting team anyone has ever played," running back Jacob Pope told an interviewer. "We don't want them looking at us as a pansy team or a schedule builder. Their idea of being a Christian is a little-bitty guy carrying a big Bible. What we do is out-hustle people, knock their heads off." Pope acknowledged that the team's reputation for hard hitting might impede its efforts at evangelization. "It's hard sometimes to show them the love of Christ after we've beat them up and down the field. You say, 'Hey, Jesus loves you,' and they don't exactly understand." The school's baseball team had already attained Division I status by the time Liberty became a university, and Falwell hoped the football team would also move from Division II to Division I by the end of the decade.[9]

Prayer was also a central focus of campus life. Three times a week the students were required to attend convocations that always began and ended with prayer and usually featured a prominent evangelical preacher or Falwell himself, and sometimes a leading conservative politician. When the choir went on the road, after setting up the sound system at the church where they were to perform, the singers would read from the Bible and pray together for an hour before their performance. Students were expected to attend Thomas Road Baptist Church or provide a letter from the pastor of another fundamentalist church if they did not. Like all other parishioners, students who attended Thomas Road were expected to tithe.[10]

As much as Falwell focused on the inner mechanics of keeping his school Christian, he also saw its potential to affect the outside world. One of the first schools at the university was the School of Journalism. "Our school of journalism . . . that is a tremendous opportunity to do what the left has done to us—that is infiltrate the media," Falwell told an interviewer in 1984. The school's students participated in the programming production for Falwell's various television and radio ventures to gain hands-on training in production techniques, but the point of acquiring expertise was not value-neutral. They were to "infiltrate the media." Unsurprisingly, given Falwell's interest in the political realm during the 1980s, his School of Government was extremely popular with incoming students.[11]

"So now we, with God's help, want to see hundreds of our graduates go out into the classrooms teaching creationism," Falwell told his congregation and the televised audience for the *Old-Time Gospel Hour* on April 11, 1982. "Of course, they'll be teaching evolution but teaching why it's invalid and why it's foolish, and then showing the proper way and correct approach to the origin of the species." These words touched off a firestorm that acutely demonstrated the challenge Falwell faced in trying to create a distinctly Christian school in a modern, pluralistic culture.[12]

Fundamentalists are deeply committed to the belief that the biblical account of Creation is a historical account of the origin of mankind. They believe that the world was created in seven twenty-four-hour days a few thousand years ago and that geological evidence that the earth is older is flawed. Efforts to legally mandate that creationism be taught in the public schools had failed. Falwell now perceived an alternate route toward bringing creationism into the public schools, and the route passed through Liberty Baptist College. The route also passed right through the First Amendment's guarantee of religious freedom.[13]

Falwell was confused. In 1982 the Virginia Board of Education was considering the accreditation of Liberty's biology curriculum. It was important to gain the accreditation. Students graduating from accredited schools were automatically certified to teach in the public schools in their subject areas. Falwell figured that if the biology program at Liberty was accredited, his graduates would be given the green light to teach creationism in the public schools. "It would give Virginia the distinction of being the first state to commit itself to academic freedom and fairness in the area of the origins of the species," Falwell told the press. The chairman of Liberty's biology department, Dr. Terry Weaver, recognized that Falwell's evangelistic promise to bring creationism into the public schools needed to be tempered. He told the state Board of Education's visiting committee, "We are going to give both sides of this important question on the origin of life an equal hearing." Among the objectives for instruction in the natural sciences, the school's catalog listed: "[showing] the scientific basis for biblical creationism."[14]

In fact, local school boards determine public school curricula, subject to approval by state authorities. And the authorities in Virginia were not prepared to approve the teaching of creationism in their public schools. Nevertheless, Falwell's enthusiastic, mistaken sermon gave his critics new ammunition to hurl at Liberty and began a debate that the school did not need in its quest for public recognition.

In advance of the next meeting of the Virginia Board of Education's Advisory Committee, the American Civil Liberties Union (ACLU) wrote to the board, urging it to deny accreditation to Liberty's biology graduates. The ACLU charged that Liberty's program was designed to "prepare students to teach religion disguised as science." The ACLU cited the catalog and Falwell's public statements to prove its case. "The Rev. Falwell made our case, we're indebted to him," Judy Goldberg, a lobbyist for the state American Civil Liberties Union, told the press. The ACLU won this round, and in May the Advisory Committee voted not to grant accreditation. "It's tyranny," Professor Weaver, head of Liberty's biology department, told the press. "To tell Liberty Baptist College that we can't teach creationism and at the same time be certified as teachers is religious oppression."[15]

Other stakeholders entered the debate. The Virginia Association for Biological Teachers was a professional association of biology teachers whose credentials would be imperiled if the Virginia board granted recognition to Liberty's program. The president of the association polled the group's seventy-six members on whether or not to oppose Liberty's certification. Fifty-seven favored doing so, while only four opposed petitioning the board on the matter. The group sent a petition that was identical to one sent by the Virginia Academy of Sciences: without naming Liberty specifically, each group urged the board not to certify any program that taught creationism on an equal footing with evolution.[16]

Falwell was out of the country, preaching in Australia, when the Advisory Committee ruled against Liberty. Upon his return, he recognized the need to dial back his pulpit commentary about the teaching of creationism and evolution at Liberty. "If I left the impression that we weren't going to teach both sides fairly, then I overstated the position of our school," Falwell told a press conference. "Both theories of the origin of life could be taught without imposing on students' beliefs and convictions." He said that he knew the difference between a university and a Sunday school, but that he was confident the full state Board of Education would overrule its Advisory Committee. "I cannot believe that the state Board of Education . . . would discriminate against a person because he or she believes in the

Bible or believes in God," Falwell said, adding that he believed the school's position was founded on academic freedom.[17]

The state Board of Education was not so easily appeased. A key issue for the board became Falwell's role at the school. He was officially the chancellor of Liberty, but in trying to determine whether there was genuine academic freedom at the school, the board wanted to know that what he said in the pulpit of his church had no real bearing on the policies of the school. Liberty's academic dean, Russell Fitzgerald, assembled documents to "show that Falwell has little involvement with college operations, curriculum decisions or hiring of faculty." Of course, Falwell's opponents could point to his prominent role in fund-raising for the school, as well as to his oft-repeated remarks about keeping the school under the church's thumb and being willing to cut off money, if needed, to ensure the doctrinal orthodoxy of the school.[18]

On the specific issue of teaching creationism, President Guillermin testified before the state Board of Education that it was not necessary to deny evolution in order to graduate from Liberty. Professor Weaver acknowledged that "Creation is not science and the Bible is not a science textbook," but he insisted that there was scientific evidence to support the creationist position. He also pointed to the high test score on state exams earned by the school's most recent graduate from the program. Guillermin and Weaver also testified that a sentence in the catalog for the Natural Sciences Department specifying that one of the objectives of the school's program was to "give the student a greater appreciation of the omnipotence and omniscience of God through a study of His creation" was under review and might be changed or dropped entirely. One board member complained, "The problem is that we've been getting conflicting signals, and those signals have been brought on by your own people," specifically Falwell. The board decided to commission a special investigation of the program by the state's superintendent of schools and delayed taking action on the certification.[19]

In September, Falwell went in person to a meeting of the State Board of Education to plead his case. Such a personal appearance ran counter to the university's strategy of downplaying his role in the school's operations, but Falwell wanted to make the case that it was the ACLU that was infringing on his rights, not the other way around. "It shocks me the ACLU would want to restrict my free speech as a pastor," Falwell told the board. But Judy Goldberg from the Virginia chapter of the ACLU countered that Falwell misstated the case. "It is not a question of whether Liberty Baptist College has every right to teach whatever theory or religious doctrine it wants," Goldberg told the board. "In fact, we strongly defend that right. But it is a question whether the state has the right to certify teachers trained to teach religious doctrine as science." Goldberg also said that Liberty was insincere in its portrayal of Falwell as a mere figurehead. "It is difficult to see how someone who is chancellor, fund-raiser, founder and pastor of the church all students at Liberty Baptist College must attend could be seen as a little old country preacher who sometimes get carried away and makes statements that are not reflective of what is really going on," Goldberg insisted. The board again punted for the time being, sending the issue back to its Advisory Committee for further study.[20]

The state superintendent's office delivered its assessment before a December meeting of the full board: it recommended that the biology program receive "provisional certification." The superintendent's office focused on the fact that the state standards did not mention creationism; they only set out requirements for adequate instruction in scientific studies, including evolution, and Liberty met those standards. There were two conditions, however. Those parts of the university catalog that included religious beliefs as among the objectives for the Natural Sciences Department had to be dropped. Additionally, a course on the "Origin of Life" in which creationism and evolution were taught as alternative theories had to be dropped from the requirements for a degree in biology, and the course had to be moved from the Biology Department to the Theology or Philosophy Department.[21]

Just when Falwell and his administrators at Liberty thought they could breathe more easily about the accreditation process, a new snag arose. In January 1984, the state's associate superintendent said he had learned that Liberty had been accredited by the Trans-National

Association of Christian Schools (TRACS) the previous September when that accrediting agency met at Lynchburg. Additionally, it was revealed that the Association of Christian Schools International (ACSI) had accredited Liberty several years earlier. Both organizations shared a commitment to the teaching of creationism and required such teaching before bestowing their approval. Indeed, the president of TRACS was also the director of the Institute for Creation Research in San Diego. And the president of ACSI, Paul Kienel, undercut Liberty's protestations, telling a Virginia newspaper, "I think it's unwise on the part of Liberty to seek state licensure of its graduating teachers. . . . I realize they want their teachers out there ministering in the public schools." Kienel added that some of Liberty's graduates "may feel called to minister in Christ's name in public schools."[22]

Recognizing that Kienel had unintentionally put his finger on precisely what worried the state Board of Education, Guillermin denied that Liberty had actually agreed to be accredited by TRACS. His position was undercut by the fact that both he and fellow university official Elmer Towns, dean of the religion school, were on TRACS's board of directors. More important, a state school official noted that if Liberty was fulfilling its obligations to TRACS, "they are espousing something that they said they weren't espousing" when they testified before the state Board of Education.[23]

Here was the dilemma brought on by the estuary that Falwell wanted Liberty to inhabit. He wanted his school to be a premier, fully accredited university, a beacon to the whole world. But his base of support, the fundamentalist churches that would provide his school with its students, wanted Liberty to teach the creationism in which they believed. He sought credit from both sides of the divide, but he could not serve two masters. In the end, he decided that he needed the approval of the state, and he would make the changes in the school's catalog and curriculum that were necessary to achieve it.[24]

Falwell hoped that his supporters would understand and continue to support the school. In an article he penned for his *Fundamentalist Journal,* Falwell wrote of Liberty's students: "They are preparing for professional careers as doctors and lawyers in some of the most prestigious schools in America, embarking upon a personal mission to impact, with Christian values and ethics, the operating rooms, clinics, courtrooms, and legislatures of America. Each graduate has been trained to personally evangelize and disciple others." And he announced plans to start a Center for Creation Studies at the school, albeit one kept separate from the Biology Department.[25]

It had been less than two years since Falwell proclaimed from the pulpit of his church that he wanted his students to go out and change the world by bringing creationism into the public schools of Virginia. Perhaps if Falwell himself had been less of a lightning rod, the ACLU and others would not have noticed. But he was in fact a lightning rod, and they did notice. In the denouement, it was not he who changed the public schools, but the public authorities who wrought changes at Liberty.

Falwell had kept the legal title to the university in the hands of the *Old-Time Gospel Hour* as a means of ensuring the school's orthodoxy. "Academics have a tendency to turn left," he warned. This created an additional, and unanticipated, legal problem for his ministries when it came time to determine their taxes. Like the struggle over creationism, the fight over Falwell's tax bill would raise profound constitutional issues, and both Falwell and his enemies would exhibit themselves at their worst and most manipulative. By the time Falwell shut down the Moral Majority to devote his energies to his Lynchburg ministries, the tax fight had been going on for almost a decade, and it would be yet another decade before the issues were resolved. In the process, Falwell would succeed in overturning a law that had been put on the Virginia legal books by none other than Thomas Jefferson.[26]

In 1980 Falwell brought suit against the tax bill levied on his ministries. Lynchburg city tax officials had entered into negotiations with the *Old-Time Gospel Hour* over the tax bill. Virginia law required that in order to be tax-exempt, a property had to be occupied, as well as owned, by the organization seeking the exemption. The *Old-Time Gospel Hour* owned all the property occupied by Liberty University, but the ministry did not really "occupy" the land; the university did. The city demanded $150,000 in back taxes on thirty-three parcels of land. Falwell's attorneys and the city reached agreement on several parcels, but the tax status of twenty-three others became the subject of litigation.[27]

Circuit court judge William Sweeney was not the kind of "liberal, activist judge" Falwell liked to denounce. This was one instance when Falwell could have used a little judicial activism. Sweeney ruled against the *Old-Time Gospel Hour* in August 1983. The judge said that Liberty Baptist College would be tax-exempt if it owned the land on which it was built, but it did not, and Falwell had declined to transfer the property's title to the school. Additionally, Judge Sweeney ruled that the *Old-Time Gospel Hour* was not "a church" as the statutes understood the term, nor was the *Gospel Hour* a tax-exempt educational or charitable institution. "While all churches are religious organizations, it does not follow that all religious organizations are churches," Sweeney ruled.[28]

Judge Sweeney also pointed out that designating the *Old-Time Gospel Hour* as a church would not qualify it for the tax exemption. In the late eighteenth century, fresh from their experience of an established church in colonial times, the Virginia legislature had adopted a law drafted by Thomas Jefferson limiting the amount of land that a church could own to four acres. Properties owned by the established Anglican Church—"glebe lands" as they were known—had conferred a great deal of wealth and power on the church in the colonial era, and after the American Revolution the new democratic government of Virginia wanted to rein in that power. Local authorities were allowed to increase the amount of land to fifty acres, and Lynchburg had designated the amount of allowable acreage at ten acres. Liberty sat on hundreds of acres.[29]

Faced with a bill for back taxes that now was more than $250,000, Falwell announced his intention to appeal the judge's decision. "Liberty Baptist College is now the only college in America that pays real estate taxes to the municipality where it resides," said Falwell. "Any

Sunday school child knows this is unfair." He noted that the Moose
Lodge and the Elks' Club were tax-exempt, but not his home for
unwed mothers. It did not seem fair, and it wasn't. But it was the law.[30]

In addition to pursuing a legal strategy to overturn Judge Sweeney's
decision, Falwell launched a separate political campaign to earn a
special tax exemption for Liberty. He decided to ask the Virginia legislature for a special tax exemption. This appeal to the legislature
came just when commentators were questioning the Moral Majority's influence in the Commonwealth, but on this issue Falwell had an
ace in the hole. He was right.

In his court ruling, Judge Sweeney had set forth the possibility
of an appeal to the legislature. "Since Thomas Road Baptist and its
ministries create a unique situation, they may wish to petition the
General Assembly for special tax exempt status," the judge wrote.
"I feel that a strong and appealing case under this section could be
made for exempting the property." But before Falwell could appeal to
the legislature, he needed the backing of Lynchburg's City Council.[31]

Falwell began to make his case in public. He noted that several
charitable organizations in Lynchburg had been given special tax-
exempt status by the legislature when, for whatever reason, their corporations originally did not fit within the tax laws. He also called
attention to the Catholic Church's many and varied ministries, in all
of which ownership was vested in the local bishop. Why should not
Liberty be treated in like fashion?[32]

Liberty University and the *Old-Time Gospel Hour* had grown
to become one of Lynchburg's leading employers. As a prelude to
making his case for a tax exemption, Falwell raised the possibility
that he might move his ministries to Atlanta. In addition to the tax
issue, Falwell claimed that there were insufficient places for Liberty's
education majors to student-teach at area schools. In 1978 Lynchburg school officials had declined to allow Liberty students into their
classrooms after parents, complaining that Falwell was continually bashing the public schools, brought the local superintendent a
recording in which Falwell called the public schools "immoral." But

recently the Lynchburg school system had changed the policy, and Liberty students were permitted to student-teach there.[33]

The threat to move to Atlanta had the desired effect. City officials noted that the ministries pumped millions of dollars into the local economy and that most of the money to support the ministries came from outside the Lynchburg area. The city's director of economic development claimed that, according to the Virginia Board of Tourism, Liberty University and Thomas Road Baptist Church were the two Lynchburg landmarks about which more visitors inquired than any other. The Virginia Restaurant Association lobbied the *Old-Time Gospel Hour* board not to move and promised its support for Falwell's tax fight with the city and the state. "I have no desire to leave this city," Falwell told the local newspaper. "I am very hopeful that our board and the city leadership can work out something that is good for both parties." But he also noted that the board would have been inclined to move had it not been for the intervention of local businessmen urging them to stay. In the event, the board postponed voting on the decision of whether or not to move to Atlanta. Falwell did not want to take that card off the table yet.[34]

Whether it was Falwell's lobbying or that of the businessmen, in September the City Council approved a request that the *Old-Time Gospel Hour* receive the special tax exemption he was seeking for three of his properties: Liberty University, the Liberty Godparent Home for unwed mothers, and the *Old-Time Gospel Hour*'s headquarters building. The City Council also recommended that Falwell's back taxes be forgiven. In addition, the local delegate to the legislature agreed to introduce a bill when the session opened in January. The chairman of the House of Delegates' subcommittee on taxation promised hearings. Taking no chances, Falwell hired some of Richmond's most seasoned lobbyists to help make his case.[35]

If Falwell had been a less polarizing public figure, the bill granting his ministries the tax exemption probably would have sailed through the Virginia legislature. But Falwell's enemies saw an opportunity to harm him. The Lynchburg chapter of the NAACP announced its opposition to the tax exemption on account of his statements attacking Bishop Tutu and other black leaders. "Reverend Falwell's repeated insults to the integrity of the Black community make it impossible for the [NAACP] to support him for fear that said support might be misconstrued by those very individuals who have been the targets of his condescending, racist obstruction to justice," said the chapter's president, Junius Haskins. He said the exemption violated the separation of church and state, which was clearly not the case unless the NAACP was prepared to exclude all religious colleges and ministries from receiving tax-exempt status. The Lynchburg Black Republicans, however, announced their support for Falwell's appeal.[36]

The bill faced other hurdles. The chairman of the relevant committee in the state Senate had recently had a nasty fight with Lynchburg's state senator, Elliot Schewel, a Democrat who was sponsoring the bill. It was also unclear whether Virginia governor Gerald Baliles would veto the bill. In 1982, when serving as the state's attorney general, he had issued a ruling denying Pat Robertson's Christian Broadcasting Network a tax exemption. The cases, as well as the two organizations, were sufficiently similar to cause concern. Another hurdle emerged when the staff who drafted the bill mistakenly included all of the *Old-Time Gospel Hour*'s properties instead of only the three properties the Lynchburg City Council had approved for a tax exemption. The lobbyists were going to have to earn their fees.[37]

On February 1, 1987, the Virginia Senate Finance Committee unanimously recommended the exemption, including a provision to forgive the back taxes. "I would summarize the opposition as criticism directed primarily at Dr. Falwell and not the merits of the bill," said the committee's chairman, Sen. Peter Babalas. Senator Schewel predicted the bill would pass the full Senate easily, which it did two weeks later on a vote of 31–9.[38]

As the House of Delegates considered the measure, Falwell went to Richmond to lobby for the proposal. He again called attention to the fact that he was only seeking the same tax status as was regularly accorded to the Catholic Church and its ministries. Against those who suggested that Falwell's church should relinquish control of the university to achieve its tax exemption, the preacher replied, "When the pope gives up control over Catholic churches, I'll give up control over Liberty University." Falwell was correct in principle, but not in fact. In the Catholic diocese of Richmond, all property was owned by the bishop, who, upon becoming bishop, was "corporation sole." And the two Catholic colleges in Virginia were owned by independent boards. Bishops and the pope exercised control over their ministries through the canon laws of the church, not the civil laws of the state. Still, Falwell was right to believe that all charitable, religious, and educational institutions should be treated similarly by the tax code.[39]

Falwell also addressed the debate in Richmond from the pulpit of his church. He said that a legislator had told him, "Jerry, I've had militant gays, I've had feminists knocking on my door, to try to do you in. I've had all kinds of characters here." Falwell said that another legislator told him that they had received more letters from Lynchburg opposing the tax exemption than letters in favor of it. He urged them to write to the members of the House of Delegates.[40]

Before the House took up the measure, Falwell agreed to drop his lawsuit against the city, a condition demanded by several legislators. Despite his best lobbying efforts, he also had to agree to a compromise that stripped the provision forgiving his past-due taxes. Legislators were worried that retroactively forgiving disputed tax bills would set a bad precedent. One of the key delegates also confessed that he did have constitutional reservations about the bill and said that the courts should look at the state's laws governing religious organizations, but since the legislature had granted similar exemptions to other religious organizations, he thought there was no rationale for denying Falwell. By a vote of 82–14, the House of Delegates passed the exemption. Falwell's spokesman, Mark DeMoss, hailed the victory. "I think it shows great professionalism to be able to separate political and ideological differences and treat the case based on the facts."[41]

The fight over the tax bill had resulted from the fact that many of Falwell's ministries, and especially his university, were technically owned by the *Old-Time Gospel Hour*. The arrangement allowed Falwell to exercise control over the university. Then, in 2002, the Ericsson cell-phone plant came on the market. The 880,000-square-foot building was adjacent to Liberty University, and it was large enough to provide the additional space for Falwell to start a law school at Liberty, one of his long-term goals. "The Liberty University School of Law will intently focus on training attorneys who will aggressively defend the religious rights of people of faith in this nation," Falwell wrote to the school's supporters. "I envision our graduates going forth to win many important battles against the anti-religious zealots at the American Civil Liberties Union."[42]

Purchasing the Ericsson building would allow Falwell to achieve another long-standing goal, one just as important as the law school project. As early as the mid-1980s, Falwell had wanted to build a new sanctuary for his church on the Liberty campus. The Ericsson building was large enough to house the church as well as the law school. But the Jefferson-era Virginia statute limiting the amount of property a church could own, tax-exempt or otherwise, was still on the books. Even if he had the money to purchase the property, which he didn't, Falwell was legally barred from doing so.[43]

Falwell may have had neither the law on his side nor the money in the bank, but he had something—or rather someone—he did not have in his earlier fight over taxes. Jerry Jr. had graduated from the University of Virginia Law School and become his father's right-hand man. He was also a very fine lawyer who had wanted to challenge the constitutionality of Jefferson's restrictions on church ownership of property. Now he had the perfect vehicle to do so. For assistance, he turned to Mat Staver, the founder of Liberty Counsel, an organization that provided legal assistance to those fighting for conservative principles in the courts.[44]

Despite Falwell's pledge to use the law school to take on the ACLU, in the matter at hand—the Virginia statutes limiting the amount of property a church could own—the ACLU sided with Falwell. In an amicus brief filed with the U.S. District Court, the ACLU claimed that the limits on property ownership "relegates them to disfavored status," in violation of the First Amendment. Staver, who was lead counsel for Falwell, welcomed the ACLU's support. "It shows that this is not a conservative-versus-liberal issue," he said. "It's a matter of constitutional rights."

In April 2002, the District Court ruled in Falwell's favor, and Thomas Road Baptist Church became the first church in the Commonwealth of Virginia to incorporate itself. Falwell secured funding from a generous donor, David Green, who purchased the Ericsson building and leased it to Falwell for a year for the sum of $1. The following year the building was deeded to the *Old-Time Gospel Hour*. Falwell had taken on Thomas Jefferson and won. In the process, he had become close with Staver, who would become the dean of the new law school. And looking ahead to a time when he would not be around to supervise his university, Falwell realized that Jerry Jr. was emerging as the most likely candidate for the job.[45]

Fund-raising continued to be a constant nightmare for Liberty University. The rising costs of providing a college education were not unique to the school, of course; many liberal arts colleges and universities struggled during the 1980s and 1990s. Falwell cultivated a stable of big donors to help keep the university afloat and, as needed, launched his own larger-than-life self into the efforts.

In 1988 Falwell sold thirty-two acres of land adjacent to Liberty's campus to developers who planned to build a Wal-Mart on the site. The developers paid $3.2 million for the property. "That's the highest per acre price for a major shopping center site that's been paid in Lynchburg," said a local banker, but the developers knew that the school would provide plenty of traffic for the store, and its location next to a major intersection on the edge of town fit with Wal-Mart's usual site selection criteria.[46]

The next year Falwell told all his employees that he expected them to join the Thomas Road Baptist Church and that, like all members, they would be expected to tithe. "If this is something you in your heart can't do, it would be better for you to not be a member of this team, rather than be forced to serve God here," Falwell told his two thousand workers. One employee, Dana Williams, announced her decision to quit to a local television crew, saying, "This is morally and spiritually wrong. I'm just as good of a Christian as anyone here, and I tithe to my regular church." Other workers agreed with Falwell that the Bible required them to tithe and that the joint church membership would help unite the employees.[47]

Williams, however, was not the only employee upset at the new requirement. Within a month of Falwell's announcement, some workers contacted the AFL-CIO about forming a union. A spokesman for the Virginia AFL-CIO said that he had received about twenty-four calls from employees of Falwell's ministries, complaining about on-site injuries, arbitrary firings, and the tithing requirement. Falwell made light of the union-organizing effort, telling his congregation at a midweek service, "Either give or join the garment union, one of the two."[48]

Thirty workers met with a union representative at the Holiday Inn near campus. "There's no question after having had two brief meetings, there's a need for something to be done," said union organizer Harold Bock after the meeting. "These people clearly need a voice. They need help." Falwell assistant Mark DeMoss went to the hotel to observe the meeting, but he was asked to leave after he identified himself as part of management. DeMoss evidently did not know it was illegal for management to conduct surveillance of such meetings. DeMoss also assured workers that there would be no repercussions from their attendance at the meeting. "From Dr. Falwell's mouth, no one would lose their job as a result of attending that meeting," DeMoss said. "He was not overly concerned and I think that's because he knows most of our people to be supportive of what we're doing and happy to be a part of it." Just as important, citing a recent Supreme Court decision, Falwell's lawyers maintained that religious organizations were exempt from standard labor laws. In the event, there was never really a prospect of garnering the support of 30 percent of the employees to hold a union election, and the attempt to organize subsided without any immediate effect.[49]

Falwell's lawyers were correct that his organizations, including the university, would probably be considered exempt from labor laws because they were essentially ministries of the church. But that argument now endangered the school on a different front. Falwell had applied for a $60 million municipal bond issue to consolidate other loans and fund new construction at Liberty. He had received approval from Lynchburg city officials. But a conservative political activist challenged the bond issue in the courts. The Industrial Development and Revenue Bond Act specifically prohibited the issuance of bonds for facilities that "provide religious training or theological education."[50]

Just as the need to get accreditation for his biology program had caused Falwell to alter Liberty's catalog and curriculum, now the need for the bonds forced Falwell into the humiliating position of having to argue that Liberty, or at least those parts of the university that would benefit from the bond issue, did not "provide religious training or theological education." Ironically, the first casualty of the campaign was tithing: Falwell testified in court that he was dropping the requirement that liberal arts professors join his church and tithe, although religion professors were still required to be members of Thomas Road Baptist. Falwell also argued that the funding for the Religion Department would be kept separate from the rest of the university and so would not benefit from the bond issue.[51]

The university also dispatched professors to the courtroom to "soften" the hard edges of Liberty's Christian identity. The dean of the Education Department declined to call Liberty a "Christian school," instead saying that it was a university "that consists primarily of Christians." Another professor testified that the school did not delete those parts of textbooks that conflicted with the school's fundamentalist theology and that professors were not "required" to support the school's doctrinal statement, only that they were expected to demonstrate their "general agreement" with the statement. The school's new chairman of the Biology Department also testified that Reverend Falwell had specifically told him not to teach creationism in biology classes.[52]

Falwell undertook other steps to secure the bond issue. In the catalog, mandatory attendance at "chapel" was changed to mandatory attendance at "convocation." The requirement that students participate in "Christian service" was altered to "community service." The admissions policies were changed as well. The previous policy stated: "The University reserves the right to refuse admission to any individual who has not received Christ as his personal Savior." In its new iteration, this became: "The prospective student is assessed according to academic background, personal moral behavior and character, personal philosophy, and compatibility with Liberty's traditions, regulations and environment." University officials downplayed the changes, noting that no one can see into another's soul, a fact that had not bothered them previously. Most important, Falwell agreed to legally separate the university from the *Old-Time Gospel Hour,* a move that he had resisted through his previous legal battles. The efforts came to naught. In January 1991, the Virginia Supreme Court ruled against the bond issue.[53]

The denial of the bond issue caused another cash crunch, which, in turn, produced another round of bad publicity. Falwell received temporary financing through two former fund-raisers for the school. But those fund-raisers received their own financial backing from Rev. Sun Myung Moon's Unification Church. Moon believed, among other eccentric tenets, that Jesus had failed in his mission to be the Messiah because he had not married and had children. Moon believed that he himself was destined to fulfill the messianic promises of Christ. Falwell took the cash and dismissed the source. "If the American Atheists Society or Saddam Hussein himself ever sent an unrestricted gift to any of my ministries," Falwell told *Christianity Today,* "be assured I will operate on Billy Sunday's philosophy: *The Devil's had it long enough,* and quickly cash the check."[54]

Other fund-raising efforts were less controversial. In 1994 the school's finances forced the college accrediting agency to place Liberty University on its "warning" list, and two years later the school was placed on probation until it solved its financial mess. Falwell went on a forty-day fast. Knowing how much Falwell liked to eat, Art Williams, who had previously donated the money for the school's football stadium, concluded that the university must really be in financial trouble and sent a check for $27 million. He followed up with another check for $25 million but insisted that his own auditors have a look at the university's books. His auditors subsequently ordered, and Falwell accepted, drastic cutbacks. One-third of the teaching faculty was let go.[55]

The controversies, the court battles, and the constant financial difficulties at Liberty University did not, however, force the school to close. Falwell continued to enjoy an enormous amount of personal loyalty from his congregation and his followers nationwide, and they continued to send their checks and their children to Lynchburg. The school continued to grow, in fits and starts dictated by funding, but it grew. And amid all the troubles there were high points to celebrate.

President George H. W. Bush became the first sitting president to deliver the commencement address at Liberty University on May 12, 1990. He and First Lady Barbara Bush flew to Roanoke on Air Force One and then flew by helicopter to the Lynchburg campus. Jerry and Macel boarded the helicopter to greet the president, and photographers captured him and Macel stepping off Marine Corps One. In his speech, President Bush, mindful of Falwell's controversial reputation, chose a perfectly anodyne topic, volunteerism. The president was in favor of it. "Individually, we can change a life. Collectively, we can change the world," Bush assured the graduates. Mindful of the attention that his appearance at Liberty would garner, Bush gave his more newsworthy commencement address earlier that day at the University of South Carolina, where he announced a new "citizens democracy corps" for eastern Europe. The South Carolina speech led the news.[56]

Nonetheless, Bush's visit to Lynchburg was a debt repaid. In shoring up support in an evangelical community that was wary of Bush's reputation for being moderate on social issues, Falwell had been critical to Bush's securing the Republican nomination in 1988. A presidential commencement address is a big deal for any university. The limelight, even if shared with South Carolina, still shone on Liberty University, and the photograph of Jerry and Macel Falwell stepping off of Marine Corps One would become a staple of Falwell's fund-raising appeals.[57]

That same year Eric Green became the first Liberty alumnus to be drafted by the National Football League. The Pittsburgh Steelers selected Green in the first round, and he went on to be selected for the Pro Bowl twice. In 1994 the school basketball team won its conference, and with that title, the team also earned an automatic berth in the NCAA tournament, although it lost in the first round. William Franklin Graham, the grandson of evangelist Billy Graham, graduated from Liberty University in 1997. His grandfather gave the commencement address and handed William his diploma. The school's debate team was a multi-year national champion.[58]

The campus continued to expand. A large indoor arena, the Vines Center, was opened in 1990, seating 10,000 people for sporting events and university ceremonies. First begun in 1989, the Williams Football Stadium was enlarged several times to a final capacity of 19,200. In addition to football games, the stadium would host the annual graduation ceremony. The DeMoss Learning Center came to dominate the academic buildings on campus. Originally built in 1985 and added on to several times, it housed the school library and several academic departments as well as dozens of classrooms.

The opening of the law school in 2004 was a major achievement for Falwell. So many of the controversies that had marked his career had ended up in a court of law. He had developed serious reservations about the ways in which modern jurisprudence dealt with religious organizations, and he wanted to prepare lawyers who could not only defend religious clients but go on to serve in the Justice Department and eventually serve as judges. In Mat Staver, who had come to Lynchburg to help Falwell overturn Virginia's ban on church incorporation and limits on property ownership, Falwell found a first-rate legal mind who shared the preacher's misgivings about First Amendment jurisprudence. In 2006 the law school received provisional accreditation, and in 2010 it was granted full accreditation by the American Bar Association.[59]

During both the successful effort to gain accreditation for Liberty's biology program and the failed struggle to secure his bond issue, Falwell appeared to trim the Christian sails of his school. He was forced to remove or change some of the arrangements and requirements he had originally placed on the school, its faculty, and its students to ensure Liberty's orthodoxy. But the Christian identity of Liberty University survived the changes in the catalog and the transfer of the creationism courses from the Biology Department to the Religion Department. The orthodoxy of the place was sturdy, even though that orthodoxy would look different in the first decade of the twenty-first century from what it had looked like in 1971.

The issue of what the civil government can, and cannot, demand of religious institutions would outlive Falwell. It remains a source of contention. When that issue lands in the courts, Liberty Counsel is virtually guaranteed to be filing an amicus brief, providing counsel, or leading the charge as a litigant. The school has followed the example of its chancellor: Falwell did not win all of his lawsuits, but he never ducked the fight.

Falwell's efforts to create a first-rate fundamentalist university were marred by controversies, many of them of his own making. Certainly, his high profile attracted enemies who considered all of his efforts pernicious influences on the culture and sought to restrict them as much as possible. But his perseverance and the indefatigable personal energy he brought to the task kept the school going. Often he spoke of his concern about continuing the task of spreading the Gospel after his own time had come. Liberty University, as both its detractors and its fans would attest, was Falwell's most significant legacy. After he shut down the Moral Majority in 1989 to pay more attention to the school and his church, he never doubted that the time and effort he spent on both were worth it. That said, in 1992 the election of Bill Clinton as president would cause Falwell to reconsider his decision to depart the political stage.

Chapter Fourteen

Back in Opposition

The Clinton Years

Falwell had shut down the Moral Majority in 1989 and spent three years focused primarily on his ministries and his university. But in 1992 the prospect of the Democrats reclaiming the White House led him to reconsider his decision to abandon the political stage. Always more effective in opposition than in power, groups like the Moral Majority had an easier time raising money and raising Cain after Clinton won the presidency.

It is not necessary to examine why Clinton made conservatives generally go ballistic to grasp why Falwell detested him so. Clinton was a southerner and a Southern Baptist, but seeking common ground was not Falwell's strength. Instead, Clinton's Baptist faith damaged Falwell's "brand" in a way that an Episcopalian or a Methodist might not have. Clinton had helped pull the Democratic Party back to the center of America's ideological spectrum, but that won him no plaudits from the right. Some thought the shift was evidence only of insincerity. And even on issues like fiscal responsibility, where Clinton took a more conservative stance than usual for a Democrat, the narcissism of small differences emerged to inflame his conservative critics.

In addition, Clinton was the first baby boomer to win the presidency, and his personal history displayed just enough dabbling in the counterculture to fill conservatives with disgust. He had smoked, though not inhaled, marijuana. He had avoided—critics said he dodged—the draft during the Vietnam War. He had gotten his start campaigning for George McGovern. And unlike Falwell, Clinton had gone to prestigious East Coast schools—Georgetown University and Yale Law School, a Rhodes Scholar at Oxford—adding a touch of anti-elitist resentment to Falwell's contempt for the man. If any more evidence was needed that Clinton was from Arkansas but not of Arkansas, there stood Hillary, a lawyer who had not abandoned her career when she became a wife and mother—and a lawyer who had worked at the very firm that had foreclosed on some of Falwell's properties. Falwell's hatred for the Clintons was venomous and would lead him into some of the most morally reprehensible behavior of his entire career.

Bill Clinton was a different kind of Democrat. While some on the left had mocked religion during the heyday of the Moral Majority, Clinton was familiar with the cadences and the content of Baptist preaching. He did not mock; he mimicked. Clinton liked to insert quotes and images from the Bible into his speeches. He related the liberal policies he advocated to the language of values he knew the electorate shared. Like Falwell himself, he always had a folksy story to use in explaining his positions and articulating his objectives.

At the 1992 Democratic National Convention, Clinton delivered an acceptance speech entitled "A New Covenant," invoking a phrase rich with religious symbolism in both the Bible and American history. Chiding President Bush for mocking "the vision thing," Clinton responded with a verse from the Book of Proverbs (29:18): "Where there is no vision, the people perish." Toward the end of the speech Clinton said, "As the Scripture says, 'Our eyes have not yet seen, nor our ears heard, nor minds imagined' what we can build." The speech was well received, and Clinton left his convention leading in the polls.[1]

Falwell was beside himself. He charged that Clinton had misquoted scripture, that the correct version of 1 Corinthians 2:9—the King James version—was "But as it is written, Eye hath not seen, nor ear heard, neither have entered into the heart of man, the things which God hath prepared for them that love Him." Falwell insisted that the scripture verse was about what God had built, not what mankind could build. "Misquoting and manipulating the Holy Scripture for political purposes should be offensive to millions of Americans who read and believe the Bible, whether they be Democrat, Republican or Independent," Falwell said in a prepared statement. He resented what he termed Clinton's "hijacking" of "covenant" language for his own political agenda, and he also questioned the distinction that Clinton had drawn in his speech between being "pro-abortion" and "pro-choice."[2]

Professor Larry Sabato at the University of Virginia recognized that Falwell was trying to blunt Clinton's appeal with evangelical voters, and he noted that Pat Robertson had issued a similar statement. "They're trying to send a signal to fundamentalist Christians that Bill Clinton may be a Baptist, but he's not their kind of Baptist," Sabato said. Falwell may have sent the signal, but it was imperfectly received. In November, Clinton won the southern states of Georgia, Louisiana, Tennessee, Kentucky, and his native Arkansas, the first Democrat to win a southern state since Jimmy Carter held on to his home state of Georgia in 1980.[3]

Within days of the election, Falwell toyed with the idea of restarting the Moral Majority. Just as important, he let it be known that he was toying with the idea. On the *Old-Time Gospel Hour* the Sunday after the election, Falwell delivered a sermon entitled "The Clinton Agenda for the Unborn and Gays." He reported receiving a "tremendous amount of contact" by phone and mail, including communications from members of Congress urging him to revive the Moral Majority, but he insisted that no decision had been made yet. In an interview with *USA Today*, Falwell worried that "we are on the threshold of national and international shame." To the *Lynchburg News*, Falwell said that if Clinton turned out to be "a reincarnation of Jimmy Carter," he would be inclined to restart the organization, but that doing so would be a "last resort."[4]

Of course, conservative evangelicals had not abandoned politics when Falwell shut down the Moral Majority. The Christian Coalition had emerged from Pat Robertson's failed presidential bid in 1988, and Ralph Reed, the Coalition's president, continued to carry the banner of Christian values onto the electoral battlefield. James Dobson's Family Research Council, started in 1981, was also emerging as a big player in national conservative politics. Neither Dobson nor Reed were pastors, however, and so, while their political involvement did not raise some of the church-state objections that Falwell's activities had occasioned, they lacked the extensive fundamentalist network that Falwell was able to use. Furthermore, Reed was a spin doctor who could never quite approximate Falwell's command of the religious idiom, and Dobson, a psychologist, also lacked the kind of pulpit oratory that Falwell brought to political debate. Both organizations carried on the work that Falwell had begun, to be sure, but neither group attained the controversial, high-profile status that Moral Majority had enjoyed in its heyday.

Among those urging Falwell to rekindle the Moral Majority flame was Martin Mawyer, who had founded the Christian Action Network. "We need individuals that can rally the forces together," Mawyer said. "The media has been looking for a marquee-type name ever since Falwell dropped out. I think he'll be great for that." Jerry Nims, the last president of the Moral Majority, agreed, saying, "The group can achieve the place it had previously, particularly with the new administration."[5]

Some conservative commentators were skeptical at the prospect of a resurrected Moral Majority. Cal Thomas, who had served as the vice president of the Moral Majority when it first began in 1979, wrote against the idea in his syndicated column: "I would advise, please, please, please don't." Thomas saw the talk of bringing the organization back as a fund-raising device. "The effort might provide some needed short-term cash for the struggling Falwell organization and for other groups," Thomas wrote. Charles Judd, another former staffer, seconded Thomas's analysis. "I'm inclined to think it's going to be a mail mill," Judd said, referring to organizations whose primary purpose is to raise money through direct-mail solicitations.[6]

At Christmastime, Falwell took to the pulpit at Thomas Road Baptist Church to preach on Judges 17:6, "In those days there was no king in Israel; every man did what was right in his own ways." Surrounded by poinsettias and faux-snow, Falwell explained that the passage applied to a time when Israel was "lawless, bloody, rootless, a time of anarchy when Israel almost lost its identity." He said that ancient Israel at that time could be described as suffering from "situational ethics." Falwell noted the chaos then engulfing the African nation of Somalia, which he attributed to the fact that the country had "no authority." He then confessed his fear that a similar fate awaited America.[7]

Falwell conducted a brief history lesson for his congregation. He recalled that he was born in 1933, in the midst of the Great Depression. He recalled World War II, and as evidence of his patriotism Falwell said that when that war was ending he was "clamoring" for the government to allow General Patton to "go on to Moscow," although it is difficult to imagine even a precocious twelve-year-old clamoring for such a geopolitical strategy. He recalled more recent events surrounding the end of the Cold War and voiced his belief that these indicated that "the birthpangs for the Lord's return are getting closer and closer together."

Having established this backdrop, he launched into a series of predictions about what his listeners could expect in the first one hundred days of the Clinton administration. The first item Falwell listed, and to which he dedicated the most time, was the prospect of gays serving in the military. As a candidate, Bill Clinton had promised to lift the ban. Falwell said that this would mean that "for the first time in our history, we will give national approval to moral perversion." He warned about the baneful consequences that would flow from permitting gays to serve in the military, joking, "I can imagine this new homosexual army who is sent out to fight the enemy instead winking at them. God have mercy." The congregation burst into laughter. Falwell also warned that Clinton intended to pass a bill granting "special rights" to gays and forcing Christian businesses and even churches to hire gays.

The rest of Falwell's laundry list was a mix of moral and political concerns. He warned that the proposed Freedom of Choice Act, which was highly unlikely to even make it out of committee, would remove all restrictions on abortion. He decried the prospect of statehood for the District of Columbia. He lamented the idea of women serving in combat. "I have no problem with Hillary going to combat but I certainly have a problem with my daughter going into combat," he told his hometown and television audience. Falwell warned against a "major move towards socialized medicine" and a downsized military and increased taxes and more "give-away programs" and a new chairman of the National Endowment for the Arts who would use taxpayer money to fund "anti-Christian art." The remedy to this catalog of woe was for Christians to pray, to get personally involved, to set the pulpits of the nation's churches "aflame," and for his people to support those ministries that stood up to the Clinton agenda. The sermon was quite a tour de force, even by Falwell's standards. He did, however, promise to pray for President Clinton and even to support him if he saw the light and broke his promise to act on the items that Falwell had just outlined.[8]

Early in 1993, Falwell sent out a mailing to potential supporters (and donors). "Dear Friend," the letter began. "Is it time to reactivate the Moral Majority? I am writing today because I am deeply concerned. Has America lost its vision of being . . . ONE NATION UNDER GOD? Are we about to become a hedonistic nation of unrestrained homosexuality, abortion, immorality, and lawlessness?" Falwell noted that homosexuality was being accepted as an alternative lifestyle and that "we are only days away from seeing the U.S. military infiltrated with gay men and lesbians." He warned that churches would be forced to hire a "quota of homosexuals." He warned that the "French abortion pill, RU–486, will soon be legalized in the U.S." The letter included a collage of headlines detailing some of the incoming administration's plans, such as "President: Ban on homosexuals will be revoked," all of them sure to alarm Falwell's fundamentalist base. It was clear that opposition to abortion and homosexuality were the two leading issues on Falwell's mind at this time. But as the spring of 1993 progressed, it also became clear that talk of reviving the Moral Majority had been, as predicted, just talk

for fund-raising purposes. Falwell took no steps to restart the organization.[9]

Falwell, of course, did not need an organization to make his
views known; while he had scaled back his political appearances,
he continued to travel across the country, speaking at fundamentalist churches. Later that year, appearing at a convention of Southern
Baptist ministers, Falwell attacked two Clinton appointees, one an
open lesbian and the other rumored to be a lesbian. "Apparently, the
president wanted 50 perverts in key places, so he wanted Roberta
Achtenberg and he wanted Donna Shalala," Falwell said. "If I had
been president and somebody said, 'We've got to have 50 perverts,'
I wouldn't know where to look. My soul, who would I check on to
get that? But Hillary knew. . . . All of these are her old friends."
Achtenberg was a parent as well as a lesbian, which offended Falwell
at every level. "She ought to be in a cage," he remarked.[10]

When President Clinton took office, he named his wife Hillary to
head a special commission to draft legislation that would guarantee
universal health insurance for all Americans, a long-standing Democratic objective. Hillary Clinton delivered her report by the end of
the summer, and in September 1993 President Clinton addressed a
joint session of Congress to deliver his proposal. "HillaryCare" was
born, and Falwell had a new issue.

Falwell produced a video about the plan to revamp the country's
health care system entitled *Prescription for Disaster*. The video featured cameos of Falwell and others discussing the proposal. A businessman from Canada shared his disgust with the health care system
in his country. A surgeon, Dr. C. Gregory Lockhart, said that having
"a medically indicated treatment refused by a bureaucrat is . . . anath-
ema to the way Americans expect their health care to be delivered."
Dr. Thomas Eppes Jr., a family practitioner, offered his opinion that
the government "has never shown it can do something as efficiently as
the private sector."

The star of the show, however, was the preacher. He announced
that the Clinton plan was "socialized medicine." Sitting in a televi-

sion studio, not standing in his pulpit, Falwell looked directly into the camera as he warned that the government would "ransom" health care and that the new law would entail federal funding of abortion. He said that if the Clinton plan was enacted, "Big Brother was watching," because the government would keep track of medical procedures, and he asserted that there was a liberal media cover-up of such negative aspects of the Clinton plan. Despite the fact that millions of Americans lacked health insurance, Falwell claimed, "It is all myth that health care is not available to the poor," citing no specifics to sustain his claim.[11]

The most repugnant part of the video, unsurprisingly, focused on gays. While videotape of two men kissing showed on the screen, Falwell complained that "unlimited coverage means that those who contract AIDS through immoral homosexual lifestyles or through dirty needles and drug abuse will receive health care without any penalty for their abusive lifestyles and you and I will be paying for their treatment with our tax dollars." In Falwell's moral universe, contracting a deadly disease was evidently not a sufficient penalty. Later in the video, Falwell said that people should be rewarded for living healthy, moral lives. "I don't smoke or drink and I don't live immorally, and most of you watching are saying, 'Amen, I do the same.' But we will pay the price for those who violate the rules of health, hygiene and decency." As Falwell spoke, a photograph of a dying AIDS patient in his hospital bed filled the screen.

The complaint that those dying from AIDS had not sufficiently paid a price for their "immoral" and "indecent" behavior was an obscene complaint. It was a measure of Falwell's diminished national influence that this video occasioned almost no protest. Nonetheless, Falwell's army of supporters, trained in the arts of political organization, assisted in the effort to defeat the Clintons' health care proposals with phone calls to members of Congress and letters to the editors of their local newspapers. The Clinton proposals would probably have failed no matter what Falwell did or did not do, but he claimed his share of the credit.

*   *   *

Falwell also lent his assistance to another anti-Clinton video in 1994, *The Clinton Chronicles*. A shortened, more concise version was produced under the title *Bill Clinton's Circle of Power*. Falwell helped finance the project, sending out a fund-raising appeal before the videos were made and promoting them on his *Old-Time Gospel Hour* show. He also helped distribute them, ordering tens of thousands of copies and packaging *Bill Clinton's Circle of Power* with his video attacking the Clintons' health care initiative. But it was one thing to question the president's policies and another to question his person. These attacks amounted to calumny.

Bill Clinton's Circle of Power opens with a disclaimer that it does not "necessarily reflect the opinions of Liberty Alliance, Inc." Viewers are then introduced to Judge Jim Johnson, a former Arkansas legislator and judge who recalls reading affidavits in a lawsuit brought by Larry Nichols, a former official with the Arkansas Development Finance Authority (ADFA). Judge Johnson says that it was in those court documents that he first learned of "Clinton's affairs with a number of bimbos." He details allegations of influence peddling, concluding that "there is less evidence against 90% of the people on death row" than there was against the Clintons.[12]

Larry Nichols then takes over and narrates the rest of the pseudo-documentary. "Bill Clinton is a liar . . . a pathological liar," Nichols intones. After describing the Clintons' influence and their instincts for political self-preservation, he warns darkly that "people are dead in Arkansas." Linda Ives is introduced, and she offers the claim that her son's murder was covered up by the Clintons, providing no evidence for the claim. Then Nichols charges that Hillary Clinton and White House lawyer Vince Foster had an affair and that Foster did not commit suicide in 1993. Nichols correctly notes that several White House officials went to Foster's office after his untimely death, but he claims, without attribution, that they were looking, not for a suicide note, but for documents relating to the Whitewater scandal then under investigation and for "love notes" from Hillary.

Nichols goes on to warn his viewers that more unseemly facts about the Clintons will be forthcoming. He claims that he knows firsthand from his time at AFDA about "special deals" for companies with ties to the Clintons, and he asserts that strong-arm tactics were used to fund-raise from those conducting business with AFDA. Nichols claims that he laid out all these charges at a press conference on the steps of the Arkansas State Capitol, but that the media declined to print his allegations.

The most serious charge leveled by Nichols is that Clinton was involved in a drug-smuggling operation at a small airport in Mena, Arkansas, but that he "can't talk about it." Nichols says that his lawyer was beaten up by "Clinton's people." When the charges made their way into the mainstream media, a congressional panel looked into them and cleared the president of any involvement in the drug-smuggling operations at Mena.[13]

Gary Parks, the son of a man who provided security at Clinton's campaign headquarters in Little Rock, charges on the video that the Clintons had his father murdered because he had video evidence of Clinton's drug use and affairs with many women. "I believe my father was assassinated," Parks says. It was later revealed that Parks's mother had received $16,000 from the producer of the video and an additional $6,000 from Nichols. Mrs. Parks also acknowledged that her husband had been involved in the drug-smuggling operation at Mena, a more likely explanation for his murder.[14]

Former congressman Bill Dannemeyer of California makes an appearance on the video. He denounces Clinton as a "draft dodging womanizer who is a pathological liar," recapitulates many of the charges detailed by Nichols, and then calls for the impeachment of the president and of Attorney General Janet Reno. The video concludes with the request that viewers write to members of Congress to demand hearings and investigations into the charges. It also offers to send them an additional copy of the video for $40 plus $3 to cover shipping and handling.

Falwell not only purchased copies of both videos but also added commentary at the end of *Bill Clinton's Circle of Power*. Adding his voice to the calls for a full-scale investigation, Falwell looks into the camera as he asks questions such as "Did Bill Clinton use taxpayer money for purposes of sexual liaisons?" and "Was Vince Foster's death a suicide or a murder?" He holds up a "Citizens' Petition to

Congress" that viewers can ask to sign for a nominal fee and shows them where their signature will appear on the formal-looking sheet of paper—"right next to mine." He promises to send the petition to the speaker of the House and the Senate majority leader.[15]

Falwell also videotaped an infomercial for the pseudo-documentaries. In the infomercial, a man identified as an investigative journalist is mostly hidden from view, to ensure his anonymity. He tells Falwell that President Clinton is responsible for many murders and that he fears for his own life, accounting for the need for anonymity. On camera, Falwell promises the journalist that "we will be praying for your safety." But the "journalist" was not a journalist at all: he was Patrick Matrisciana, the man who produced *The Clinton Chronicles*. Matrisciana would later tell journalists that the scene was Falwell's idea, a claim disputed by Falwell's son Jerry Jr.[16]

Matrisciana later admitted that he had paid several of the people leveling allegations against the Clintons as "expert witnesses." "We did not pay people to tell lies," Matrisciana told *Salon,* which had obtained copies of his firm's financial records. "We paid people so that they would no longer have to be afraid to tell the truth. Most of the folks whom we have paid money have been the victims of political persecution and political oppression. These people [told] . . . the truth, and we wanted to compensate them for that." Nichols received more than $89,000 from Citizens for Honest Government. Falwell's spokesman, Mark DeMoss, said the preacher knew nothing about such payments.[17]

DeMoss was less clear about Falwell's connection to Matrisciana and the videos. He claimed that Falwell had not been involved in *The Clinton Chronicles* until it was already completed and that he had merely tried to promote it; DeMoss was overlooking the fund-raising appeal that specifically said the money raised would be used to produce the video. He also neglected to grapple with the fact that Falwell appears on-screen in *Bill Clinton's Circle of Power*. DeMoss at one point said that Falwell had known Matrisciana for twenty years, but later he suggested that the two had only met "about twice."[18]

Falwell was challenged by a fellow Baptist minister, Tony Campolo, who was also a friend of the Clintons. In a letter to Falwell that

Campolo released to the press, he wrote, "You have challenged the president of the United States to respond to the charges and issues raised in the video. As his [Clinton's] personal friend I am asking you to allow me time on your TV show to respond to these charges." DeMoss said the request was denied. In Little Rock, Falwell had been scheduled to speak at a conference at Clinton's own Immanuel Baptist Church, but the conference had to be moved when the pastor objected. "I saw Falwell promoting the tapes that have been proven to be scurrilous. I could not, with good conscience, go along with it any longer," Rev. Rex Horne told the press.[19]

Some of Falwell's friends took issue with his promotion of the video. William Bennett, the former Education secretary who had given a speech at Liberty University, said the videos were "below the pale, beyond the pale," in an appearance on *The Cal Thomas Show*. Bennett, no friend of the Clintons, added, "The problem with this sort of thing is that there are lots of credible criticisms to make about Bill Clinton. When you start to get into bizarre stuff that I think lacks any substantiation whatsoever, you discredit responsible criticism."[20]

Not all of Falwell's political statements during the 1990s focused on the president he so detested. He had developed a new, more immediate way to communicate his views on a wide variety of issues, introducing "Falwell Fax Online," which he described as a "weekly fax-briefing exclusively for America's pastors and Christian leaders who may use this information without attribution." These short, one- or two-page faxes carried news of Falwell's activities and comments from the preacher on the topics of the day.

The Republican Party had won big in the 1994 midterm elections, but Clinton's landslide reelection in 1996 was an invitation for the GOP to engage in some soul-searching. One of the debates that emerged was between those who wanted the party to deemphasize the polarizing social issues such as abortion or gay rights and instead focus on economic issues like cutting taxes and improving the economy. Not surprisingly, Falwell was adamant that the Republicans not backtrack on their commitment to the issues he had first brought to the table, along with millions of evangelical voters, in 1980.

"If the Republican Party is to flourish it must continue to be the party of the family and the unborn!" Falwell announced in a "Falwell Fax Online" message sent from the Philippines, where he was preaching. He gave his approval to a measure being pushed by the Republican National Committee (RNC) that would deny funding to any candidate who failed to support the ban on partial-birth abortion. Among those arguing for the proposal was conservative evangelical and Missouri senator John Ashcroft. Arizona senator John McCain and Texas governor George W. Bush opposed the measure. Falwell was loath to be on the opposite side of an issue from the Bushes. "Whatever the outcome of the looming vote, it is good to see that abortion has returned to the forefront of the party. Even if this measure is not passed, it has put a much-needed scare into the handful of pro-choice candidates in the party!" This was hardly a line drawn in the sand.[21]

The Republican National Committee, on a vote of 114–43, decided not to adopt the proposal cutting funds off for those who did not support the ban. Instead, the RNC passed a resolution condemning partial-birth abortion and Clinton's veto of the measure. Falwell said that he agreed with this outcome and quoted Illinois representative Henry Hyde, who had stated, "We can have a resolution that condemns this barbarism, that condemns a president who is so insensitive as to support it, but let us try to maintain every vote we can get because you win by addition, you do not win by subtraction." This was not expert moral reasoning, but it was smart politics.[22]

In 1998 Falwell had to differentiate himself from some of the more extreme elements within the anti-abortion movement. Operation Rescue advocated direct protesting at abortion clinics and physically preventing women from entering. Their tactics sometimes crossed the line between protest and intimidation, and they were quick to denounce anti-abortion groups that did not support their more extreme stance and tactics. One of the group's leaders, Flip Benham, came to Lynchburg to protest at a clinic, where he was arrested. Falwell denounced Benham's tactics and agreed to reimburse the Lynchburg police for the costs they incurred. Benham was less than gracious and began a protest at the gates of Liberty University. Benham accused Falwell of being "soft on porn" because of a book in the university bookstore that Benham thought was risqué. Having had enough of Benham and his friends, Falwell called them "thugs and thieves."[23]

Falwell faced more criticism from his right when he denounced Rev. Fred Phelps, pastor of the Westboro Baptist Church in Topeka, Kansas. Phelps came to national prominence when he and his parishioners protested at the funeral of Matthew Shepard, a young man who had been murdered in Wyoming because he was gay. Phelps and his supporters carried signs that read "God Hates Fags" and similar messages at the funeral, believing it was wrong to give a Christian burial to a homosexual. In an appearance on *Larry King Live,* Falwell had denounced Phelps's tactics and said that he believed God loves everyone, even if He does not approve of everything they do. This led Phelps to mount a protest outside Thomas Road Baptist Church. "We're just preaching the Bible—and not this kissy-pooh stuff Falwell is putting out," Phelps told reporters as he stood outside the church.[24]

"I would think the cause of Christ would be better served if they were home in church today," Falwell told reporters as he arrived at Thomas Road. "Even those most unenlightened believe God is love. . . . The practice of homosexuality is wrong. But I don't think it's any more wrong than heterosexual promiscuity," Falwell said. He did not approach the protesters, nor did he speak of them in his sermon. The parishioners at Thomas Road seemed nonplussed by the protests. "I don't think we can say we agree with them," parishioner Don Sloan told a reporter. "Their interpretation of the Bible is totally different. When Christ died on the cross, he died for all men." Another parishioner dismissed Phelps and his group as "a bunch of fools."[25]

Falwell, of course, had not softened his position on the role of gays in society. He used his "Falwell Fax Online" to applaud the results of a voter referendum in Maine that repealed a gay rights ordinance in that state. He warned that such popular defeats for gay rights supporters at the local level would lead them to try to secure passage of a federal nondiscrimination law, and he urged his supporters to write their members of Congress to oppose any such measure. Falwell disclosed that he had sent three staffers to "infiltrate" a large gay rights march in Washington and said that the videotape made by the staffers contained unbelievable things. "Sodom and Gomorrah had nothing on the march," Falwell wrote. He promised to infiltrate an upcoming gay rights march as well.[26]

On January 21, 1998, most of the major networks had dispatched their anchors or principal reporters to Havana, Cuba, where Pope John Paul II was to begin his first-ever visit to the island nation. But that morning they were all recalled to Washington for breaking news. The nation was introduced to Miss Monica Lewinsky.

Falwell was not the only person appalled by the allegations against the president, but he was one of the most fervent in his commentary on each and every aspect of the scandal. When the news first broke about the relationship, and as Lewinsky began negotiations with prosecutors to secure her testimony, Falwell urged that no grant of immunity to the former White House intern be granted. Another week he asked that prosecutors also examine the circumstances surrounding the death of Commerce secretary Ron Brown, who was killed in an airplane crash in Croatia two years earlier, feeding the conspiracy theorists who believed that Brown was killed.[27]

Falwell saw the scandal as confirming all the things he had ever believed about the Clintons. When President Clinton tried to avoid testifying, citing executive privilege, Falwell claimed that the president's response would "give the certain impression of stonewalling. Of course, stonewalling is one of the things this president does best, but voters have been unwilling to look beneath the surface of Clinton's six years of excuses and self-justifications." He also dismissed the Clintons' complaints that the charges against the president were politically motivated. "Blaming their opponents is nothing new for the Clintons," Falwell wrote in one of his faxes.[28]

Even though Falwell had been largely out of the political lime-light for almost a decade, his name still served as shorthand in liberal political circles for nefarious conservative influences. In an interview on *The Today Show,* First Lady Hillary Clinton mentioned Falwell by name when she said that the charges against her husband were the result of a "vast right-wing conspiracy." A Clinton political adviser also called Falwell "the biggest liar in the country." Falwell denied involvement in any conspiracy. "I can tell you unconditionally that I have had absolutely nothing to do with any conspiracy against the White House," Falwell wrote in an article. "I have never met White-water independent counsel Kenneth Starr, Monica Lewinsky, Gen-nifer Flowers or any of the other women who are alleged to have had affairs with the president." Falwell also claimed not to have rehearsed his role in *The Clinton Chronicles*.[29]

In August, after President Clinton testified before a grand jury and publicly admitted having had an "inappropriate relationship" with Lewinsky, Falwell appeared on Jesse Jackson's CNN talk show to discuss the scandal. He suggested that the president should resign or be impeached because he had lost the ability to lead the nation. He also took swipes at the Clintons' marriage. "I do not see with Bill and Hillary the loving commitment one to another. I see rather an arrangement," Falwell told Jackson. He speculated that if Hill-ary had "gotten tougher with him, I mean from Day One, maybe he might be a different person today. No husband should be allowed to live the animal-like life he has lived." He admitted, however, that he did not know the Clintons personally.[30]

Of course, Clinton was impeached on a party-line vote in the House, confirming the views of most Americans that the charges were a Republican witch hunt. The president was acquitted by a bipartisan vote in the Senate. With the whole sordid "Monicagate" episode in the past, the country could hope for calmer waters. The nation was prosperous at home and at peace abroad and seemed exhausted from the political mudslinging.

The Clinton presidency was frustrating for Falwell politically, but it was good for his ministry. His brand of over-the-top political attacks had always been more effective in opposition. As much as he enjoyed the perks of power when his friends were in the White House, he seemed to equally revel in the political brawling occasioned by his opponents' political ascent. And when he gave voice to what many conservative evangelicals were thinking during the Clinton years, they responded with financial support.

Additionally, technology came to his aid as cable and satellite television allowed his *Old-Time Gospel Hour* to appear in many markets he had been forced to abandon during the budget crunches after the PTL scandal. The "Falwell Fax Online" was an inexpensive way for him to communicate with a network of conservative pastors and supporters. However controversial the Clinton videos had been, the videotapes used by Liberty University for its home learning courses brought needed revenue to the school at very little cost.

In fact, after all the turmoil of earlier times, Falwell's church and university seemed to be on the strongest footing since before the PTL scandal, largely because of the efforts of Jerry Falwell Jr. to bring order to his father's often scattered management. Jonathan Falwell had joined the Thomas Road Baptist Church staff as an associate minister in the 1990s. Both sons made smart investments—Jonathan in a video-processing business and Jerry Jr. in real estate—and both were also beginning their own families, to the delight of new grandparents Jerry and Macel. Both sons kept a very low profile, however, as they were still being groomed. Their father remained the face of the ministries.[31]

Falwell was getting on in years, and he might have been inclined to grasp the spirit of the nation and become content with less contentiousness. He was in his sixty-fifth year when the Clinton impeachment controversy came to an end. He could have been forgiven for wanting to find some quietude. But this was Jerry Falwell, so predictions of a noncontroversial future were bound to be proven wrong. Soon they were.

Chapter Fifteen

Falwell's Last Years

Controversy and Consolation

The last decade of Falwell's life was a combination of controversy and consolation. He continued to rage against homosexuals, but also found himself hosting a "summit on nonviolence" at which gays and evangelicals sat down together to discuss lessening the vitriol that characterized the relationship between the two groups. In the wake of the terrorist attacks on September 11, 2001, Falwell found himself embroiled in controversy once again, this time over his remarks about Islam and the role of Providence in the attacks.

In the background, death was knocking at the door and he knew it, but he chose to ignore advice to take care of his physical well-being. Falwell was constitutionally incapable of healthy eating. He continued to have cheddar cheese omelets with sausage for breakfast at the Bob Evans restaurant, where he was usually joined by his friend and associate Ron Godwin, who had returned to Lynchburg to assist Falwell. His schedule continued to include cross-country trips to preach at churches, preaching at Thomas Road Baptist on Sundays and at the university's three weekly convocations, fundraising trips, and meetings with administrators and donors. It was a hectic schedule for any man, but for a man in his sixties it was

extraordinary. He would continue to do too much until he took his
last breath.

A recent study claims that abortion and homosexuality are the "glue"
that holds the religious right coalition together. Both issues had long
been staples of Falwell's sermons and his fund-raising appeals. Both
were among the four issues originally identified by the Moral Majority as its core concerns. On all the leading political issues the nation
faces today, only with abortion and homosexuality do popular positions continue to track closely with high degrees of religiosity.[1]

In the more than twenty years since Falwell had traveled to
Florida to help Anita Bryant in her successful crusade against a
gay rights ordinance in Dade County, Falwell had warned repeatedly against the dangers that gays posed to the traditional family.
He based his opposition to homosexuality squarely on his reading of the Bible and would frequently cite Sodom and Gomorrah
as examples of what awaited a country that embraced homosexuality. Falwell also lent credence to some of the more sinister, and
unfounded, attitudes toward gays, such as the charge that the so-
called gay agenda included recruiting young children to participate
in the gay lifestyle.

The AIDS epidemic changed profoundly how gays were treated
by the rest of American society. Here was a disease that entailed horrible suffering and shockingly early death for thousands. For many
Americans, AIDS was an invitation to compassion. In 1987, when a
prominent Catholic priest, Father Michael Peterson, was dying from
AIDS, his boss, Archbishop James Hickey of Washington, visited
the dying priest daily and then presided at his funeral, where he was
joined by hundreds of priests and six other bishops. In remarks at
the end of the funeral, Hickey, known for his conservative views on
homosexuality and other sexual issues, compared the sufferings of
Father Peterson from AIDS to the sufferings of Christ on the Cross.
In a letter sent to all the American bishops just before Peterson died,
Hickey wrote that his "illness reminds us in a personal way of the
terrible human tragedy of AIDS in our midst. His suffering chal-

lenges us to reach out with renewed conviction and compassion . . .
not condemnation."[2]

Others used the deadly disease to frighten and ostracize. Falwell's approach to the disease more clearly fell into this camp. He
had warned in his anti–health care reform video that AIDS patients
would receive treatment without "any penalty for their abusive lifestyles." From the pulpit of his church, he cited talk radio host Rush
Limbaugh to the effect that letting gays serve in the military would
cost the government too much money because of the cost of caring
for veterans who had AIDS. In 1994, in a mailing sent out to supporters of the Liberty Alliance, Falwell wrote that the "Clinton administration is set to award thousands and thousands of immigration visas
to foreigners who are infected with the lethal, fatal and deadly **AIDS
virus**—so they can come to America! . . . That's right. The Clinton
administration is putting the health, welfare, public safety and life
of every American at risk . . . just so these homosexuals can hold
an Olympic Games for gays and lesbians and transvestites and bi-
sexuals and pedophiles and sodomites and exhibitionists and cross
dressers and every other sexual deviant on the planet with perverted
proclivities!" The fund-raising appeal warned that these "deviants"
would infect Americans with the AIDS virus before leaving, "defame
your pastors," "invade your neighborhoods," and "recruit your children."[3]

Not all of Falwell's assaults on gays were so venomous. In early
1999, Falwell took on Tinky-Winky, one of the stars of a British children's show, *The Teletubbies*. The wildly popular television show for
preschool children featured four "Teletubbies," who were played by
four actors wearing brightly colored, oversized costumes with televi-
sions on their stomachs and geometric symbols on their heads. The
four Teletubbies romped over a magical landscape in every episode,
engaging in very simple plots and exclaiming "uh-oh" to each other.

Falwell's *Liberty Journal* discerned a sinister agenda regarding
Tinky-Winky. "He is purple—the gay-pride color; and his antenna
is shaped like a triangle—the gay-pride symbol," noted the February
issue. If that was not enough, Tinky-Winky carried a magic bag that
Falwell's editors thought looked suspiciously like a purse. The article

accused the producers of intentionally putting "subtle depictions" of gay sexuality in the show and said that such role-modeling of the gay lifestyle was "damaging to the moral lives of children." The company that produced the show laughed off Falwell's suspicions: "It's a children's show, folks," said Itsy Bitsy Entertainment spokesman Steve Rice. "To out a Teletubby in a pre-school show is kind of sad on his part. I really find it absurd and kind of offensive." Falwell said that he had had nothing to do with the *Liberty Journal* article. "I certainly never criticized Tinky Winky in any way," he assured a reporter.[4]

It was against this backdrop of comic misunderstanding and strangely un-Christian venom that Mel White approached Falwell about toning it down. White, a professor at Fuller Theological Seminary in Pasadena, California, had worked for Falwell and other prominent evangelists as a ghostwriter. He had first come to Lynchburg in 1986 to work on Falwell's anti-abortion book, *If I Should Die Before I Wake*. The two men liked each other immediately and formed an effective collaboration. Then White stayed on with Falwell to ghostwrite his autobiography. Unbeknownst to Falwell at the time, White had separated from his wife and was living with a man, struggling with his decision about whether or not to come out of the closet.

In 1991, on Christmas Eve, White wrote Falwell a long letter in which he disclosed his homosexuality and recalled a conversation with Falwell in which the preacher had admitted that he was close friends with a gay man who was in a committed relationship. In White's recollection of that conversation, Falwell had said, "I'm not going to put him in a corner if he doesn't put me in one." White then called attention to a recent fund-raising appeal from Falwell in which gays were called "perverts." After touting Falwell's influence, White asked plaintively, "Did anyone think about the confusion, the anguish and the despair that the letter's simplistic, judgmental, and erroneous position creates for [gays] and for their families?" Falwell did not reply.[5]

In October 1998, the torture and murder of a young gay man,

Matthew Shepard, captured the nation's attention. It was the protests at Shepard's funeral by Reverend Phelps and Falwell's subsequent denunciation of Phelps that brought the Wichita pastor to protest at Thomas Road Baptist. The tragedy also prompted White to suggest to Falwell that they convoke a summit dedicated to nonviolence between White's gay evangelical organization, Soulforce, and Falwell and his ministries. The two men met in August 1999. Falwell agreed to "take a more careful look" at the letters being sent out over his signature. More surprisingly, he agreed to host the summit in Lynchburg in October.

Two hundred members of Soulforce arrived in Lynchburg on October 23. Falwell brought two hundred members of his organizations as well. Tragically, a different kind of balance had been achieved the month before when a man shouting anti-Christian expletives burst into a Fort Worth, Texas, church and killed seven parishioners. Falwell was able to call for denunciations of violence against Christians too. Both Falwell and White went out of their way before the event to demonstrate mutual respect. "My goal is not to demean [Falwell], ridicule him or call him the village idiot," White said, "but to help him understand the truth as I know it and as he knows it." For his part, Falwell acknowledged that "through the years, evangelicals, Jerry Falwell included, have been too strident in their condemnations of the [homosexual] lifestyle to the point that we were not communicating adequate love to the gays and lesbians themselves."[6]

The summit drew plenty of media attention: outside the auditorium where the meeting was held, television camera crews lined the driveway of Liberty University. Protesters from both gay rights groups and evangelical organizations protested the meeting. One gay rights leader denounced White, saying that the gay rights movement wanted no "assistance" from Falwell. In reply to the evangelical protesters, Falwell quipped, "Like a bull in a china closet, I just keep doing what I think is right."[7]

Inside the hall, Falwell said that they had not gathered to debate the inerrancy of the Bible or their differing positions on the morality of homosexuality. Several times he repeated his position that the Bible condemned homosexuality and that he could never abandon his views on the subject. He compared the summit to his frequent speeches before Jewish organizations: he never denied his belief in the necessity of Christian faith for salvation, but he would tell Jewish groups that his belief did not prevent them from finding common ground. He promised to make sure that he examined everything that was being said and taught by his ministers and professors "to make sure we're talking about issues, not persons." Falwell noted that both he and White had taken heat for the meeting, "but someone must find a way to sit down as friends, the same way Jesus sat down, the friend of sinners, and that includes all 400 of us today."[8]

Behind the lectern were photographs of people who had been killed because they were gay. Falwell invoked their memory and claimed that "inside both camps there are . . . people more interested in peace than in war, in glorifying God than in getting their point across." He mentioned his friendship with Larry Flynt and noted that his ministries helped alcoholics and unwed mothers even though he disapproved of alcohol and sex outside of marriage. Those ministries, however, "show that we love people no matter what we think of their behavior. We have not done that with you. We apologize for that. We ask your forgiveness for that."

Falwell again called attention to the risk that both he and White were taking. He said that he had already received lots of mail about the event. "And I'm not gonna answer my mail until it's over," Falwell joked. "Do I have some mail to answer! From the people who pay my bills." Despite the occasional defensiveness in his speech, Falwell was supremely gracious. "I don't want you to leave here ever, ever, ever again thinking I don't love you and I'm gonna do my best not to say anything or do anything that will make you think that."[9]

It did not take long for Falwell to hedge his bets. The next week, on the *Old-Time Gospel Hour,* Falwell said that five of the gay people who had attended the summit had decided to abandon their lifestyle. White tracked down the claim and found it groundless. True or not, the claim allowed Falwell to tell those who opposed his summit that good had come from it. The next week, on the same show, he repeated his belief that the purpose of the summit had been to reach sinners. "We haven't been reaching them because we've been yelling at them," he told his congregation and television audience. He said that, as a Bible-based church, "we can never sanction their behavior, never approve their lifestyle but love them with an unconditional love." He again compared the proper stance toward gays as the stance his ministry took toward alcoholics and unwed mothers. He repeated these arguments in a letter to his supporters in early December. "Hate the sin, but love the sinner" was not going to satisfy many gays and lesbians, but it was better than the venom of Reverend Phelps.[10]

Early in January, at a Liberty University convocation, Falwell again discussed the summit. "That wasn't unusual. That was unbelievable. Only God could have done that," Falwell told the students. Now, in addition to the five he mentioned previously, Falwell claimed that "several" of the gay participants "contacted us and . . . are making progress spiritually away from the gay and lesbian lifestyle and into Christ." This justification for hosting the summit fit nicely with Falwell's self-image as a celebrity: His many media appearances allowed him to bring people he might not otherwise reach to Christ.[11]

It was a foregone conclusion that Falwell would support George W. Bush's bid for the White House in 2000. Although he had largely stayed off the political stage for more than ten years, he joined with other conservative Christians in launching an effort to register yet more evangelical voters. He went to the National Press Club to announce the effort to register ten million new voters, an ambitious goal, and his appearance garnered plenty of publicity, but many doubted his ability to deliver. His former colleague Cal Thomas dismissed the effort. "What's out there has been registered. There's no untapped mother lode that can magically be called up," Thomas said. "It's the mushy middle that determines the election. This is just about getting people to send in money."[12]

Bush's advisers were acutely aware that those in the "mushy middle" described by Thomas were not the kind of voters likely to be swayed by an appeal from Falwell and other religious right leaders. At the Republican National Convention in August, social conservatives and their issues were kept off the podium and on the back burner. Some were especially distressed when Rep. Jim Kolbe of Arizona addressed the convention in prime time to discuss trade issues. Kolbe was openly gay. A group of Texas delegates stood in silent prayer during Kolbe's speech to protest. Prominent conservatives such as Alan Keyes, Pat Robertson, and Falwell himself were not given prime-time speaking slots.[13]

Falwell had always been politically savvy in his way, and he dismissed the complaints of those who thought the Republicans were not indulging in enough red meat. "Some of our people have just got to grow up," Falwell told the *New York Times*. "Our crowd needs to get into the battle, keep their mouths shut and help this man win." To another reporter, Falwell said, "Some of our good conservative friends would not be satisfied if Jesus were the candidate, but overall I haven't sensed this much excitement among religious conservatives since Ronald Reagan." The platform was steadfastly pro-life and pro-family, as Falwell noted, and the selection of Richard Cheney as Bush's running mate had pleased conservatives. According to one reporter at the convention, "Pat Robertson and Jerry Falwell are as giddy about Bush as a Texas cheerleader."[14]

Falwell's verbosity did get the best of him in one, relatively minor dustup at the Republican convention. Writing in his Liberty Alliance newsletter, Falwell had voiced his pleasure at the selection of Cheney as Bush's running mate and sought to defuse criticism regarding Cheney's daughter, who was openly gay. "It is ludicrous to judge a man based on one errant, but loved, family member." *USA Today* picked up the comment and said that it caused a "minor furor," but Falwell said that no such furor had happened. He noted that the one word "errant" could not be taken out of context and that, as a Baptist minister, he had no apologies to make about considering homosexuality "errant."[15]

The issue of gay rights surfaced during the vice presidential debate in October. In response to a question about gays enjoying all the rights that other citizens enjoyed, Cheney said, "I think we ought to do everything we can to tolerate and accommodate whatever kind of relationships people want to enter into," but he acknowledged that same-sex marriage was "a tougher problem"; in any event, he noted, Bush would be setting policy, not he. Cheney also suggested that the issue should be left to the states, not the federal government.

Falwell joined in with other social conservatives in criticizing Cheney's apparent nod toward gay marriage. "I disagree with Mr. Cheney on his suggestion that the states should be allowed to sanction any relationship they wish." He added that Cheney "could have given a firmer and stronger answer." The issue did not have legs, however, as conservatives saw the need to drop it, and whenever Cheney was asked specifically about his daughter, he replied succinctly that she was entitled to her privacy.[16]

Falwell had been content to stay in the background during the election for fear that his polarizing personality would affix itself to Bush, but that reticence evaporated when Bush, having gained the White House after the Supreme Court ended the recount of votes in Florida, started selecting his cabinet. "As far as I'm concerned, the worst thing Mr. Bush could do is bring Democrats into his administration or reach out to Governor Whitman or Governor Ridge for key positions when these people do not believe what his constituency believes or what he believes," Falwell told an interviewer. New Jersey governor Christine Todd Whitman and Pennsylvania governor Tom Ridge were both pro-choice. In fact, Bush would select Whitman to oversee the Environmental Protection Agency and Ridge would later become secretary of the newly established Department of Homeland Security. In neither capacity would the former governors have any say in abortion or other social issues. At the Justice Department, Bush installed conservative darling Sen. John Ashcroft as attorney general, an appointment that more than satisfied social conservatives.[17]

The social conservatives who had harbored doubts about George Bush's commitment to their agenda were proven wrong, and Falwell's support for him was justified, as Bush emerged as one of the most conservative presidents in memory. On the first major issue of concern to social conservatives, Bush decided in August 2001 to ban the use of federal funds for research using embryonic stem cells. Not only that, Bush announced the decision in the first Oval Office address of his presidency. That decision, however, and indeed the entire social agenda of the religious right, was about to be over-shadowed by something no one had foreseen—the terrorist attacks of September 11, 2001.

The instinct to never decline a media appearance had served Falwell well, allowing him to spread his message, as he often said, with his opponents paying the bill. But in the days after September 11, 2001, this instinct cost Falwell dearly.

Falwell made an appearance on Pat Robertson's show, *The 700 Club,* two days after the attacks on New York and Washington. Like all Americans, they were discussing the terrorist attacks, how they could have happened, and what these events portended for the future. "God continues to lift the curtain and allow the enemies of America to give us probably what we deserve," Falwell said. Robertson voiced his agreement.

Falwell recalled the Supreme Court "expelling" God from the public schools. But then he swung for the fences. "I really believe that the pagans, and the abortionists, and the feminists, and the gays and the lesbians who are actively trying to make that an alternative lifestyle, the ACLU, People For the American Way—all of them who have tried to secularize America—I point the finger in their face and say, 'You helped this happen,'" Falwell told Robertson. Coming just two days after the attack, when emotions were running high to begin with, these words could scarcely have been more inflammatory. He had just laid the murder of three thousand souls at the feet of his political opponents.[18]

The outrage was immediate and comprehensive. A spokesman for the ACLU said, "We are not dignifying it with a response." Ralph Naes, president of People For the American Way, said that Falwell's remarks were "absolutely inappropriate and irresponsible," and furthermore, they ran directly contrary to President Bush's call for the nation to unite in the face of the tragedy. When asked about Falwell's comments, White House spokesman Ken Lisaius said, "The president believes that terrorists are responsible for these acts. He does not share those views, and believes that those remarks are inappropriate." Strangely, even Robertson, who had nodded and voiced his agreement with Falwell during the interview, subsequently issued a press release calling Falwell's comments "totally inappropriate."[19]

The preacher, however, was not backing down. He told an interviewer that on *The 700 Club* show he was "making a theological statement, not a legal statement. I put all the blame legally and morally on the actions of the terrorists." He dug in on his central theme, however, saying that the "secular and anti-Christian environment left us open to our Lord's [decision] not to protect." He explained that if America "does not repent and return to a genuine faith and dependence on [God], we may expect more tragedies, unfortunately." Falwell added that he regretted the fact that his remarks, when taken out of context, "have detracted from the spirit of this day of mourning."[20]

Falwell recognized, however, that sticking by his comments was costing him more in the court of public opinion than he was prepared to pay. He issued a press release that stated, "I had no intention of being divisive. I was sharing my burden for revival in America on a Christian TV program, intending to speak to a Christian audience from a theological perspective about the need for national repentance." He appeared on Geraldo Rivera's cable television show a few nights later to say, "This is not what I believe and I therefore repudiate it and ask God's forgiveness and yours." Falwell pleaded that he had been tired when he did the interview with Robertson, having gotten little sleep the night before, a point made subsequently by his supporters. A few weeks later Falwell sat down with a reporter from the *Washington Post* to explain that his *700 Club* remarks were "a complete misstatement of what I believe and what I've preached for nearly 50 years." He said that no mortal can know when God is or is not judging a nation. In between the two interviews, his ministries sent out a fund-raising appeal signed by Falwell's son Jonathan, asking donors to show their support for his father. "Satan has launched a hail of fiery darts at dad!" the younger Falwell wrote.[21]

In fact, Falwell had made what is known as a "Kinsley gaffe," named for writer Michael Kinsley, who wrote that in Washington a real gaffe is when a politician says what he really believes, but usually refrains from saying because it would be politically disadvantageous to do so. Falwell had always preached that only devotion to God, moral living, and support for Israel could earn God's protection of a nation. And he believed that those he listed—the ACLU, gays and lesbians, abortion providers, and so on—were all turning America away from God. What Falwell misunderstood was not that he was unable to discern the will of God, but that giving voice to such a sentiment was divisive at the exact moment when Americans wanted to rally together. Falwell, of course, had made a career of being divisive, his protestations notwithstanding. The reason for his retractions now had nothing to do with what he believed. A more likely explanation is that, finding himself standing all alone, condemned for moral obtuseness even by his closest allies, including President Bush, he decided to walk back his controversial remarks.

As he walked back his remarks, Falwell made a singularly important admission. He told an interviewer that "as a matter of fact, most of the heat I've taken has not been because of the statement. It's from people who are upset that I apologized. Thousands of people of faith unfortunately agreed with the first statement." This "heat" was from Falwell's own people, the men and women who watched his show or sat in the pews of Thomas Road Baptist Church and agreed with his initial assignation of blame. Falwell had not only given voice to their sentiments but had helped to shape those sentiments. Ultimately, the reason for all the controversy about Falwell's statement about 9/11 was not that he misspoke, but that people knew he had really meant what he said.

Falwell would differ with President Bush again the following year when, once again, he gave voice to the true sentiments of his flock. Bush had gone out of his way to avoid any denunciations of Islam as America attacked Afghanistan and prepared to attack Iraq. The president went to a mosque with a group of American Muslims to denounce anti-Muslim bigotry and spoke frequently about the nation's long alliance with Saudi Arabia and other moderate Muslim countries. Bush wanted his wars in the Middle East to be seen as strategic wars, not crusades, knowing that if they were cast in religious terms they would be virtually impossible for America to win.

Appearing on the CBS news show *60 Minutes,* Falwell took a different approach to the issue. "I think Mohammed [the founder of Islam] was a terrorist," Falwell told correspondent Bob Simon. "I read enough, by both Muslims and non-Muslims, [to decide] that he was a violent man, a man of war." Falwell contrasted the founder of Islam with Moses and Jesus, who "set the example for love. . . . I think Mohammed set an opposite example."

Falwell found himself on the defensive yet again. "I sincerely apologize that certain statements of mine . . . were hurtful to the feelings of many Muslims," Falwell said after the remarks received wide publicity. "I intended no disrespect to any sincere, law-abiding Muslim." He went on *The Phil Donohue Show* to clarify his statements, arguing that Simon had interviewed him for an hour and a half and that they had only spent a few moments at the end discussing Islam. Falwell told Donohue he had recently read a biography of Mohammed, written by a Muslim. "And I was a little shocked at what he wrote about his prophet. And then I unwisely—you know, I've been with you and I 35 years. So I should have a little sense by now. . . . And I said just what I said. I knew when I said it, that was a bad choice of words."

A leading scholar pointed out that, the apologies notwithstanding, the damage had been done already. "What Americans don't realize," said Akbar Ahmed, chairman of the Islamic Studies Department at American University, "is that remarks like this are flashed all over the Muslim world, and they are doing very serious damage to U.S. interests." Indeed, within days Muslim youths protesting Falwell's statement ignited a riot in Solapur, India, leaving eight people dead and some ninety injured.[22]

Falwell was not the only evangelical leader to stoke the flames of anti-Muslim bigotry. Pat Robertson called Mohammed an "absolute wild-eyed fanatic" and a "killer." The past president of the Southern Baptist Convention, Rev. Jerry Vines, called Mohammed a "demon-possessed pedophile." John Green, a professor at Akron University, noted that there had been "rumblings" within the evangelical community when Bush had gone to the mosque and called Islam a "religion of peace." Green said, "I suspect that it's just become more and more acceptable for evangelical leaders to speak out against Islam."[23]

The controversies surrounding Falwell's remarks about 9/11 and his subsequent characterization of Mohammed were the last great controversies of his life. And they were quintessentially Falwellian. Never able to resist a catchy phrase, unalert to the cost of divisiveness, rooted in a fundamentalist, often Manichaean, dualistic worldview, Falwell's comments garnered the attention they were designed to capture—but were so over-the-top that he had to walk them back.

Falwell's health began to deteriorate in 2005. In February of that year, he suffered cardiac arrest and was resuscitated. The next month, after a quiet night at home, Falwell shouted for Macel to drive him to the hospital. She wanted to call an ambulance, but he insisted that she drive. Halfway there, he slumped over unconscious. Macel herself collapsed once they reached the hospital and Jerry was put on a ventilator. He recovered from both attacks and went to the Cleveland Clinic, where doctors inserted stents in his coronary arteries. He appeared to recover completely, and he even evidenced more energy than before the operations.[24]

The ordeal led Falwell to think more clearly about how his ministries would transition after him. In 2005, for the first time, his son Jonathan preached at Thomas Road Baptist Church. Jerry Jr. was intimately involved in all of his father's decisions and had taken an especially large role at Liberty University. Jonathan was named copastor of Thomas Road Baptist Church, and Jerry Jr. was named vice chancellor of Liberty. It was clear that when Falwell's time came, the church would be entrusted to Jonathan and the university to Jerry Jr.[25]

In the meantime, Falwell reclaimed his pulpit and continued to appear on television shows and give interviews. He strongly backed George W. Bush's reelection effort, but just as important, the Republicans recognized that the army of evangelical voters Falwell had once galvanized could not be taken for granted. Bush's strategist,

Karl Rove, drew up plans to mobilize evangelical voters, an effort that was aided by the fact that eleven states had ballot measures on same-sex marriage that year. In the key swing state of Ohio, two and a half million anti–gay marriage leaflets were distributed at some seventeen thousand churches the week before the election. President Bush visited smaller cities in rural Ohio in an effort to turn out the vote. On election day, four million more evangelicals voted than had done so four years before, assuring Bush's reelection and also defeating gay marriage in all eleven referenda.[26]

Falwell's main focus, however, remained in Lynchburg. He was exultant when the law school at Liberty University opened in 2004. "We plan to turn out conservative lawyers the same way Harvard turns out liberals," Falwell told an interviewer. He drove his SUV around campus, developing a new prank of revving the motor at students as they walked in front of the vehicle. He equipped his SUV with an especially loud horn that he would blow at unsuspecting pedestrians. He achieved one of his long-standing ambitions in 2006 when, on the fiftieth anniversary of his starting Thomas Road Baptist Church in the old Donald Duck plant, the congregation moved into its new six-thousand-seat sanctuary in the Ericsson building. His church was now a part of Liberty's campus.[27]

On May 15, 2007, Falwell began his day as he had every day for fifty years, with prayer at home. Then, in keeping with another, newer tradition, he drove over to the Bob Evans restaurant for a breakfast meeting with Ron Godwin. The two went over their lists of things to do, with most of the attention focused on the upcoming graduation ceremonies at Liberty University. Then Falwell went to his office in the Carter Glass mansion on campus. When Macel tried to call him but received no answer, she remembered that Jerry often forgot to turn his phone back on. When he missed an 11:00 A.M. meeting, his assistants became worried, and one of them entered his office to find Falwell unconscious on the floor. Jonathan rushed over from his office. Paramedics tried to revive him, and he was rushed to the hospital, where more efforts were made to resuscitate him. This time the doctors' efforts failed. Jerry Falwell was dead.[28]

Epilogue

The night after Jerry Falwell died, author and devout atheist Christopher Hitchens appeared on Fox News with Ralph Reed, whose Christian Coalition had carried the evangelical banner into the political realm after Falwell disbanded the Moral Majority in 1989. Hitchens called Falwell "a vulgar fraud, a crook," and celebrated his demise. Reed said he considered Falwell an "agent of change," a man who was "one of the most important historical figures of the last fifty years"; Reed was clearly delighted at the effects of Falwell's career.

Hitchens was wrong on two counts. First, Falwell was no fraud: he truly believed in his fundamentalist vision of the Christian faith and of that faith's importance for American politics, religion, and culture. Second, Hitchens also refused to acknowledge how important religion was and is to American culture, and so he was incapable of grasping, or admitting, Falwell's significance. Even if Falwell was loathsome to some, like Hitchens, that was not the most interesting thing about him.

It was one of the distinguishing characteristics of Falwell's critics that they often let the emotions he provoked get in the way of their own balanced judgments. Hitchens's postmortem churlishness was not his finest hour, and Yale president Bart Giamatti's attack on Falwell was not his finest hour either. Falwell never let political disagreements get in the way of developing personal relationships, as witnessed by the odd-couple friendships he enjoyed with Larry

Flynt and Sen. Ted Kennedy. Some of Falwell's critics, like Hitchens, descended into demonization and could not grant him the personal respect he was usually capable of granting others. When Falwell demonized people, it was in the abstract: the abortionists, the gays, the secular humanists. One of the reasons he was so persuasive to many was that he did not indulge in the vulgar personal attacks that so often were hurled at him.

Reed's assessment was closer to the mark, and he had reason to know. In the ten years of the Moral Majority's existence, the Republicans won every presidential contest. After 1989, the year the Moral Majority folded and Reed's Christian Coalition was formed, the GOP lost the popular vote in the next three elections; not until 2004, when Karl Rove mounted a Falwell-like strategy to turn out evangelical voters, did the Republican candidate win the election. Reed understood that Falwell's efforts to galvanize evangelical voters had changed not only the electorate but the face of American religion. If, before Falwell, the face of politically active religion was most likely to be that of William Sloane Coffin, or Father Drinan, or the Berrigan brothers, or someone else from the left side of the political spectrum, after Falwell, religious activity in politics was more often associated with Falwell and his followers on the right.

Falwell's baptizing of the American right not only brought millions of previously uninvolved voters into the political sphere but raised issues that are still at the center of America's political debates. During the 2009–10 congressional battle over health care reform legislation, the last issue to be overcome was abortion funding. During the early 2011 negotiations to avert a government shutdown, the conservative Christian attempt to defund Planned Parenthood was the last hurdle to be overcome. In thirty-one states, attempts to pass a referendum to legalize gay marriage or civil unions have met with failure as evangelicals have flocked to the polls to defend traditional marriage. The issues that brought Falwell and his followers out of the political wilderness remain on the front burner of American politics.

Just as important as Falwell's effort to bring issues of specific moral concern into the public square was his success in educating evangelical voters in the basic principles of modern conservatism and turning those principles into orthodoxy. The conservative aversion to big government, originally an outgrowth of Falwell's anticommunism, has persisted long since communism collapsed in Europe. The exception to the big government rule, a larger Pentagon budget, has become an article of faith for evangelical voters, and in the post-9/11 political landscape the pro-military stance has been joined by a hostility to Islam that sometimes takes on the tenor of a modern-day crusade.

Falwell's impact on the language and policies of the modern Republican Party were on full display in President George W. Bush's acceptance speech to the Republican National Convention in 2004. Framing his speech with biblical allusions, he began with a list of key conservative principles and introduced each one with the words, "I believe. . . ." Speaking not far from ground zero, Bush did not say that New York had "recovered" from the attacks of September 11, 2001, but that it had been "resurrected." Most important, Bush's rhetoric captured the strange combination of humility and ferocity that likewise characterized Falwell's pulpit oratory, mesmerizing their followers and frustrating their critics. Indeed, the entire 2004 convention looked like an expanded, more high-tech version of one of Falwell's 1970s "I Love America" rallies.

The commitment to laissez-faire economics, the aversion to taxes, and the hostility to government regulation have taken on a canonical status within the contemporary conservative movement. There can be disagreement about many things within conservative circles, but anything that contains even a whiff of restriction on private business is seen as a form of heresy. This orthodoxy combines with an expropriated patriotism, so that those who differ are considered not only wrong but un-American. Solemn pledges are demanded that candidates will uphold this orthodoxy, and a coterie of talking heads, from Grover Norquist to Sean Hannity, who wrote the introduction to Macel Falwell's book about her husband, serve as high priests at the no-tax altar, enforcing the political orthodoxy on those who might be tempted to stray. And today's free market zealots, like Falwell, never think to examine the degree to which an unrestrained market places enormous economic pressures on families, forces women into the workforce, disrupts local, especially rural, economies, and generally undermines the traditional values that evangelicals celebrate.

The most significant recent political development, the emergence of the Tea Party movement in 2009 and its electoral successes in the 2010 midterms, was obviously not Falwell's doing. But his fingerprints are all over the Tea Party. The emphasis on American exceptionalism, tinged with religious connotations and fervor, is straight out of any one of Falwell's sermons. The expropriation of the Founders that is the hallmark of Tea Party historiography similarly characterized Falwell's entire career, from choosing to model the Thomas Road Baptist Church sanctuary on a Jeffersonian design to insisting that America was a "Christian nation." When Falwell later attempted to discipline himself and avoid the term "Christian nation"—an effort at which he was never completely successful—he did so not because he had acquired a more nuanced historical sensibility but because he did not wish to offend conservative Jewish Americans.

Falwell's commitment to Israel and his many meetings with Jewish leaders helped eviscerate the ugly stain of anti-Semitism on the American right. It was part of the baptism. Falwell's reasons for supporting Israel were exclusively religious in nature, but he gave them political expression and succeeded in making a commitment to Israel a central tenet of Republican Party orthodoxy. There is a reason why Sarah Palin, Mike Huckabee, and other GOP leaders have made highly public treks to Israel in recent years: going there gives them a chance to establish their pro-Israel bona fides. Before Falwell, there was no such need for candidates trying to garner conservative support.

Electoral politics was only one venue in which Falwell sought to enact his vision for America, and his successes on election days were not always accompanied by triumphs in other areas. The free speech rights embedded in the First Amendment trumped his concern for decency when the Supreme Court unanimously ruled against him in his lawsuit against Larry Flynt. Falwell's desire to propagate creationism could not overcome the requirement of the Commonwealth of Virginia that accredited science teachers be capable of teaching science, not religion, in the state's science classrooms. And at the end of the day, Falwell was unable to see *Roe v. Wade* overturned. His influence was not absolute, and American politics contained powerful counterforces that obstructed his efforts.

Falwell's legacy manifests itself in other ways as well. For example, once President Barack Obama signed the health care reform law, the first lawsuit filed against it came from Liberty University, on the grounds that it would require the school to indirectly pay for abortion coverage in its insurance plans. The school has more than thirteen thousand students on campus and some fifty thousand enrolled in online courses. Its graduates include Shannon Bream, the Supreme Court reporter for *Fox News*, Ben Parkhill, senior strategist to Mississippi governor Haley Barbour, and Tony Perkins, the head of the Family Research Council and one of the religious right's most formidable public advocates. Republican staffers on Capitol Hill include many Liberty alumni. Falwell's "Joshua Generation" has been trained and sent out to carry on his work.

The political landscape continues to reflect Falwell's influence, but his most enduring impact may have been reshaping both the self-image of fundamentalist Christians and the perception of Christianity held by the mainstream culture. In some more secularized Western countries, changing the face of Christianity might not make a difference in society. If French Christians or Swedish Christians were to transform themselves as fundamentalist American Christians did under Falwell's tutelage, the sociocultural effects in France and Sweden might be minimal. In America, changing the perception and self-perception of Christianity is a big deal.

The separationist doctrine that had kept fundamentalist Christians in a self-imposed cultural exile through much of the twentieth century did not survive Jerry Falwell's ministry. Once Falwell perceived that Christians could not look the other way while America descended into what he considered moral anarchy—and that isolation would not protect them from the encroachments of a secular state—he knew Christians had to become engaged and get involved: speaking out, urging television stations not to air morally repugnant shows and boycotting companies that underwrote such shows, training law enforcement personnel in methods for rooting out pornography, rescuing young women who faced a crisis pregnancy and might be tempted to procure an abortion, encouraging congregants to run for local school boards, removing objectionable textbooks from the curriculum, and a host of other activities that Falwell and his ministries undertook. To be a good Christian it was no longer enough to maintain personal purity. After Falwell, fundamentalists and conservative evangelicals understood that they had to try to restore moral purity to the culture. Within a very few years, fundamentalists went from being cultural isolationists to being cultural activists.

The society these new activists entered, however, was pluralistic in the extreme. The tenets of fundamentalism that provided certainty to those who already believed were not shared by nonfundamentalists. Falwell, and fundamentalists in general, had two options. The first was to try to create a synthesis between their belief system and modern political and cultural ideas. Fundamentalism is better at creating tautologies, however, than at generating a cultural and intellectual synthesis. It lacks the suppleness and the intellectual architecture to fashion the kind of rapprochement with modernity that sustained political engagement requires.

Instead, Falwell went with the second option: denuding fundamentalist theology of its specifically doctrinal elements and reaching for a common moral denominator. He reduced religion to ethics. In his public speaking engagements on political matters, he did not cite chapter and verse from scripture, opting instead to articulate moral postulates that conformed to his conservative principles. The fundamentalist persona became bifurcated: at home and in the church the emphasis remained on doctrine and scripture, while in the public square the emphasis was on a morality that had to compete with other moral visions. This free market of moral ideas was not the kind of free market to which Falwell's heart warmed.

The precepts of Christian morality are far from self-evident. Indeed, their authority comes not from their efficacy but from their divine origin. Disconnected from their roots in doctrinal claims, they must withstand the scrutiny of the public square on their own. And in the last half of the twentieth century, in America's consumer-driven, spread-eagle capitalist economy, there were all manner of more accessible avenues to personal happiness and fulfillment to tempt people away from the Christian moral vision. What Falwell, of all people, should have recognized is that the Christian moral vision lacks the power to attract and to save.

Falwell gave many reasons for his decision in 1989 to shut down the Moral Majority and focus on his church and his university. He claimed that the Moral Majority had accomplished its mission. He was doubtless exhausted by the near-constant travel that his Moral Majority schedule imposed on him. But perhaps the best reason to abandon the public square and concentrate on his ministry and his school would have come from this inability to find a way to bring his faith into the public square. Falwell never put it this way, but perhaps he recognized that a faith that does not generate culture is a dead faith, and he needed to create a community where that faith could flourish. At Thomas Road Baptist Church and Liberty University, this was precisely what he endeavored to do.

The church and, especially, the university were vastly different from the separationist network of fundamentalist schools and churches that existed throughout most of the twentieth century. They were outward-looking, not inward-looking. While they still maintained a decidedly defensive posture vis-à-vis the mainstream culture, they were designed to engage that culture and change it, not to remove Christians from it. Falwell put evangelization back into evangelism, and the institutions he built reflected that change. Cultural change is a slower process than electoral change, but in America fundamentalist churches continue to grow, or at least maintain their numbers, while most other denominations decline, and Liberty University has become the flagship university for conservative Christians at a time when older denominational schools, such as Baylor and Wake Forest, have seen their distinctively religious character challenged by conservative Christians.

To be clear, fundamentalists could have been brought into the mainstream of American life in any one of a number of ways. They were a great untapped electoral resource, and a different pastor could have tapped their votes. But the way in which fundamentalists did enter the mainstream culture was through the ministries and the political activities of Jerry Falwell. Through all the vicissitudes that accompany the starting of major enterprises like a university, a megachurch, and a political organization, Falwell gave direction to conservative Christians. He created a platform from which they could get engaged, he energized them, he gave them their talking points, he raised the money and staffed the operations, he set the tone and assaulted the airwaves. The baptizing of the American right could have been accomplished by someone else, but in fact it was accomplished by Falwell.

Cultural forces always provoke a reaction. Indeed, Falwell's career can be seen as a reaction to the religious and secular left. But his career also provoked a reaction as seen in the increasing number of Americans who decline to identify themselves as religious at all, those who reply "none" when asked about their religious affiliation. The "nones" are actually growing faster than the evangelicals, and they are almost exclusively younger in age. Falwell became the face of Christianity to many Americans, and many Americans turned away from it. They did not merely reject his politics; his politics was such a part of his religion that they rejected both. The baby, as it were, was thrown out with the baptismal water.

Falwell's legacy, then, is a mixed one. He remade the Republican Party, which today suffers from the fact that, in an increasingly diverse electorate, it is now perceived as too white, too southern, too conservative, and too Christian. He remade the fundamentalist church, and he dragged fundamentalists into the public square, where they remain a force to be reckoned with. He provoked many Americans to see a lack of religious affiliation as preferable to accepting his brand of conservative Christianity. And in spite of himself, he aided the reduction of religion to ethics that frustrated, rather than enhanced, his evangelizing activities. But one thing is undeniable. Falwell mattered, and the changes he wrought continue to shape the culture in which we Americans live today.

Acknowledgments

I am grateful in the first place to Leon Wieseltier, literary editor of *The New Republic*, who first suggested the idea of writing a biography of Reverend Falwell. Leon also was the first person to publish my writings in his pages, so my debt to him is incalculable.

My agent, Andrew Stuart, and my editor, Roger Freet, were encouraging throughout the process of researching and writing this book and it is a better book for their efforts. Christina Bailly and Suzanne Quist, both at HarperOne, were patient and enormously helpful.

The staffs at several libraries and archives were unfailingly gracious. This book could not have been written without the assistance of the good people who work at the archives at Liberty University and People For the American Way, as well as the knowledgeable and helpful staff at the Library of Congress, the Prince George's County Memorial Library, and the John K. Mullen Library at the Catholic University of America. Mel White and Daryl Lach were exceedingly kind in opening their private archives of both video and documentary resources to me.

My thinking about religion and politics has been shaped by conversations with a host of friends and family, all of whom are far smarter than myself. I am especially indebted to the insights, and the generosity in sharing their knowledge, extended to me by Lisa Adams, Dayna McDermott Arriola, Peter Berkowitz, Michelle Boorstein, MaryAnn Brownlow and Beth Judy, John Carr, Isaac

Chotiner, Dennis Coday, William D'Antonio, E. J. Dionne, Joshua DuBois, Jerry Filteau, Paul and Debbie Fitzgerald, Tom Fox, Rick Garnett, John Gehring, Laurie Goodstein, Cathy Grossman, Jane Hampton, Hendrick Hertzberg, Sister Carol Keehan, Alexia Kelley, Mollie McCusic and Tom Rosshirt, Colin McEnroe, Rocco Palmo, Tom Roberts, Fred Rotondaro, Kathy Saile, Linda Sanchez, Stephen Schneck, Mark Silk, George Stephanopoulos, Amy Sullivan, Jim Sullivan, Sister Mary Ann Walsh, Benjamin Wittes, Albert Wojtcuk, Alan Wolfe, and Rachel Zoll. The late Joe Feuerherd encouraged me in this project, suggested important sources, and offered me a professional home in the pages of the *National Catholic Reporter*. I miss him very much.

Very few people have been as blessed as I have been to enjoy the friendship and the ministry of so many intelligent and holy priests. I am indebted, as a writer and as a soul, to the Reverend Monsignor Lorenzo Albacete; the Reverend Monsignor Henry Archambault; the Reverend John Ashe; the Reverend Monsignor Edward Arsenault; the Most Reverend Stephen Blaire; the Reverend Anthony Chandler; the Reverend Drew Christiansen, S.J.; the Reverend Charles Currie, S.J.; the Most Reverend J. Augustine DiNoia, O.P.; the Reverend G. Dennis Gil; the Most Reverend Roberto Gonzalez Nieves, O.F.M.; the Reverend Gene Hemrick; the Reverend Jack Hurley; the Reverend Monsignor Ronald Jameson; the Reverend Cletus Kiley; the Reverend Monsignor Paul Langsfeld; the Very Reverend Lawrence LaPointe; the Reverend Robert Maloney, C.M.; the Reverend James Martin, S.J.; the Reverend Jay Scott Newman; the Most Reverend David O'Connell, C.M.; His Eminence Sean Patrick Cardinal O'Malley, O.F.M. Cap.; the Reverend Anthony Pogorelc, S.S.; the Reverend Monsignor Kevin Randall; the Reverend Thomas Reese, S.J.; the Reverend Kevin Regan; the Reverend Ron Roberson; and the Reverend Robert Washabaugh.

Writing is a solitary activity, and the life of the writer would be impossible without the support of special friends. In addition to those listed above, I must extend a special note of gratitude to Lisa Farnsworth, who has always been more of a sister to me than a friend; to the Reverend Monsignor Charles Antonicelli, who is the brother I never had; and to Kirk Burke Hamilton, whose friendship has made me a far better person than I was before. Gale Lockland has been my friend since childhood and I can't imagine life without the prospect of sharing its triumphs and travails with her.

My mentor in history, and my model for writing biography, was Monsignor John Tracy Ellis, who has gone to God. And I often wonder if I would have been lost to the life of faith had it not been for the ministry of the late Reverend Joseph Kugler in my early years. How I wish they were both here to critique this book! I am so mindful of their presence in my work and in my life, and of their heavenly intercession.

Working from home would be intolerable without the companionship of Ambrose, my St. Bernard; Bernie, my black Labrador; and Clementine, my Border collie. They are the most wonderful beasts.

I have dedicated this book to my father, Felix Winters. There are no words to describe the depths of his faith nor the good works that faith brings forth. He is stubborn in the Lord and I admire him more than I can say.

Michael Sean Winters
Hampton, Connecticut

Notes

Chapter 1: The Prodigal

1. Jerry Falwell, *An Autobiography*, Lynchburg, Va.: Liberty House Publishers, 1997, pp. 48–50; Dinesh D'Souza, *Falwell: Before the Millennium*, Chicago: Regnery Gateway, 1984, pp. 37–39; Jerry Strober and Ruth Tomczak, *Jerry Falwell: Aflame for God*, Nashville: Thomas Nelson Publishers, 1979, pp. 15–16; "Falwell, Booed and Heckled, Holds a Town Hall Dialogue," *New York Times*, December 12, 1984.
2. Falwell, *An Autobiography*, pp. 62–64.
3. Falwell, *An Autobiography*, p. 28.
4. Falwell, *An Autobiography*, pp. 34–36; D'Souza, *Falwell*, p. 38.
5. Falwell, *An Autobiography*, pp. 53–57; Strober and Tomczak, *Jerry Falwell*, p. 16.
6. Falwell, *An Autobiography*, pp. 81–83, 87.
7. Falwell, *An Autobiography*, pp. 87–88, 53–54.
8. Darrell Laurent, *Remembering Lynchburg and Central Virginia*, Charleston, S.C.: History Press, 2005, pp. 17–19.
9. Laurent, *Remembering*, pp. 21–24.
10. Laurent, *Remembering*, pp. 25–27.
11. Dirk Smillie, *Falwell Inc.: Inside a Religious, Political, Educational, and Business Empire*, New York: St. Martin's Press, 2008.
12. William Leuchtenburg, *The White House Looks South: Franklin D. Roosevelt, Harry S. Truman, Lyndon B. Johnson*, Baton Rouge: Louisiana State University Press, 2005, pp. 42–43, 50.
13. Leuchtenburg, *The White House Looks South*, pp. 37, 53, 124.
14. Leuchtenburg, *The White House Looks South*, p. 58.
15. Leuchtenburg, *The White House Looks South*, pp. 122, 127, 135–37.
16. Taylor Branch, *Parting the Waters: America in the King Years, 1954–1963*, New York: Simon & Schuster, 1988, pp. xi, 13.
17. Michael J. Klarman, *From Jim Crow to Civil Rights: The Supreme Court and the Struggle for Racial Equality*, New York: Oxford University Press, 2004, pp. 171–73.
18. Leuchtenburg, *The White House Looks South*, p. 171; Morris J. MacGregor, *Steadfast in the Faith: The Life of Patrick Cardinal O'Boyle*, Washington, D.C.: Catholic University Press, 2006, pp. 173–74, 194–95.
19. Falwell, *An Autobiography*, p. 58.

20. Timothy Snyder, *Bloodlands: Europe Between Hitler and Stalin*, New York: Basic Books, 2010.

21. Falwell, *An Autobiography*, pp. 73–74, 80.

22. Falwell, *An Autobiography*, pp. 87, 93–94, 99–100; Strober and Tomczak, *Jerry Falwell*, p. 18.

23. Macel Falwell, *Jerry Falwell: His Life and Legacy*, New York: Howard Books, 2008, p. 16; Falwell, *An Autobiography*, pp. 105–6.

24. Falwell, *An Autobiography*, pp. 111–13; Strober and Tomczak, *Jerry Falwell*, p. 20.

25. Falwell, *An Autobiography*, pp. 107–9.

26. Falwell, *An Autobiography*, p. 113.

27. Falwell, *An Autobiography*, pp. 113–15.

28. Susan Friend Harding, *The Book of Jerry Falwell*, Princeton, N.J.: Princeton University Press, 2000, pp. 88–90.

Chapter 2: The Road to Damascus

1. Jerry Falwell, *An Autobiography*, Lynchburg, Va.: Liberty House Publishers, 1997, pp. 118–21.

2. Falwell, *An Autobiography*, pp. 120–21.

3. Falwell, *An Autobiography*, pp. 122–23.

4. Falwell, *An Autobiography*, pp. 132–33; Jerry Strober and Ruth Tomczak, *Jerry Falwell: Aflame for God*, Nashville: Thomas Nelson Publishers, 1979, p. 22; Macel Falwell, *Jerry Falwell: His Life and Legacy*, New York: Howard Books, 2008, p. 28.

5. Falwell, *An Autobiography*, pp. 133–37.

6. Dinesh D'Souza, *Falwell: Before the Millennium*, Chicago: Regnery Gateway, 1984, p. 77.

7. Jerry Falwell, *Building Dynamic Faith*, Nashville: Thomas Nelson Books, 2005, pp. 65–69.

8. D'Souza, *Falwell*, pp. 144–45, 149.

9. Marsden, *Religion and American Culture*, New York: Harcourt Brace Jovanovich, 1990, pp. 53–58.

10. Marsden, *Religion and American Culture*, pp. 59–61.

11. Marsden, *Religion and American Culture*, p. 66.

12. James Tunstead Burtchaell, *The Dying of the Light: The Disengagement of Colleges and Universities from Their Christian Churches*, Grand Rapids, Mich.: Eerdmans, 1998, p. 358.

13. Burtchaell, *The Dying of the Light*, p. 93; Edwin S. Gaustad, *A Documentary History of Religion in America Since 1865*, Grand Rapids, Mich.: Eerdmans, 1993, p. 7.

14. Gaustad, *Documentary History of Religion*, p. 184; Deirdre M. Moloney, *American Catholic Lay Groups and Transatlantic Social Reform in the Progressive Era*, Chapel Hill: University of North Carolina Press, 2002, pp. 169–70; Marsden, *Religion and American Culture*, p. 97.

15. Burtchaell, *The Dying of the Light*, pp. 46, 362, 369; Marsden, *Religion and American Culture*, pp. 118–21.

16. Allan Lichtman, *White Protestant Nation: The Rise of the American Conservative Movement*, New York: Grove Press, 2008, pp. 26–30; Marsden, *Religion and American Culture*, pp. 99, 118–21.

17. Marsden, *Religion and American Culture*, pp. 171–72, 177–78, 181.
18. Marsden, *Religion and American Culture*, pp. 183–84.
19. Gaustad, *A Documentary History of Religion*, pp. 395–97.
20. Gaustad, *A Documentary History of Religion*, p. 186; Harding, *The Book of Jerry Falwell*, pp. 67–69.
21. Harding, *The Book of Jerry Falwell*, p. 62.
22. Harding, *The Book of Jerry Falwell*, pp. 61–62, 74–76; Marsden, *Religion and American Culture*, p. 258.
23. Marsden, *Religion and American Culture*, pp. 213–14; Lichtman, *White Protestant Nation*, pp. 196–97.
24. Lichtman, *White Protestant Nation*, p. 219.
25. Falwell, *Jerry Falwell*, p. 29.
26. Falwell, *An Autobiography*, pp. 157, 166.
27. John Killinger, *The Other Preacher in Lynchburg*, New York: St. Martin's Press, 2009, p. 121.
28. Falwell, *An Autobiography*, pp. 157–58.
29. Falwell, *An Autobiography*, pp. 159–60.
30. Strober and Tomczak, *Jerry Falwell*, p. 28; Falwell, *An Autobiography*, p. 169.
31. Falwell, *An Autobiography*, pp. 173–75.
32. Strober and Tomczak, *Jerry Falwell*, pp. 28–29; Falwell, *An Autobiography*, pp. 182–83.
33. Falwell, *An Autobiography*, pp. 175–76, 184–85.

Chapter 3: The Preacher

1. Macel Falwell, *Jerry Falwell: His Life and Legacy*, New York: Howard Books, 2008, pp. 36–37; Jerry Falwell, *An Autobiography*, Lynchburg, Va.: Liberty House Publishers, 1997, pp. 185–86.
2. Falwell, *An Autobiography*, pp. 186–88.
3. Falwell, *An Autobiography*, pp. 189–92, 194; Falwell, *Jerry Falwell*, p. 40.
4. Falwell, *An Autobiography*, pp. 194–95, 207.
5. Falwell, *An Autobiography*, pp. 209, 212.
6. Falwell, *An Autobiography*, pp. 212–14.
7. Falwell, *An Autobiography*, pp. 215–18.
8. Falwell, *An Autobiography*, p. 219.
9. John Killinger, *The Other Preacher in Lynchburg*, New York: St. Martin's Press, 2009, pp. 83–84.
10. Falwell, *An Autobiography*, pp. 219–20; Dinesh D'Souza, *Falwell: Before the Millennium*, Chicago: Regnery Gateway, 1984, p. 67.
11. Falwell, *An Autobiography*, pp. 220–21.
12. Falwell, *An Autobiography*, pp. 230–31; Jerry Strober and Ruth Tomczak, *Jerry Falwell: Aflame for God*, Nashville: Thomas Nelson Publishers, 1979, p. 33.
13. Falwell, *An Autobiography*, pp. 223–24.
14. Falwell, *An Autobiography*, p. 224.
15. Falwell, *An Autobiography*, p. 233.
16. Falwell, *An Autobiography*, pp. 213, 215, 224; Strober and Tomczak, *Jerry Falwell*, p. 29.
17. "Segregation or Integration, Which?," reprinted in "Word of Life" newsletter, Jones Memorial Library, Lynchburg, Va.

18. Allan Lichtman, *White Protestant Nation: The Rise of the American Conservative Movement,* New York: Grove Press, 2008, pp. 225–26; Marsden, *Religion and American Culture,* p. 43.

19. Falwell, *An Autobiography,* pp. 238–39.

20. Falwell, *An Autobiography,* pp. 241–42.

21. Falwell, *An Autobiography,* p. 249.

22. Falwell, *An Autobiography,* p. 250.

23. Falwell, *An Autobiography,* pp. 250–51.

24. Falwell, *An Autobiography,* pp. 251–52.

25. Falwell, *An Autobiography,* pp. 252–53.

26. Falwell, *An Autobiography,* pp. 253–55.

27. Falwell, *An Autobiography,* p. 319; "A Treasure Lost," *Lynchburg Living,* September–October 2009.

28. "A Treasure Lost," *Lynchburg Living.*

29. Falwell, *An Autobiography,* pp. 282–83.

30. Falwell, *An Autobiography,* pp. 313–14.

31. Laurant, Darrell, *Remembering Lynchburg and Central Virginia,* Charleston: History Press, 2005, pp. 57–59.

32. Jerry Falwell, "Ministers and Marches," sermon preached at Thomas Road Baptist Church, March 21, 1965, Jones Memorial Library. The pamphlet states that the sermon was preached in 1965, but Macel Falwell's book places the sermon in 1964, and Falwell's autobiography places it in 1964 at one point and later claims that the sermon was given in 1965.

Chapter 4: Family of Faith

1. Macel Falwell, *Jerry Falwell: His Life and Legacy,* New York: Howard Books, 2008, pp. 29, 32.

2. Falwell, *Jerry Falwell,* pp. 31–32; Jerry Falwell, *An Autobiography,* Lynchburg, Va.: Liberty House Publishers, 1997, pp. 226–27.

3. Falwell, *An Autobiography,* pp. 268–69; Falwell, *Jerry Falwell,* pp. 48–50.

4. Falwell, *Jerry Falwell,* p. 50; Falwell, *An Autobiography,* pp. 269–70.

5. Falwell, *An Autobiography,* pp. 270, 273–74.

6. Falwell, *An Autobiography,* pp. 274–75.

7. Falwell, *Jerry Falwell,* pp. 52–55.

8. Falwell, *Jerry Falwell,* pp. 56–58.

9. Jerry Falwell, *The New American Family: The Rebirth of the American Dream,* Dallas: Word Publishing, 1992, p. 47.

10. Jerry Falwell, *Listen, America,* New York: Doubleday, 1980, p. 110.

11. Falwell, *Listen, America,* pp. 61–62.

12. Falwell, *An Autobiography,* pp. 279–80.

13. Falwell, *Jerry Falwell,* p. 63.

14. Falwell, *Jerry Falwell,* p. 64; Falwell, *An Autobiography,* pp. 280–81.

15. Falwell, *An Autobiography,* pp. 283–84, 288, 296–97.

16. Falwell, *Jerry Falwell,* pp. 69–70.

17. Falwell, *Jerry Falwell,* pp. 72–73.

18. Allan Lichtman, *White Protestant Nation: The Rise of the American Conservative Movement,* New York: Grove Press, 2008, pp. 224–26.

19. Lichtman, *White Protestant Nation*, p. 270.

20. Lichtman, *White Protestant Nation*, p. 313; Marsden, *Religion and American Culture*, New York: Harcourt Brace Jovanovich, 1990, pp. 103–19.

21. Marsden, *Religion and American Culture*, p. 131; Lichtman, *White Protestant Nation*, pp. 313–15.

22. "81 Attend Christian Academy," *Lynchburg Daily News*, August 29, 1967; Dinesh D'Souza, *Falwell: Before the Millennium*, Chicago: Regnery Gateway, 1984, p. 84.

23. D'Souza, *Falwell*, p. 38.

24. D'Souza, *Falwell*, pp. 83–84; Jerry Strober and Ruth Tomczak, *Jerry Falwell: Aflame for God*, Nashville: Thomas Nelson Publishers, 1979, p. 37.

25. Falwell, *An Autobiography*, p. 289.

Chapter 5: Building a Religious Empire

1. Dinesh D'Souza, *Falwell: Before the Millennium*, Chicago: Regnery Gateway, 1984, p. 85.

2. D'Souza, *Falwell*, p. 85; Dirk Smillie, *Falwell Inc.: Inside a Religious, Political, Educational, and Business Empire*, New York: St. Martin's Press, 2008, p. 52; Jerry Falwell, *An Autobiography*, Lynchburg, Va.: Liberty House Publishers, 1997, p. 335.

3. Falwell, *An Autobiography*, pp. 65–66.

4. Allan Lichtman, *White Protestant Nation: The Rise of the American Conservative Movement*, New York: Grove Press, 2008, p. 150; *Lynchburg Daily News*, advertisement for Thomas Road Baptist Church, August 6, 13, 20, and 27, 1967.

5. *Lynchburg Daily News*, advertisement for Thomas Road Baptist Church, August 6, 13, 20, and 27, 1967; see sermon titles in Liberty University Archives (LUArchives) catalog of holdings.

6. "Redeeming the Time," sermon preached August 10, 1975, LUArchives, OTGH–148.

7. "Sins That Cause Sickness," sermon preached August 24, 1975, LUArchives, OTGH–150.

8. "God's Plan for Supporting God's Work," sermon preached September 7, 1975, LUArchives, SE–101.

9. Jerry Strober and Ruth Tomczak, *Jerry Falwell: Aflame for God*, Nashville: Thomas Nelson Publishers, 1979, pp. 43–44.

10. Richard Marius, *Martin Luther: The Christian Between God and Death*, Cambridge, Mass.: Belknap Press of Harvard University Press, 1999, p. 307; James Tunstead Burtchaell, *The Dying of the Light: The Disengagement of Colleges and Universities from Their Christian Churches*, Grand Rapids, Mich.: Eerdmans, 1998, pp. 4–5.

11. Strober and Tomczak, *Jerry Falwell*, p. 49; Falwell, *An Autobiography*, p. 421.

12. D'Souza, *Falwell*, pp. 84–85; Burtchaell, *The Dying of the Light*, pp. 357–58; "Liberty Baptist Students Seen as Foundation of New Nation," *Richmond Times-Dispatch*, May 9, 1982; "The Moral Majority's Higher Education: Falwell U," *Boston Phoenix*, August 4, 1981; Smillie, *Falwell Inc.*, pp. 74–75.

13. Smillie, *Falwell Inc.*, pp. 73–74.

14. Smillie, *Falwell Inc.*, pp. 76–77; Strober and Tomczak, *Jerry Falwell*, pp. 45–47.

15. "Liberty Baptist Students Seen as Foundation of New Nation," *Richmond Times-Dispatch,* May 9, 1982; Smillie, *Falwell Inc.,* p. 75; Strober and Tomczak, *Jerry Falwell,* p. 46.

16. Falwell, *An Autobiography,* pp. 330–31; D'Souza, *Falwell,* p. 85.

17. D'Souza, *Falwell,* pp. 86–87; "College Aims to Be Fundamentalism's Notre Dame," *New York Times,* October 4, 1981; Falwell, *An Autobiography,* pp. 332–35.

18. Falwell, *An Autobiography,* pp. 336–37; Smillie, *Falwell Inc.,* pp. 79–80.

19. Smillie, *Falwell Inc.,* pp. 79–80; D'Souza, *Falwell,* pp. 86–87; Strober and Tomczak, *Jerry Falwell,* p. 85.

20. Smillie, *Falwell Inc.,* pp. 80–81.

21. Smillie, *Falwell Inc.,* pp. 81–82; Falwell, *An Autobiography,* p. 354; "Falwell Method Questioned," *Denver Post,* June 6, 1981.

22. Smillie, *Falwell Inc.,* p. 81.

23. Smillie, *Falwell Inc.,* pp. 88–89.

24. Smillie, *Falwell Inc.,* p. 89.

25. Smillie, *Falwell Inc.,* pp. 88, 90–91.

26. Falwell, *Jerry Falwell,* pp. 146–47; Strober and Tomczak, *Jerry Falwell,* pp. 76–77.

27. "The Moral Majority's Higher Education: Falwell U," *Boston Phoenix,* August 4, 1981.

28. "Liberty Baptist Students Seen as Foundation of New Nation," *Richmond Times-Dispatch,* May 9, 1982.

29. Smillie, *Falwell Inc.,* pp. 91–92; Strober and Tomczak, *Jerry Falwell,* pp. 79–80.

Chapter 6: Wading into the Religious-Political Estuary

1. Michael Sean Winters, *Left at the Altar: How the Democrats Lost the Catholics and How the Catholics Can Save the Democrats,* New York: Basic Books, 2008, pp. 130–33, 142; Martin Durham, *The Christian Right: The Far Right and the Boundaries of American Conservatism,* Manchester, U.K.: Manchester University Press, 2000, pp. 84–89.

2. Durham, *The Christian Right,* p. 115.

3. Durham, *The Christian Right,* pp. 139–41.

4. Jerry Falwell, "Our Citizenship as Americans," sermon preached March 7, 1976, LUArchives, OTGH–179.

5. Jerry Falwell, *An Autobiography,* Lynchburg, Va.: Liberty House Publishers, 1997, pp. 357–60.

6. "Conditions Corrupting America," sermon preached May 16, 1976, LUArchives, OTGH–192.

7. Falwell, *An Autobiography,* pp. 363–64.

8. Durham, *The Christian Right,* pp. 4–5; Allan Lichtman, *White Protestant Nation: The Rise of the American Conservative Movement,* New York: Grove Press, 2008, pp. 221–22, 240.

9. Merrill Simon, *Jerry Falwell and the Jews,* Middle Village, N.Y.: Jonathan David Publishers, 1984, pp. 9, 14–16.

10. Simon, *Jerry Falwell and the Jews,* pp. 5–6; "The Gospel According to Falwell," *Atlanta Constitution,* August 23, 1980.

11. Falwell, *An Autobiography,* pp. 400–401.

12. Durham, *The Christian Right,* p. 43.

13. Jerry Strober and Ruth Tomczak, *Jerry Falwell: Aflame for God,* Nashville: Thomas Nelson Publishers, 1979, p. 180.

14. Durham, *The Christian Right,* p. 43; Strober and Tomczak, *Jerry Falwell,* pp. 180–82.

15. Durham, *The Christian Right,* pp. 43–44; Strober and Tomczak, *Jerry Falwell,* pp. 179–80.

16. Strober and Tomczak, *Jerry Falwell,* pp. 183–85.

17. Jerry Falwell, "Conditions Corrupting America," sermon preached May 16, 1976, LUArchives, OTGH–192; Dirk Smillie, *Falwell Inc.: Inside a Religious, Political, Educational, and Business Empire,* New York: St. Martin's Press, 2008, pp. 95–96.

18. Falwell, *An Autobiography,* pp. 303–5; 316–18.

19. Falwell, *An Autobiography,* pp. 318–20; D'Souza, *Falwell,* p. 81.

20. William Leuchtenburg, *The White House Looks South: Franklin D. Roosevelt, Harry S. Truman, Lyndon B. Johnson,* Baton Rouge: Louisiana State University Press, 2005, pp. 321, 325.

21. Durham, *The Christian Right,* pp. 7–8, 24–25; Lichtman, *White Protestant Nation,* pp. 280–90.

22. "Conditions Corrupting America," sermon preached May 16, 1976, LU-Archives, OTGH–192; *American Opinion* (May 1979).

23. Alexis de Tocqueville, *Democracy in America,* translated by Harvey C. Mansfield and Delba Winthrop, Chicago: University of Chicago Press, 2000, p. 552; Falwell, *An Autobiography,* pp. 368–69.

24. *Old-Time Gospel Hour,* October 19, 1980 (transcript), People For the American Way (PFAW) Archives.

25. D'Souza, *Falwell,* pp. 96–97, 99–100.

26. Thomas Byrne Edsall, with Mary D. Edsall, *Chain Reaction: The Impact of Race, Rights, and Taxes on American Politics,* New York: W. W. Norton, 1992, pp. 131–32.

27. Edsall, *Chain Reaction,* p. 132; "Right Religion Right Politics?," *Home Missions* (September–October 1980); William Martin, *With God on Our Side: The Rise of the Religious Right in America,* New York: Broadway Books, 1996, pp. 191–92; Durham, *The Christian Right,* pp. 105–6.

28. Durham, *The Christian Right,* pp. 10–11.

29. Edsall, *Chain Reaction,* pp. 18, 130–31.

30. Edsall, *Chain Reaction,* pp. 35–36; D'Souza, *Falwell,* pp. 96–97, 99–100.

Chapter 7: Starting the Moral Majority

1. Dinesh D'Souza, *Falwell: Before the Millennium,* Chicago: Regnery Gateway, 1984, p. 109; Jerry Falwell, *An Autobiography,* Lynchburg, Va.: Liberty House Publishers, 1997, p. 384.

2. "'Christian New Right's' Rush to Power," *New York Times,* August 18, 1981.

3. William Martin, *With God on Our Side: The Rise of the Religious Right in America,* New York: Broadway Books, 1996, pp. 201–2; Susan Friend Harding, *The Book of Jerry Falwell,* Princeton, N.J.: Princeton University Press, 2000, pp. 74–75.

4. Dirk Smillie, *Falwell Inc.: Inside a Religious, Political, Educational, and Business Empire,* New York: St. Martin's Press, 2008, p. 98.

5. Falwell, *An Autobiography*, p. 385; "Spirit of Truth or Spirit of Error," sermon preached February 11, 1976, LUArchives, MW–113.
6. Martin, *With God on Our Side*, p. 62; Falwell, *An Autobiography*, p. 386.
7. D'Souza, *Falwell*, p. 111.
8. Falwell, *An Autobiography*, p. 388; D'Souza, *Falwell*, pp. 111–12.
9. Martin, *With God on Our Side*, pp. 202–3.
10. William R. Price and James J. H. Goodman, *Jerry Falwell: An Unauthorized Profile*, Lynchburg, Va.: Paris & Associates, 1981, p. 27; Falwell, *An Autobiography*, p. 388.
11. Martin, *With God on Our Side*, p. 204.
12. "Rev. Falwell Inspires Evangelical Vote," *New York Times*, August 20, 1980.
13. Price and Goodman, *Jerry Falwell*, p. 25.
14. Price and Goodman, *Jerry Falwell*, p. 25.
15. Price and Goodman, *Jerry Falwell*, p. 26; Smillie, *Falwell Inc.*, p. 102.
16. Harding, *The Book of Jerry Falwell*, p. 27.
17. "The Gospel According to Falwell," *Atlanta Constitution*, August 23, 1980; Smillie, *Falwell Inc.*, pp. 102, 104.
18. Smillie, *Falwell Inc.*, p. 100.
19. "Ultraconservative Evangelicals a Surging New Force in Politics," *New York Times*, October 17, 1980.
20. *Moral Majority Report*, October 15, 1980.
21. "Group of Evangelical Protestants Takes Over the GOP in Alaska," *New York Times*, June 8, 1980; *Moral Majority Report*, October 15, 1980.
22. "Politics from the Pulpit: Fundamentalists Take Aim at Carter and Liberals Nationwide," *Time*, October 13, 1980.
23. Harding, *The Book of Jerry Falwell*, p. 79.
24. "Politics from the Pulpit," *Time*.
25. "Politics from the Pulpit," *Time*.
26. Falwell, *An Autobiography*, p. 391; "Falwell Strives for Role as Political Kingmaker," *Washington Star*, July 3, 1980.
27. Falwell, *An Autobiography*, p. 360.
28. *Moral Majority Report*, October 15, 1980.
29. Martin, *With God on Our Side*, p. 200.
30. John Killinger, *The Other Preacher in Lynchburg*, New York: St. Martin's Press, 2009, pp. 31–33.
31. "Right Religion, Right Politics?," *Home Missions* (September–October 1980).
32. "Right Religion, Right Politics?," *Home Missions*.
33. "Falwell Strives for Role as Political Kingmaker," *Washington Star*, July 3, 1980.
34. Dobson and Hinson, *The Seduction of Power*, p. 48.
35. D'Souza, *Falwell*, p. 117.
36. Lou Cannon, *Governor Reagan: His Rise to Power*, New York: Public Affairs, 2003, pp. 14, 209ff; John Patrick Diggans, *Ronald Reagan: Fate, Freedom and the Making of History*, New York: W. W. Norton, 2007, p. 22.
37. Cannon, *Governor Reagan*, pp. 118–19, 124.
38. "'Christian New Right's' Rush to Power," *New York Times*, August 18, 1980; Cannon, *Governor Reagan*, pp. 473–75; D'Souza, *Falwell*, pp. 126–27.
39. "Right Religion, Right Politics?," *Home Missions*.
40. Cannon, *Governor Reagan*, p. 481.
41. Brian Kaylor, "Anniversary of Bailey Smith's Harmful Moment in Baptist-Jewish

Relations," EthicsDaily.com, August 23, 2010, available at: http://www.bap
tists4ethics.com/news.php?viewStory=16564.

42. Goodman and Price, *Jerry Falwell*, pp. 1–3.
43. "'Anecdote' Hurts Falwell Credibility," *Washington Star*, August 23, 1980;
"Allen Agrees with White House on Falwell Fabrication," *The Baptist Messenger* (Oklahoma), August 21, 1980.
44. "'Anecdote' Hurts Falwell Credibility," *Washington Star*, August 23, 1980.
45. "Politics from the Pulpit," *Time*.
46. Jerry Falwell, *Listen, America*, New York: Doubleday, 1980, pp. 3–6.
47. Falwell, *Listen, America*, pp. 6–7, 8–10, 11, 15.
48. Falwell, *Listen, America*, pp. 15–17.
49. Falwell, *Listen, America*, pp. 25, 26, 33; *Moral Majority Report*, October 15, 1980.
50. Falwell, *Listen, America*, pp. 67, 87.
51. "Politics from the Pulpit," *Time*; "Rev. Falwell Inspires Evangelical Vote," *New York Times*, August 20, 1980.
52. Jerry Falwell, sermon delivered on *Old-Time Gospel Hour*, October 19, 1980 (transcript), PFAW Archives.
53. "The Christian Bill of Rights," sermon delivered on *Old-Time Gospel Hour*, October 26, 1980 (transcript), PFAW Archives.
54. Jerry Falwell, sermon delivered on *Old-Time Gospel Hour*, October 19, 1980 (transcript), PFAW Archives.

Chapter 8: Proximity to Power

1. "Reagan Easily Beats Carter," *New York Times*, November 5, 1980; "The Collapse of a Coalition," *The Washington Post*, November 5, 1980.
2. Jerry Falwell, *An Autobiography*, Lynchburg, Va.: Liberty House Publishers, 1997, p. 390; Dinesh D'Souza, *Falwell: Before the Millennium*, Chicago: Regnery Gateway, 1984, pp. 129–30; William Martin, *With God on Our Side: The Rise of the Religious Right in America*, New York: Broadway Books, 1996, p. 220.
3. Martin, *With God on Our Side*, p. 236; Dirk Smillie, *Falwell Inc.: Inside a Religious, Political, Educational, and Business Empire*, New York: St. Martin's Press, 2008, p. 103.
4. "Evangelical Leaders Hail Election and Ask Continuation of Efforts," *New York Times*, January 28, 1981.
5. Falwell, *An Autobiography*, p. 391.
6. Martin, *With God on Our Side*, pp. 226, 228.
7. Martin, *With God on Our Side*, pp. 236–37; Ed Dobson and Edward E. Hindson, *The Seduction of Power: Preachers, Politics, and the Media*, Ada, Minn.: Fleming Revell Co., 1988, pp. 35–36.
8. JoAnn Gaspar, "More Reaganite Women Needed in the Reagan Administration," *Conservative Digest*, February 1981.
9. Lou Cannon, *President Reagan: The Role of a Lifetime*, New York: Simon & Schuster, 1991, pp. 49–51; Falwell, *An Autobiography*, p. 391.
10. Cannon, *President Reagan*, p. 87; "Falwell Says Budget, Taxes Should Come First on Hill," *Washington Star*, April 20, 1981.
11. "Falwell Says Budget, Taxes Should Come First on Hill," *Washington Star*.

12. Cannon, *President Reagan*, pp. 241–42.

13. "Moral Majority Focusing on Local Concerns," *Washington Star*, February 21, 1981.

14. "Moral Majority Establishes Beachhead in New York," *New York Times*, February 5, 1981.

15. "Maryland's Religious Lobby Loses First Test," *Washington Post*, February 1, 1981.

16. "Case of 'Dirty Cookies' Spurs Legislative Hoax," *Baltimore Sun*, January 8, 1981.

17. "Local Group, Political Views Discussed by Rev. Falwell," *San Jose Mercury*, March 8, 1981.

18. "What the Moral Majority Is Not," advertisement in *The Washington Post*, March 23, 1981.

19. Transcript 04241, *The Phil Donahue Show*, July 1981.

20. Martin, *With God on Our Side*, p. 223.

21. Martin, *With God on Our Side*, pp. 222–23, 225.

22. Martin, *With God on Our Side*, p. 226; Dobson and Hindson, *The Seduction of Power*, p. 31.

23. "Falwell Criticizes AWACS Sale," *Washington Star*, April 23, 1981; Martin, *With God on Our Side*, p. 224.

24. "Moral Majority Leader to Headline Local Rally," *Billings Gazette*, March 11, 1981.

25. "Stockman's Favorite Defeated in Michigan by Right-Wing Rival," *Washington Star*, March 26, 1981.

26. "Beyond the Election, Moral Majority Is Active," *Jackson News*, May 6, 1981; "Moral Majority Inc. Spreads Its Wings," *Meridian Star*, June 2, 1981.

27. "Falwell Tabloid Distributed in Martinsburg Newspaper," *Hagerstown* (Maryland) *Morning Herald*, May 23, 1981.

28. "Virginia Vetoes Called Moral Majority Victory," *Raleigh* (North Carolina) *News and Observer*, March 29, 1981.

29. "No-Frills Academy Thrives in Fairfax," *Washington Post*, March 29, 1981.

30. "Sex-Education Film Is Attacked," *Washington Post*, April 1, 1981.

31. "Sex Ed—More or Less," *Peoria Journal Star*, May 8, 1981.

32. "Parents' Groups Purging Schools of 'Humanist' Books and Classes," *New York Times*, May 17, 1981.

33. "Theologians, Scientists Shouldn't Argue on Evolution, Falwell Says," *Chattanooga* (Tennessee) *Times*, May 1, 1981.

34. "Falwell Evolution Special," *Old-Time Gospel Hour* (transcript), June 7, 1981, PFAW Archives.

35. "Censorship: What Johnny Can't Read," *Washington Post*, Summer Education Review, April 19, 1981.

36. "TV Monitors Plan Sponsor Pressure," *New York Times*, May 27, 1981.

37. Moral Majority fund-raising letter, July 15, 1981, PFAW Archives; *Moral Majority Report*, June 22, 1981.

38. D'Souza, *Falwell*, p. 138.

39. "Moral Majority Mixes Politics, Religion on Child Rearing," *Franklin Daily Journal*, June 1, 1981.

40. "Danks Rejects Free Trip to Anti-Porn Conference," *Jackson News*, August 5, 1981.

41. "In Slap at Falwell, Va. Senate Tells Students to Study Statutes," *Washington Post,* February 4, 1981.
42. "Moral Majority Policies Criticized by McGovern," *Worcester Gazette,* March 12, 1981.
43. Judy Mann, "When a Public Official Ignores Human Suffering," *Washington Post,* April 3, 1981.
44. Richard Cohen, "The Moral Majority and I Agree—On One Issue," *Washington Post,* May 12, 1981.
45. Pat Bouchard, "One Person's Viewpoint," *Palos Heights Regional,* July 23, 1981.
46. "New Right Loses Followers," *Roanoke Times & World News,* September 25, 1981.
47. "Corbin Joins Majority's Opponents," *Flint Journal,* March 30, 1981.
48. "Dr. William Sloane Coffin: Theologian Adds to Discussion on Moral Majority," *Arkansas Gazette,* May 24, 1981.
49. "Protest Against Moral Majority Emerges at Baptist Conference, Dallas," *New York Times,* March 26, 1981.
50. "Drift Away from Fundamentalism Splits Ranks of Southern Baptists," *New York Times,* March 28, 1981.
51. Cannon, *President Reagan,* pp. 722–23; John Patrick Diggins, *Ronald Reagan: Fate, Freedom, and the Making of History,* W. W. Norton and Company, 2007, p. 315; "Reagan Names Woman to Supreme Court," *Washington Post,* July 8, 1981.
52. D'Souza, *Falwell,* p. 133.
53. "Reagan Names Woman to Supreme Court," *Washington Post.*
54. "Reagan Choice for Court Decried by Conservatives but Acclaimed by Liberals," *Washington Post,* July 8, 1981.
55. "Reagan Choice for Court Decried by Conservatives," *Washington Post.*
56. "Baker Vows Support for Nominee," *New York Times,* July 8, 1981.
57. Michael Sean Winters, *Left at the Altar: How the Democrats Lost the Catholics and How the Catholics Can Save the Democrats,* New York: Basic Books, 2008, pp. 139–41.
58. "Goldwater Tells Opponents of O'Connor Nomination to 'Back Off,'" *New York Times,* July 10, 1981; "Falwell Speaks at Broadway Baptist Church," *Memphis Commercial Appeal,* August 27, 1981.
59. "Packwood Vents Ire upon Moral Majority," *Portland Oregonian,* August 19, 1981; "The American Conservatives' Two Faces," *Chicago Tribune,* July 12, 1981; "Falwell Snaps Back at Goldwater," *Dallas Times Herald,* September 17, 1981; D'Souza, *Falwell,* pp. 133–34.
60. "Why State and Religion Do Not Mix," *Grand Forks Herald,* July 14, 1981; "Pope Falwell," *Greensboro News,* July 22, 1981; "Moral Majority's Outrage," *Hartford Courant,* July 12, 1981.

Chapter 9: The Moral Majority Matures

1. Jerry Falwell, *Listen, America,* New York: Bantam Books, 1980, p. 71; Lou Cannon, *President Reagan: The Role of a Lifetime,* New York: Simon & Schuster, 1991, p. 241.
2. Cannon, *President Reagan,* pp. 37–38.
3. Cannon, *President Reagan,* p. 260.

4. "Jerry Falwell Crosses the Line in 'Religious' Electioneering," *Los Angeles Times,* December 19, 1983; "Falwell Says U.S. Beginning Rebirth," *Arkansas Democrat,* February 23, 1983; Jerry Falwell, *Old-Time Gospel Hour,* March 20, 1983, quoted in PFAW letter to Vice President George Bush, May 16, 1983; "Falwell: Not the Time for Arms Freeze," *Rutland* (Vermont) *Daily Herald,* April 20, 1983.
5. "U.S. Headed Back to God, Falwell Says," *Savannah* (Georgia) *News,* May 2, 1983; "Falwell: A Winner of Hearts," *Cincinnati Enquirer,* July 10, 1983.
6. "Special Briefing Opposing an Immediate Nuclear Freeze," June 1983, PFAW Archives.
7. "Reverend Jerry Falwell on 'Morning Break,'" May 19, 1983 (transcript), PFAW Archives; "Falwell on 'Panorama,'" September 21, 1983 (transcript), PFAW Archives.
8. "Falwell Attacks Trudeau," *Washington Post,* March 13, 1982.
9. "In '60s, '70s, USA 'Nearly Went to Hell'" (interview with Falwell), *USA Today,* December 20, 1983.
10. CBS, *60 Minutes,* November 13, 1983 (transcript), PFAW Archives.
11. Winters, *Left at the Altar,* pp. 157–58.
12. "Falwell Expresses Confidence in '84 Reagan-Bush Victory," *West Palm Beach Post,* April 21, 1983; "Jerry Falwell Crosses the Line in 'Religious' Electioneering," *Los Angeles Times,* December 19, 1983.
13. "Falwell Trip to El Salvador Gets Administration OK," *Lynchburg News,* September 7, 1983.
14. "Falwell Asks More Aid for Salvador," *Lynchburg News,* September 15, 1983; "Falwell Backs More Aid to Salvador," *Washington Times,* September 16, 1983.
15. "Falwell Backs More Aid to Salvador," *Washington Times.*
16. "In '60s, '70s, USA 'Nearly Went to Hell'" (interview with Falwell), *USA Today.*
17. Robert Calvo, "The Church and the Doctrine of National Security," in *Churches and Politics in Latin America,* edited by Daniel Levine, Beverly Hills, Calif.: Sage Publications, 1979, p. 149.
18. William Martin,*With God on Our Side: The Rise of the Religious Right in America,* New York: Broadway Books, 1996, p. 229.
19. "Pastor Launches National Private 'War on Poverty,'" *Los Angeles Times,* March 30, 1981.
20. ABC News, "Helping the Poor—Church or State?" *Nightline,* December 23, 1982 (transcript), PFAW Archives.
21. "In '60s, '70s, USA 'Nearly Went to Hell'" (interview with Falwell), *USA Today.*
22. Jerry Falwell, *An Autobiography,* Lynchburg, Va.: Liberty House Publishers, 1997, pp. 370–72; "Falwell Unwed Mothers Home Is Antiabortion Tactic," *Washington Post,* April 15, 1984.
23. "Save-A-Baby" (undated brochure), PFAW Archives.
24. "Just for Variety," *Variety,* December 5, 1983.
25. "Falwell Urges Readers to Ignore Penthouse Report on Ministries," *Lynchburg News,* October 1, 1981.
26. Rodney A. Smolla, *Jerry Falwell v. Larry Flynt: The First Amendment on Trial,* New York: St. Martin's Press, 1988, pp. 12–13.

27. Smolla, *Jerry Falwell v. Larry Flynt*, pp. 11, 13; Dinesh D'Souza, *Falwell: Before the Millennium*, Chicago: Regnery Gateway, 1984, p. 137; "Moral Issues Will Get a Second Chance" (interview with Jerry Falwell), *USA Today*, October 18, 1982.

28. "Concerns About In-Vitro Process," *Lynchburg News & Daily Advance*, January 16, 1982.

29. "Falwell Starts Daily Column," *Lynchburg News & Daily Advance*, February 22, 1982; "Falwell Tapes TV Message," *Lynchburg News & Daily Advance*, February 22, 1982.

30. "New Magazine Started for Fundamentalists," *Richmond Times-Dispatch*, September 11, 1982.

31. "Moral Majority Leader Knocks 'Silent Pulpits,'" *Fort Lauderdale Sun-Sentinel*, September 25, 1981; "Falwell: Abortion the Issue of the '80s," *Philadelphia News*, September 28, 1981; "A Visitor Interview," *Our Sunday Visitor*, December 13, 1981.

32. "Falwell Backs Reagan's Re-election with Caution," *Washington Times*, September 22, 1983.

33. Murray Rothbard, "Viewpoint: The Moral Majority and the Public Schools," *Reason*, September 1981.

34. "Head of Yale Calls Moral Majority 'Peddlers of Coercion' on 'Values,'" *New York Times*, September 1, 1981; D'Souza, *Falwell*, pp. 147–48.

35. Jerry Falwell, "The Four Hot Buttons That Cause the Greatest Controversy," sermon preached September 13, 1981 (transcript), PFAW Archives.

36. "Yale Head Decries Moral Majority, and Is Accused of Bias and Bigotry," *Washington Post*, September 2, 1981; "Mugging Mr. Falwell," *Dallas News*, September 3, 1981; "Moral Majority Goblins," *Wall Street Journal*, September 2, 1981.

37. "Yale and the Moral Majority," *Washington Post*, September 8, 1981.

38. "GU President Assails Moral Majority and Reagan's Program," *Washington Post*, October 2, 1981; John Killinger, *The Other Preacher in Lynchburg*, New York: St. Martin's Press, 2009, pp. 97–98.

39. "Moral Majority, Pro and Con: Organization Spokesman, Foe Debate at Akron U," *Akron Beacon Journal*, September 30, 1981.

40. "Moral Majority Official Gets Flak," *Watsonville* (California) *Register*, October 11, 1983.

41. D'Souza, *Falwell*, pp. 7–8; Falwell, *An Autobiography*, pp. 393–94.

42. Jerry Falwell, letter to *Moral Majority Report* subscribers, April 15, 1981, PFAW Archives.

43. "Moral Majority Doubles Income, but Still Has Deficit," *Lynchburg News*, December 10, 1981.

44. "Falwell and Moral Majority Declare War in City's 'Perverted Act,'" *Washington Post*, September 10, 1981; "Congressmen Who Voted for Sodomy," *Moral Majority Report*, October 19, 1981, PFAW Archives.

45. Moral Majority, "Urgent Legislative Alert," November 19, 1981, PFAW Archives.

46. D'Souza, *Falwell*, p. 142.

47. "Falwell Preparing to Fund Candidates," *Evansville* (Indiana) *Press*, February 4, 1983.

48. "Falwell to Assist Candidates," *Lynchburg News,* February 9, 1983; "Falwell Forms Million-Dollar PAC," *Moral Majority Report,* March 1983.

49. "Conservative Voter Drive Starts," *Winston-Salem Journal,* July 7, 1983.

50. "Falwell Calls Recent Black Voter Registration Campaign 'Racist,'" *Montgomery Advertiser Daily,* September 20, 1983.

51. "Moral Majority Not Backing Crane," *Lynchburg News & Daily Advance,* August 28, 1983.

52. "Falwell at Word of Life Backs Reagan Leadership," *Plattsburgh* (New York) *Press-Republican,* June 21, 1983.

53. "School Prayer Impasse Solved," *Washington Times,* July 13, 1983; "Prayer Left Unanswered," *Time,* April 2, 1984; "Jerry Falwell Vows to Continue Prayer Fight," *Phoenix Republic,* March 24, 1984.

54. "Wrong Number," *New York Times,* May 19, 1983.

55. Macel Falwell, *Jerry Falwell: His Life and Legacy,* New York: Howard Books, 2008, p. 164.

56. "Kennedy Addresses Falwell's Students," *Washington Times,* October 4, 1983.

57. Falwell, *An Autobiography,* p. 403; "Falwell Calls Kennedy's Speech Excellent," *Lynchburg News,* October 4, 1983.

58. "The Man Who Came to Dinner," *Washington Post,* October 9, 1983.

59. "Kennedy *Is* a Threat to the Survival of the Republic," *Human Events,* October 22, 1983.

60. *Moral Majority Report,* November 1983.

61. "Personalities," *Washington Post,* January 26, 1984; "Falwell Met with Kennedy," *Lynchburg News,* January 26, 1984; Falwell, *Jerry Falwell,* pp. 164–65.

62. "Jackson Tries to Befriend Fundamentalists in Meetings with Coalition, Jerry Falwell," *Washington Post,* December 24, 1983.

63. "Falwell Lauds Jackson but Supports Reagan," *Akron Beacon Journal,* January 7, 1984.

64. "Falwell Backs Reagan's Re-election with Caution," *Washington Times,* September 22, 1983; "Jerry Falwell Predicts Reagan Will Run, Win," *Dallas Morning News,* December 1, 1983.

65. "'Religious Right' Won't Be as Excited About Reagan Campaign in 1984," *Santa Barbara News Press,* March 6, 1984.

66. "Baptists Convene Here; Reagan to Speak," *Washington Post,* April 13, 1984; "Hecklers Interrupt Reagan Speech at Gathering of Fundamentalists," *New York Times,* April 15, 1984; "Baptist Fundamentalism '84" (official program), PFAW Archives.

67. "Falwell Foresees Judicial Clout for Reagan," *Philadelphia Inquirer,* April 24, 1984.

68. "'Amoral' Groups Threaten Nation, Falwell Declares," *Washington Post,* June 9, 1984.

69. "Falwell Avoids Controversial Ordinance," *Lynchburg Daily News & Advance,* June 16, 1984.

70. "Objecting Conscientiously," *Fundamentalist Journal,* July–August 1984.

71. "Jerry Falwell—Republican Convention Benediction—1984," August 22, 1984 (transcript), PFAW Archives.

72. "Falwell Addresses GOP Platform Committee," *Moral Majority Report,* September 1984.

73. "I Love America" Committee (PAC), "The Hotline Report," September 1984, PFAW Archives.
74. "Falwell Says No to Christian State," *Lynchburg News & Daily Advance,* September 10, 1984.
75. "Falwell Says Debate Failed to Add Votes for Mondale," *Chicago Tribune,* October 10, 1984.
76. "Peace Through Strength Backers Rally; Soviets 'Would Love' Mondale Presidency, Rev. Falwell Says," *St. Louis Democrat,* October 1, 1984.
77. "Falwell Says Debate Failed to Add Votes for Mondale," *Chicago Tribune,* October 10, 1984; "Falwell Disputes Mondale's Debate Allegations," *Marshall* (Texas) *News-Messenger,* October 11, 1984.
78. "His Influence Just Average, Falwell Says at City Club," *Cleveland Plain Dealer,* October 13, 1984.
79. "Moral Majority Welcomes Partisan Gibes," *Washington Times,* October 19, 1984.
80. "Falwell Urges Voters to Oppose Abortion," *New York Times,* November 5, 1984; "Falwell's PAC: Trading Bibles for Dollars Yields Few Cents for Political Candidates," *PACs & Lobbies,* November 7, 1984.
81. "Falwell Views on Election Part of Networks' Coverage," *Lynchburg News,* November 4, 1984; "Falwell's Opinion in Demand," *Lynchburg News,* November 7, 1984.
82. "Concerned with Morals, Not State Politics Says Falwell," *Nashville Tennessean,* November 17, 1981.
83. "Falwell Strives for Role as Political Kingmaker," *Washington Star,* July 3, 1980; "Base of Support Dying for Moral Majority?" *Denver Post,* July 10, 1981.
84. "Moral Majority: Falwell Wants 'Always to Be the Underdog,'" *Pueblo Chieftain & Star-Journal,* April 23, 1983.
85. "Falwell Backs Reagan's Re-election with Caution," *Washington Times,* September 22, 1983.
86. "A Visitor Interview" (interview with Jerry Falwell), *Our Sunday Visitor,* December 13, 1981.
87. "Falwell Defends Softened Stances," *Fort Worth Star-Telegram,* February 25, 1982.
88. "In '60s, '70s, USA 'Nearly Went to Hell,'" *USA Today.*
89. "A Visitor Interview" (interview with Jerry Falwell), *Our Sunday Visitor.*
90. Larry King, "Falwell Regret; An Official Pitch" ("People" column), *USA Today,* October 29, 1984.
91. "A Visitor Interview" (interview with Jerry Falwell), *Our Sunday Visitor.*
92. "Objecting Conscientiously," *Fundamentalist Journal,* July–August 1984.

Chapter 10: The First Amendment

1. Rodney A. Smolla, *Jerry Falwell v. Larry Flynt: The First Amendment on Trial,* New York: St. Martin's Press, 1988, p. 1.
2. Smolla, *Jerry Falwell v. Larry Flynt,* p. 116.
3. Smolla, *Jerry Falwell v. Larry Flynt,* pp. 2–3.
4. Smolla, *Jerry Falwell v. Larry Flynt,* pp. 7–8.
5. Gene Owens, "Falwell vs. Hustler: Who's First in Bad Taste?," *Roanoke Times & World-News,* November 27, 1983.

6. "Falwell Sues Publisher Flynt over Fake Ad in Hustler Magazine," *Washington Post,* November 1, 1983.
7. "Falwell's Lawyer, Plump, Flamboyant," *Lynchburg News,* December 5, 1984.
8. Smolla, *Jerry Falwell v. Larry Flynt,* pp. 10–12.
9. "Falwell's Lawyer, Plump, Flamboyant," *Lynchburg News.*
10. Bob Colacello, "Larry Flynt, Hustling the American Dream," *Vanity Fair,* February 1984.
11. "Falwell Suit Against Hustler Heads to Trial," *Washington Post,* December 2, 1984.
12. Darrell Laurant, "Falwell-Flynt: The First Chapter Was a Little Weird," *Lynchburg News,* December 5, 1984.
13. "Jury Clears Flynt of Libel, Awards Falwell $100,000," *Washington Post,* December 10, 1984; Smolla, *Jerry Falwell v. Larry Flynt,* p. 96.
14. "Falwell Wins Copyright Fight," *Washington Times,* August 13, 1986.
15. "Jury Clears Flynt of Libel, Awards Falwell $100,000," *Washington Post.*
16. "Jury Clears Flynt of Libel, Awards Falwell $100,000," *Washington Post;* "Falwell Says Verdict Draws Line for Publication," *Lynchburg News,* December 10, 1984.
17. "Rev. Falwell and Mr. Flynt" (editorial), *Washington Post,* December 12, 1984.
18. Smolla, *Jerry Falwell v. Larry Flynt,* pp. 221–28.
19. Smolla, *Jerry Falwell v. Larry Flynt,* pp. 184–88, 195–201.
20. Smolla, *Jerry Falwell v. Larry Flynt,* pp. 178–80.
21. "Falwell Likes New Court Make-up," *Birmingham Post-Herald,* June 20, 1986.
22. Smolla, *Jerry Falwell v. Larry Flynt,* pp. 286, 289.
23. "Court, 8–0, Extends Right to Criticize Those in Public Eye; Falwell Rebuffed," *New York Times,* February 25, 1988; "Excerpts from High Court's Affirmation of Speech Protections."
24. "Court, 8–0, Extends Right to Criticize Those in Public Eye; Falwell Rebuffed," *New York Times;* "Outrageous Speech? Yes, and Free," *New York Times,* February 26, 1988.
25. "Larry Flynt: My Friend, Jerry Falwell," *Los Angeles Times,* May 20, 2007.
26. Macel Falwell, *Jerry Falwell: His Life and Legacy,* New York: Howard Books, 2008, pp. 177–79; "Larry Flynt: My Friend, Jerry Falwell," *Los Angeles Times.*
27. "Larry Flynt: My Friend, Jerry Falwell," *Los Angeles Times;* Falwell, *Jerry Falwell,* p. 179.

Chapter 11: The Perils of Power

1. "Falwell Fund-Raiser Sentenced for Cheating Orem Woman," *Salt Lake City Tribune,* December 12, 1984.
2. "Falwell List Misleading, Many Claim," *Milwaukee Journal,* April 13, 1985.
3. "Falwell Says Letters Show Aid Threatened," *Lynchburg News,* June 24, 1986.
4. "Now Falwell on the Griddle over Famine Fund-Raising," *Arlington Heights* (Texas) *Daily Herald,* March 30, 1987; "Falwell Takes Issue; Newspaper Stands by Story on Sudan Relief Solicitations," *Roanoke Times & World-News,* June 3, 1986; "Falwell Method Questioned," *Denver Post,* June 6, 1981.
5. "Falwell Looks to Future with Tunnel Vision," *Dayton Daily News,* March 17, 1985; "Notebook: Lord Help Us," *The New Republic,* April 29, 1985.
6. "Gay Bests Falwell in Court Test," *Sacramento Bee,* September 25, 1985.

7. "California Judge Orders Falwell to Pay $5,000," *Lynchburg News,* September 26, 1985.
8. ABC News, *Nightline,* July 31, 1985 (transcript), PFAW Archives.
9. ABC News, *Nightline,* July 31, 1985 (transcript), PFAW Archives.
10. "Falwell Blames $1 Million Gift Drop on Media," *Nashville Tennessean,* October 11, 1985.
11. ABC News, *Nightline,* October 31, 1986 (transcript), PFAW Archives.
12. Allan Lichtman, *White Protestant Nation: The Rise of the American Conservative Movement,* New York: Grove Press, 2008, pp. 421–22; "Cardinal O'Connor, 80, Dies; Forceful Voice for Vatican," *New York Times,* May 4, 2000.
13. Jerry Falwell, letter to rabbis, February 26, 1985, PFAW Archives.
14. "Falwell Apologizes to Rabbis for Urging 'Christianized' America,'" *Miami Herald,* March 14, 1985.
15. "Falwell's Apology to the Jewish Community at the 85th Annual Convention of the Rabbinical Assembly," April 9, 1985 (transcript), PFAW Archives.
16. "Falwell Attempts to Mend Interfaith Fences," *Washington Post,* April 4, 1985.
17. "Falwell Says Foe Exploited Judge's Bias," *Sacramento Bee,* April 18, 1986.
18. "Falwell Address to National Religious Broadcasters Association," *Moral Majority Report,* March 1985.
19. "May 26, 1985, Falwell Live on South Africa" (transcript), in undated PFAW memo.
20. "South African Sanctions Issue Divides U.S. Conservatives," *Washington Post,* August 22, 1985.
21. "Soviet African Role Veiled, Falwell Says," *Washington Times,* May 29, 1985.
22. "South Africa Unrest May Result in Soviet Takeover, Falwell Says," *Lynchburg News,* September 13, 1985; "Botha Sees South African Churchmen and Falwell," *New York Times,* August 29, 1985.
23. "Botha Sees South African Churchmen and Falwell," *New York Times,* August 29, 1985.
24. "Falwell Gives Qualified Apology for Calling Bishop Tutu a Phony," *New York Times,* August 24, 1985; "Inquiry, Topic: South Africa" (interview with Bishop Desmond Tutu), *USA Today,* August 25, 1985.
25. "Jesse Jackson and Jerry Falwell Square Off on S. Africa," *Washington Times,* August 22, 1985.
26. "Jackson and Falwell on 'Nightline,'" *New York Times,* September 4, 1985; "Jackson-Falwell Clash Gets High Rating," *Washington Times,* September 6, 1985.
27. "Jerry Falwell's Crusade" and "Jerry Falwell Spreads the Word," *Time,* September 2, 1985.
28. "Virginia Beach Tells Falwell He's Too Political for Festival," *Washington Times,* August 29, 1985; "Internal Rifts Blur Fundamentalist War on Pornography," *Fort Worth Star Telegram,* September 11, 1985; "Liberty Baptist Dropped," *Fayetteville* (North Carolina) *Times,* November 6, 1985.
29. "Local Black Leaders Lash Out at Falwell," *Lynchburg News,* August 22, 1985; "Many Think Falwell Should Stick to Preaching, Cut Out Politicking," *Lynchburg News,* August 22, 1985; "Contributions to Falwell Show Drop," *Lynchburg News,* September 26, 1985.
30. *Baltimore Sun,* August 22, 1985; *Los Angeles Times,* August 22, 1985; *Washington Post,* September 12, 1985.

31. "Special Report: South Africa, The Untold Story," *Fundamentalist Journal*, October 1985.
32. "Falwell Gets Marcos' VIP Welcome in Manila, Urges U.S. to Support Philippines," *Baltimore Sun*, November 12, 1985; "Falwell Says Philippines a Paradise," *Lynchburg News*, November 13, 1985; "Philippine 'Paradise' Description by Falwell Draws Multiple Outcry," *Louisiana United Methodist Weekly*, November 22, 1985.
33. "More Falwell Follies," *Pittsburgh Post-Gazette*, November 19, 1985; "Philippine 'Paradise' Description by Falwell Draws Multiple Outcry," *Louisiana United Methodist Weekly*, November 22, 1985.
34. "Jerry Falwell Spreads the Word," *Time*, September 2, 1985.
35. "Falwell Backs Durette's Bid for Governorship," *Lynchburg News*, April 25, 1985.
36. "Fundamentalist Leader Endorses Durette," *Roanoke Times & World-News*, September 21, 1985; "Durette Says He Shares Moral Majority Values," *Norfolk Virginian-Pilot*, September 21, 1985.
37. "Is Falwell's Political Influence Waning?," *Anderson* (South Carolina) *Independent-Mail*, December 9, 1985.
38. "Is Falwell's Political Influence Waning?," *Anderson Independent-Mail;* "Virginia Polls and Politicians Indicate Falwell Is Slipping in His Home State," *New York Times*.
39. "Virginia Polls and Politicians Indicate Falwell Is Slipping in His Home State," *New York Times*.
40. "Democrats Hope to Use Falwell to Foil GOP," *Washington Post*, February 12, 1986; "Democrats Make Falwell an Issue," *Cincinnati Post*, March 19, 1986.
41. "Dr. Falwell Forms 'Liberty Federation,'" *Liberty Report*, January 1, 1986.
42. "Statement by Jerry Falwell," Nation Press Club, January 3, 1986, PFAW Archives.
43. "'Moral Majority' Name Changed to Boost Image," *Washington Post*, January 7, 1986.
44. "'Moral Majority' Name Changed to Boost Image," *Washington Post;* "Falwell Aims for a Larger Majority," *Insight*, January 20, 1986.
45. "A Vision for the Future, Not a Tired Agenda," *The Christian Century*, January 22, 1986.
46. "Falwell's Shift May Help GOP," *Lynchburg News*, September 18, 1986.
47. "Falwell to Shift Emphasis from Politics to Pulpit," *Lynchburg News*, September 17, 1986.
48. "Falwell's Shift May Help GOP," *Lynchburg News*.
49. Falwell, *Jerry Falwell*, pp. 214–16.
50. "Who Holds the Power Outside Washington," *U.S. News & World Report*, May 20, 1985.
51. "Big Reagan Man on Campus," *Washington Post*, April 24, 1986; "Reaganite Says Strong Values Needed," *Lynchburg News*, May 6, 1986.
52. "A Bad Grant at Justice," *Washington Post*, March 5, 1986; Federal Election Commission, report for the "I Love America" Committee for the period April 1–June 30, 1986, June 30, 1986, PFAW Archives; "Simon 'a Bigot' Falwell Charges," *Carbondale-Herrin Southern Illinoisan*, June 22, 1986.
53. "Is Falwell Endorsing Bush Run Already?" *Washington Times*, February 6, 1985.
54. "Guess Who's Going Abroad with Bush," *New York Times*, March 1, 1985;

"Bush Gives Falwell a Vote of Confidence—Sort Of," *San Francisco Examiner,* September 12, 1985.

55. "Who Should Succeed Reagan?," *Policy Review,* Summer 1986.

56. "Robertson Missing the Evangelist Vote," *Lynchburg News & Daily Advance,* August 25, 1986.

57. "An 'Entrepreneurial' Approach to Religion and Political Action," *St. Louis Post-Dispatch,* December 18, 1985.

58. Dirk Smillie, *Falwell Inc.: Inside a Religious, Political, Educational, and Business Empire,* New York: St. Martin's Press, 2008, pp. 104, 106; "Falwell Blames $1 Million Gift Drop on Media," *Nashville Tennessean,* October 11, 1985; "Moral Majority: Political Organization Still Going Strong, Falwell Says," *Lynchburg News,* October 17, 1985; "Falwell Ministries Collected $84 Million in '86," *Lynchburg News,* April 22, 1987.

59. Smillie, *Falwell Inc.,* p. 105.

60. "Doing a Number on Falwell," *Washington Post,* January 5, 1986.

61. "Falwell Trims Ministry," *Lynchburg News,* March 29, 1986; "Liberty University Purchases Academy of Music Theater," *Lynchburg News,* November 9, 1985; "Gospel Hour Agrees to Turn Control of Trust to Bank," *Lynchburg News,* February 12, 1987.

62. "Falwell Pushes Up Satellite Schedule," *Lynchburg News,* February 23, 1986; "Liberty Broadcasting Network Established," *Fundamentalist Journal,* March 1986.

63. "Falwell Blames $1 Million Gift Drop on Media," *Nashville Tennessean;* "U.S. Is Healing Spiritually, Falwell Tells Ironton Church," *Huntington* (West Virginia) *Herald-Dispatch,* June 24, 1985; "In Akron, Falwell Lashes Out at Critics," *Akron Beacon Journal,* September 27, 1985; Jerry Falwell, "Church Planting," sermon preached September 6, 1981, LUArchives, OTGH-464.

64. "Falwell Cheers on Christian Educators," *Orange County* (California) *Register,* October 31, 1986.

65. "Anti-Abortion Forces, in a Change of Tactics, Offer Alternative Care," *Wall Street Journal,* March 10, 1986.

Chapter 12: Scandal and Retrenchment

1. Jerry Falwell, *An Autobiography,* Lynchburg, Va.: Liberty House Publishers, 1997, pp. 429–30.

2. Dirk Smillie, *Falwell Inc.: Inside a Religious, Political, Educational, and Business Empire,* New York: St. Martin's Press, 2008, pp. 106–7.

3. Falwell, *An Autobiography,* pp. 430–31.

4. Falwell, *An Autobiography,* pp. 433–35.

5. Falwell, *An Autobiography,* pp. 435–36.

6. Falwell, *An Autobiography,* pp. 436–37.

7. "Falwell Says Bangor Baptist Will Survive Despite Chaos," *Bangor News,* January 15, 1986.

8. "Falwell Says Bangor Baptist Will Survive Despite Chaos," *Bangor News.*

9. Falwell, *An Autobiography,* pp. 439–40.

10. Falwell, *An Autobiography,* pp. 441–44.

11. Falwell, *An Autobiography,* pp. 444–45; Smillie, *Falwell Inc.,* p. 108; "Some Questions for Falwell," *Lynchburg News,* April 30, 1987.

12. "Falwell Ministries Collected $84 million in '86," *Lynchburg News,* April 22, 1987; Falwell, *An Autobiography,* pp. 446–47.

13. Falwell, *An Autobiography,* pp. 446–47.

14. Falwell, *An Autobiography,* pp. 448–49, 457, 464–65; "PTL Meeting Leaves Falwell Firmly in Control," *Richmond News-Ledger,* April 29, 1987.

15. "Falwell Asks Supporters for $25 Gifts," *Greensboro* (North Carolina) *News,* April 20, 1987; "The Faces of Jerry Falwell," *Charlotte Observer,* June 14, 1987.

16. Falwell, *An Autobiography,* pp. 432, 457; Smillie, *Falwell Inc.,* pp. 108–9.

17. Falwell, *An Autobiography,* pp. 451, 463–64.

18. "Didn't Trick Bakker into Leaving PTL, Falwell Says," *Los Angeles Times,* May 28, 1987.

19. "Falwell Opposes Criminal Investigations of Bakker," *Los Angeles Times,* June 9, 1987; "Falwell Expected Attack by Bakker," *Lynchburg News,* May 29, 1987.

20. Falwell, *An Autobiography,* pp. 466–68.

21. Falwell, *An Autobiography,* pp. 449, 454–55, 468; Jerry Falwell press conference, November 3, 1987 (transcript), PFAW Archives.

22. Falwell, *An Autobiography,* p. 469.

23. "Donations to Falwell Ministry Drop," *Lynchburg News,* November 30, 1988; "Falwell's Offerings Hit Slump," *Washington Post,* December 3, 1988.

24. "Falwell Pulls TV Hour Off 50 Stations," *Cincinnati Enquirer,* October 8, 1987; "Unpaid Bills Cancel Falwell's Program," *Washington Times,* February 24, 1988.

25. Smillie, *Falwell Inc.,* pp. 110–11; "Falwell's Ratings Slip," *Lynchburg News,* May 13, 1988.

26. Smillie, *Falwell Inc.,* pp. 116–18.

27. Smillie, *Falwell Inc.,* pp. 122–29.

28. Smillie, *Falwell Inc.,* p. 125.

29. "Falwell Political Funds Shifted to Religious Arms," *New York Times,* August 23, 1987; "Falwell Denies Fund Diversion," *Washington Post,* August 25, 1987.

30. "Falwell Denies Fund Diversion," *Washington Post.*

31. "Loans Made Between Falwell Organizations," *Washington Post,* August 27, 1987.

32. "Atlanta Man to Head Moral Majority; Falwell Quitting as President to Concentrate on Va. Church," *Atlanta Constitution,* November 4, 1987.

33. Jerry Falwell press conference, November 3, 1987 (transcript), PFAW Archives.

34. "Columnist Predicts Moral Majority's End," *Spartanburg Herald-Journal,* November 6, 1987.

35. "The Moral Majority's Hart Attack," *Washington Post,* January 15, 1988.

36. "In Grove City Vote, GOP Shows Its Racist Stripes," *In These Times,* March 30–April 5, 1988.

37. "In Grove City Vote, GOP Shows Its Racist Stripes," *In These Times;* Tommy Robinson, op-ed piece, "Falwell Distorting Rights Act," *Arkansas Gazette,* March 23, 1988; "Congress Overrides Reagan's *Grove City* Veto," *Congressional Quarterly,* March 26, 1988; "Coalition Fights Falwell Effort," *Chicago Tribune,* March 19, 1988.

38. "Congress Overrides Reagan's *Grove City* Veto," *Congressional Quarterly;* Tommy Robinson, op-ed piece, "Falwell Distorting Rights Act," *Arkansas Gazette,* March 23, 1988; "Coalition Fights Falwell Effort," *Chicago Tribune,* March 19, 1988.

39. "Magazine Pictures Wright as Vampire," *Houston Chronicle,* March 27, 1988.
40. "Charges a 'Badge of Honor,' North Says at Liberty U," *Washington Post,* May 3, 1988.
41. "Donations Request Gets Wide Play," *Lynchburg News,* May 6, 1988.
42. "Falwell Backs Bush, Says Moral Majority Will Take Active Part," *Birmingham News,* June 20, 1988; "Falwell Pushes Bush Bid in Sevier," *Knoxville Journal,* June 21, 1988.
43. "Falwell's Retirement from Politics Is Short," *Lynchburg News,* August 18, 1988.
44. "Falwell Gratified by Bush Inauguration," *Lynchburg News,* January 21, 1989.
45. "Moral Majority Ready to Close, Falwell Says," *Chicago Sun Times,* June 12, 1989.
46. "Moral Majority Ready to Close, Falwell Says," *Chicago Sun Times;* "Moral Majority's Work Is Done, so Falwell Sets End," *Birmingham News,* June 12, 1989.
47. Michael Sean Winters, *Left at the Altar: How the Democrats Lost the Catholics and How the Catholics Can Save the Democrats,* New York: Basic Books, 2008, pp. 120–21.
48. "Moral Majority Ready to Close, Falwell Says," *Chicago Sun Times,* June 12, 1989; "Falwell Disbands Moral Majority to Focus on Ministry, University," *Richmond Times-Dispatch,* June 12, 1989.
49. "Friends, Foes Agree Time for Moral Majority Past," *Memphis Commercial-Appeal,* June 13, 1989; Tom Baxter, "Falwell's Legacy in Doubt," *Atlanta Journal Constitution,* June 18, 1989.
50. "The Moral Majority," *New York Times,* June 18, 1989.
51. "Falwell's Unfinished Mission," *Norfolk Virginian-Pilot,* June 13, 1989; "Moral Majority Makes Its Exit," *Roanoke Times & World-News,* June 14, 1989; "Epitaph for Intolerance," *Raleigh News & Observer,* June 15, 1989.
52. Robert D. Putnam and David E. Campbell, *American Grace: How Religion Divides and Unites Us,* New York: Simon & Schuster, 2010, pp. 375, 383.
53. Putnam and Campbell, *American Grace,* pp. 388–95.
54. Putnam and Campbell, *American Grace,* pp. 120–33.

Chapter 13: Liberty University

1. "Liberty Baptist College Will Get New Name," *Lynchburg News,* April 13, 1985; "Students Flock to Liberty University," *Washington Post,* May 7, 1985; "News Briefs: Virginia," *USA Today,* December 20, 1985.
2. "Where Is Jerry Falwell Headed in 1986?" *Christianity Today,* February 21, 1986.
3. Jerry Falwell, sermon preached April 21, 1976, LUArchives MW 105; "Keep Contraceptives Away from Teen-agers," *USA Today,* March 20, 1985.
4. "Censored: Falwell Yanks Stories from Student Newspaper," *Lynchburg News,* April 17, 1986.
5. "LBC Halts, Then Allows YAF Leaflets," *Lynchburg News,* April 13, 1983; "LBC Group Wants Reagan Official Fired," *Lynchburg News,* April 19, 1983.
6. John Killinger, *The Other Preacher in Lynchburg,* New York: St. Martin's Press, 2009, pp. 122–25; "Teacher Fired over Article Sues Falwell," *Washington Times,* July 16, 1982.

7. "Save the Nation," *Old-Time Gospel Hour* videocassette, Mel White Video Archives.

8. "Liberty Baptist Students Seen as Foundation of New Nation," *Richmond Times-Dispatch*, May 9, 1982.

9. "Liberty U. Hits First, Saves Later," *Washington Post*, October 5, 1985.

10. "Liberty U. Hits First, Saves Later," *Washington Post;* "College Aims to Be Fundamentalism's Notre Dame," *New York Times*, October 4, 1981.

11. "Falwell Considers White House a 'Bully Pulpit,'" *Ontario* (California) *Daily Report*, March 22, 1984.

12. "Falwell: Va. May Allow Creationism Teaching," *Washington Post*, May 20, 1982; "Falwell Backs Off Earlier Statement," *Lynchburg News*, June 2, 1982.

13. Edwin S. Gaustad, *A Documentary History of Religion in America Since 1865*, Grand Rapids, Mich.: Eerdmans, 1993, pp. 583–84.

14. "Falwell: Va. May Allow Creationism Teaching," *Washington Post*, May 20, 1982; "Civil Liberties Union Against Biology Teachers from LBC," *Lynchburg News*, May 20, 1982.

15. "Falwell May Lose Fight on Biology Program," *Washington Post*, May 22, 1982.

16. "Biology Teachers Oppose Request for Certification," *Lynchburg News*, June 10, 1982.

17. "Falwell Backs Off Earlier Statement," *Lynchburg News*, June 2, 1982.

18. "LBC Officials to Outline Falwell's Role," *Lynchburg News*, June 18, 1982; "LBC Officials to Downplay Falwell's Role," *Lynchburg News*, June 18, 1982.

19. "Evolution Ban Denied," *Roanoke Times & World-News*, July 2, 1982; "LBC Pushes Certification," *Lynchburg News*, July 2, 1982.

20. "Falwell Defends Biology Course," *Norfolk Ledger-Star*, September 24, 1982; "Board Splits on LBC Certification," *Lynchburg News*, September 25, 1982.

21. "State Points Out Differences but Certifies LBC Course," *Lynchburg News*, December 11, 1982.

22. "LBC Biology Program Hits New Snag," *Lynchburg News*, January 6, 1984; "Education Program Has Christian Backing," *Roanoke Times & World-News*, January 7, 1984.

23. "LBC Ties Delay State's Decision on Accreditation," *Lynchburg News*, January 7, 1984.

24. "Board Delays Vote on Biology Program at Va. Baptist College," *Washington Post*, May 31, 1984; "Education Board Delays LBC Decision," *Lynchburg News*, June 22, 1984; "LBC Biology Majors Say Free Discussion Stifled," *Lynchburg News*, September 25, 1984.

25. "Jerry Falwell Comments," *Fundamentalist Journal*, December 1985; "LBC Planning Center to Study Creationism," *Lynchburg News*, September 29, 1984.

26. "Falwell Lobbies in Assembly for Three Tax Exemptions," *Washington Post*, February 13, 1987.

27. "City Negotiating with Gospel Hour to Shrink Tax Suit," *Lynchburg News*, November 14, 1981; "Falwell Says Some Taxes to Be Paid," *Lynchburg News*, February 10, 1983; "Gospel Hour to Appeal Ruling," *Lynchburg News*, August 13, 1983.

28. "Gospel Hour to Appeal Ruling," *Lynchburg News*.

29. "Gospel Hour to Appeal Ruling," *Lynchburg News*.

30. "Gospel Hour to Appeal Ruling," *Lynchburg News*.

31. "Falwell Could Petition Legislature for Exemption," *Lynchburg News*, August 29, 1986.

32. "Falwell Could Petition Legislature for Exemption," *Lynchburg News*.

33. "Falwell Plans to Keep Post with Church," *Lynchburg News*, August 18, 1986.

34. "No One Doubts Falwell's Departure Would Be Deeply Felt," *Lynchburg News*, August 23, 1986; "Gospel Hour Delays Decision on Moving," *Lynchburg News*, August 25, 1986.

35. "Legislator Says Hearing Likely on Tax Break for Gospel Hour," *Lynchburg News*, November 20, 1986; "Gospel Hour Hires Two High-Powered Lobbyists," *Lynchburg News*, January 16, 1987.

36. "Local NAACP Opposes Falwell Tax Exemption," *Lynchburg News*, January 14, 1987.

37. "Gospel Hour Hires Two High-Powered Lobbyists," *Lynchburg News*, January 16, 1987; "1982 Ruling Could Affect Falwell Request," *Lynchburg News*, January 21, 1987; "Mistake Made in Gospel Hour Bill," *Lynchburg News*, January 23, 1987.

38. "Gospel Hour Bill Glides Through Senate Panel," *Lynchburg News*, February 2, 1987.

39. "Falwell States His Case Personally," *Lynchburg News*, February 13, 1987; "Legislators Asked to Note Catholic Tax Arrangement," *Lynchburg News*, February 13, 1987.

40. "Delegate Wants Back Taxes Paid," *Lynchburg News*, February 17, 1987.

41. "Gospel Hour Finally Drops Tax Appeal," *Lynchburg News*, January 29, 1987; "Falwell Loses on Retroactive Portion of Bill," *Lynchburg News*, February 19, 1987; "House OKs Tax Break for Gospel Hour," *Lynchburg News*, February 24, 1987.

42. "Accreditation for an LU Law School Likely to Take Years," *Lynchburg News*, October 19, 2002; Smillie, *Falwell Inc.*, p. 139.

43. Smillie, *Falwell Inc.*, pp. 138–39; "Falwell, Thomas Road Baptist Church Buy Ericsson Building," *Lynchburg News*, November 8, 2002.

44. Smillie, *Falwell Inc.*, p. 139.

45. Smillie, *Falwell Inc.*, pp. 140–42; Macel Falwell, *Jerry Falwell: His Life and Legacy*, New York: Howard Books, 2008, pp. 220–23; "Falwell, Thomas Road Baptist Church Buy Ericsson Building," *Lynchburg News*.

46. "Old-Time Gospel Hour Sells Land to Wal-Mart," *Lynchburg News*, November 19, 1988.

47. "Falwell Tells Workers to Join Church, Tithe," *Fort Worth Star Telegram*, March 11, 1989.

48. "Some Falwell Workers Might Join Union," *Lynchburg News*, March 23, 1989.

49. "Falwell Employees Hold Discussions About Union," *Lynchburg News*, March 24, 1989; "Falwell Lawyer Attacks Union Plan," *Lynchburg News*, March 25, 1989.

50. Smillie, *Falwell Inc.*, pp. 128–29; "Challenge Made in LU Bond Bid," *Lynchburg News*, November 18, 1989.

51. "Tithing's End Won't Surprise Some," *Lynchburg News*, January 11, 1990.

52. "LU Professors Soften School's Christian Stand," *Lynchburg News*, January 12, 1990.

53. "Falwell Says Tax-Free-Bond Issue Will Sever College from Ministry," *Washington Times*, January 19, 1990; "Church-State Questions Vex Falwell's Uni-

versity," *Christianity Today,* February 19, 1990; "Falwell: Mature LU Ready for Transfer," *Lynchburg News,* October 7, 1989; "Falwell College's Tax-Free Bond Issue Barred," *Washington Times,* January 14, 1991; Smillie, *Falwell Inc.,* p. 129.

54. "Finance: Moon-Related Funds Filter to Evangelicals," *Christianity Today,* February 9, 1998; Smillie, *Falwell Inc.,* pp. 130–31.
55. Smillie, *Falwell Inc.,* pp. 132–35.
56. "Bush Backs E. Europe Aid 'Corps,'" *Washington Post,* May 13, 1990.
57. Falwell, *Jerry Falwell,* p. 150.
58. Falwell, *Jerry Falwell,* pp. 150, 155; "In Final 64, This School Has a Prayer," *New York Times,* March 18, 1994; "Liberty Plays Host to Grahams Galore," *Washington Times,* May 5, 1997.
59. "School of Law Receives Full Accreditation in Record Time," *Liberty Journal,* no. 2, 2010.

Chapter 14: Back in Opposition

1. "Acceptance Speech to the Democratic National Convention by Governor Bill Clinton from Arkansas," July 16, 1992, available at: http://www.4president .org/speeches/billclinton1992acceptance.htm.
2. "Falwell: Clinton Misquoted Bible," *Lynchburg News,* July 22, 1992.
3. "Falwell: Clinton Misquoted Bible," *Lynchburg News.*
4. "Falwell May Resurrect Moral Majority," *Washington Times,* November 8, 1992; Jerry Falwell, "The Clinton Agenda for the Unborn and Gays," sermon preached November 8, 1992, White Video Archives; "Religious Activists Feeling a Renewed Political Calling," *USA Today,* November 12, 1992; "Religious Right Hopes Clinton Swells Ranks," *Washington Post,* November 8, 1992.
5. "Moral Majority: Can It Relive Days of Glory?," *Lynchburg News,* November 13, 1992.
6. "Moral Majority: Can It Relive Days of Glory?," *Lynchburg News.*
7. Jerry Falwell, "The First 100 Days: The Radical Departure and the Christian Response," *Old-Time Gospel Hour* (videocassette), White Video Archives.
8. Falwell, "The First 100 Days," *Old-Time Gospel Hour.*
9. Jerry Falwell, undated mailing (early 1993), PFAW Archives.
10. "Falwell Blasts Clinton During Meeting with Southern Baptists," *Church and State,* December 1993.
11. Liberty Alliance, *Prescription for Disaster* (videocassette), White Video Archives.
12. Citizens for Honest Government, *Bill Clinton's Circle of Power* (videocassette), distributed by Liberty Alliance, White Video Archives; "Falwell Selling Videotape That Fiercely Denounces Clinton," *Washington Post,* May 21, 1994; Dirk Smillie, *Falwell Inc.: Inside a Religious, Political, Educational, and Business Empire,* New York: St. Martin's Press, 2008, p. 131.
13. "The Falwell Connection," *Salon,* March 1998.
14. *Bill Clinton's Circle of Power,* "The Falwell Connection," *Salon,* March 1998.
15. *Bill Clinton's Circle of Power.*
16. "The Falwell Connection," *Salon;* Smillie, *Falwell Inc.,* pp. 131–32.
17. "The Falwell Connection," *Salon.*
18. "The Falwell Connection," *Salon.*
19. "Evangelical Leader Petitions to Rebut Anti-Clinton Tapes," *Washington Post,*

January 27, 1995; "Falwell Challenged on Anti-Clinton Tapes," *Christian Century,* February 15, 1995; "Jerry Falwell Preaches Anti-Clinton Message in President's Home State of Arkansas," *Church and State,* December 1994.

20. "Bennett Slams Falwell," *Washington Times,* June 30, 1994.
21. "Falwell Fax Online," January 16, 1998, PFAW Archives.
22. "Falwell Fax Online," February 6, 1998, PFAW Archives.
23. "Falwell Denounces Operation Rescue," *Christianity Today,* May 18, 1998.
24. "Protesters Greet Falwell Congregation; Anti-Gay Group Upset over Minister's Remarks on TV," *Richmond Times-Dispatch,* November 30, 1998.
25. "Protesters Greet Falwell Congregation," *Richmond Times-Dispatch.*
26. "Falwell Fax Online," February 13, 1998, PFAW Archives.
27. "Falwell Fax Online," February 6 and 13, 1998, PFAW Archives.
28. "Falwell Fax Online," February 20, 1998, PFAW Archives.
29. Jerry Falwell, "Am I Leading a 'Vast Right-Wing Conspiracy'?," *Liberty Journal,* March 1998.
30. "The Clergy, Monicagate and the 'Arrangement,'" *Washington Times,* August 30, 1998.
31. Smillie, *Falwell Inc.,* pp. 144–45,149–50.

Chapter 15: Falwell's Last Years

1. Robert D. Putnam and David E. Campbell, *American Grace: How Religion Divides and Unites Us,* New York: Simon & Schuster, 2010, pp. 384–88.
2. "As Father Michael Peterson Lay Dying of AIDS, the Catholic Church Showed That It Cared for One of Its Own," *People,* May 11, 1987.
3. Liberty Alliance, letter from Jerry Falwell, June 1994, PFAW Archives.
4. "Gay Tinky Winky Bad for Children," BBC Online Network, February 10, 1999; "Bearing No Malice Against Mr. Winky," *Washington Times,* February 26, 1999.
5. Mel White, *Stranger at the Gate,* New York: Penguin, 1994, pp. 250, 291–96.
6. "Leaders Decry Rising Hostility to Christians," *Washington Post,* September 19, 1999; "A Dialogue in Lynchburg," *Washington Post,* October 22, 1999.
7. "Falwell Shares Peace Meal with Gay Christians," *Washington Times,* October 24, 1999; "Tension and Snubs, Some Conciliation as Falwell, Gays Meet," *USA Today,* October 25, 1999.
8. "Falwell; Soulforce," October 1999, White Video Archives.
9. "Falwell; Soulforce."
10. Jerry Falwell, *Old-Time Gospel Hour* sermon preached November 6, 1999, White Video Archives; Jerry Falwell, "The Ministry Is Not Compromising on Homosexuality," letter dated December 3, 1999, PFAW Archives.
11. Jerry Falwell, *Old-Time Gospel Hour* sermon preached January 29, 2000, White Video Archives.
12. "He's Ba-a-a-ck!," *Church and State,* May 2002; "Hard Right Burning for Bush?," *The Nation,* August 7–14, 2000.
13. "Biding Time, Conservatives Hold Breath and Brimstone," *New York Times,* August 3, 2000.
14. "Biding Time," *New York Times;* "Social Conservatives Stay Off Stage in Hopes of Payback After Election," *Chicago Tribune,* August 3, 2000; "Hard Right Burning for Bush?," *The Nation,* August 7–14, 2000.
15. Liberty Alliance, newsletter, August 3, 2000, PFAW Archives.

16. "Cheney Defends Gay Rights Stance; GOP Right Objects," *Los Angeles Times,* October 10, 2000.

17. "Many on Right Are Urging No Compromise on Cabinet," *New York Times,* December 15, 2000.

18. "God Gave U.S. 'What We Deserve,' Falwell Says," *Washington Post,* September 14, 2001; "Falwell Apologizes for Remarks," *Washington Post,* September 18, 2001.

19. "U.S. 'Secular' Groups Set Tone for Terror Attacks, Falwell Says," *New York Times,* September 14, 2001; "God Gave U.S. 'What We Deserve,' Falwell Says," *Washington Post;* "Falwell Apologizes for Remarks," *Washington Post;* "Falwell's Finger-Pointing Inappropriate, Bush Says," *New York Times,* September 15, 2001.

20. "U.S. 'Secular' Groups Set Tone for Terror Attacks, Falwell Says," *New York Times;* "God Gave U.S. 'What We Deserve,' Falwell Says," *Washington Post.*

21. Jerry Falwell Ministries, "Why I Said What I Said," September 17, 2001 (press release), PFAW Archives; "Jerry Falwell's Awkward Apology," *Washington Post,* November 18, 2001; Macel Falwell, *Jerry Falwell: His Life and Legacy,* New York: Howard Books, 2008, pp. 208–11.

22. "Christian Leaders' Remarks Against Islam Spark Backlash," *Washington Post,* October 15, 2002.

23. "Christian Leaders' Remarks Against Islam Spark Backlash," *Washington Post.*

24. Falwell, *Jerry Falwell,* pp. 212–13, 223–27.

25. Dirk Smillie, *Falwell Inc.: Inside a Religious, Political, Educational, and Business Empire,* New York: St. Martin's Press, 2008, pp. 146–47; Falwell, *Jerry Falwell,* p. 227.

26. "State of the Union: The Evangelical Vote," BBC News, November 9, 2004, available at: http://news.bbc.co.uk/2/hi/3992067.stm.

27. "Falwell Asks Christians to Support President," *Washington Times,* September 30, 2004; "Falwell Has High Hopes as Law School Opens," *Dallas Morning News,* August 24, 2004; Smillie, *Falwell Inc.,* p. 164; Falwell, *Jerry Falwell,* pp. 229–31.

28. Falwell, *Jerry Falwell,* pp. 237–40.

Index

Abdnor, James, 157
abortion: Biblical references, 98–99;
Catholic Church and, 96–97, 117,
118, 158; Civil Rights Restoration Act
amendment and, 319–20; Clinton and,
357; Falwell and, 5, 7, 98–99, 116,
117–19, 137, 153, 154, 159, 167–68,
186–87, 196, 197, 357, 366–68,
376, 390; government funding, 180,
367, 390, 393; Human Life Amendment, 227, 240; as "national sin," 99;
non-evangelicals and, 139; Operation Rescue and extremists, 367–68;
partial-birth, 367; as polarizing issue,
366; as political litmus test, 186–87,
322, 324, 325; pro-choice, 118, 305,
325, 327, 357, 367, 381; Reagan and,
158, 187–93; religious right/Moral
Majority and pro-life, 96–98, 110,
114, 117–19, 120, 129, 158, 159,
172, 305, 374; Republican Party and,
117, 322, 324; Right-to-Lifers, 160,
163, 190, 238; *Roe v. Wade*, 7, 96–98,
117, 139, 160, 172, 187, 227, 268,
393; Save-A-Baby ministry, 212, 240,
300, 302
Achtenberg, Roberta, 361
Acts of the Apostles, 57–58; chapter 1,
49–50
Ahmed, Akbar, 385
Allen, Jimmy, 145
Alvis, Josh, 25
American Civil Liberties Union (ACLU),
337, 339, 341, 347–48, 382
American South, 18–24, 35–36, 40–41,
110; Democrats and, 6, 18–21, 106–7,
114, 357; high esteem for military,
124; patriotic fervor in, 108–9; racial
issues, 20–24, 37–38, 57, 106, 114;
Republicans and, 106–7, 157
Ammerman, Nancy, 325
Anderson, John, 130, 142, 157

Anderson, Paul, 80
Ankerberg, John, 306, 307, 311
anti-Semitism, 8–9, 36, 100–101, 143–44,
164, 392; Falwell and, 281–83, 392.
See also Jews and Israel
Armey, Richard, 298
Armstrong, Ben, 309
Ashcroft, John, 367, 381
Assemblies of God, 306, 307, 309

Babalas, Peter, 345
Bachmann, Michele, 6
Baker, Howard, 299
Baker, James, 161
Bakker, Jim and Tammy Faye, 11,
305–13, 318, 326
Baliles, Gerald, 292, 345
Bangor Baptist Church, 308
Baptist Bible College, Springfield, Mis-
souri, 33–34, 38, 40, 41–45
Baptist Bible Fellowship, 40, 48–49, 200,
301
Baptists, 4, 33–34, 35, 37, 61, 185–86;
anti-apartheid protests, 283; church-
state separation and, 113, 282; criti-
cism of Falwell and Moral Majority,
133–134, 184–85; "priesthood of
the believer," 134; secularization of
Baptist colleges, 85
Barbour, Haley, 393
Barer, Raymond, 237
Barringer, Vann, 69
Barry, Marion, 237
Baxter, Tom, 325
Begin, Menachem, 101
Bell, Terrell, 333
Bellah, Robert, 124, 185
Benham, Flip, 367–68
Bennett, William, 297, 366
Berlin, Isaiah, 2, 154
Bernardin, Joseph, 204
Bible: abortion referenced in, 98–99;